FIRST EDITION

RACE AND ETHNICITY

CONSTANCY IN CHANGE

EDITED BY

Milton Vickerman
University of Virginia

and Hephzibah V. Strmic-Pawl
Manhattanville College

Bassim Hamadeh, CEO and Publisher
Kassie Graves, Director of Acquisitions
Jamie Giganti, Senior Managing Editor
Jess Estrella, Senior Graphic Designer
Lara Braff, Specialist Acquisitions Editor
Michelle Piehl, Project Editor
Alexa Lucido, Licensing Coordinator
Allie Kiekhofer and Rachel Singer, Associate Editors

Printed in the United States of America

ISBN: 978-1-63487-489-2 (pbk) / 978-1-63487-490-8 (br)

cognella | ACADEMIC PUBLISHING

TABLE OF CONTENTS

PART 6

RACISM IN POPULAR CULTURE
205

TO OUR STUDENTS,

who have made us better people.

RACE & ETHNICITY

WHY IT MATTERS

MILTON VICKERMAN AND
HEPHZIBAH V. STRMIC-PAWL

R ace and racism are crucial issues in US society. Without understanding these issues, it is impossible to understand much of what happens in the country's politics, its justice system, its cultural dynamics, and everyday interactions. This statement seems bold, even counterintuitive, in light of the oft-stated claim that much racial progress has been made since the successes of the Civil Rights Movement; so much progress, in fact, that it is sometimes claimed that Americans do not even see race anymore (Pew Research Center 2010). For many Americans, Barack Obama's election as president in 2008 provided the final proof of American post-racialism. His victory symbolized the "hope and change" in race relations that many had longed for but never thought they would see (Lane and Jost 2011).

Despite the fact that the president's approach to race has been largely colorblind (Kennedy 2011), his post-election fortunes have gradually deflated post-racial optimism. Indeed, his rise to power provoked attacks that were often both implicitly and explicitly racist. These attacks have implied that Obama is racially inferior and unfit to hold the office of President. For instance, some of the president's opponents have asserted the need to "take back their country" (Rich 2010). Although this slogan could be read in a number of ways, its use in conjunction with the first African American president in American history implies fears of racial change. It also implies that African Americans are outsiders and should remain so. Shortly after President Obama took office, the Birther movement manufactured the lingering pseudo-controversy over his American identity by insisting on his disqualification for the American presidency because of his putative foreign birth and his supposed Muslim identity (Pham 2015). Concurrently, the Tea Party movement caricatured the president and the first lady using crude racist slogans that harked back to slavery and Jim Crow. These depictions of the Obamas are not confined to the Tea Party, however, as they are ubiquitous on the Internet.

As the Obama presidency has proceeded, the racial climate in the United States has become more tense. A pattern of controversial shootings of African Americans, largely by White police, has led to more recognition within a White—usually resistant—public that race is indeed a pressing issue in American society (Norton and Sommers 2011; Robertson, Davey, and Bosman 2015). In June 2015, White supremacist Dylann Roof drove home this point by murdering nine praying Black parishioners in Charleston, South Carolina's famous Emanuel African Methodist Episcopal Church. His self-described manifesto, discovered after the rampage, laid bare that his hatred of African Americans motivated the murders. Race and racism are stilly highly relevant and charged issues in today's society, and a sociological analysis of these issues will help to decipher the problems and the solutions.

The Social Construction of Race

Race is determined by society's available racial categories, and racial categories are invented by society by assigning meaning to phenotypical traits. Race is not a biological given; rather race is interpreted through our cultural lens. Evidence that race is a social construction—meaning it varies by time and place—is clearly available. The "one-drop rule" is the classic example in American history (Davis 2001; Malcomson 2000). The "one-drop rule" dictated that being "Black" meant having only the slightest trace of African ancestry, but because the exact proportion to determine "Black" identity varied from state to state, a "Black" individual could become White (or vice versa) simply by crossing state lines (Williams 1996). The US Census racial categories are a second example of the social construction of race since, over time, the Census has constantly adjusted the number of racial categories offered to the American public as well as re-categorized communities as different races. As of the 2000 Census, Americans can indicate that they belong to multiple racial categories, resulting in 63 possible racial categories on the Census (Carl 2012; Jones and Bullock 2012; Lee 1993).

Taking account of ethnicity complicates matters even further. Weber (1998) understood ethnicity as a broad category around which individuals develop feelings of historical blood bonding, based on multiple criteria. Biology was only one of these. However, the confluence of European immigration to the United States and the punitive policies adopted by the nation toward people of color, such as African Americans, Asians, Hispanics, and Native Americans, has led to the peculiar American distinction between ethnicity as culture and race as biology. In contemporary American society, Hispanics are perhaps the clearest example of this conventional distinction since, for instance, the Census asks them to state whether or not they are "Hispanic"—an ethnic identity—and then their race—Asian, Black, White, and so on. However, the race/ethnicity, biology/culture distinction is not as clear-cut as it seems, since there is evidence that some ethnic groups are being racialized and some racial communities prefer an ethnic identity. For instance, some Hispanics view themselves as constituting a race (Gonzalez-Barrera and Lopez 2015) and there is a tendency for Americans to speak of Muslim Americans as if they constitute some unitary, essential group (Bayoumi 2008). Conversely, "racial" groups, such as African Americans, also exhibit distinctive cultures and could also be viewed in ethnic terms. Moreover, historically, the United States Census Bureau has often conflated racial and ethnic categories (Carl 2012; Lee 1993). The upshot, and very important to remember, is that ethnicity is as much of a social construct as is race (Nagel 1999).

Structured Racial Inequality

Typically, Americans believe that racism—the persecution of people based on a belief in their inherent inferiority—is an individual-level problem. They also tend to emphasize that the quality of the interaction between groups of individuals—race relations—has improved since the successes of the Civil Rights Movement in the 1960s. However, this focus on individual-level racism misses the deeper truth that racism is also structural, or institutional, which means that resources are distributed along racial and ethnic lines such that Whites systematically enjoy a disproportionate share, and people of color a lesser share, of these resources (Desmond and Emirbayer 2010; Roithmayr 2014). This inequality has persisted over decades, whereas race relations have improved relatively more quickly, giving the false impression that America's racial problems are a thing of the past. Whites are particularly apt to believe this, but people of color tend to express greater skepticism (Bobo 2011; The Pew Research Center 2013; Tankersely 2015).

Structural racism is insidious and difficult to combat because ill will toward particular groups is often hard to detect in the internal routines of institutions. Nevertheless, the normal behavior of institutions may systematically harm these groups. The criminal justice system is a good example of this truth. Mandatory minimum sentences established in the 1980s called for five years in prison for possession of five grams of crack cocaine, but required five hundred grams of powder cocaine to trigger the same sentence: a 100 to 1 disparity. This policy has resulted in the systematic imprisonment of thousands of African Americans, who are more likely to use crack cocaine, while Whites are more likely to use powder cocaine (Gao 2014; US Sentencing Commission 2011). Drug sentencing disparities continue, though the crack-cocaine ratio was reduced to 18:1 in 2010 by the US Sentencing Commission. The reasons for the sentencing disparities remain unresolved, since the US Congress has always denied a racial motive (Easley 2011). The important point is that in this, and in other instances of institutional racism, many Americans express confusion that a seemingly relentless stream of social ills continues to afflict African Americans despite the achievement of anti-discrimination laws and policies. Structural racism explains this discrepancy, but its invisibility causes Americans to blame individuals or cultures, rather than the system. This misunderstanding of the true source of the country's racial problems is a characteristic feature of the contemporary American racial landscape.

Future Trends

Unlike institutional racism, Americans easily grasp that the country's demographics are changing because of the massive influx of Hispanic, Asian, Caribbean, African, Middle Eastern, and other non-White immigrants since the 1960s. There are also higher birth rates among these immigrants and increasing marriage and cohabitation across racial and ethnic lines. These changes will likely alter our perception of race in America. For instance, race relations, which have long revolved around a Black/White binary, are evolving to incorporate multiple racial and ethnic groups in American society. Similarly, the meaning of race seems likely to undergo modification as society grapples with racial and ethnic diversity (Humes, Jones, and Ramirez 2011).

The shape of society's future racial structure has been the subject of much speculation. Researchers have proposed a number of competing models. Post-racialism—the idea that race will not matter in the future—is the most idealistic of these, and is not supported by many scholars (Vickerman 2013). Other possibilities include the development of a White/non-White frame, in which White Americans maintain their dominance of society and all people of color are excluded. A third possibility is that American society will come to revolve around a Black/non-Black frame, which is a modified version of the Black/White framework in which all people of color except for African Americans are absorbed into the White mainstream (Bean, Lee, and Bachmeier 2013). A fourth possibility is the growth of a tri-racial "Latinization" frame, in which African Americans and some other people of color with low economic means (e.g., Hmong Americans) occupy the bottom rungs of society. Meanwhile, Whites continue to dominate the society but "Whiteness" is expanded to incorporate a select few minority groups (e.g., Latinos with light features and some Asians who have higher socioeconomic status). In between these extremes we will have "Honorary Whites," groups such as Middle Eastern Americans and Indian Americans who are held by the theory to be neither Black nor White, but who also enjoy some of the trappings of Whiteness (Bonilla-Silva 2004).

Despite uncertainty over the future racial configuration of American society, all the models discussed, with the exception of post-racialism, posit that African Americans will continue to experience unique deprivation—though they may also underestimate rising hostility towards Latinos and Muslims as these populations grow in size. With respect to African Americans the argument made by the various models is that racial circumstances in the United States may change for the better but, as the sociologist Richard Alba (2010) has put it, Blacks remain the "hard case" where race is concerned. This point is not to argue against significant improvements in the fortunes of African Americans since the 1960s. For instance, if 27 percent of the African American population resides in poverty, 73 percent does not, and the Black poverty rate has declined noticeably over time (DeNavas-Walt and Proctor 2014). More pointedly, the Black middle class has grown significantly in the post–Civil Rights period (Lacy 2007; Pattillo-McCoy 1999; Vickerman 2013; Wilson 1978). It could be argued that Barack Obama is the exemplar of the success of this middle class. Yet, as noted at the beginning, African Americans continue to bear the weight of the criminal justice system, whether in the form of racial profiling, extremely high rates of incarceration, or questionable police shootings. They also experience low wealth accumulation and lower educational attainment than do other groups. (Alexander 2012; Bobo 2011; Cole 1999; DeNavas-Walt and Proctor 2013; FBI 2015). As a result of all this, racially speaking, the America of the future will be a changed place; one that Americans living in the early twentieth century would hardly recognize. It will exhibit more racial diversity and possibly more tolerance, but this tolerance should not be taken for granted or overstated. Patterns of racism that have been inscribed into the grooves of American history will not be soon overcome.

Approach of Book

This book is carefully organized and uses a scaffolding approach for the most accessible and successful learning. Rather than providing too many readings for each section of the book that then require selective assignments, we have designed the book with the required readings needed to understand each topic. There are nine main sections that follow a progressive logic, both in terms of concepts that build upon one another and that largely follow a chronological order. The book begins with the history and definitions of race, and then lays the crucial foundation that race is a social construction, not a biological one. We then proceed to discuss immigration and assimilation as they form the racial landscape. The next section provides several theories for understanding racism and, in particular, provides readings on the nuanced and complex racial discrimination that is the hallmark of contemporary racism. The following three sections address why race continues to be a matter of significant import by looking at structured racial inequality, race in popular culture, and contemporary systems of oppression. The last two sections of the book address the changes in race and racism, and how to combat racism. By following the order of the book as it is outlined, you will be able to successfully build upon your knowledge while learning the complexities of race and racism.

The book, overall, has two primary learning goals.

1. Grasp the fundamentals of race and racism.
    Race is a social construction that is both changing and fixed, and inherently tied to the problems of a racial hierarchy and racial discrimination.

2. Be comfortable having a conversation about race and racism.
    In our contemporary world, many of us would rather avoid the conversation about race, whether because we believe it is not a problem and/or because we are afraid to offend someone or appear racist. But avoiding the conversation about race is like playing a game of peek-a-boo; we may close our eyes in order to not see what is in front of us, but that does not mean the issue disappears. Race and racism will be with us even if we choose not to see it. In order to end racism, we have to learn how to discuss it; thus, the second learning goal of this book is to have you confidently discussing race and racism.

To achieve these learning goals, we have integrated several features in the book that enhance the readings. The book opens with a list of key terms that are necessary for navigating a course on race. This list is not exhaustive but rather provides the terms that frame conversations on race and that are useful toward understanding all the readings. This list should be used as a reference throughout the book, and a close familiarity with the concepts by the end of the book would indicate successful learning of the material. Another major feature is section introductions. More than just overviews, these introductions frame the sections and address why the readings are important. At the end of each introduction are also three learning objectives, denoted by the heading "As You Read"; these points can be used to guide the reader to the broad, main points. As you read the book, you should also look for the "Reflect and Consider" feature at the end of each reading; they provide analytical questions and investigative statements to contemplate. A fun feature is "Highlights," which are the last reading of each section. Highlights are recent stories and reports that showcase important racial trends, news stories on contemporary events, or critical commentary on highly relevant issues. The Highlights, chosen from a range of news sources, accent the information in the readings for that section and provide alternative avenues for critical information on race outside of formal, academic papers. Another feature, which comes at the end of each section, is "Read, Listen, Watch, Interact!" This feature provides a range of additional sources related to each section's reading; a key way to relate to the readings more closely and in an engaged manner. At the end of the book is a section entitled "Investigate Further," which provides a set of further readings related to each section of the book. This list consists of readings that review the literature, highlight an important part of the literature, and/or are particularly accessible starting points for learning more about each respective issue. The list of readings certainly should not be taken as being exhaustive or even a list of the most important or more cited works, but is a starting point for delving more into the research. Investigate Further also has a list of resources that are useful for accessing contemporary statistics. As a set, we hope these additional features provide a wide variety of uses: in research papers, classroom assignments, reading comprehension, group dialogue, group projects, and/or personal, further exploration.

FEATURES OF THE BOOK

- **As You Read:** Look for bulleted learning objectives, denoted by the phrase "As you read," at the end of each section introduction. These objectives will help guide you toward the main points of the readings and the information you should know after completing that section's readings.
- **Highlights:** A "Highlight" is put at the end of each section; they are contemporary resources that connect to that section's readings and highlight an issue that is in the news today.
- **Investigate Further:** At the end of the book is a list of readings related to each section of the book. These readings will be helpful if you are interested in a particular issue and want to investigate it further.
- **Key Terms:** At the beginning of the book is a list of forty key terms. These terms are ones that are referenced throughout the book and with which you should be most familiar by the end of the course.
- **Reflect and Consider:** Look for this feature at the end of each reading. These critical thinking questions and statements are meant to deepen your understanding of racial issues.
- **Read, Listen, Watch, Interact!** This section is a list of four types of additional resources to help you engage with the reading. "Read" additional readings, "Listen" to audio clips, "Watch" small clips and full feature films, and "Interact" with online interactive sources to connect with the material directly.
- **Section Introductions:** At the beginning of each section is a section introduction. These introductions provide a framework for why the readings are important and give brief reading summaries.

References

Alba, Richard. 2010. *The New Chance for a More Integrated America*. Cambridge: Harvard University Press.

Alexander, Michelle. 2012. *The New Jim Crow: Mass Incarceration in the Age of Colorblindness*. New York: The New Press.

Bayoumi, Moustafa. 2008. *How Does It Feel to Be a Problem?* New York: Penguin.

Bean, Frank D., Jennifer Lee, and James D. Bachmeier. 2013. "Immigration and the Color Line at the Beginning of the 21st Century." *Daedalus* 142 (3): 123–40.

Bobo, Lawrence. 2011. "Somewhere Between Jim Crow and Post-Racialism: Reflections on the Racial Divide in America Today." *Daedalus* 140 (2): 27.

Bonilla-Silva, Eduardo. 2004. "From Bi-Racial to Tri-Racial: Towards a New System of Racial Stratification in the USA." *Ethnic and Racial Studies* 27 (6): 931–50.

Carl, John D. 2012. *A Short Introduction to the U.S. Census*. Boston: Pearson.

Cole, David. 1999. *No Equal Justice: Race and Class in the American Criminal Justice System*. New York: The New Press.

Davis, F. James. 2001. *Who Is Black? One Nation's Definition*. University Park, PA: The University of Pennsylvania Press.

DeNavas-Walt, Carmen, and Bernadette D. Proctor. 2013. "US Census Bureau, Current Population Reports," P60–249, *Income and Poverty in the United States*: Washington, DC: US Government Printing Office.

Desmond, Matthew, and Mustafa Emirbayer. 2010. *Racial Domination, Racial Progress*. New York: McGraw-Hall.

Easley, Jonathan. 2011. "The Day the Drug War Really Started." http://www.salon.com/2011/06/19/len_bias_cocaine_tragedy_still_affecting_us_drug_l aw/print.

Federal Bureau of Investigation (FBI). 2014. "Bias Breakdown." https://www.fbi.gov/news/stories/2014/december/latest-hate-crime-statistics-report-released.

Gao, George. 2014. "Chart of the Week: The Black-White Gap in Incarceration Rates." Pew Research Center. http://www.pewresearch.org/fact-tank/2014/07/18/chart-of-the-week-the-black-white-gap-in-incarceration-rates/

Gonzalez-Barrera, Ana, and Mark Hugo Lopez. 2015. "Is Being Hispanic a Matter of Race, Ethnicity or Both?" Pew Research Center. http://www.pewresearch.org/fact-tank/2015/06/15/is-being-hispanic-a-matter-of-race-ethnicity-or-both/.

Humes, Karen, Nicholas A. Jones, and Roberto R. Ramirez. 2011. "Overview of Race and Hispanic Origin: 2010." Washington, DC: US Census Bureau.

Jones, Nicholas, and Jungmiwha Bullock. 2012. "The Two or More Races Population: 2010." Washington, DC: US Census Bureau.

Kennedy, Randall. 2011. *The Persistence of the Color Line*. New York: Pantheon Books.

Lacy, Karyn. 2007. *Blue Chip Black*. Berkeley: University of California Press.

Lane, Kristin, and John T. Jost. 2011. "Black Man in the White House: Ideology and Implicit Racial Bias in the Age of Obama." In *The Obamas and a (Post) Racial America?* edited by Gregory S. Park and Matthew W. Hughey, 48–69. New York: Oxford University Press.

Lee, Sharon M. 1993. "Racial Classification in the U.S. Census: 1890–1990." *Ethnic and Racial Studies* 16 (1): 75–94.

Malcomson, Scott. 2000. *One Drop of Blood*. New York: Farrar Straus Giroux.

Nagel, Joane. 1999. "Constructing Ethnicity: Creating and Recreating Ethnic Identity and Culture." In *Majority and Minority*, edited by Norman Yetman, 57–71. Boston: Beacon.

Norton, Michael I., and Samuel R. Sommers. 2011. "Whites See Racism as a Zero-Sum Game That They Are Now Losing." *Perspectives on Psychological Science* 6 (3): 215–18.

Patillo-McCoy, Mary. 1999. *Black Picket Fences*. Chicago: University of Chicago Press.

Pew Research Center. 2010. "Almost All Millennials Accept Interracial Dating and Marriage," February 1. http://www.pewresearch.org/2010/02/01/almost-all-millennials-accept-interracial-dating-and-marriage/.

Pew Research Center. 2013. "I Have a Dream, 50 Years Later," August 22. http://www.pewsocialtrends.org/2013/08/22/chapter-1-i-have-a-dream-50-years-later/#treatment-of-blacks-by-the-courts-police-seen-as-less-fair.

Pham, Vincent. 2015. "Our Foreign President Barack Obama: The Racial Logics of Birther Discourses." *Journal of International and Intercultural Communication* 8 (2): 86–107.

Rich, Frank. 2010. "The Rage Is Not About Health Care." *New York Times*, March 27. http://www.nytimes.com/2010/03/28/opinion/28rich.html.

Robertson, Campbell, Monica Davey, and Julie Bosman. 2015. "Calls to Drop Confederate Emblems Spread Nationwide." *New York Times*, June 23. http://www.nytimes.com/2015/06/24/us/south-carolina-nikki-haley-confederate-flag.html.

Roithmayr, Daria. 2014. *Reproducing Racism*. New York: NYU Press.

Tankersely, Jim. 2015. "Half of White Americans See No Racism Around Them." *Washington Post*, June 18. http://www.washingtonpost.com/blogs/wonkblog/wp/2015/06/18/half-of-american-whites-see-no-racism-around-them/.

US Sentencing Commission. 2011. "US Sentencing Commission Votes Unanimously to Apply Fair Sentencing Act of 2010 Amendment to the Federal Sentencing Guidelines Retroactively," June 30. http://www.ussc.gov/ Legislative and Public Affairs/ Newsroom/Press Releases/20110630 Press Release.pdf.

Vickerman, Milton. 2013. *The Problem of Post-Racialism*. Houndsmills, Basingstoke, Hampshire, UK: Palgrave-MacMillan.

Weber, Max. 1998. "Ethnic Groups." In *New Tribalisms: The Resurgence of Race and Ethnicity*, edited by Michael W. Hughey. New York: NYU Press.

Williams, Gregory. 1996. *Life on the Color Line*. New York: Penguin.

Wilson, William J. 1978. *The Declining Significance of Race*. Chicago: University of Chicago Press.

KEY TERMS

As you read, use these terms to guide you through the sociological language of race and ethnicity.

Affirmative action

Assimilation

Blackness

(US) Census

Color-blind

Color-blind racism

Colorism

Critical race theory

Cultural relativism

De jure racism

Discrimination

Ethnicity

Eugenics

Ideology

"Illegal" immigrant

Immigration

Institutional racism

Interracial

Intersectional analysis

Intraracial

Hegemony

Model minority

Multiculturalism

Multiracial (or biracial)

Nationality

Nativism

Oppression

People of color

Post-racial

Prejudice

Race

Racial hierarchy

Racial identity

Racialization

Racism

Reparations

Scientific racism

Segregation

White privilege

White supremacy

THE FOUNDATIONS OF RACE

M ost of us go into a room and automatically identify people's races—or at least, our perception of people's racial identities. Race is so infused into today's society that it's difficult to think of a time when it did not exist. Yet, race is a relatively new idea. So, when did race begin, and how? As Peter Wade shows in the first reading, "Race," modern ideas about race emerged gradually after the fifteenth-century expansion of Europeans across the globe, and then took on a variety of meanings. These ideas developed in response to economic needs and were influenced by Europeans' religious beliefs, as well as their preconceived notions about non-Europeans. Over time, European cultural prejudices against dark skin transformed into rigid ideologies revolving around phenotype (physical looks), innate character, and intelligence. These ideologies then resulted in European-dominated hierarchies that relegated non-Europeans to a place of inferiority in those societies.

In North America, Native Americans quickly found themselves occupying this inferior role and experienced, as a result, centuries of oppression, ranging from early forms of ethnic cleansing to genocide. By the second half of the seventeenth century, the enslavement of Africans in Virginia had framed American social relations for centuries to come. The equating of "Blackness" with degradation and inferiority spurred, as its opposite, the development of the idea of "Whiteness." By the end of the eighteenth century, this concept had become law and associated Whiteness with privilege, citizenship, and Protestant Christianity.

By the late nineteenth century, Americans had come to rely on science to explain race, but the second reading, "American Anthropological Association Statement on Race," shows that race scientists' conclusions reflected prevailing racist sentiment rather than fact. Their science was tainted by pre-existing judgments about the innate superiority and inferiority of particular groups.

Eugenics, a system of population control, was a particularly dangerous form of this scientific racism because its call to sterilize people of color and the poor (including White women) was adopted by many states. The goal was the prevention of offspring the eugenicists believed were "feebleminded," or in other words, genetically inferior. Simultaneously, eugenicists encouraged wealthy and White Anglo-Saxon Protestants to have more children.

Eugenicist thought led to the sterilization of thousands of women in the United States, influenced the passage of restrictive immigration laws, and culminated in the Nazi's genocidal policies during World War II. As Wade shows in the first reading, after the war, the devastating consequences of these policies, coupled with generalized attacks on racism, led to a backlash against eugenics and scientific racism in general. As a result, scholars, policy makers, and much of the general public gradually came to believe that society constructs race. Nevertheless, as discussed in the Highlight, "Eugenics Are Alive and Well in the United States," the practice of eugenics continues, but it is hidden from public view.

AS YOU READ

- Examine the origins and creation of "race."
- Explain connections between and among colonization, religion, and science in the creation of racial categories.
- Recognize race as a concept connected to ideologies and stratification.

RACE

BY PETER WADE

Rather than starting with a definition of race which would seem to create a nice objective area of analysis against which previous approaches to the idea might then be judged more or less adequate, I will start with a look at how the term has changed in meaning over time, so that we can see what it has come to mean (without perhaps completely divesting itself of all its previous semantic cargo), rather than what it 'really' means.[1]

Race until 1800

Michael Banton (1987) gives a very useful outline of changing 'racial theories'. The word race entered European languages in the early sixteenth century. Its central meaning was what Banton calls *lineage*, that is a stock of descendants linked to a common ancestor; such a group of people shared a certain ancestry which might give them more or less common qualities. This usage was predominant until roughly 1800. The overall context was a concern with classifying living things and there was discussion and disagreement about why things were different, how permanently they were different and so on. In the concept of race as lineage, the role of appearance was not necessarily fundamental as an identifier. Thus one 1570 English usage referred to 'race and stock of Abraham', meaning all the descendants of Abraham. This included Moses who had two successive wives; one of these was a Midianite (descendant of Midian, a son of Abraham); the other was a black Ethiopian woman. All the sons of Moses by these two women would be of 'his race', whatever their appearance (Banton, 1987: 30).

In general terms, the Bible supplied the framework for thinking about difference: the theory of monogenism was accepted—all humans had a common genesis, being the progeny of Adam and Eve. The main explanations for human difference were environmental and this was seen as affecting both the social and political institutions of human society and bodily difference—often the two were not really seen as separate.

For example, the Swedish botanist Linnaeus (1707–78), whose *System of Nature* was published in 1735, divided up all living things into species and genera, setting the basis for later classifications of difference. He presented various accounts of the internal subdivisions of the genus *Homo*. In one such (Hogden, 1964: 425), 'Americans' were characterised thus: 'Copper-coloured, choleric, erect. Paints self. Regulated by custom'. What we would call cultural and physical features are presented together, showing that they were not necessarily seen as very different, but also showing that what we would now call cultural traits were seen as 'natural': such differences were *naturalised* without being *biologised* (see next section, below).

Banton argues that the use of the term race was quite rare between the sixteenth and eighteenth centuries—the period of the scientific revolution and the Enlightenment—and that ideas about the inferiority of non-European peoples, such as Africans, were not very widespread, especially among the major thinkers of the time. Thus he sees the oft-quoted Edward Long, son of a Jamaican planter, whose *History of Jamaica* (1774) is frequently claimed as showing typically racist attitudes, as an exception rather than the rule. Equally, he argues that Thomas Jefferson, who famously advocated abolition in his *Notes on the State of Virginia* (1787), may have thought of the gulf between blacks and whites in terms of species difference, but was criticised by others for his views.

Banton's concern here is to contest 'presentism', the judging of the ideas of previous historical eras by the standards of our own. This, he argues, tends to lump all these different people together indiscriminately as 'racists', thus losing sight of the complex ways people thought about difference.

This is all very well, but Banton presents us with a history of ideas which is rather divorced from its social context. Audrey Smedley (1993) gives a rather different picture in which the guiding thread of ideas about the supposed *superiority* of Europeans, or whites, runs through the varying and complex ways of conceiving of human difference. The Bible may have implied mono genesis, but it also provided a means for asserting that Africans were inferior. Different peoples were said to be the descendants of the various sons of Noah and Africans were sometimes argued to be the sons of Ham, cursed by Noah for having seen him when he was drunk and naked.[3] In medieval theology, blackness was often linked to the devil and sin, and Africans were often held to be inferior even during the early stages of this period (Jordan, 1977, Pieterse, 1992). Throughout the period Banton refers to, Europeans were generally thought of as more civilised and superior.

Smedley's account—like many others—lays emphasis on the social, economic and political conditions in which the ponderings about human difference took place: explorations of Africa, the conquest of the New World, colonialism, slavery. Following a lead set by Horsman's study of Anglo-Saxons' ideas about fulfilling their 'manifest destiny' of superior political leadership based on freedom and democracy (Horsman, 1981), she focuses on the English and suggests various factors that made them particularly prone to exclusivist ideas of themselves as superior. These factors included the relative isolation of north-eastern European peoples from Greek and Roman knowledge, at least until the Renaissance; the rise from the sixteenth century of capitalism, secularism and possessive individualism (based on ideas of personal autonomy, the importance of property-owning and the accumulation of wealth); the importance given to hierarchy, often defined in economic terms; and the English experience with the sixteenth- and seventeenth-century colonisation of the Irish who had already been relegated to the status of savages (that is, as supposedly bestial, sexually licentious, undisciplined, etc.). This sort of background set the scene for the brutal encounter of the English with the Africans and the native inhabitants of the New World, the usurpation of land as private property and the conversion of Africans into chattels.

Hall (1992b) makes a more general argument about Europe as a whole. He emphasises how the idea of Europe as an entity emerged during this period, from broader and more inclusive concepts of Christendom—which included, for example, black Christian Ethiopians seen as allies in holy wars against Islam (Pieterse 1992: ch. 1). During the fifteenth century, non-European Christians were gradually excluded from the domain of Christendom itself and by the sixteenth century Europe had replaced Jerusalem as the centre of the known world. Despite internal wars and quarrels, Europe was being drawn together by mercantile capitalism and technological development (see also Jones, 1981). It was also being increasingly defined in opposition to Others—Africans, native Americans. The image of the wild man, the savage who reputedly existed on the peripheries of Europe (Taussig, 1987: 212), and of the infidel who had been fighting Christendom for the Holy Land were being increasingly supplemented and displaced by the image of the paganism and savagery located in Africa and the New World—although in all cases, ambivalence (for example, of hate and desire) attached to such images.

In short, then, ideas about human difference, while they may have involved a concept of race that was diverse, contested and even not very central, were certainly powerfully structured by ideas of European superiority. Kant (1724–1804), the philosopher whose influence has been so important in Western thought, may not have written much directly about race, but he did comment thus: 'the fellow was quite black from head to foot, a clear proof that what he said was stupid', and David Hume (1711–76) could also state that 'the Negro' was 'naturally inferior to the whites' (Goldberg, 1993: 31–2).

Goldberg (1993) also paints a broad picture. He sees the concept of race as emerging with modernity itself—'*race* is one of the central conceptual inventions of modernity' (1993: 3)—and as intertwined with basic ideas about morality. Whereas in previous eras, morality was defined in terms of virtue and correct behaviour, or of the prevention of sin, in the modern period, and with the Discoveries, people began talking in terms of stocks or breeds of humans people with engrained, *natural* qualities. Human identity and personhood became increasingly defined by a discourse of race, certain races became defined as non-rational or aesthetically inferior (lacking in the 'natural' balance of beauty and harmony) and race could define certain people as fit for slavery.

Race in the nineteenth century

Banton (1987) then moves on to consider the concept of race as *type*. This concept, which built on existing ones and developed in diverse and contested ways during the nineteenth century, was based on the idea that races were permanent, separable types of human beings with innate qualities that were passed on from one generation to the next. Now everyone (or thing) that was alike in nature and appearance was thought to have descended from a common ancestor. Moses' sons, in this view, would not belong to the stock and race of Abraham: some would be considered to belong to the black race, while others might be mixed race, Semites or perhaps Caucasians. Within this overall view, typologies of humankind proliferated and there was heated debate about whether types were separate species or not. Polygenism—the theory that different human types had separate origins—gained ground, despite its divergence from Biblical teachings. Ideas about evolutionary change (in a pre-Darwinian sense), which had been present in the seventeenth century in concepts of the gradual progression from primitive forms of human life (of which the 'lower' peoples were often thought to be exemplars) towards supposedly superior forms, were adapted to ideas about racial types as stages on an evolutionary scale. Racial types were hierarchically ordered, as racial 'lineages' had been before, but now the basis of the hierarchy was thought of in terms of innate differences of 'biology', the term proposed by Lamarck, among others, in 1802 to describe the scientific study of living organisms (Mayr, 1982: 108). 'Natural' differences were increasingly seen as specifically 'biological' differences.

Stocking (1982: ch. 2) compares two French scientists of the early nineteenth century, Degerando and Cuvier. In his writings, Degerando hardly mentioned race and saw difference as environmental, although he did see 'primitive' peoples as being examples of previous stages in progression of humans towards European perfection. Cuvier, sign of things to come, expounded a 'static non-evolutionary tradition of comparative anatomy', and spent his time collecting (or rather stealing) bones and skulls for comparative measurement to assess racial difference. This was an early example of a whole industry of anatomical measurement, designed to specify racial typologies, with great attention being paid to the skull since brain size was held to correlate with superior intelligence. Although many of the practitioners of this science were medics and naturalists, anthropology was often the label they used for their investigations.

This was the age of scientific racism when 'even for self-proclaimed egalitarians, the inferiority of certain races was no more to be contested than the law of gravity to be regarded as immoral' (Barkan, 1992: 2-3). The conceptual centrality which Goldberg asserts for race can also be seen in this statement by Robert Knox, Scottish medic and author of *The Races of Men* (1850): 'That race is everything, is simply a fact, the most remarkable, the most comprehensive, which philosophy has ever announced. Race is everything: literature, science, art—in a word, civilisation depends on it' (cited in Pieterse, 1992: 49).

The context for the rise of this science—and science it was held to be, even if it was bad science and immoral by today's standards—was the abolition of slavery and the slave trade. There is no easy correlation here, because the apogee of scientific racism was the end of the nineteenth and the beginning of the twentieth centuries, whereas first the slave trade then slavery itself were mostly abolished by 1863.[4] Also, some racial theorists were opposed to slavery on humanitarian grounds, while, conversely, some southern US slave-holders opposed racial typologies on religious grounds (Banton, 1987: 9, 45). But it is no coincidence that just as abolitionist opinion gained dominance in Europe, making the institutionalised inferiority of blacks morally insecure, theories began to emerge that could justify the continued dominance over blacks (not to mention native Americans, Asians and Orientals) in terms of supposedly innate and permanent inferiority and now with the full power of scientific backing. In any case, slavery was partly opposed in terms of its unsuitability for a modern industrial society based on free wage labour (Eltis, 1987), rather than because it oppressed black people, so opposing slavery was no guarantee of a positive stance on racial equality.

The other main social context was the rise of imperialism which, following on from the first main phase of colonialism between about 1450 and 1800 based mainly on settler colonies and mercantile capitalism, began in the nineteenth century to expand rapidly into Asia, Africa and the Pacific with less direct settlement and more emphasis on the extraction and cultivation of raw materials and on the sale of industrial goods. Goldberg continues his analysis of the intertwining of ideas of moral philosophy and racial theory in Western thought by arguing that, in the nineteenth century, utilitarianism became central and that, although the concept of race might not be directly invoked, the principles of utility and the collective good allowed authoritarian rule in which the most rational—the white colonisers—decided on rational grounds what was best for the less rational—the black colonised. Thus John Stuart Mill, the great exponent of utilitarianism, who followed his father into the colonial service in India where 6,000 civil servants controlled vast areas of the subcontinent, preached the need to govern the lower, less civilised orders (1993: 35).

Race in the twentieth century

The twentieth century saw a period of changes and contradictions during which the meanings attached to the term race varied very widely. On the one hand, eugenics emerged as a convergence of science and social policy, the term coined at the turn of the century by Francis Galton, scientist and cousin of Charles Darwin. It was based on scientific racism and the idea that the reproductive capacities of biologically 'unfit' individuals (for example, the insane) and, more generally, the 'inferior races' should be restricted, just as the breeding of domestic livestock might try to eliminate unwanted traits. The movement had quite a strong influence in Europe and the USA and also affected Latin America (Stepan, 1991); by the time it became part of Nazi policy in the 1930s, it had lost much ground elsewhere. On the other hand, however, this period also saw the dismantling of scientific racism.

The latter trend had several sources. Darwin's evolutionary theories indicated that it was no longer possible to think in terms of permanent racial types: breeding populations adapted over time. However, these ideas, published as early as 1871 (*The Descent of Man*) took a long time to impact and did not scotch scientific racism; rather the latter adapted to the former with the development of social evolutionism according to which superior, 'fitter' races were more 'successful' in terms of their capacity to dominate others (Stocking, 1982: ch. 6).

Franz Boas, the anthropologist, also played an important role in challenging scientific racial typologies (Stocking, 1982: ch. 8). A Jew with a background in physics, he left the anti-Semitism of late nineteenth-century Germany and migrated to the US where he did anthropometric research—measuring heads, like many others were doing at the time. He discovered that variation in head dimensions over a lifetime or between contiguous generations exceeded that found between 'races'. The very techniques of scientific racism could be used to undermine its theories. Boas went on to challenge theories of innate racial difference and hierarchy, but it would be wrong to see Boas as the hero single-handedly overthrowing scientific racism. Students of his—such as Ashley Montagu—were also very influential. More broadly, the rediscovery of Mendelian inheritance in 1900 paved the way for the establishment of the science of genetics. Mendel, hitherto a little known Austrian monk, had discovered forty years earlier that specific traits (in sweet peas) were controlled by specific elements (that is, genes) which were passed from one generation to another as independent components; this meant that the idea of 'type', based on a collection of traits passed as an unchanging bundle down the generations, was untenable.

The social context for these changes was varied: imperialism continued apace, legal racial segregation was solidly in place in the US and was gaining ground in South Africa, and the rise of the women's movement and working-class militancy aroused conservative fears of social degeneration which fed into the social reform drive of the eugenics movement. On the face of it, then, there was little reason why scientific racism should be undone. But science had its own dynamic here and the facts that were mounting about inheritance and anthropometry simply no longer fitted into the racial typology paradigm. The racist ideology and atrocities of the Nazi regime in Europe and the upheavals of the Second World War, followed by the black civil rights movement in the US protesting against legal racial segregation, supplied the political drive finally to dismantle scientific racism. This was epitomised in the post-war UNESCO declarations on race which boldly stated that humans were fundamentally the same and that differences of appearance were just that and did not indicate essential differences in, say, intellect.

What happened, then, to the term race in this context? Many biologists, geneticists and physical anthropologists—but not all—have reached the conclusion that, biologically speaking, races do not exist. Genetic variation exists, but it is very difficult to take a given gene or set of genes and draw a line around its distribution in space to define a 'race'; nor can a term such as 'black' or 'white' be pinned down genetically in anything approaching a clear way. Furthermore, most psychologists agree that humans are, on average, the same in terms of their mental capacities; individual variation exists, of course, but there are no significant variations that correlate with categories such as 'black', 'Amerindian', 'white', 'African', 'European' and so on (Lieberman and Reynolds, 1996). Therefore, many natural scientists and the vast majority of social scientists agree that races are social constructions. The idea of race is just that—an idea. The notion that races exist with definable physical characteristics and, even more so, that some races are superior to others is the result of particular historical processes which, many would argue, have their roots in the colonisation by European peoples of other areas of the world.

Note

1. There are many sources on the history of the concept of race. See, for example, Banton (1987), Barkan (1992), Reynolds and Lieberman (1996), Smedley (1993), Stepan (1982).

References

Barkan, Elazar (1992) *The Retreat of Scientific Racism: Changing Concepts of Race in Britain and the United States between the World Wars* (Cambridge: Cambridge University Press).

Bauer, Arnold (1984) 'Rural Spanish America, 1870-1930', in Leslie Bethell (ed.) *The Cambridge History of Latin America,* vol. 4, pp. 151–86 (Cambridge: Cambridge University Press).

Eltis, David (1987) *Economic Growth and the Ending of the Transatlantic Slave Trade* (Oxford: Oxford University Press).

Goldberg, D. (1993) *Racist Culture: Philosophy and the Politics of Meaning* (Oxford: Blackwell).

Hall, Stuart (1992b) 'The West and the Rest: discourse and power', in S. Hall and B. Gieben (eds) *Formations of Modernity,* pp. 275–332 (Milton Keynes: Open University Press).

Hodgen, Margaret (1964) *Early Anthropology in the Sixteenth and Seventeenth Centuries* (Philadelphia: University of Pennsylvannia Press).

Horsman, Reginald (1981) *Manifest Destiny: The Origins of American Racial Anglo-Saxonism* (Cambridge: Harvard University Press).

Jones, E.L. (1981) *The European Miracle: Environments, Economics, and Geopolitics in the History of Europe and Asia* (Cambridge, Cambridge University Press).

Jordan, Winthrop (1977) *White over Black: American Attitudes towards the Negro, 1550–1812* (New York: Norton).

Lieberman, Leonard and Reynolds, Larry T. (eds) (1996) 'Race: the deconstruction of a scientific concept', in L.T. Reynolds and L. Lieberman (eds) *Race and Other Misadventures: Essays in Honor of Ashley Montagu in his Ninetieth Year,* pp. 142–73 (Dix Hills, NY: General Hall Inc.).

Mayr, Ernst (1982) *The Growth of Biological Thought: Diversity, Evolution and Inheritance* (Cambridge, Mass.: Harvard University Press).

Pieterse, J. Nederveen (1992) *White on Black: Images of Africa and Blacks in Western Popular Culture* (New Haven: Yale University Press).

Smedley, Audrey (1993) *Race in North America: Origin and Evolution of a World View* (Oxford: Westview).

Stepan, Nancy (1991) *'The Hour of Eugenics': Race, Gender and Nation in Latin America* (Ithaca: Cornell University Press).

Stocking, George (1982) *Race, Culture and Evolution: Essays on the History of Anthropology* (2nd edn Chicago: Chicago University Press).

Taussig, Michael (1987) *Shamanism, Colonialism and the Wild Man: A Study in Terror and Healing* (Chicago: Chicago University Press).

REFLECT AND CONSIDER

- Why did scientific racism attain such influence in the late nineteenth and early twentieth century?
- Why does Wade assert that race is an idea?

AAA STATEMENT ON RACE

BY AMERICAN ANTHROPOLOGICAL ASSOCIATION

The following statement was adopted by the AAA Executive Board on May 17, 1998, acting on a draft prepared by a committee of representative American anthropologists. It does not reflect a consensus of all members of the AAA, as individuals vary in their approaches to the study of "race." We believe that it represents generally the contemporary thinking and scholarly positions of a majority of anthropologists.

In the US both scholars and the general public have been conditioned to viewing human races as natural and separate divisions within the human species based on visible physical differences. With the vast expansion of scientific knowledge in this century, however, it has become clear that human populations are not unambiguous, clearly demarcated, biologically distinct groups. Evidence from the analysis of genetics (eg, DNA) indicates that there is greater variation within racial groups than between them. This means that most physical variation, about 94%, lies within so-called racial groups. Conventional geographic "racial" groupings differ from one another only in about 6% of their genes. In neighboring populations there is much overlapping of genes and their phenotypic (physical) expressions. Throughout history whenever different groups have come into contact, they have interbred. The continued sharing of genetic materials has maintained all of humankind as a single species.

Physical variations in any given trait tend to occur gradually rather than abruptly over geographic areas. And because physical traits are inherited independently of one another, knowing the range of one trait does not predict the presence of others. For example, skin color varies largely from light in the temperate areas in the north to dark in the tropical areas in the south; its intensity is not related to nose shape or hair texture. Dark skin may be associated with frizzy or kinky hair or curly or wavy or straight hair, all of which are found among different indigenous peoples in tropical regions. These facts render any attempt to establish lines of division among biological populations both arbitrary and subjective.

Historical research has shown that the idea of race has always carried more meanings than mere physical differences; indeed, physical variations in the human species have no meaning except the social ones that humans put on them. Today scholars in many fields argue that race as it is understood in the USA was a social mechanism invented during the 18th century to refer to those populations brought together in colonial America: the English and other European settlers, the conquered Indian peoples, and those peoples of Africa brought in to provide slave labor.

From its inception, this modern concept of race was modeled after an ancient theorem of the Great Chain of Being which posited natural categories on a hierarchy established by God or nature. Thus race was a mode of classification linked specifically to peoples in the colonial situation. It subsumed a growing ideology of inequality devised to rationalize European attitudes and treatment of the conquered and enslaved peoples. Proponents of slavery in particular during the 19th century used race to justify the retention of slavery. The ideology magnified the differences among Europeans, Africans and Indians, established a rigid hierarchy of socially exclusive categories underscored and bolstered unequal rank and status differences, and provided the rationalization that the inequality was natural or God-given. The different physical traits of African-Americans and Indians became markers or symbols of their status differences.

As they were constructing US society, leaders among European-Americans fabricated the cultural/behavioral characteristics associated with each race, linking superior traits with Europeans and negative and inferior ones to blacks and Indians. Numerous arbitrary and fictitious beliefs about the different peoples were institutionalized and deeply embedded in American thought.

Early in the 19th century the growing fields of science began to reflect the public consciousness about human differences. Differences among the racial categories were projected to their greatest extreme when the argument was posed that Africans, Indians and Europeans were separate species, with Africans the least human and closer taxonomically to apes.

Ultimately race as an ideology about human differences was subsequently spread to other areas of the world. It became a strategy for dividing, ranking and controlling colonized people used by colonial powers everywhere. But it was not limited to the colonial situation. In the latter part of the 19th century it was employed by Europeans to rank one another and to justify social, economic and political inequalities among their peoples. During World War II, the Nazis under Adolf Hitler enjoined the expanded ideology of race and racial differences and took them to a logical end: the extermination of 11 million people of "inferior races" (eg, Jews, Gypsies, Africans, homosexuals and so forth) and other unspeakable brutalities of the Holocaust.

Race thus evolved as a world view, a body of prejudgments that distorts our ideas about human differences and group behavior. Racial beliefs constitute myths about the diversity in the human species and about the abilities and behavior of people homogenized into racial categories. The myths fused behavior and physical features together in the public mind, impeding our comprehension of both biological variations and cultural behavior, implying that both are genetically determined. Racial myths bear no relationship to the reality of human capabilities or behavior. Scientists today find that reliance on such folk beliefs about human differences in research has led to countless errors.

At the end of the 20th century, we now understand that human cultural behavior is learned, conditioned into infants beginning at birth, and always subject to modification. No human is born with a built-in culture or language. Our temperaments, dispositions and personalities, regardless of genetic propensities, are developed within sets of meanings and values that we call "culture." Studies of infant and early childhood learning and behavior attest to the reality of our cultures in forming who we are.

It is a basic tenet of anthropological knowledge that all normal human beings have the capacity to learn any cultural behavior. The American experience with immigrants from hundreds of different language and cultural backgrounds who have acquired some version of American culture traits and behavior is the clearest evidence of this fact. Moreover, people of all physical variations have learned different cultural behaviors and continue to do so as modern transportation moves millions of immigrants around the world.

How people have been accepted and treated within the context of a given society or culture has a direct impact on how they perform in that society. The racial world view was invented to assign some groups to perpetual low status, while others were permitted access to privilege, power and wealth. The tragedy in the US has been that the policies and practices stemming from this world view succeeded all too well in constructing unequal populations among Europeans, Native Americans and peoples of African descent. Given what we know about the capacity of normal humans to achieve and function within any culture, we conclude that present-day inequalities between so-called racial groups are not consequences of their biological inheritance but products of historical and contemporary social, economic, educational and political circumstances.

REFLECT AND CONSIDER

- Why is the observation that greater genetic variation exists within racial groups than between them important?
- Examine how race is an ideology about human difference.

HIGHLIGHT

EUGENICS ARE ALIVE AND WELL IN THE UNITED STATES

BY PAUL CAMPOS, *TIME*

SUMMARY

In this article from *TIME*, Campos argues that eugenics, a practice thought to have been discredited because of its association with Nazism, has continued in California. Between 2006 and 2010, 148 female prisoners were sterilized without their permission. However, these revelations have been met with only muted response, a response that leads the author to conclude that the American public needs to be re-educated about one of the darker chapters of recent American history.

EXCERPT FROM
"EUGENICS ARE ALIVE AND WELL IN THE UNITED STATES"

Informed consent is a concept at the core of both liberal democracy and the ethical practice of medicine. That is just one reason why a new report that, between 2006 and 2010, at least 148 women were sterilized illegally in California prisons should deeply disturb us. The report found the inmates were given tubal ligations without the prison administrators bothering to get the case by case authorization for the procedures, required by law, from a state board. The point of this requirement is to have state officials outside of the prison review whether a proposed sterilization is genuinely consensual. (At least one woman has complained that she was coerced by prison officials into having the procedure). Judging from the comments being made on even many liberal internet sites regarding this story, it seems a refresher course in one of the darker sides of American history is in order (A typical reaction: "So ridiculous making this procedure so difficult. Every woman who walks in the door of a prison should be encouraged with times cuts and subsidies to get sterilized.")

 READ THE REST OF THE ESSAY:

bit.ly/eugenicstime

READ, LISTEN, WATCH, INTERACT!

READ

 Indian Affairs, Frequently Asked Questions
U.S. Department of the Interior
READ AT bit.ly/indianaffairs

 Boarding Schools: Struggling with Cultural Repression
National Museum of the American Indian
READ AT bit.ly/nativewords

LISTEN

 Navigating the Lines Between Ethnicity and Identity
NPR, 4.18.2013
LISTEN AT bit.ly/ethnicityidentity

 Lincoln's Second Inaugural
This American Life, 4.4.1997
LISTEN AT bit.ly/lincolninaugural

WATCH

Race the Power of an Illusion, Episode I: "The Difference Between Us"

California Newsreel, 2003
AVAILABLE AT bit.ly/raceillusion

Slavery and the Making of America

PBS, 2005
AVAILABLE AT bit.ly/slaveryamerica

Slavery by Another Name

PBS, 2012
AVAILABLE AT bit.ly/slaveryname

The Journey of Man

C-Span, 2003
AVAILABLE AT bit.ly/journeygenetic

INTERACT

U.S. Mexican War, Interactive Timeline, 1846-1848

PBS
INTERACT AT bit.ly/usmexicanwar

Photographs and Postcards of Lynching in America

Without Sanctuary
INTERACT AT bit.ly/lynchingamerica

THE SOCIAL CONSTRUCTION OF RACE

What is your definition of race? Do you connect race to phenotypical features such as skin tone, eye color, or hair texture? Since most of us "determine" another's racial identity through physical features and/or the race of one's parents, it would appear that race is biological; however, race is a *social construction*.

The fundamental way that we know race is a social construction is that it varies by time and location—that is, the classification of people into racial categories is not consistent historically or regionally. For example, in 1890 the Census used the category "quadroon" to represent people who were one-fourth black; however, this category is not one we would consider using today. Likewise, race varies by region; for instance, a person who has a light complexion might be classified as Latino in California (where the Latino population is higher), Black in Alabama (where the Black population is higher), and multiracial in New York (where there is a range of races, ethnicities, and nationalities). Thus, rather than being defined as biological, race is a set of phenotypical characteristics to which society assigns socially significant meanings—therefore race has power only so long as society continues to give it power.

The readings for this section clearly outline why race is a social, not biological, construction. It is important to be unwavering in your knowledge of this fact, because race has so often been co-opted by movements to rationalize social inequality. Plantation slavery and genocide of Native Americans were defended by ideologies that Whites were morally, intellectually, and biologically superior to all other races. In contemporary times, some continue to suggest that Whites and Asians have higher IQs and aptitudes for success than Blacks and Latinos. Yet, there are *no* biological connections between race and social success—any correlations between races and social outcomes are a consequence of the ways in which racial groups are systematically provided or denied opportunities.

Kenneth Prewitt, in "Immigrants and the Changing Categories of Race," outlines the ways that racial categories have changed throughout time and the connections between the rise of racial categories and corresponding ideologies about immigrant groups. This conversation is continued in the following reading by Michael Omi and Howard Winant in the foundational reading "The Theory of Racial Formation." Omi and Winant provide the useful concepts of *racialization* and *racial project*s to evaluate how racial categories are created, modified, and disappear as social conditions change. Race is a "master category" that shapes the "history, polity, economic structure and culture of the United States," but it is also both fixed and fluid, as race has to adapt as society evolves. The Highlight, "Why Do So Many Americans Think They Have Cherokee Blood," provides a good example of how racial/ethnic identities are fluid and socially constructed.

AS YOU READ

- Explain how race is a social construction.
- Discuss how races have changed over time.
- Express how race is central to society.

IMMIGRANTS AND THE CHANGING CATEGORIES OF RACE

BY KENNETH PREWITT

It is instructive to compare the ease with which a racial classification was introduced into our statistical system with the resistance resulting from an occupational classification. In preparing for the nation's first decennial census, James Madison proposed a question to classify America's working population into agriculture, commerce, or manufacturing (Cohen 1982).[1] The new Congress rebuffed his initiative, registering both a technical and a philosophical objection. Technically, said the congressional opponents, the categories were imprecise, because, after all, the same person could fall into all three sectors—being a farmer who manufactured nails on the side and traded those he did not need to a neighboring farmer who made ax handles. More philosophically, Madison's critics held that an occupational classification would admit to, and perhaps even excite, differing economic interests. This very possibility challenged eighteenth-century thought that took society to be a harmonious whole, and viewed the task of governing as that of divining a common good rather than that of managing conflicting interests. The harmonious whole that was blind to occupational differences was not, of course, color-blind. In the color-coded language that becomes prominent in the nineteenth century, the earliest census separates the black, red, and white population groups.

I take from the 1790 census a larger lesson. To divide the population into its several race groups was unquestioned. The categories could change, but not the need for the classification itself (see, e.g., Nobles 2000). In 1820 "free colored persons" was added to the census form (as, by the way, was Madison's occupation question). After the Civil War, interest in shades of color led the census to classify people as mulatto, quadroon, and octoroon, motivated by a race science that viewed race mixing as detrimental to the moral fiber of the nation itself. New immigrant groups began to appear in census categories around the same time. Chinese and Japanese were counted in 1890. Later, in 1920, Filipinos, Koreans, and Hindus appeared on the census form. Before 1930, Mexicans were counted as white, but in 1930 were separately counted as a race. This was quickly dropped when the government of Mexico complained, and Mexicans remained "white" until the category Hispanic origin appeared in the 1980 census (and has remained in every census since), though as I note in more detail below, labeled an ethnic rather than racial group.[2] Following statehood for Hawaii, Hawaiian and part-Hawaiian appear on the 1960 census form, though statehood for Alaska did not generate a specific category for Aleut and Eskimo until 1980.

America's changing demography is traced to both immigration and imperialism, the latter resting on purchase as well as conquest. The Louisiana Purchase brought Creoles into America's population. The purchase of the Russian colony of Alaska in 1867 added the Inuit, the Kodiak, and other Alaskan natives. The Mexican-American War in midcentury added the nation's first large Mexican population. The Spanish-American War later in the century added Puerto Rico, other Caribbean islands, and their peoples, as well as Guam and the Philippines. When Hawaii was annexed in 1898, its native Pacific Islander population fell under American rule. Although population increases that resulted from conquest and purchase were relatively small, they added substantially to the country's racial diversity, completing David Hollinger's "racial pentagon" (1995) by adding brown and yellow to the eighteenth-century population base of white, black, and red.

The nineteenth- and early twentieth-century immigration story is less about race than about national origin and religion, though these traits were often "racialized" as in the swarthy southern Europeans or the Jewish race. The well-known story is how a permissive immigration policy that brought workers to a growing economy was combined with civic exclusion, denial of citizenship, and limited rights (Smith 1997, Zolberg 2005). And when people with nativist tendencies in American political life worried that the internal borders were not holding, permissive immigration was brought to a sharp and sudden halt (Chan 1991, Hing 1993). The restrictive 1924 legislation drew specifically on the census to set limits that effectively denied entry to those national origin groups that had dominated immigration flows for the previous half century (Anderson 1988).

From the founding period through the Second World War, racial classification in our official statistical system interacted with two politically related policy narratives. One, the three-fifths clause, entrenched slaveholding interests until the Civil War, and then, even as three-fifths gave way to a full count of African Americans, entrenched a Jim Crow society and continued disproportionate power for the South in Congress and the Electoral College. The census made room for Southern blacks, but voting rolls and polling booths did not (Keyssar 2000). The second policy narrative is the racially constructed policy that excluded Asians, Mexicans, Hawaiians, Puerto Ricans, and other minorities from civic life, and then, with the Immigration Act of 1924, sought to wind the demographic clock back to Anglo dominance (Haney Lopez 1996). These policy narratives eventually gave way to a liberalization of immigration and a reopening of America's gates with the Immigration and Nationality (McCarran-Walter) Act of 1952—which lifted the ban on immigration set by the 1924 Act, but kept stringent quotas on immigrants from particular sending countries (e.g., the limit on Japanese immigrants was set at 128 persons per year)—and the 1965 Hart-Cellar Act amendments to the 1952 legislation, which effectively ended the discriminatory national origin-based quota system.

If state-sanctioned discrimination is the central policy narrative linked to racial classification for more than a century and a half, the 1960s ended it only in part. Discrimination was to end, but not classification itself or its tight coupling to national policy. That is, the long period that precedes the civil rights legislation of the 1960s and the shorter period that immediately follows it rest on two propositions: First, that there should be a racial classification system that assigns every American to one and only one of a small number of discrete ethnoracial groups. The second proposition is that this racial classification system should be designed to serve public policy purposes. Where earlier policies had been discriminatory, new civil rights policies were intended to right those wrongs and benefit groups that had been "historically discriminated against." Belonging to a racial minority becomes a basis from which to assert civic rights. In this task, statistical proportionality became a much-deployed legal and administrative tool. Soon, the nation was enmeshed in a new form of politics. Equal opportunity becomes proportional representation. Disparate impact gains an important place in legal reasoning. Institutional racism enters the political vocabulary. Individual rights came to share political space with group rights.

Accompanying this shift in vocabulary and focus was a broadened understanding of civil rights, which was quickly adjudged to be about more than redressing the legacy of slavery. It was about all "groups historically discriminated against"—including, especially, Native Americans, Hispanics, and Asians. Civil rights became minority rights, and references to black-white were supplanted by references to people of color. Even this was too narrow a construction. The minority rights revolution came to encompass other groups historically discriminated against, in particular, women and the disabled (Skrentny 2002).

Statistical proportionality was central to this steady broadening of the civil rights agenda. Through legislation like the Civil Rights Act of 1964 and the Voting Rights Act of 1965 and the subsequent Supreme Court interpretations of these laws, the discriminatory and exclusionary nature of society came to be determined by examining whether certain groups were statistically underrepresented in colleges and universities, in the better jobs, in winning government contracts, in home mortgages, and in elected office. Underrepresentation was accepted as an indicator of denied social justice.

The census racial classification system that gave rise to concepts of underrepresentation and to statistical proportionality as a juridical and administrative tool had a small number of discrete categories—white, black, Indian, Asian and, as an ethnic category, Hispanic. But with the census classification scheme steadily accumulating more policy weight, the categories themselves could hardly be left to chance. The "politics of classification" changed, drawing fresh energy from multicultural identity politics. These politics brought many advocacy groups to issues that had generally been the preserve of statistical agencies (Anderson 1988, Espiritu 1992, Nobles 2000).

Fueling these politics is a broad public question. Why do we have an official ethnoracial classification? For much of American history, the answer was self-evident: the classification helped in the design and implementation of discriminatory and exclusionist policies. When these policies were radically challenged and eventually dismantled, the policy use of classification remained in place. Except now it was historical wrongs and ongoing discrimination that were made tractable to policy intervention.

Recent developments have begun to confuse this basic understanding of the policy function of ethnoracial classification. Today the country has a less sure or agreed-upon answer to why we preserve the racial classification system, at least in its current broad outline, which essentially carries forward race categories that date to the seventeenth century.

Conclusions

The ethnoracial classification system that currently underpins official statistics in the United States is unstable and will undergo additional changes. Elsewhere I have argued that the distinction between race and ethnicity as used in official statistics is itself suspect (Prewitt 2005). This argument gains even more force when considering the great diversity of national origin, linguistic, and religious groups that have made their way to American shores since immigration policy was liberalized in 1965. Certainly the presumption that there are only two ethnic groups in the United States—Hispanic and Non/Hispanic—makes little sense. Nor should we expect every recently arrived group to feel comfortable in one of the preexisting five primary race groups. So what gets added, by what criteria, and in response to what political pressure? Hovering over these issues is the broader question of the purpose to be served by the classification system: enforcement or affirmation? Perhaps there is a way to realize both of these functions. I have suggested elsewhere a way to preserve the enforcement purpose with one question on the census form, and yet respond to the demands for affirmation and identity expression through another question on the form (Prewitt 2005). Whether that is practical remains to be tested.

The only certainty I see in the future of racial classification is a politics that includes a much more active role by recent immigrants, especially by Hispanics and Asians, than has historically been the case. This is not to say that how to incorporate immigrants into preexisting classification is a new consideration in statistical policy. It is not, but compared to the nineteenth and early twentieth century, the politics today are much more open. Who "owns" the racial classification system? No one and everyone is probably the answer, and immigration scholars will need to be attentive to how different groups politically position themselves as the classification system again comes under review.

Notes

1. For a discussion of Madison's failed proposal, see Cohen 1982, pp. 159–64.
2. The politics behind this decision were intense, as reflected in U. S. Commission on Civil Rights report, *Counting the Forgotten* (1974).

REFLECT AND CONSIDER

- How does the system of racial and ethnic classification illustrate the social construction of these categories?
- Has the rise of multicultural identity politics made the Black/White framework irrelevant for understanding race?

THE THEORY OF RACIAL FORMATION

BY MICHAEL OMI AND HOWARD WINANT

Race as a Master Category

It is now widely accepted in most scholarly fields that race is a *social construction*. Simply stating that race is socially constructed, however, begs a number of important questions. How is race constructed? How and why do racial definitions and meanings change over time and place? And perhaps most important, what role does race play within the broader social system in which it is embedded?

With respect to this last question, we advance what may seem an audacious claim. We assert that in the United States, *race is a master category*—a fundamental concept that has profoundly shaped, and continues to shape, the history, polity, economic structure, and culture of the United States. Obviously, some clarification is in order. We are not suggesting that race is a transcendent category—something that stands above or apart from class, gender, or other axes of inequality and difference. The literature on intersectionality has clearly demonstrated the mutual determination and co-constitution of the categories of race, class, gender, and sexual orientation. It is not possible to understand the (il)logic of any form of social stratification, any practice of cultural marginalization, or any type of inequality or human variation, without appreciating the deep, complex, comingling, interpenetration of race, class, gender, and sexuality. In the cauldron of social life, these categories come together; they are profoundly transformed in the process.[1]

We hold these truths of intersectional analysis to be self-evident. But we also believe that race has played a unique role in the formation and historical development of the United States. Since the historical encounter of the hemispheres and the onset of transatlantic enslavement were the fundamental acts of race-making, since they launched a global and world-historical process of "making up people" that constituted the modern world, race has become the *template* of both difference and inequality. This is a world-historical claim, but here we develop it only in the context of the United States.

We suggest that the establishment and reproduction of different regimes of domination, inequality, and difference in the United States have consciously drawn upon concepts of difference, hierarchy, and marginalization based on race. The genocidal policies and practices directed towards indigenous peoples in the conquest and settlement of the "new world," and towards African peoples in the organization of racial slavery, combined to form a template, a master frame, that has perniciously shaped the treatment and experiences of other subordinated groups as well. This template includes not only the technologies (economic, political, cultural) of exploitation, domination, and deracination; it also includes the technologies of resistance: self-activity (James et al., 1958); "*liberté, égalité, fraternité*," sisterhood, and abolition democracy (Du Bois 2007 [1935]).

Consider the questions of class and gender. Historically in the United States, race has provided a master category for understanding the definition of class and the patterns of class consciousness, mobilization, and organization. Class stratification in the United States has been profoundly affected by race and racism, and the reproduction of class inequalities is inextricably linked to the maintenance of white supremacy. Race has shaped the meaning of such concepts as work and worker, labor and employment, master and servant, supervisor and subordinate (Roediger 2007 [1991]). Race is a fundamental organizing principle of social stratification. It has influenced the definition of rights and privileges, the distribution of resources, and the ideologies and practices of subordination and oppression. The concept of race as a marker of difference has permeated all forms of social relations. It is a template for the processes of marginalization that continue to shape social structures as well as collective and individual psyches. Drawing upon social psychology and mind science research that explores mechanisms of "othering," john a. powell and Stephen Menendian assert: "Without being identical, most of the forms of marginalization and stratification in society share a common set of heuristics and structure, which is patterned on race" (powell and Menendian n.d.).

From conquest and slavery on, racial parallels and racial "crossings" have shaped gender relations. Women and slaves were at best lower-status humans, at worst not human at all. They were both subject to chattelization. Their labor was coerced and unremunerated; they were physically brutalized. Although there were, of course, very distinct and widely varied experiences of subordination among different classes of women and of blacks, the objectification of both groups was near-total. Repression of women's autonomy, intellect, and bodily integrity was obsessive and often violent (Beauvoir 1989; Federici 2004). Blacks, Indians, and women were afforded very little recognition: Their entry into the public sphere, corporeal integrity, and intellectual capacity was strenuously denied. In political and legal theory, the sexual contract and the racial contract have been extensively compared (Goldman 1911; Rubin 1975; Pateman 1988; Mills 1999).

The corporeal distinction between white men and the others over whom they ruled as patriarchs and masters, then, links race to gender, and people of color to women. Whether they were defined by their racial status (as enslaved or "free," black, Indian, *mestiza*), or by the patriarchal family (as daughters, wives, mothers), they were corporeally stigmatized, permanently rendered as "other than," and the posessions of, the white men who ruled. As in the case of class distinctions, evolving gender distinctions coincided in important ways with racial ones. In part, this too was corporeal: Perhaps at the core of intersectionality practice, as well as theory, is the "mixed-race" category. Well, how does it come about that people can be "mixed"? What does the presence of mixed people mean for both white and male supremacy?

In short, the master category of race profoundly shaped gender oppression. It's fascinating that this pattern of combined political influence and political tension, which was established in the antebellum intersection between abolitionism and early feminism and reproduced during the struggle for women's suffrage and against Jim Crow at the turn of the 20th century, was then reiterated again in the post-World War II years in "intersectional" alliance and conflict between the civil rights movement and "second-wave" feminism. To be sure, there were many "intersections" between the two patterns described here. The tense and ultimately ruptural relationship between "first-wave" feminism and the black freedom movement around the turn of the 20th century is perhaps the best-known example: The (white) women's suffrage movement broke with its former black allies, abandoning black women (and black men too) in the process, as the Jim Crow system was institutionalized in the United States. Southern states' ratification of the 19th Amendment was conditional on their continued denial of black voting rights. Such black women activists as Ida B. Wells, Mary Church Terrell, and Anna Julia Cooper, as well as many lesser-known figures, fiercely denounced this as a betrayal. Of course, it reflected the pervasive white racism of the epoch (see Crenshaw 1991; Cooper 1998; Collins 2008 [1999]; Davis 2011 [1983]).

While race is a template for the subordination and oppression of different social groups, we emphasize that it is also a template for resistance to many forms of marginalization and domination. The new social movements of the 1960s and 1970s, for example—the women's movement, the student movement, the anti-war movement, the gay liberation movement—were inspired by and consciously drew upon the black movement's theoretical insights, strategies, and tactics to organize their specific constituencies, make political demands, and challenge existing practices of exclusion and subordination. These movement challenges underscore the dual-edged and dynamic qualities that inhere in the social category of race. These qualities are, once again, economic, political, and cultural technologies. They involve asserting previously stigmatized identities, "fusing" previously "serialized" groups (Sartre 2004), creating "commons" where resources can be shared. "Making up people" racially, then, has been "portable" across U.S. history. It has spread from one oppressed group to another and proved transferable to other marginalized identities, social cleavages, and political struggles.

Before we can consider and fully evaluate the notion of race as a master category of social organization in the United States, we need to think about how race itself is defined, what meanings are attached to it, and how it is deployed to create, reproduce, or challenge racist structures. The process of race making, and its reverberations throughout the social order, is what we call *racial formation*. We define racial formation as *the sociohistorical process by which racial identities are created, lived out, transformed, and destroyed.*

Racialization

Race is often seen as a social category that is either objective or illusory. When viewed as an objective matter, race is usually understood as rooted in biological differences, ranging from such familiar phenomic markers as skin color, hair texture, or eye shape, to more obscure human variations occurring at the genetic or genomic levels. When viewed as an illusion, race is usually understood as an ideological construct, something that masks a more fundamental material distinction or axis of identity: our three paradigms of ethnicity, class, and nation typify such approaches. Thus race is often treated as a metonym or epiphenomenon of culture (in the ethnicity paradigm), inequality and stratification (in the class paradigm), or primordial peoplehood (in the nation paradigm).

On the "objective" side, race is often regarded as an *essence*, as something fixed and concrete. The three main racial classifications of humans once posed (and now largely rejected) by physical anthropology—Negroid, Caucasoid, and Mongoloid—are examples of such an essentialist perspective. Another example is "mixed-race" identity: To consider an individual or group as "multiracial" or mixed race presupposes the existence of clear, discernible, and discrete races that have subsequently been combined to create a hybrid, or perhaps mongrel, identity. Here race is functioning as a metonym for "species," although that connection is generally not admitted in the present day.

While race is still popularly understood as essence, it has also been viewed as a mere *illusion*, especially in more recent accounts. As a purely ideological construct, race is considered to be unreal, a product of "false consciousness." As we have seen in our discussion of class paradigms of race, both orthodox (neoclassical) economics and orthodox Marxism viewed race this way. For the former, it was an irrational distraction from pure, market-based considerations of value in exchange; for the latter it was an ideological tool that capitalists (or sometimes privileged white workers) deployed to prevent the emergence of a unified working-class movement. In the current period, colorblind ideology—expressed, for example, in affirmative action debates—argues that any form of racial classification is itself inherently racist since race is not "real."

We are critical of both positions: race as essence and race as illusion. Race is not something rooted in nature, something that reflects clear and discrete variations in human identity. But race is also not an illusion. While it may not be "real" in a biological sense, race is indeed real as a social category with definite social consequences. The family, as a social concept, provides an intriguing analogy to grasp the "reality" of race:

> We know that families take many forms... Some family categories correspond to biological categories; others do not. Moreover, boundaries of family membership vary, depending on individual and institutional factors. Yet regardless of whether families correspond to biological definitions, social scientists study families and use membership in family categories in their study of other phenomena, such as well-being. Similarly, racial statuses, although not representing biological differences, are of sociological interest in their form, their changes, and their consequences.
>
> (American Sociological Association 2003, 5)

We cannot dismiss race as a legitimate category of social analysis by simply stating that race is not real. With respect to race, the Thomases's sociological dictum is still in force: "It is not important whether or not the interpretation is correct—if men [sic] define situations as real, they are real in their consequences" (Thomas and Thomas 1928, pp. 571–572).

One of our aims here is to disrupt and reorganize the rigid and antinomic framework of essence-versus-illusion in which race is theorized and debated. We understand race as an unstable and "decentered" complex of social meanings constantly being transformed by political struggle. With this in mind, we advance the following definition: *Race is a concept that signifies and symbolizes social conflicts and interests by referring to different types of human bodies.*

Although the concept of race invokes seemingly biologically based human characteristics (so-called phenotypes), selection of these particular human features for purposes of racial signification is always and necessarily a social and historical process. Indeed, the categories employed to differentiate among human beings along racial lines reveal themselves, upon serious examination, to be at best imprecise, and at worst completely arbitrary. They may be arbitrary, but they are not meaningless. Race is strategic; race does ideological and political work.

Despite the problematic nature of racial categorization, it should be apparent that there is a crucial and non-reducible *visual dimension* to the definition and understanding of racial categories. Bodies are visually read and narrated in ways that draw upon an ensemble of symbolic meanings and associations. Corporeal distinctions are common; they become essentialized. Perceived differences in skin color, physical build, hair texture, the structure of cheek bones, the shape of the nose, or the presence/absence of an epicanthic fold are understood as the manifestations of more profound differences that are situated *within* racially identified persons: differences in such qualities as intelligence, athletic ability, temperament, and sexuality, among other traits.

Through a complex process of selection, human physical characteristics ("real" or imagined) become the basis to justify or reinforce social differentiation. Conscious or unconscious, deeply ingrained or reinvented, the making of race, the "othering" of social groups by means of the invocation of physical distinctions, is a key component of modern societies. "Making up people," once again. This process of selection, of imparting social and symbolic meaning to perceived phenotypical differences, is the core, constitutive element of what we term "racialization."

We define racialization as *the extension of racial meaning to a previously racially unclassified relationship, social practice, or group.* Racialization occurs in large-scale and small-scale ways, macro- and micro-socially. In large-scale, even world-historical settings, racialization can be observed in the foundation and consolidation of the modern world-system: The conquest and settlement of the western hemisphere, the development of African slavery, and the rise of abolitionism, all involved profuse and profound extension of racial meanings into new social terrain. In smaller-scale settings as well, "making up people" or racial interpellation (a concept drawn from Althusser 2001 [1971]) also operates as a quotidian form of racialization: Racial profiling for example, may be understood as a form of racialization. Racial categories, and the meanings attached to them, are often constructed from pre-existing conceptual or discursive elements that have crystallized through the genealogies of competing religious, scientific, and political ideologies and projects. These are so to speak the raw materials of racialization.

To summarize thus far: Race is a concept, a representation or signification of identity that refers to different types of human bodies, to the perceived corporeal and phenotypic markers of difference and the meanings and social practices that are ascribed to these differences.

It is important to emphasize that once specific concepts of race are widely circulated and accepted as a social reality, racial difference is not dependent on visual observation alone. Legal scholar Osagie Obasogie makes the intriguing point that iterative social practices give rise to "visual" understandings of race, even among those who cannot see. The respondents in his study, blind since birth, "see" race through interpersonal and institutional socializations and practices that shape their perceptions of what race is (Obasogie 2013). Thus race is neither self-evident nor obvious as an ocular phenomenon. Instead racialization depends on meanings and associations that permit phenotypic distinction among human bodies.

Some may argue that if the concept of race is so nebulous, so indeterminate, so flexible, and so susceptible to strategic manipulation by a range of political projects, why don't we simply dispense with it? Can we not get "beyond" race? Can we not see it as an illusory thing? Don't we see how much mischief has occurred in its name? These questions have been posed with tremendous frequency in both popular and academic discourse.[2] An affirmative answer would of course present obvious practical difficulties: It is rather difficult to jettison widely held beliefs, beliefs which moreover are central to everyone's identity and understanding of the social world. So the attempt to banish the concept as an archaism is at best counterintuitive. But a deeper difficulty, we believe, is inherent in the very formulation of this schema, in its way of posing race as a *problem*, a misconception left over from the past, a concept no longer relevant to a "post-racial" society.

A more effective starting point is the recognition that despite its uncertainties and contradictions, the concept of race continues to play a fundamental role in structuring and representing the social world. The task for theory is to capture this situation and avoid both the utopian framework that sees race as an illusion we can somehow "get beyond," as well as the essentialist formulation that sees race as something objective and fixed, a biological given. We should think of race as an element of social structure rather than as an irregularity within it; we should see race as a dimension of human representation rather than an illusion. Such a perspective informs what we mean by racial formation.

Since racial formation is always historically situated, understandings of the meaning of race, and of the way race structures society, have changed enormously over time.

Racial Projects

Race is a "crossroads" where social structure and cultural representation meet. Too often, the attempt is made to understand race simply or primarily in terms of only one of these two analytical dimensions. For example, efforts to explain racial inequality as a purely social structural phenomenon either neglect or are unable to account for the origins, patterning, and transformation of racial meanings, representations, and social identities. Conversely, many examinations of race as a system of signification, identity, or cultural attribution fail adequately to articulate these phenomena with evolving social structures (such as segregation or stratification) and institutions (such as prisons, schools, or the labor market).

Race can never be merely a concept or idea, a representation or signification alone. Indeed race cannot be discussed, cannot even be *noticed*, without reference—however explicit or implicit—to social structure. To identify an individual or group racially is to locate them within a socially and historically demarcated set of demographic and cultural boundaries, state activities, "life-chances," and tropes of identity/difference/(in)equality. Race is both a social/historical structure and a set of accumulated signifiers that suffuse individual and collective identities, inform social practices, shape institutions and communities, demarcate social boundaries, and organize the distribution of resources. We cannot understand how racial representations set up patterns of residential segregation, for example, without considering how segregation reciprocally shapes and reinforces the meaning of race itself.

We conceive of racial formation processes as occurring through a linkage between structure and signification. *Racial projects* do both the ideological and the practical "work" of making these links and articulating the connection between them. *A racial project is simultaneously an interpretation, representation, or explanation of racial identities and meanings, and an effort to organize and distribute resources (economic, political, cultural) along particular racial lines.* Racial projects connect what race *means* in a particular discursive or ideological practice and the ways in which both social structures and everyday experiences are racially *organized*, based upon that meaning. Racial projects are attempts both to shape the ways in which social structures are racially signified and the ways that racial meanings are embedded in social structures.

Racial projects occur at varying scales, both large and small. Projects take shape not only at the macro-level of racial policy-making, state activity, and collective action, but also at the level of everyday experience and personal interaction. Both dominant and subordinate groups and individual actors, both institutions and persons, carry out racial projects. The imposition of restrictive state voting rights laws, organizing work for immigrants', prisoners', and community health rights in the ghetto or barrio are all examples of racial projects. Individuals' practices may be seen as racial projects as well: The cop who "stops and frisks" a young pedestrian, the student who joins a memorial march for the slain teenager Trayvon Martin, even the decision to wear dreadlocks, can all be understood as racial projects. Such projects should not, however, be simply regarded and analyzed as discrete, separate, and autonomous ideas and actions. Every racial project is both a reflection of and response to the broader patterning of race in the overall social system. In turn, every racial project attempts to reproduce, extend, subvert, or directly challenge that system.

Racial projects are not necessarily confined to particular domains. They can, for example, "jump" scale in their impact and significance. Projects framed at the local level, for example, can end up influencing national policies and initiatives. Correspondingly, projects at the national or even global level can be creatively and strategically recast at regional and local levels. Projects "travel" as well. Consider how migration recasts concepts of race, racial meaning, and racial identity: Immigrants' notions of race are often shaped in reference to, and in dialogue with, concepts of race in both their countries of origin and settlement. Thus migrants can maintain, adopt, and strategically utilize different concepts of race in transnational space (Kim 2008; Roth 2012).

At any given historical moment, racial projects compete and overlap, evincing varying capacity either to maintain or to challenge the prevailing racial system. A good example is the current debate over the relevance of "colorblind" ideology, policy, and practice; this provides a study of overlapping and competing racial projects.

Racial projects link signification and structure not only in order to shape policy or exercise political influence, but also to organize our understandings of race as everyday "common sense." To see racial projects operating at the level of everyday life, we have only to examine the many ways in which we "notice" race, often unconsciously.

One of the first things we notice about people when we meet them (along with their sex) is their race. We utilize race to provide clues about *who* a person is. This fact is made painfully obvious when we encounter someone whom we cannot conveniently racially categorize—someone who is, for example, racially "mixed" or of an ethnic/racial group with which we are not familiar. Such an encounter becomes a source of discomfort and momentarily a crisis of racial meaning.

Our ability to interpret racial meanings depends on preconceived notions of a racialized social structure. Comments such as "Funny, you don't look black" betray an underlying image of what black should look like. We expect people to act out their apparent racial identities. Phenotype and performativity should match up. Indeed we become disoriented and anxious when they do not. Encounters with the black person who can't dance, the Asian American not proficient in math and science, or the Latina who can't speak Spanish all momentarily confound our racial reading of the social world and how we navigate within it. The whole gamut of racial stereotypes testifies to the way a racialized social structure shapes racial experience and socializes racial meanings. Analysis of prevailing stereotypes reveals the always present, already active link between our view of the social structure—its demography, its laws, its customs, its threats—and our conception of what race means.

Conversely, the way we interpret our experience in racial terms shapes and reflects our relations to the institutions and organizations through which we are embedded in the social structure. Thus we expect racially coded human characteristics to explain social differences.

"Making up people" once again. Temperament, sexuality, intelligence, athletic ability, aesthetic preferences are presumed to be fixed and discernible from the palpable mark of race. Such diverse questions as our confidence and trust in others (for example, salespeople, teachers, media figures, and neighbors), our sexual preferences and romantic images, our tastes in music, films, dance, or sports, and our very ways of talking, walking, eating, and dreaming become racially coded simply because we live in a society where racial awareness is so pervasive.

To summarize the argument so far: The theory of racial formation suggests that society is suffused with racial projects, large and small, to which all are subjected. This racial "subjection" is quintessentially ideological. Everybody learns some combination, some version, of the rules of racial classification, and of their own racial identity, often without obvious teaching or conscious inculcation. Thus are we inserted in a comprehensively racialized social structure. Race becomes "common sense"—a way of comprehending, explaining, and acting in the world. A vast web of racial projects mediates between the discursive or representational means in which race is identified and signified on the one hand, and the institutional and organizational forms in which it is routinized and standardized on the other. The interaction and accumulation of these projects are the heart of the racial formation process.

Because of the pervasion of society by race, because of its operation over the *longue durée* as a master category of difference and inequality, it is not possible to represent race discursively without simultaneously locating it, explicitly or implicitly, in a social structural (and historical) context. Nor is it possible to organize, maintain, or transform social structures without simultaneously engaging, once more either explicitly or implicitly, in racial signification. Racial formation, therefore, is *a synthesis, a constantly reiterated outcome*, of the interaction of racial projects on a society-wide level. These projects are, of course, vastly different in scope and effect. They include large-scale public action, state activities, and interpretations of racial conditions in political, artistic, journalistic, or academic fora,[3] as well as the seemingly infinite number of racial judgments and practices, conscious and unconscious, that we carry out as part of our individual experience.

The concept of racial projects can be understood and applied across historical time to identify patterns in the *longue durée* of racial formation, both nationally and the entire modern world. At any particular historical moment, one racial project can be hegemonic while others are subservient, marginal, or oppositional to it. White supremacy is the obvious example of this: an evolving hegemonic racial project that has taken different forms from the colonial era to the present.

Notes

1. The notion of *intersectionality* was advanced by legal scholar Kimberlé W. Crenshaw, who argued that both oppression and resistance are always situated in multiple categories of difference (Crenshaw 1989). Failure to grasp how categories of race, gender, sexuality, and class dynamically interact and shape one another, she asserted, led to a fragmented politics:

   > Feminist efforts to politicize experiences of women and anti-racist efforts to politicize experiences of people of color have frequently proceeded as though the issues and experiences they each detail occur on mutually exclusive terrains. (Crenshaw 1991, 1242)

   Two other key intersectionality theorists should be mentioned. Patricia Hill Collins emphasizes the mutual determination of race, gender, and class in her survey and theoretical synthesis of the themes and issues of black feminist thought. Collins invented the phrase "matrix of domination" to describe the "overall social organization within which intersecting oppressions originate, develop, and are contained" (Collins 2008 [1999] 227–228). Evelyn Nakano Glenn argues that race and gender are relational concepts in an interlocking system, providing a historical examination of citizenship and labor in the United States between 1870 and 1930. Glenn argues that these categories cannot be understood separately, but are defined and given meaning in relationship to each other: "Race and gender share three key features as analytic concepts: (1) they are relational concepts whose construction involves (2) representation and material relations and (3) in which power is a constitutive element" (Glenn 2002, 12–13). In many respects, race is gendered and gender is racialized. Inequality is always racialized and gendered as well. There are no clear boundaries between the "regions" of hegemony, so political conflicts will often invoke some or all these themes simultaneously.

2. "The truth is that there are no races; there is nothing in the world that can do all we ask race to do for us.... The evil that is done is done by the concept, and by easy—yet impossible—assumptions as to its application" (Appiah 1992, 45). Appiah's eloquent and learned book fails, in our view, to dispense with the race concept, despite its anguished attempt to do so; this indeed is the source of its author's anguish. We agree with him as to the non-objective character of race, but fail to see how this recognition justifies its abandonment.

3. We are not unaware, for example, that publishing this work is itself a racial project.

REFLECT AND CONSIDER

- Why is it important to understand race as a "master category"?
- How do the concepts of "racialization" and "racial projects" help us understand the creation and maintenance of racial categories?

HIGHLIGHT

WHY DO SO MANY AMERICANS THINK THEY HAVE CHEROKEE BLOOD: THE HISTORY OF A MYTH

BY GREGORY D. SMITHERS, *SLATE*

SUMMARY

Native Americans have important claims to their racial and/or tribal identity; after hundreds of years of oppression, there are few resources offered to tribal members as a small effort at reparations. Identification with a tribe(s) also keeps valuable histories and cultures alive. In this article, Smithers briefly reviews Cherokee history and the ways in which Whites have muddled that history in order to falsely claim Cherokee ancestry. This pattern of choosing one's racial or ethnic identity is a good example of the social construction of race.

EXCERPT FROM "WHY DO SO MANY AMERICANS THINK THEY HAVE CHEROKEE BLOOD"

"I cannot say when I first heard of my Indian blood, but as a boy I heard it spoken of in a general way," Charles Phelps, a resident of Winston-Salem in North Carolina, told a federal census taker near the beginning of the 20th century. Like many Americans at the time, Phelps had a vague understanding of his Native American ancestry. On one point, however, his memory seemed curiously specific: His Indian identity was a product of his "Cherokee blood." ... These tales of family genealogies become murkier with each passing generation, but like Phelps, contemporary Americans profess their belief despite not being able to point directly to a Cherokee in their family tree.

READ THE REST OF THE ESSAY:

bit.ly/cherokeeslate

READ, LISTEN, WATCH, INTERACT!

READ

The Importance of Collecting Data and Doing Social Scientific Research on Race

American Sociological Association. 2003.
READ AT bit.ly/asaracedata

Race: About

United States Census Bureau.
READ AT bit.ly/racecensus

LISTEN

People of Color with Albinism Ask: Where Do I Belong?

Morning Edition, 12.7.2015, NPR
LISTEN AT bit.ly/albinismbelong

Race

Radiolab, Season 5, Episode 3
LISTEN AT bit.ly/raceradiolab

Your Family May Once Have Been a Different Color

Robert Krulwich (with Nina Jablonski). 2.2.2009, NPR
LISTEN AT bit.ly/skincolorevolution

WATCH

Decoding Our Past Through DNA, Jessica Alba's Mexican Roots
Henry Louis Gates, Finding Your Roots. Episode 10, Season 2. PBS.
AVAILABLE AT bit.ly/dnaalba

Jefferson's Blood [Last half hour]
Frontline, PBS.
AVAILABLE AT bit.ly/Jeffersonsblood

Race the Power of an Illusion, Episode III: "The House We Live In"
California Newsreel, 2003.
AVAILABLE AT bit.ly/raceillusion

Skin Deep
Smithsonian Channel, 2010
AVAILABLE AT bit.ly/skindeepdoc

INTERACT

A Genetic Atlas of Human Admixture History
Garrett Hellenthal, George Busby, Gavin Band, James Wilson, Cristian Capell, Daniel Falush and Simon Myers.

INTERACT AT bit.ly/atlashuman

Measuring Race and Ethnicity Across the Decades: 1790–2010
United States Census Bureau, 2015.
INTERACT AT bit.ly/raceacrosstime

What Census Calls Us: A Historical Timeline
Pew Research Center, 2015
INTERACT AT bit.ly/censustimeline

STRUCTURING AMERICAN IDENTITY THROUGH IMMIGRATION

Immigration is a now a topic that is familiar to most if not all of us. Continuing debates over Mexican immigration and refugees from abroad are common on the news and at dinner tables. In fact, even a cursory glance at any street in America's big cities is all that is needed to show how racially and ethnically diverse society has become. The demographics in the United States are changing because of higher fertility rates in some communities, rising rates of racial intermarriage, and continuing immigration. Immigration is particularly important, because it ushers in millions of people from around the globe into the United States every year, most of whom are from Africa, Asia, Latin America, the Caribbean, and the Middle East.

These post-1965 immigrants are only the latest wave of immigrants to come to America. Before the 1970s, most immigrants originated in Europe, but the first reading, "The United States: A Nation of Immigrants," by Peter Kivisto explains that the particular region of Europe mattered. The initial European migrants from Western Europe came to the US bounded by their desire to practice Protestantism but the second set of European immigrants, between 1880-1920, from Eastern, Central, and Southern Europe encountered much hostility in the United States. Scientific racism, very influential during this period, held that these later immigrants were inferior to the initial White Anglo Saxon Protestants immigrants. American immigration policy enshrined this principle into law between 1924 and 1965 in the National Origins System, which gave preference to Western Europeans, while discouraging immigration from other parts of the world.

As Portes and Rumbaut argue in the second reading, "The Three Phases of US Bound Immigration," the Immigration Act of 1965 reversed this focus on race, centering it, instead, on the principle of the reunification of families and occupational merit. This policy shifted the migrant stream away from Europe and facilitated the entrance of large numbers of Asians, Latin Americans, and people from the Caribbean; it ushered in the racial and ethnic diversity with which Americans are now so familiar. Meanwhile, adding to this diversity, Mexicans, exploited as low-cost labor since the nineteenth century, increasingly came to be categorized as "illegals." As Joseph Nevins illustrates in "The Ideological Roots of the 'Illegal' as Threat and the Boundary as Protector," the issue of illegality has only grown in importance, coming to preoccupy present-day discourse on immigration.

The question whether and how undocumented and non-White immigrants will be absorbed into American society, a process we refer to as "assimilation," underlies much of the debate surrounding present-day immigration. As Peter Kivisto shows, racism made this a problem for central, southern, and eastern European immigrants, but they gradually assimilated. However, they were deemed White, whereas most immigrants today are not. The question then becomes whether post-1965 immigrants can emulate Central, Southern, and Eastern Europeans in their mobility process. As explained in the third reading by Mary Waters, Van C. Tran, Philip Kasinitz, and John H. Mollenkopf, "Segmented Assimilation Revisited," they are unlikely to follow the pathway of early immigrants. Instead, today's immigrants will, as predicted by segmented assimilation theory, become absorbed into American society in different ways and at different levels.

Anny Bakalian and Mehdi Bozorgmehr, in "Immigration Patterns, Characteristics, and Identities," discuss Muslim Americans, a fast-growing group that often experiences hostility because of confusion over their origins, perceived foreign-ness, and the American public's tendency to link them to terrorism. Another group that often faces immigrant stereotypes is Asian Americans. Chou and Feagin, in "The Reality of Asian American Oppression," show that Asian Americans' exemplary socioeconomic performance as a "model minority" does not shield them from experiencing a great deal of discrimination. The Highlight "Future Immigration Will Change the Face of America by 2065" shows that Asians will double their proportion of the American population by 2065, and no group will constitute a demographic majority.

AS YOU READ

- Explain why central, southern, and eastern European immigrants faced difficulty assimilating into American society.
- Assess how assimilation has varied among central, southern, and eastern European immigrants and post-1965 immigrants.
- Describe the relationship between immigration and the racial hierarchy.

THE UNITED STATES: A NATION OF IMMIGRANTS

BY PETER KIVISTO

Historian Oscar Handlin (1973) once claimed that he set out to write the history of American immigration and discovered it was the history of America. While this was an overstatement insofar as indigenous peoples—American Indians and Mexicans in the southwest—were not immigrants and Africans, though migrants, were not voluntary immigrants, nonetheless there is considerable truth to his claim. Indeed, the vast majority of the 281,000,000 residents of the nation either migrated themselves or, more often, are the offspring of earlier immigrants. They originated from a vast array of countries, with the largest numbers originating from various locales in Europe, Latin America, and Asia.

Each of the successive waves of immigration that has shaped American history has had its own distinctive ethnic character. Thus, immigrants from western Europe characterized the first major wave—from about 1820 up to the Civil War. The second wave, extending from around 1880 until the imposition of immigration restrictions in 1924, was not only considerably larger than the first, but its composition differed insofar as large numbers originated from eastern and southern Europe. The third wave, which commenced after the passage of the Immigration and Nationality Act of 1965, differed yet again as the main contributing nations to this surge of immigration were Latin American and Asian.

Immigrants were key to the evolving understanding of what it meant to be an American. National identity was forged within the reality that as a settler nation with an ever-changing ethnic composition, an overarching American identity had to be in some way reconciled with a multitude of particular ethnic identities. Historian John Higham (1999: 40) has described the situation in comparative terms in the following way:

> The truly distinctive feature of immigration to the United States is its extraordinary and continuing diversification from the early eighteenth century to the present. Other immigrant-receiving countries have tended to draw from a few favored ethnic backgrounds. ... In contrast, the United States has continually attracted new groups and has thereby avoided a fixed division between an immigrant people and an older native population. As the country became more accessible to less familiar immigrant types, by fits and starts it made room for them.

Higham goes on to identify a number of factors that served to mitigate potential conflicts between and among ethnic groups. These include the fact that because the nation was rich in resources and land, it offered opportunities to newcomers and in the process blunted ethnic competition. The vast frontier of the nineteenth century contributed to this situation, and served as an impetus to geographic mobility that prevented particular ethnic groups from associating corporate ethnic life with particular social spaces. This meant that the United States would not be burdened with the intractable ethnic conflicts that are rooted in competing territorial claims. While these factors are important, for our purposes the third factor he discusses—political access—is critical. Higham (1999: 41) observes that:

> The United States presented itself to the world as a universal nation, a home for all peoples. ... This American self-image was enormously magnetic. It implied that nationality was not exclusive, that citizenship would be widely available, and that class and ethnic boundaries would be soft and permeable. The invitation to newcomers (at first to white males only) to participate in political life on equal terms with other citizens gave outsiders some leverage in using the power of suffrage and the protection of courts. It encouraged white ethnic groups to organize, to make their weight felt, and so to use a system of liberty under law.

As Higham notes, the inclusiveness of the new republic has its limits. In connecting these ideals to reality, as we shall see in the following sections, newcomers were not always welcome and were forced to confront considerable ethnocentric animus. Moreover, for those not considered to be white, the reality of their experience was the antithesis of the universal nation ideal.

A dialectical tension existed between the ideal of inclusion and actual demands for exclusion. Nowhere was this better seen than in the way democracy was initially conceived. Bernard Bailyn (1967: 60) has pointed out that though a "contagion of liberty" swept the new republic, at the same time fears were expressed about the presumed dangers that would result if political power were granted to "weak or ignorant" people. Thus, although the nation was conceived as a democracy, who was and who was not eligible for citizenship became a crucial concern. Citizenship, and how it was granted or denied, became a major means of incorporating some groups into not only the American political system, but also into social life in general, while at the same time excluding others. In most of the nation's history of incorporation and exclusion, race served as the most powerful determinant shaping policies regarding citizenship.

Thus, for the millions of European immigrants who entered the US during the nineteenth and early twentieth centuries, the "invention of the white race" and their progressive inclusion within the parameters of this racial designation proved crucial to their ability to become full-fledged Americans (Allen 1994; see also Roediger 1991). This is seen vividly in the case of the Irish. They were the first among the voluntary immigrants to confront intense nativist hostility, giving rise to such anti-Irish organizations as the Know-Nothings (Higham 1970). Viewed as a social problem, they were accused of being inclined to alcoholism and criminal activity. Their burgeoning numbers in major cities combined with their inclination to be involved in political activities fueled anxiety about their potential impact on American democracy. In this regard, critics contended that their Catholicism was inherently authoritarian and thus antithetical to democracy. Moreover, the Irish were often depicted in the popular imagination in racial terms. Cartoonist Thomas Nast, for example, portrayed them as racially similar to Africans, and it was not uncommon for them to be referred to as "white niggers." This term reflects their racially ambiguous status in the nineteenth century. Not surprisingly, part of the strategy designed by the Irish to promote their inclusion and to combat prejudice directed against them was to become unambiguously white. In so doing, the Irish sought to distance themselves from outsider groups by embracing the white supremacist oppression and exclusion of American Indians and African Americans. They acquiesced to the claim that the dominant culture was to be construed in terms of a core that was white, Anglo-Saxon in origin, and Protestant in religion, or in other words WASP.

WASP hegemony, European immigrants, and the melting pot

Throughout the nineteenth century and past the middle of the twentieth, the melting-pot metaphor was the most influential and enduring characterization of ethnic relations in the US. Yet, as Philip Gleason (1964) has pointed out, this symbol of fusion has also led to considerable confusion. During the formative decades of the new republic, French immigrant J. Hector St. John de Crèvecoeur (1904 [1782]: 39) wrote about the American experience as involving newcomers from various nations being "melded into a new race of men." Though such ideas gained common currency in the nineteenth century, it was not until the Jewish playwright Israel Zangwill's play, *The Melting Pot,* was staged in 1908 that the metaphor received its most explicit and popular articulation. Here again one encounters the idea that the American, though the composite product of individuals from various national origins, is someone qualitatively distinct from those particular origins. Thus, the American is the product of the fusion of diverse peoples with distinctive cultural perspectives. The confusion Gleason refers to involves three points. First, it is not clear whether the melting pot is intended as a description of what is an inevitable process of incorporation or as a prescription of what ought to be achieved in promoting a unified national identity. Second, it is not clear whether the idea refers only to cultural fusion or to biological fusion (that is, intermarriage) as well. Finally, it is not entirely clear whether the immigrant alone is transformed by the melting pot, or whether their presence also transforms the host society.

What was clear was that the melting pot served to justify the Americanization campaigns particularly characteristic of the early decades of the twentieth century. These campaigns were intended to eradicate all vestiges of the new arrivals' cultural heritages, while simultaneously instilling in them what were considered to be appropriate American attitudes, beliefs, and behaviors. Nowhere was this position more vividly evident than in the activities of industrialist Henry Ford's "Sociology Department," which ran training schools in his automobile plants for immigrant workers. The purpose of the schools was to teach the English language and to study in preparation for citizenship. Workers enrolled in the program took pledges that they would only speak English, and they proclaimed themselves intent on becoming "100 percent" American—rather than remaining a hyphenated American. In practical terms, this perspective required a willingness and ability on the part of immigrants to accept and to emulate the hegemonic WASP culture.

An ongoing issue confronting the political representatives of the dominant culture was to determine whether in fact particular groups had the requisite capacity and desire to become American in the WASP sense of the term. In other words, they had to determine which groups were capable of fusing or blending into the fabric of American society and which were "unmeltable." The two primary criteria employed in making these determinations were race and religion. The result was that the subsequent social history of immigrants of European origin diverged considerably from that of all others. But this is not to suggest that Europeans should be seen as a homogeneous whole. Indeed, within the composite European population, various groups experienced considerable levels of prejudice and discrimination during their early years in the US, while others managed rather quickly to gain acceptance (Jaret 1999).

While religion was a crucial variable, with the arrival of waves of Catholics and Jews between 1880 and 1924 being seen by nativists as a serious threat to the "righteous empire" created by Protestants, the saliency of race was also a key factor. As noted above about the Irish, southern and eastern Europeans also tended to be described in racial terms: the Nordic peoples of western Europe were contrasted to a variety of presumed racial inferiors, including Mediterraneans, Slavs, and Jews. Racialist thought was used by those urging immigrant restriction legislation. Their fears were articulated by Madison Grant in his diatribe, *The Passing of the Great Race* (1916: 92), when he wrote that as a consequence of the arrival of these newcomers, "Our jails, insane asylums, and almshouses are filled with this human flotsam and the whole tone of American life, social moral, and political, has been lowered and vulgarized by them."

The divide between acceptable and unacceptable Europeans emerged as the consequence of the particular character of national identity that took form during the period between the American Revolution and the Civil War. During the nineteenth century, the new nation set out with an expansionist mission to control much of the continent from the Atlantic to the Pacific, finding in the doctrine of Manifest Destiny an ideological justification for a policy of conquest. The United States was resource rich but population poor, while economic development required both resources and an expanding population. This was the case during the earlier agrarian era, but population growth became even more crucial as the nation began to industrialize in the nineteenth century. Thus, in order to attract an adequate labor supply, the nation established liberal immigration policies and continued the practices begun during the colonial era of investing heavily in the Atlantic slave trade.

Despite its general openness to newcomers, during this early phase of nation-building, the voluntary immigrants came overwhelmingly from western Europe, with the British constituting the dominant group. Over a million immigrants had already arrived by the time of the first census in 1790, with fully 89 percent of this population originating from England and Scotland. At slightly under 6 percent, the Germans were the second largest group. Among the other groups represented during the early years of the republic were the Irish, Dutch, French, and Scandinavians. The sheer size of the British population, combined with the legacy of colonial rule, stamped the British heritage on the political, cultural, and social fabric of the emerging nation. The economic domination of the British coalesced with political domination. British laws, institutions, and political sensibilities were transplanted to America. To provide but one example of what this meant, British hegemony was such that the language question never managed to rise to the level of genuine political debate during the nineteenth century, and as a result no law was passed that mandated English as the official language of the nation. It was simply assumed to be (Kivisto 1995: 117–24).

Between 1790 and 1820, the level of immigration was relatively modest, with an estimated 250,000 people arriving from western Europe during these three decades. The number picked up dramatically thereafter, with sizeable immigrant streams coming from not only Britain, but also Germany and Ireland. Though there were considerable differences among the British, as a whole they not surprisingly adapted quickly to the new environment, blending into the host society so rapidly that they became, as Charlotte Erickson (1972) has characterized them, "invisible immigrants." These new arrivals settled in the urban centers of the northeast and became the key component in the move into the frontier, first in the middle west and later onward to the Pacific coast.

The Germans, too, played a major role in the settlement of the middle west. With sufficient social and individual capital to be economically successful, the German population—diverse in terms of religious affiliation and political persuasion—established a vibrant ethnic community while exhibiting a willingness to develop social relationships outside of the confines of German America. By the latter part of the nineteenth century, the Germans were well positioned in the hierarchy of ethnic groups in America. In this regard, their experience parallels that of most other western European groups. The Irish were the exception. As noted above, this was in no small part due to the fact that they were Catholic in a chiefly Protestant nation (Jones 1960: 147–57). Moreover, the idea that they were racially distinct from the British further served to place them in a disadvantageous location in the ethnic hierarchy.

All of this changed dramatically after 1880, during which time the industrialization of the economy intensified and the demand for unskilled laborers in the manufacturing sector grew. Although immigrants continued to arrive from western Europe, their numbers were not sufficient to meet demand. The slack was taken up by immigrants from other parts of Europe. Indeed, between 1890 and 1930, the number of immigrants from eastern and southern Europe exceeded those from western Europe. The largest groups to arrive during this major immigration were Italians, Jews (from various countries in Europe, but particularly from Poland and Russia), and Poles. However, immigrants came from a wide range of countries, including Albanians, Byelorussians, Bulgarians, Croatians, Czechs, Estonians, Finns, Greeks, Hungarians, Macedonians, Montenegrins, Portuguese, Romanians, Russians, Serbians, Slovaks, Slovenes, Spaniards, and Ukrainians. Taken as a whole, as table 3.1.1 indicates, the foreign born reached a level of 14.8 percent of the total population during this period.

These "strangers in the land" (Higham 1970) were culturally, religiously, and linguistically diverse, but what was most significant to native-born Americans were their differences *vis-à-vis* those who had arrived prior to the Civil War. These were the people Madison Grant accused of constituting a cultural threat and a social problem. They confronted in varying degrees prejudice, discrimination, and social marginalization. In many instances, efforts to gain an economic foothold that allowed for upward social mobility proved to be difficult. In response to their presence, an increasingly powerful movement to limit or altogether ban further mass immigration took root. It managed to influence immigration legislation from the 1890s forward, during which time a series of measures were taken to make admission to the US more difficult and to raise the barrier for those seeking to become citizens. These efforts to limit immigration culminated in an initial quota law in 1921 and a more stringent one passed in 1924, known as the National Origins Act. Although immigration was not altogether prohibited, the result was that with the passage of this law, the migratory movement from Europe on a grand scale came to a halt. Economic and political factors served to reinforce this situation, as the Depression of the 1930s followed by the Second World War proved to be disincentives to would-be immigrants.

TABLE 3.1.1 US foreign-born population, 1890–2000

YEAR	NUMBER (IN MILLIONS)	PERCENT
2000	28.4	10.4
1990	19.8	7.9
1970	9.6	4.7
1950	10.3	6.9
1930	14.2	11.6
1910	13.5	14.7
1890	9.2	14.8

Source: US Census Bureau 2001.

Southern and eastern Europeans occupied an interstitial and ambiguous place in American society. Nowhere was this better reflected than in the social distance studies [...] that were conducted by Emory Bogardus (1933). In these studies of comparative levels of social acceptance of various groups, whereas western Europeans were the most readily accepted and non-Europeans (including blacks, Asians, Turks, and others) were the least readily accepted, these groups found themselves somewhere in the middle. Not surprisingly, the ethnic communities that they created expended considerable time and energy attempting to convince the larger society—and perhaps themselves—that they were in fact fully capable of being assimilated into American society (Overland 2000). Part of these campaigns entailed efforts to convince the host society that they were indeed white. Over time, as the members of these groups adjusted to their new homeland and became acclimated to it, immigrants and their offspring relied less and less on their ethnic communities to sustain them. Rather, they began to look to the institutions of the larger society and began to involve themselves in their activities. This occurred more quickly for some groups and at a slower pace for others, depending in no small part on the variations in the levels of prejudice and discrimination that confronted particular groups. What all of these groups shared in common was easy access to full citizenship rights, which served as a major vehicle for becoming American on terms where they had a voice in defining precisely what that meant.

References

Allen, Theodore W. 1994. *The Invention of the White Race*. vol. 1. *Racial Oppression and Social Control*. London: Verso.

Bailyn, Bernard. 1967. *The Ideological Origins of the American Revolution*. Cambridge. MA: The Belknap Press of Harvard University Press.

Bogardus, Emory. 1933. "A Social-distance Scale." *Sociology and Social Research*. 17 (Jan.–Feb.): 265–71.

de Crèvecoeur, J. Hector St. John. 1904 [1782]. *Letters from an American Farmer*. New York: Fox. Duffield.

Erickson, Charlotte. 1972. *Invisible Immigrants: The Adaptation of English and Scottish Immigrants in Nineteenth-Century America*. Coral Gables. FL: University of Miami Press.

Gleason, Philip. 1964. "The Melting Pot: Symbol of Fusion or Confusion?" *American Quarterly*. 16(1): 20–46.

Grant, Madison. 1916. *The Passing of the Great Race*. New York: Charles Scribner's Sons.

Handlin, Oscar. 1973. *The Uprooted*. Boston: Little, Brown & Co.

Higham, John. 1999. "Cultural Responses to Immigration." Pp. 39–61 in Neil J. Smelser and Jeffrey C. Alexander (eds.). *Diversity and Its Discontents*. Princeton. NJ: Princeton University Press.

Jaret, Charles. 1999. "Troubled by Newcomers: Anti-Immigration Attitudes and Action During Two Eras of Mass Immigration to the United States." *Journal of American Ethnic History*. 18(3): 9–39.

Kivisto, Peter. 1995. *Americans All: Race and Ethnic Relations in Historical. Structural and Comparative Perspectives*. Belmont. CA: Wadsworth.

Overland, Orm. 2000. *Immigrant Minds, American Identities: Making the United States Home, 1870–1930*. Urbana: University of Illinois Press.

Roediger, David R. 1991. *The Wages of Whiteness: Race and the Making of the American Working Class*. New York: Verso.

REFLECT AND CONSIDER

- In what sense was the White race "invented" during nineteenth century America?
- How were nineteenth century European immigrants transformed from strangers into "Americans"?

THE THREE PHASES OF US BOUND IMMIGRATION

BY ALEJANDRO PORTES AND RUBEN RUMBAUT

Rebound: 1970–2010

The 1960s were a period of prosperity and atonement in America. The failure of the post–World War II years to integrate African Americans and Mexican Americans into the social and economic mainstream finally came back with a vengeance. In the midst of economic prosperity and global hegemony, the relegation of one-fifth of the American population to a caste-like status could no longer continue. The urban riots and the parallel civil rights movement wrought major changes in the nation's institutional framework. Predictably, black mobilizations in the Southeast and riots in cities everywhere were accompanied by parallel protests in the Southwest by its large Mexican American population. Both groups reacted to the patent injustice of being used as the backbone of the low-wage labor market and as foot soldiers in the nation's wars without ever being granted access to its opportunities.

Fortunately, the nation's political leaders at the time recognized this and took a series of measures to remedy the situation. Civil rights legislation and the War on Poverty, launched by President Lyndon Johnson, followed in short order. Embedded in the new national mood to atone for past racial injustices was the initiative to eliminate the last vestiges of the racist provisions of the 1924 National Origins Act. Thereafter, access to the United States would be based on two fundamental criteria: family reunification and occupational merit. National origin would not enter the picture, except for a per-country limit set on a universalistic basis. In 1952, provisions to exclude Asians had been repealed in a bill passed over President Truman's veto. The 1965 amendments completed the task. These events opened the door to immigration from all countries, setting a cap of 20,000 per country and a global limit of 290,000.[1] Children under twenty-one years of age, spouses, and parents of U.S. citizens were exempt from those numerical limits.

In the floor debates over the new legislation, cosponsor Emanuel Celler (D–New York) argued that few Asians and Africans would actually come since they had no families to reunite with. President Johnson reassured critics of the bill's benign consequences: "This bill that we sign today is not a revolutionary bill. It does not affect the lives of millions," he declared. Secretary of State Dean Rusk anticipated only eight thousand immigrants from India over five years and few thereafter. Senator Edward Kennedy argued that the ethnic mix of the country would not be altered.[2] Subsequent history was to prove these predictions deeply wrong.

A year before this legislation was passed and in the same mood of atonement, the *bracero* agreement with Mexico was repealed. Opponents argued that the program subjected Mexican workers to systematic exploitation by unscrupulous American employers and corrupt Mexican officials. Its elimination would also create new employment opportunities for native workers.[3] The lofty spirit in which these pieces of legislation were crafted did not envision what their actual consequences would be. Denied access to braceros, U.S. ranchers and farmers did not hire native workers but turned to the same Mexican workers now rebaptized as clandestine migrants. As also shown in table 6, apprehensions of "illegal aliens" at the border shot up with the end of the Bracero Program, rising year by year and reaching more than half a million by 1972.

A second unexpected consequence of the 1965 act was that it provided a new avenue for unauthorized migrants to legalize their situation. Clandestine Mexican workers who wanted to stay on this side of the border could now make use of various legal means, paramount among them marriage to a U.S. citizen or permanent resident. A study of Mexican migration conducted in the early 1970s found that, by 1973, 70 percent of legal Mexican migrants had already lived in the United States for one year or more: "Clearly, most of the men in this sample did not face legal entry into the United States as strangers or newcomers. Instead the vast majority were 'return immigrants' coming back to places and people that had long before become established parts of their lives."[4]

A third consequence of the 1965 act was to open the professional labor market to foreigners. As Representative Celler would have it, few Africans and Asians had families to reunite with, but they had occupational qualifications, and Asians, in particular, took full advantage of the meritocratic provisions of the new system. As we will see, a major consequence was to bifurcate the immigration stream into flows targeting different segments of the American labor market. Thereafter, both the composition of the foreign population in America and its impact on the receiving society and economy would become far more nuanced and complex.

Industrial Restructuring and the Hourglass

As in the 1920s, it took time for the new Immigration Act of 1965 to be implemented. Immigration continued at low levels during the 1960s so that, as shown in figure 3.2.1, the foreign-born population reached its lowest absolute and relative numbers in 1970. It was only after that year that the momentous effect of the reform was to be felt. Framers of the 1965 amendments could not possibly have foreseen it, but the new system paved the way for a segmentation of future immigration flows reflecting the bifurcation of the American economy and labor markets in the decades to come.

As seen previously, the United States generated a vast demand for industrial labor during the late nineteenth century and the first three decades of the twentieth century. Indeed, this was the reason why European immigrants, first, and southern black migrants, second, were recruited and came in such vast numbers to northern American cities. The availability of industrial jobs and the existence of a ladder of occupations within industrial employment created the possibility of gradual mobility for the European second generation *without need* for an advanced education. This continued labor demand was behind the rise of stable working-class communities, where supervisory and other preferred industrial jobs afforded a reasonable living standard for European ethnics. As has also been seen, their gradual mobility into the higher tiers of blue-collar employment and then into the white-collar middle class furnished the empirical basis for subsequent theories of assimilation.

Beginning in the 1970s and accelerating thereafter, the structure of the American labor market started to change under the twin influences of technological innovation and foreign competition in industrial goods. The advent of Japan as a major industrial competitor took American companies by surprise, accustomed as they were, to lacking any real foreign rivals in the post–World War II era. As two prominent students of American deindustrialization concluded: "What caused the profit squeeze was mainly the sudden emergence of heightened international competition—a competition to which U.S. business leaders were initially blind. … In the manufacturing sector a trickle of imports turned into a torrent. The value of

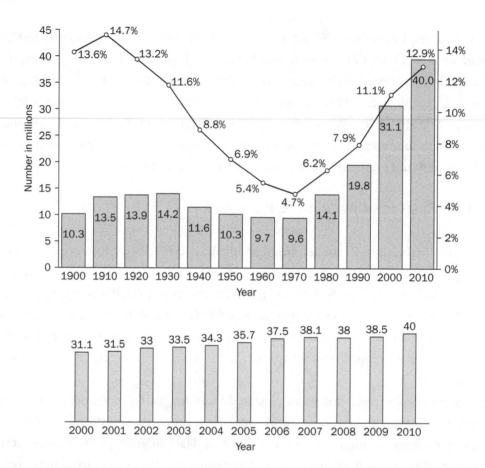

FIGURE 3.2.1. The evolution of the foreign-born population of the United States. *Top:* Number and percentage. *Sources:* Decennial census for 1900 to 2000; and U.S. Census Bureau, American Community Survey, 2010. *Bottom:* Total immigrant population, 2000–2010 (millions). *Sources:* 2000 decennial census; and U.S. Census Bureau, American Community Surveys, 2001–10.

manufactured imports relative to domestic production skyrocketed—from less than 14 percent in 1969 to nearly triple that, 38 percent, only ten years later." [5]

Caught in this bind, many companies resorted to the "spatial fix" of moving production facilities abroad in order to reduce labor costs. Technological innovations made the process easier by lowering transportation barriers and making possible instant communication between corporate headquarters and production plants located abroad. The garment industry represents a prime example of this process of restructuring. While fashion design and marketing strategies remained centralized in the companies' American headquarters, actual production migrated, for the most part, to industrial zones in the less-developed world. [6]

Industrial restructuring and corporate downsizing brought about the gradual disappearance of the jobs that had provided the basis for the economic ascent of the European second generation. Between 1950 and 1996, American manufacturing employment plummeted, from more than 33 percent of the labor force to less than 15 percent. The slack was taken up by service employment, which skyrocketed from 12 percent to almost 33 percent of all workers. Service employment is, however, bifurcated between menial and casual low-wage jobs commonly associated with personal services and the rapid growth of occupations requiring advanced technical and professional skills. These highly paid service jobs are generated by knowledge-based industries linked to new information technologies and those associated with the command and control functions of a restructured capitalist economy.[7]

The growth of employment in these two polar service sectors is one of the factors that stalled the gradual trend toward economic equality in the United States and then reversed it during the following decades. Between 1960 and 1990 the income of the top decile of American families increased in constant (1986) dollars from $40,789 to $60,996. In contrast, the income of the bottom decile barely budged, from $6,309 to $8,637. The income of the bottom half of families, which in 1960 represented about 50 percent of the income of those in the top decile, declined by almost 10 percent relative to this wealthiest group in the following thirty years. By 2000 the median net worth of American households had climbed to about $80,000. However, almost half of households (44 percent) did not reach $25,000, and exactly a third had annual incomes below this figure. More than half of American families (57 percent) did not own any equities at all, falling further behind in terms of economic power.[8] The trend continued during the first decade of the twenty-first century, with gaps in household wealth (net worth) becoming wider still. By 2009, the net worth of black and Hispanic households (which among homeowners is largely based on their home equity) was largely wiped out in the wake of the collapse of housing prices and a deep recession. Net worth among Hispanics dropped to a miniscule $6,300, and the average wealth of white households was twenty times that of Hispanic households—the widest wealth gap in twenty-five years. Economic inequality—as measured by the Gini index and related indicators—reached Third World levels by 2010.[9]

In this changed market, high demand exists, at the low end, for unskilled and menial service workers and, at the high end, for professionals and technicians—with diminishing opportunities for well-paid employment in between. Figure 3.2.2. illustrates this changed situation. Contemporary immigration has responded to this new "hourglass" economy by bifurcating, in turn, into major occupational categories. As we have seen, the end of the Bracero Program rechanneled the low-skill agricultural flow from Mexico, Central America, and the Caribbean into the category of "illegal aliens." Simultaneously, the occupational preference provisions of the 1965 Immigration Act paved the way for major professional and technical flows originating primarily in Asia. Subsequent legislation added flexibility and volume to this form of immigration. The increasing heterogeneity of the contemporary foreign-born population in the wake of these legal and labor-market changes requires additional emphasis as a counterpart of the common popular description of immigration as a homogeneous phenomenon.

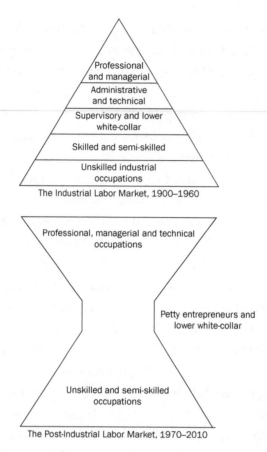

FIGURE 3.2.2. Changing labor markets.

Notes

1. Tienda, "Demography"; Massey and Pren, "Unintended Consequences"; Rumbaut, "Origins and Destinies."

2. Tienda, "Demography," 11–12.

3. Samora, *Los mojados;* Massey, Durand, and Malone, *Beyond Smoke and Mirrors.*

4. Portes and Bach, *Latin Journey,* 126.

5. Harrison and Bluestone, *The Great U-turn,* 8.

6. Gereffi, "International Trade"; Fernández-Kelly, *For We Are Sold.*

7. U.S. Census Bureau, *U.S. Employment Data: 1950–1997.*

8. See Karoly, *The Trend in Inequality*, 1–5.

9. Massey, *Categorically Unequal.*

REFLECT AND CONSIDER

- ■ Why can the Hart-Cellar Act of 1965 be described as an "atonement"?
- ■ What is the relationship between immigration and the economy?

THE IDEOLOGICAL ROOTS OF THE "ILLEGAL" AS THREAT AND THE BOUNDARY AS PROTECTOR

BY JOSEPH NEVINS

A preoccupation with unauthorized migrants and boundary enforcement—at least in a sustained manner with widespread popular support—is of relatively recent origin. The national platform of the Republican Party, for example, did not mention immigration enforcement for the first time until 1980. It was not until four years later that the party affirmed the right of the United States to control its boundaries and voiced concern about illegal immigration. In like fashion, the Democratic Party's national platform did not even mention illegal immigration until 1996, when it took a similar stand to the Republicans. That is not to say that unauthorized immigration had not hitherto been of any concern. As demonstrated previously, there were a number of points in twentieth-century U.S. history prior to the 1970s when unauthorized immigration and boundary enforcement did raise state and public concern, such as during World War II and in 1954 with Operation Wetback. But what is striking—at least as indicated by media coverage—is how shallow that concern has been on a popular level, until relatively recently. Not surprisingly, as official and popular concerns have grown, so have the levels of institutionalization of the U.S.–Mexico boundary and associated enforcement practices. At the same time, the labeling of unauthorized immigrants—again, as manifested by media coverage—has changed.

At the time of the creation of the Border Patrol in 1924, major media outlets generally referred to unauthorized immigrants (to the extent that the media talked about them at all) as simply "aliens." However, by 1954—the time of Operation Wetback—the term "wetback" was most popular, with the term "illegal" (as in "illegal alien") being the second most common label. As media interest in the boundary and unauthorized immigration increased significantly beginning in the 1970s, a considerable shift was evident in the language employed to describe unauthorized immigrants as demonstrated by media coverage around the time of Mexican President José Lopez-Portillo's visit to Washington, DC, in February 1977. On the basis of an analysis of major media outlets, "illegal" was the term most commonly ascribed to unauthorized immigrants (in 76 percent of the cases). The term "wetback" was present in only 3 percent of the cases, whereas it was the label of choice in 39 percent of the cases identified in the media items examined from 1954 (Nevins 1998). This shift is not surprising given a growing perception beginning in the 1960s that labels such as "wetback" were disrespectful (at best) or racist. The INS began to prohibit the use of such terms in the early 1960s (Botts 1997: 11). The growth in the use of the term "illegal" continued into the 1990s. Although the Carter administration in the late 1970s forbade the use of the term "illegal alien," instead using terms such as "undocumented worker" or "undocumented alien" (Botts 1997: 11–13; McDonald 1997: 84), this linguistic sensitivity quickly disappeared in official circles. State authorities now almost exclusively use the term "illegal" in public and official discussions to describe unauthorized immigrants—a development replicated in public discourse as a whole.

The rise in emphasis on the legality of migrants coincided with a substantial increase in national media coverage of issues relating to unauthorized immigration and boundary control. A review of the annual indices of the *New York Times* from the 1970s, for example, found a considerable change in the number of articles that discussed extralegal immigration over the course of the decade. From 1970 to 1972, the *Times* published an average of slightly more than 8.5 articles per year on the subject. During the next eight years (1973–1980), a time of economic recession and increasing activism by politicians and state actors toward unauthorized immigration and boundary enforcement, it produced an average of more than 57 articles annually, an increase of more than 650 percent. Only about 15 percent of the articles during the 1970–1972 period discussed unauthorized immigration specifically from Mexico, whereas the figure reached 36 percent between 1973 and 1980. On an absolute scale, the average number of articles (on an annual basis) that linked unauthorized immigration to Mexico increased from 1.3 in the 1970–1972 period to 20.6 from 1973 to 1980. Most of the articles dealing with extralegal immigration from Mexico (and many of those dealing with illegal immigration more generally) explicitly or implicitly discussed the U.S.–Mexico boundary and its enforcement. In this sense, the articles contributed to a growing awareness of the boundary, thus making it (and alleged problems associated with the international divide) more meaningful in the collective mind of the U.S. public.

As the labels applied to unauthorized migrants changed and the amount of media coverage increased, the actual content of the reporting transformed in terms of their representation. The media coverage surrounding the Carter–Lopez-Portillo summit in 1977, for instance, manifested an increasing tendency to associate unauthorized immigrants with criminal activity and a declining standard of living for U.S. citizens (Nevins 1998). Another study revealed a significant increase from the period 1959–1972 to that of 1973–1986 in the number of articles suggesting that "illegals" were overwhelming the United States in terms of sheer numbers, that illegal immigration was a Mexican problem, that unauthorized immigrants were a financial burden to U.S. taxpayers and were taking jobs away from U.S. workers, and that immigration was purely a (U.S.) domestic issue that could be solved through unilateral action (Walters 1990: 10–12). The cover of the December 1974 issue of *The American Legion Magazine*, for example, contained a cartoon image of U.S. territory being overrun by an influx of immigrants for an article entitled "Our Illegal Alien Problem." The cover depicted the vast majority of the immigrants by means of a throng of cartoon-like Mexicans with sombreros smashing through U.S. boundary blockades, overrunning boundary inspectors, and flooding into buildings with descriptive signs such as "schools," "welfare department," "medical aid," and "jobs" (Ardman 1974).

Media coverage of unauthorized immigration reached such a level in the 1970s that the Gallup Organization found in a 1976 poll conducted for the INS that over half of those polled had recently read or heard something about "the problem of illegal aliens." The figure was particularly high—over two-thirds—in the West and in states that bordered Mexico (Fernández and Pedroza 1982: 4).

U.S. News & World Report was especially aggressive in highlighting the alleged threat unauthorized migrants presented to U.S. society. The January 17, 1972, issue, for example, contained a report entitled "Surge of Illegal Immigrants Across American Borders" in which it stated that the number of unauthorized immigrants in the United States could be high as 10 million and reported that they pay no taxes (a patently false claim), contribute to the flow of U.S. dollars out of the country, and take jobs from U.S. citizens. A July 23, 1973, report from the same magazine carried the provocative title "'Invasion' by Illegal Aliens and the Problems They Create." The magazine also indirectly suggested that unauthorized Mexican immigrants were less desirable than the European immigrants who arrived in the United States in the late nineteenth and early twentieth centuries.

The mass media clearly helped to construct the image of an immigration and boundary enforcement crisis. As a 1977 *Time* magazine report described ominously:

> The U.S. is being invaded so silently and surreptitiously that most Americans are not even aware of it. The invaders come by land, sea and air. They fly commercial and private aircraft; they jump ship or sail their own boats; they scale mountains and swim rivers. Some have crawled through a mile-long tunnel; others have squeezed through the San Antonio sewerage system. No commandos or assault troops have shown more ingenuity and determination in storming a country that tries to keep them out.
>
> (*Time* 1977: 26)

The invasion, according to *Time*, was largely Mexican in nature. The report stated that "[s]ome 80% of the illegal aliens now living in America come from Mexico." (At that time, about two-thirds of the unauthorized immigrant population was of Mexican origin: Morris and Mayio 1982: 4.) The article quoted INS Commissioner Chapman warning that "We have become the haven for the unemployed of the world. I think it's going to be catastrophic" (*Time* 1977: 26). Such thinking continued to inform public and official perceptions and representations of unauthorized immigration and boundary through the early to mid-1990s when the notion of an illegal immigration crisis re-emerged with a vengeance.

The perception of the illegal alien as a significant threat to the American social fabric emerged most strongly in California during the debate surrounding Proposition 187. Somewhat surprisingly, however, a linking of crime with unauthorized immigrants was not a major theme in the media around the time of Proposition 187. The most common pro-187 theme emphasized the illegal nature of unauthorized immigration, often arguing that the United States should not reward those who break the law with social benefits, and that the survival of the U.S. immigration regime requires a strong distinction between legal and illegal forms of immigration. It was local and federal government officials who most frequently put forth this argument.

The second most popular argument in favor of the measure was one that argued that unauthorized immigrants take scarce social services and undermine the American socio-economic fabric in the process. Kitty Calavita (1996) refers to this position as "balanced-budget conservatism," a stance that blames immigrants as well as government spending (but almost exclusively social spending) and budget deficits, rather than deindustrialization or economic restructuring and the dismantling of the social safety net, for prevailing economic and social problems.

A minority of media items voicing support for Proposition 187 argued for the need of the United States to protect itself from threats from without, often contending that unauthorized immigration was leading to the creation of a "Third World" country in the United States, was "balkanizing" American society, and/or was undermining the country's culture (implicitly a European-American one). Others justified cracking down on unauthorized immigration by employing pro-environment and neo-Malthusian population perspectives, blaming a supposed oversupply of immigrants for traffic congestion, air pollution, and overburdened schools (see Ling-Ling 1994; also Camarota 1997; Reimers 1998). In this manner, the environment provided a host of unflattering metaphors (such as "pollution" and "contamination") to attach to immigrants (Gabriel 1998: 122). Similarly, racialized fears of immigrant criminality, hyper-fertility among women of Mexican origin, and potential cultural and even political conquest by immigrants disrespectful of (implicitly white) American territorial sovereignty were also important elements of the discourse (see Gabriel 1998: 117–123; Jacobson 2008). As quoted in one *Los Angeles Times* article, Ruth Coffey, the head of a Long Beach-based group called Stop Immigration Now, wrote, "I have no intention of being the object of 'conquest,' peaceful or otherwise, by Latinos, Asians, blacks, Arabs, or any other group of individuals who have claimed my country" (quoted in Martinez and McDonnell 1994: A1; also see Suro 1996).

Such views dominated much of the pro-187 literature emanating from grassroots, pro-restrictionist groups. And they also were very prominent in a number of right-wing periodicals (see Gabriel 1998). These views echo those of a number of right-wing groups and publishing houses that began promoting the issue of illegal immigration at the beginning of the 1980s. Two of the most prominent organizations were the Federation for American Immigration Reform (FAIR) and the American Immigration Control Foundation (AICF). Before immigration became a hot issue, self-identified "paleoconservatives" were waging the anti-immigrant war, while most of the Right was preoccupied with its anti-communist crusade. Paleoconservatives rejected economic questions around immigration, instead focusing on the putative threat that the influx of nonwhite immigrant groups was creating for U.S. cultural homogeneity. The focus on cultural homogeneity was a central focus of immigration restriction groups during this time, such as U.S. English. In 1986, for example, California's Proposition 63, an Official English amendment, passed with 73 percent voting in favor (Diamond 1996: 156–58; also see Lewis 1979: 141–44).

It is important to point out here that the various themes are not equal in terms of their effectiveness, as certain ones "have a natural advantage because their ideas and language resonate with larger cultural themes" (Gamson and Modigliani 1987: 169). And it is probably the fear of "third worldization" that dovetails best with the long history of nativism in the United States, demonstrating that negative perceptions about the "Other" were very much present in public discourse about unwanted immigrants—especially so-called illegals—in the 1990s.

A number of the themes raised by the so-called paleoconservatives were at home with a large sector of the U.S. population. An August 1993 Gallup Poll, for example, reported that more than 60 percent of Americans felt that there were too many immigrants from Latin American, Asia, and Arab countries. And almost the same number stated that the presence of immigrants from Mexico, Haiti, Iran, and Cuba created problems for the United States (McDonald 1997: 69).

Negative stereotypes about Mexicans, and Latin Americans more generally, have a long history in the United States (see Schmidt 1997). It is impossible to separate these deeply rooted stereotypes from support for measures favoring more restrictive measures against immigrants—authorized or not. As the historian Robin D. G. Kelley argues:

> Anti-immigrant sentiment ... is not just about class anger, because there really is no mobilization against Canadians or European immigrants taking what are essentially skilled jobs. It is about dark people, whether wetbacks or some invisible Pacific Rim empire run by sneaky Chinese. The history of conquest, repatriation in the Southwest, stereotypes of "Latin" hypersexuality, even racialized and gendered myths of the welfare mother, are fundamental to understanding anti-immigrant sentiment, the English-only movement, and pro-Proposition 187.
>
> (Kelley 1997: 120–21)

Indeed, how else can we understand the significant differential between ethno-racial groups in terms of support for certain types of immigration restrictionist measures, such as Proposition 187? While about 67 percent of white voters in California supported the measure, only about half of African-American and Asian-American voters did so. And only 23 percent of Latino voters approved of the proposition (Chávez 1997: 63) despite the fact that Latinos opine to a degree similar to whites that rates of immigration should be lower and that enhanced boundary enforcement is desirable (Binder et al. 1997; Gutiérrez 1995). Clearly, the historical weight of white supremacy and anti-Mexican sentiment, outlined earlier, informed voting patterns.

A racialized notion of the nation was a central component to debates surrounding illegal immigration in the early 1990s. As the former Republican presidential candidate Pat Buchanan wrote, "Proposition 187 [is about] ... the deepest, most divisive issues of our time: ethnicity, nation, culture." Buchanan called for "a timeout on immigration" to have the time to assimilate those who are already here (thus resurrecting the idea of racial indigestion), lest Quebec-like secession result in the U.S. Southwest and interethnic conflict intensify (Buchanan 1994). Such sentiments were and are very common among pro-restrictionist activists and groups that organized in favor of Proposition 187 and continue to agitate in favor of enhanced boundary policing. Voice of Citizens Together (VCT), for example, based in Sherman Oaks, California, had an ad in the November 4, 1996, issue of the *Los Angeles Times* warning that "A VOTE FOR BILL CLINTON AND THE DEMOCRATS MAY BE A VOTE TO RETURN CALIFORNIA TO MEXICO." When Cruz Bustamente became speaker of the California Assembly and Antonio Villaraigosa became Majority Leader of the Assembly, the VCT's newsletter (November/December 1996) proclaimed that "Mexicans Take Over State Assembly." A widely circulated 1995 book, *Alien Nation* by Peter Brimelow—a senior editor of *Forbes* and *National Review*—openly called upon the United States to revert back to its pre-1965 immigration policies, when racial and ethnic factors were primary, to ensure the survival of the United States as a white, English-speaking country where European values reign.

The proponents of such views almost always vehemently deny that the views are racist in nature. But such disavowals do not mean that racism is not present; "on the contrary, that is the way racism usually works" (Lipsitz 1998: 215). Although few people in contemporary American society subscribe to biology- or religion-based theories of racial inferiority or superiority—indeed, the vast majority of whites surely reject such views and espouse universalistic views of human equality—that does not mean that racism is not still very much present. In 1990, for example, not long before Brimelow's book was published, a National Opinion Research Report disclosed that 50 percent of U.S. whites viewed blacks as innately lazy as well as less intelligent than whites, while 56.3 percent felt that blacks preferred welfare to employment (Lipsitz 1998: 19).

What have changed over the course of U.S. history are the forms that racism takes and the social purposes that it serves (Lipsitz 1998). A cultural argument has come to dominate racist discourse since roughly the 1950s, one that does *not* contend that any defined people does not have a capacity equal to that of other groups. Instead, those arguing this line of thought assert that marginalized groups have proven unable (or unwilling) to realize their capacity because of their inferior culture and/or because they have not learned or they do not practice what it takes to succeed (Blaut 1992).

References

Ardman, Harvey. 1974. "Our Illegal Alien Problem." *American Legion Magazine* 97(6): 6–9+.

Binder, Norman E., J.L. Polinard, and Robert D. Winkle. 1997. "Mexican American and Anglo Attitudes toward Immigration Reform: A View from the Border." *Social Science Quarterly* 78(2): 324–37.

Blaut, James M. 1992. "The Theory of Cultural Racism." *Antipode* 24(4): 289–99.

Botts, Gene. 1997. *The Border Game: Enforcing America's Immigration Laws.* Phoenix: Quest Publishing Group.

Camarota, Steven A. 1997. "Reducing Greenhouse Gases: The Vital Immigration Angle." (Op-ed), *San Diego Union-Tribune*, November 28.

Carter, Bob, Marci Green, and Rick Halpern. 1996. "Immigration Policy and the Racialization of Migrant Labour: The Construction of National Identities in the USA and Britain." *Ethnic and Racial Studies* 19(1): 135–57.

Chávez, Leo R. 1997. "Immigration Reform and Nativism: The Nationalist Response to the Transnationalist Challenge." Pp. 61–77 in *Immigrants Out!: The New Nativism and the Anti-Immigrant Impulse in the United States*, ed. Juan F. Perea. New York: New York University Press.

Diamond, Sara. 1996. "Right-Wing Politics and the Anti-Immigration Cause," *Social Justice* 23(3): 154–68.

Doty, Roxanne L. 1996. "Sovereignty and the Nation: Constructing the Boundaries of National Identity." Pp. 121–47 in *State Sovereignty as Social Construct*, eds. Thomas J. Biersteker and Cynthia Weber. Cambridge, UK: Cambridge University Press.

Fernández, Celestino, and Lawrence R. Pedroza. 1982. "The Border Patrol and News Media Coverage of Undocumented Mexican Immigration during the 1970s: A Quantitative Content Analysis in the Sociology of Knowledge." *California Sociologist* 5(2): 1–26.

Gabriel, John. 1998. *Whitewash: Racialized Politics and the Media*. London: Routledge.

Gutiérrez, David G. 1995. *Walls and Mirrors: Mexican Americans, Mexican Immigrants, and the Politics of Ethnicity*. Berkeley: University of California Press.

Jacobson, Robin Dale. 2008. *The New Nativism: Proposition 187 and the Debate over Immigration*. Minneapolis: University of Minnesota Press.

Kelley, Robin D. G. 1997. *Yo' Mama's Disfunktional!: Fighting the Culture Wars in Urban America*. Boston: Beacon Press.

Lewis, Sasha G. 1979. *Slave Trade Today: American Exploitation of Illegal Aliens*. Boston: Beacon Press.

Ling-Ling, Yeh. 1994. "The Welcome Mat Is Threadbare." (Op-ed), *Los Angeles Times*, April 13.

Martinez, Gene, and Patrick J. McDonnell. 1994. "Prop. 187 Backers Counting on Message, Not Strategy." *Los Angeles Times*, October 30: A1+.

McDonald, William F. 1997. "Illegal Immigration: Crime, Ramifications, and Control (the American Experience)." Pp. 65–86 in *Crime and Law Enforcement in the Global Village*, ed. William McDonald. Cincinnati: Anderson Publishing.

Nevins, Joseph. 1998. "California Dreaming: Operation Gatekeeper and the Social Geographical Construction of the 'Illegal Alien' along the U.S.–Mexico Boundary." Ph.D. Dissertation, Department of Geography, University of California, Los Angeles, December.

____. 1998. *Unwelcome Strangers: American Identity and the Turn against Immigration*. New York: Columbia University Press.

Suro, Roberto. 1996. *Watching America's Door: The Immigration Backlash and the New Policy Debate*. New York: Twentieth Century Fund Press.

Time. 1977. "Getting Their Slice of Paradise." May 2: 26+.

Walters, Jana. 1990. "Illegal Immigration: The Making of Myth." (Unpublished paper completed for a graduate seminar in sociology at the University of Texas at Austin).

REFLECT AND CONSIDER

■ Why does it matter what undocumented immigrants are called?

■ Why do questions of race and nation come up in the debate over undocumented immigration?

SEGMENTED ASSIMILATION REVISITED: TYPES OF ACCULTURATION AND SOCIOECONOMIC MOBILITY IN YOUNG ADULTHOOD

BY MARY C. WATERS, VAN C. TRAN, PHILIP KASINITZ, AND JOHN H. MOLLENKOPF

Introduction

The study of the "new second generation"—children born to post-1965 immigrants in the U.S.—has expanded rapidly as they have entered adulthood. Understanding how they are integrating into American society is both theoretically important and a key policy issue. Since the children of immigrants are now one tenth of the American population and one fifth of those under 18, their fate is enormously important to the future of the country.

It is important not only to understand trends for the second generation as a whole, but why some of its members are succeeding and others doing poorly. What factors lead the children of immigrants to do better than their parents and what factors lead to downward social mobility? Drawing on data from the study of the Immigrant Second Generation in Metropolitan New York[*], this paper examines how types of acculturation shape socioeconomic outcomes among young adult respondents.

Theories of Straight-Line and Segmented Assimilation Revisited

Two major theories—straight-line assimilation and segmented assimilation—point to different processes underlying second generation outcomes. The standard assimilation theory is associated with the founders of the Chicago School of Sociology, who studied the integration of the first and second generation European immigrants in the early 20th century (Park and Burgess 1925). This model argues that assimilation processes will enable each succeeding generation to show upward social mobility in education and occupation, be more integrated into the American mainstream, and show less ethnic distinctiveness in language use, residential concentration, and intermarriage patterns (Warner and Srole 1945).

Segmented assimilation theory emerged as an alternative to this model in the 1990s and has been enormously influential. Formulated by Alejandro Portes and his collaborators and elaborated and tested empirically by Portes and Ruben Rumbaut (Portes and Zhou 1993; Portes and Rumbaut 2001), this approach argues that starkly different outcomes are possible for the second generation. Its members can end up "ascending into the ranks of a prosperous middle class or join in large numbers the ranks of a racialized, permanently impoverished population at the bottom of society" (Portes, Kelly and Haller 2005:1004).

Segmented assimilation theory posits three possible outcomes for the second generation: upward assimilation, downward assimilation, and upward mobility combined with persistent biculturalism. These paths correspond to three processes that summarize the relations between immigrant children, their parents, and the wider ethnic community—consonant, dissonant, and selective acculturation. Consonant acculturation occurs when the children and parents both learn American culture and gradually abandon their home language and "old country" ways at about the same pace. As these children enter the American mainstream, they achieve upward mobility with the support of their parents. Dissonant acculturation occurs when children

---

[*]For a detailed description of the study, refer to the Methodological Appendix in Kasinitz et al (2008).

learn English and adopt American ways far faster than do their immigrant parents. Portes and Rumbaut (2001) argue that this process can lead to downward assimilation when young people confront racial discrimination, bifurcated labor markets, and often nihilistic inner city young people on their own, without strong parental authority or community support. The third process, selective acculturation, leads to upward assimilation and biculturalism. This occurs when parents and children both gradually learn American ways while remaining embedded, at least in part, in the ethnic community. It is characterized by "preservation of parental authority, little or no intergenerational conflict, and fluent bilingualism among children" (Portes and Rumbaut 2001:52). Portes and his collaborators argue that selective acculturation is especially important for groups facing discrimination

> ... because individuals and families do not face the strains of acculturation alone but rather within the framework of their own communities. This situation slows down the process while placing the acquisition of new cultural knowledge and language within a supportive context. (Portes and Rumbaut 2001:54)

Segmented assimilation theory also stresses the importance of parental human capital (including parents' education and income), modes of incorporation (state definitions of immigrant groups, eligibility for welfare, degree of discrimination and antipathy towards immigrant groups), and family structure (single vs. married couple families as well as multigenerational vs. nuclear family living arrangements). Although less explicitly stated, the model also points to the varying degrees of transnational connection among immigrant groups as an important element of the context of reception.

This theory has inspired a large volume of work on immigrant incorporation. The concept of "modes of incorporation", for instance, has been extremely useful in systematizing how varying political and cultural reactions to immigrant groups shape their individual experiences. Yet the most innovative causal mechanism of the theory—selective acculturation—has not been as closely examined as one would expect. This is unfortunate because this aspect of the segmented assimilation approach most clearly separates it from other accounts of immigrant incorporation. After all, standard sociological models of status attainment predict that children from two-parent households will have better outcomes, as whites will compared to Blacks and Hispanics, given the reality of ongoing racial discrimination in the U.S. It also predicts that the children of parents with high levels of education and income will do well, on average.

Where segmented assimilation departs from these standard interpretations is in predicting two specific outcomes as in part the result of intra-family dynamics—that downward assimilation occurs not because of the failure to Americanize, but of doing it too quickly (dissonant acculturation), and that upward mobility is possible for those with low income or poorly educated parents who stay at least partially tied to the "ethnic" community. In these two predictions, segmented assimilation stands the standard sociological account of assimilation on its head. For at least some immigrants, it argues that quickly coming to share American (or at least lower class American) ways is bad for the second generation, while holding on to immigrant distinctiveness can turn out to be an advantage.

In response to this approach, Alba and Nee (2003) formulated a new version of (more or less) straight line assimilation for the post-1965 immigrants. Retaining many key insights from earlier theorists, Alba and Nee predict that most members of the contemporary second generation will experience gradually increasing social integration and upward mobility. In contrast to the segmented assimilation model, they find little support for the notions that many will experience "downward assimilation" or that embeddedness in dense ethnic networks will prove beneficial. In contrast to earlier versions of straight line assimilation, however, Alba and Nee reject the overly prescriptive assertion that the second generation must adopt "American norms" and stress that the American "mainstream" is highly dynamic and heterogeneous. Drawing on segmented assimilation and other contemporary accounts, they understand the variation in immigrants' pre-migration backgrounds, current positions within a highly stratified American society and emphasize the importance of historically contingent contexts of reception.

Types of Acculturation and Socioeconomic Mobility

Many studies in the U.S. and increasingly in Europe show support for the theory of segmented assimilation, including work arising from the Children of Immigrants Longitudinal Study (CILS) and important case studies of particular second generation groups including Vietnamese (Zhou and Bankston 1998), West Indians (Waters 1999; Vickerman 1999), Chinese (Zhou and Kim 2006), Salvadorans (Menjívar 2000), and Haitians (Stepick 1998; Zéphir 2001). There is close to universal agreement that American society is not an undifferentiated whole—and in that sense immigrants clearly assimilate into one of its *segments*. Virtually all studies show that the children of immigrants do not follow a single trajectory and that second generation outcomes are highly contingent on the segment of American society into which they are being incorporated (Greenman and Xie 2008).

That said, one key point of disagreement between Alba and Nee's reformulated assimilation theory and segmented assimilation theory is whether the processes and mechanisms that led the previous waves of European immigrants in the early part of the 20th century to successfully integrate will work for the current wave of immigrants and their children. Indeed, while segmented assimilation claims that the non-white racial status of most current immigrants and the very different economy they face in 21st century America puts them and their children at greater risk. Waldinger and Perlmann (1998), Perlmann and Waldinger (1997) and Gratton (2002) have all criticized segmented assimilation's characterization of past. Further, many studies of the contemporary second generation find little evidence of second generation decline or downward assimilation (Boyd, 2002; Farley and Alba (2002), Hirschman (2001), Smith (2003), Waldinger and Feliciano (2004), and Kasinitz et al. (2008, 2004, 2002).

Of course, segmented assimilation does not predict universal downward mobility any more than classic assimilation predicts universal upward mobility. Alba and Nee (2001) and Portes and Zhou (1993) both argue that some members of the second generation will do well compared to their parents, while others will not. Both theories posit that racial discrimination will make it much more difficult for those defined as non-white to achieve upward mobility in America's racially stratified economy. The difference between the two approaches lies in which *mechanisms* the theories suggest lead to successful outcomes for the second generation. Alba and Nee (2003) posit that similar historical processes will blur the differences between the immigrant groups and the mainstream. Segmented assimilation argues that, especially for non-white poor immigrants, maintaining ethnic differences with the American mainstream—selective acculturation—will lead to successful outcomes for the second generation.

References

Abada, Teresa; Hou, Feng; Ram, Bali. Ethnic differences in educational attainment among the children of Canadian immigrants. Canadian Journal of Sociology 2009;34(1):1–28.

Alba, Richard; Nee, Victor. Remaking the American Mainstream: Assimilation and Contemporary Immigration. Cambridge, MA: Harvard University Press; 2003.

Boyd, Monica. Educational attainments of immigrant offspring: success or segmented assimilation? International Migration Review 2002;36(4):1037–60.

Crul, Maurice; Thomson, Mark. The second generation in Europe and the United States: how is the transatlantic debate relevant for further research on the European second generation? Journal of Ethnic and Migration Studies 2007;33(7):1025–1041.

Farley, Reynolds; Alba, Richard. The new second generation in the United States. International Migration Review 2002;36(3):669–701.

Gans, Herbert J. Acculturation, assimilation and mobility. Ethnic and Racial Studies 2007;30(1):152–64.

Gratton, Brian. Race, the children of immigrants, and social science theory. Journal of American Ethnic History 2002;21(4):74–84.

Greenman, Emily; Xie, Yu. Social Science Research. Vol. 37. 2008. Is assimilation theory dead? the effect of assimilation on adolescent well-being; p. 109-37.

Hirschman, Charles. The educational enrollment of immigrant youth: a test of the segmented-assimilation hypothesis. Demography 2001;38(3):317–36. [PubMed: 11523261]

Kasinitz, Philip; Mollenkopf, John H.; Waters, Mary C.; Holdaway, Jennifer. Inheriting the City: The Children of Immigrants Come of Age. New York: Russell Sage Foundation; 2008.

Kasinitz, Philip; Mollenkopf, John; Waters, Mary C. Becoming New Yorkers: Ethnographies of the New Second Generation. New York: Russell Sage Foundation; 2004.

Kasinitz, Philip; Mollenkopf, John; Waters, Mary C. Becoming American/becoming New Yorkers: immigrant incorporation in a majority minority city. International Migration Review 2002;36(4): 1020–36.

Menjívar, Cecilia. Fragmented Ties: Salvadoran Immigrant Networks in America. Berkeley, CA: University of California Press; 2000.

Park, Robert E.; Burgess, Ernest. The City. Chicago, IL: The University of Chicago Press; 1925.

Perlman, Joel; Waldinger, Roger. Second generation decline? children of immigrants, past and present—a reconsideration. International Migration Review 1997;31(4):893–922. [PubMed: 12293209]

Portes, Alejandro; Fernandez-Kelly, Patricia; Haller, William. Segmented assimilation on the ground: the new second generation in early adulthood. Ethnic and Racial Studies 2005;28(6):1000–40.

Portes, Alejandro; Rumbaut, Ruben G. Legacies: The Story of the Immigrant Second Generation. Berkeley, CA: University of California Press; 2001.

Portes, Alejandro; Min, Zhou. The New Second Generation: Segmented Assimilation and its Variants. The Annals 1993;530(1):74–96.

Smith, James. Assimilation across the Latino generations. American Economic Review 2003;93(2):315–19.

Stepick, Alex. Pride against prejudice: Haitians in the U S. Boston, MA: Allyn and Bacon Publishers; 1998.

Vickerman, Milton. Crosscurrents: West Indian Immigrants and Race. New York: Oxford University Press; 1999.

Waldinger, Roger. Did manufacturing matter? The experience of yesterday›s second generation: a reassessment. International Migration Review 2007;41(1):3–39.

Waldinger, Roger; Feliciano, Cynthia. Will the new second generation experience 'downward assimilation'? Segmented assimilation re-assessed. Ethnic and Racial Studies 2004;27(3):376–402.

Waldinger, Roger; Perlman, Joel. Second generations: past, present, future. Journal of Ethnic and Migration Studies 1998;24(1):5–24.

Warner, W Lloyd; Srole, Leo. The Social Systems of American Ethnic Groups. New Haven: Yale University Press; 1945.

Waters, Mary C. Black Identities: West Indian Immigrant Dreams and American Realities. New York: Russell Sage Foundation; 1999.

Zéphir, Flore. Trends in Ethnic Identification among Second-Generation Haitian Immigrants in New York City. Westport, CT: Bergin and Garvey; 2001.

Zhou, Min. Segmented assimilation: issues, controversies and recent research on the new second generation. International Migration Review 1997;31(4):975–1008. [PubMed: 12293212]

Zhou, Min; Bankston, Carl L. Growing Up American: How Vietnamese Children Adapt to Life in the United States. New York: Russell Sage Foundation; 1998.

Zhou, Min; Xiong, Yang Sao. The multifaceted American experiences of the children of Asian immigrants: lessons from segmented assimilation. Ethnic and Racial Studies 2005;28(6):1119–52.

Zhou, Min; Kim, Susan S. Community forces, social capital, and educational achievement: the case of supplementary education in the Chinese and Korean immigrant communities. Harvard Educational Review 2006;76(1):1–29.

REFLECT AND CONSIDER

- How does classical assimilation theory explain mobility compared to segmented assimilation theory?
- Is there an American mainstream into which immigrants can assimilate?

IMMIGRATION PATTERNS, CHARACTERISTICS, AND IDENTITIES

BY ANNY BAKALIAN & MEHDI BOZORGMEHR

Contested Classifications and Identities

Sociologists define "minority groups" by the following criteria: (1) members suffer various disadvantages at the hands of a majority population; (2) they are easily identified by a visible characteristic; (3) their status is ascribed; (4) they have group consciousness; and (5) by choice or necessity they tend to be endogamous, confining their primary group relations (i.e., friendships and marital partners) to fellow members. These conditions apply to some degree to Middle Eastern Americans. Many share visible physical characteristics—olive skin, dark hair, prominent facial features—and outsiders have difficulty distinguishing people of the differing nationalities. For example, an Iranian is rarely distinguished from an Egyptian or a Lebanese. After 9/11, even Filipinos, Mexicans, and other Hispanics have been mistakenly victimized. Though Middle Eastern Americans are ascribed a broadly "Middle Eastern" status, their individual and group consciousness is more ethnic than pan-ethnic. Nostalgia for their native culture (e.g., cuisine, music, theater, sense of humor) spurs many to seek the company of their compatriots. These factors as a whole point to Middle Easterners as a sociological minority group.[1]

Individuals of Middle Eastern descent identify themselves by national (e.g., Iranian, Israeli), ethnic (e.g., Arab), or ethno-religious (e.g., Armenian, Druze, Jewish) categories. South Asian Muslims, such as Bangladeshis, Pakistanis, and Indians, on the other hand, favor a religious label. The term *Middle Eastern* entered the American lexicon only after 9/11 and has been more frequently used in the media since. Though immigrants from Iran, Israel, and Turkey tend to generally identify with their national origin as Iranian, Israeli, and Turkish, the ethno-religious minority populations from within those countries, such as Armenians from Iran, tend to identify themselves as Armenian or Armenian Iranian.

There is much disagreement as to what the term *Arab American* means. Does it imply a primordial connection to the Arab world? Does it refer to a shared cultural heritage that includes the Arabic language, beliefs about the primacy of the family and the values of respect for elders, hospitality, generosity, and honor? Or does it have a political connotation with regard both to nations of origin, in terms of support for the "Arab cause" in the Middle East, and to efforts to mobilize as an ethnic group in the United States? The identity of Arabic-speaking immigrants to North America and their descendants in the last century has fluctuated with the social and political changes in both their countries of origin and the host society.[2]

If someone were to ask the early Arabic-speaking immigrants to America how they thought of themselves, they would have probably identified first with their family, next with their village or town of origin, and last with their sect.[3] The Ottomans had organized their society along religious lines, better known as the *millet* (people) system (see Cahnman 1944). This made sectarian affiliation, mainly for the non-Muslim populations, more consequential for one's well-being.

Many of the early immigrants were either Armenians or Christian Arabs.[4] The latter included Maronites, Antiochian/Syrian Orthodox, Melkites, and Protestants.[5] Most were from the Ottoman province of Syria, which was made up of Syria proper, Mount Lebanon, and Pales-tine. Eric Hooglund (1987b, 88) writes, "In a new country, where they were surrounded by different peoples who identified themselves on the basis of ethnicity, it became necessary for the Arabic-speaking immigrants to find a similar identity. As early as the 1890s they had begun to refer to themselves as 'Syrians.'" These Christians tended to use the term *Arab* to identify native Muslims of Syria. Therefore, *Syrian* came to identify an Arabic speaker who was from the ancient Syrian churches rather than a Muslim. Hooglund adds that U.S. immigration officials promoted the label *Syrian* as an ethnicity because they favored providing designations of nationality to varied groups from multiethnic empires. Common practice also designated the Arabic language as

"Syrian," and in 1899 the United States officially adopted this term for Arabic speakers from Ottoman Syria. Today most immigrants from the Middle East are Muslim,[6] but some Jews have also emigrated from the Arab world.[7] Immigrants from the three non-Arab countries in the Middle East—Iran, Israel, and Turkey—tend to be newcomers.[8]

Race has been a central issue in the question of citizenship since the formation of the United States. The Naturalization Act of 1790 made any free white persons of satisfactory character eligible for naturalization after a two-year residence. After the Civil War, aliens of African descent were also eligible to become U.S. citizens (Zolberg 2006). However, as large numbers of immigrants, including Middle Easterners, arrived in the latter part of the nineteenth century, their "whiteness" became a contentious issue. According to Tehranian (2008), between 1878 and 1952 (when naturalization laws changed), fifty-two cases were litigated after immigration officials denied an immigrant the right to become a U.S. citizen on the basis of race. These cases presented the first challenge for the federal government in dealing with the Middle Easterners, and the subsequent jurisprudence settled their classification as white.

In 1910, the U.S. Census Bureau classified Syrians, Palestinians, Armenians, Turks, and others from the eastern Mediterranean as "Asiatics": that is, nonwhite. However, thanks to the editors of the Arabic press in New York City, Syrians galvanized support and raised funds to fight this decision. Several cases came before the courts across the United States with the argument that Syrians were Caucasians, therefore white. Naff (1985, 257) summarizes the conclusion of the case of George Dow of Charleston, South Carolina, in 1914: "After deliberating, the court accepted the definition of the Dillingham Report of the Immigration Commission, namely that 'Physically the modern Syrians are of mixed Syrian, Arabian, and even Jewish blood. They belong to the Semitic branch of the Caucasian race, thus widely differing from their rulers, the Turks, who are in origin Mongolian.'" Before that, the federal court in Georgia had allowed a Syrian with a dark complexion to be naturalized (*In re Najour*).[9] Similar cases were settled for Armenians with *In re Halladjian* in 1909 and *United States v. Cartozian*, on whose behalf the anthropologist Franz Boas testified in 1924–25 (Alexander 2005, 112–18; see also Suleiman 1987, 44; Younis 1995, Appendix 4, "The Syrian Naturalization Issue").[10] However, the Syrians' Caucasian identity was predicated on their Christian faith. In 1942, the naturalization of Ahmed Hassan was disputed in a court in Detroit. His case was resolved with the stipulation that Arab Muslims were white but only when their religious affiliation was left undeclared. Thus Muslims became "honorary whites" (Gualtieri 2001). As these cases illustrate and as Tehranian (2008) explains, those who won their lawsuit were able to show good character, Christian faith and beliefs, association with the upper class, educational credentials, wealth, English proficiency, intermarriage—that is, generally, an ability to pass as white in a cultural sense.

Helen Samhan (1999) argues that race has remained an issue for Arab Americans. In an article appropriately entitled "Not Quite White," she demonstrates that "Arabs who contest, resent, or misunderstand their white classification … in school and medical forms, job and loan applications, political caucuses, polls, even market surveys" are denied all identity and are classified as the "other" who is not counted. She illustrates her point by citing, among others, the "1988 national longitudinal study of eighth graders" that overreported the Asian/Pacific Islander category by 15 percent because of the (mistaken) inclusion of students of Middle Eastern descent (219). Because of this error, the voices of these Arab American students were silenced.

Suad Joseph contends that Arab Americans, in spite of their white citizenship, go "against the grain of the nation" (1999, 257). She avoids racial or color designations in claiming difference but asserts that the situation is more subtle and damning because Arabs are painted as the opposite of the independent, autonomous, individual, modern, and free person (260). Several Arab American scholars have applied the racial formation perspective to explain the relentless stereotyping and escalating scapegoating of Arab and Muslim Americans, especially after 9/11 (Naber 2000; Alsultany 2005; Cainkar 2006). Using representations of Arabs in the media before 9/11, Nadine Naber argues that Muslims and Arabs are considered "tainted" but not enough to be colored: "While Arab Americans … have been forced into the binary classification 'either entirely white or entirely non-white,' … [they] do not quite fit into the U.S.'s either/or racial labeling system" (2000, 51). She believes that distortions have racialized Arab Americans "through religion rather than phenotype" (53).

Evelyn Alsultany (2005) draws on Edward Said's *Orientalism,* which argues that identity is constructed in relation to the "other," and on Michael Omi and Howard Winant's (1994) theory that racial formation is the outcome of historical and sociological processes to contend that Arab and Muslim Americans are racialized. Since the beginning of the "War on Terror," the U.S. media have turned these populations into the "enemy-other," terrorist noncitizens in opposition to American citizens. Racializing Muslims as dangerous extremists produces national unity through fear, which in turn leads to public endorsements of government initiatives such as the PATRIOT Act, detentions, deportations, and special registration. According to Alsultany, speeches by government officials, television dramas, talk shows, and nonprofit advertising create the "feeling" that the United States is, in contrast to reality, "unique, harmonious, equal, democratic, in relation to other countries" (2005, 5). Alsultany borrows from Omi and Winant (1994) to emphasize politics' influence in establishing difference, arguing that "racialization is not solely based on phenotype but relies heavily on racing politics and religion" (Alsultany 2005, 7).

According to Louise Cainkar (2006), Arab Americans have experienced increased marginalization and racialization since the 1960s. This is not due to "the domestic distribution of power and resources" (273) or even religious differences and distinctive institutions formed by

Arab immigrants. Rather, international political developments, America's relationship to the region, and the media's negative depictions of Arabs as violent have led to their exclusion from political and civic life and a heightened incidence of discrimination and hate crimes against them.

Cainkar's historicizing of Arab American marginalization fits in well with Omi and Winant's theory of racial formation: "[The] sociohistorical process by which racial categories are created, inhabited, transformed, and destroyed … is a process of historically situated *projects* in which human bodies and social structures are represented and organized. … [It is linked] to the evolution of hegemony, the way in which society is organized and ruled. … From a racial formation perspective, race is a matter of both social structure and cultural representation" (Omi and Winant 1994, 55–56; emphasis in original). Similarly, Bonilla-Silva notes in *Racism without Racists* (2006) that contemporary racism is covert discriminatory behavior embedded within systematic, institutionalized structures. A racial ideology then becomes a political instrument that justifies the status quo and those in power.

Andrew Shryock explores the racialization of Arab and Muslim Americans though a more critical lens. Analyzing the DAAS data on racial and ethnic identification, he finds that the vast majority of respondents (70 percent) identified as "Arab American" and the remaining 30 percent offered about "one hundred" alternative identities. "Not a single person opted for an extant 'racial' alternative: no one said white, black, Asian, or even 'of color'" (2008, 89). On the basis of these findings, Shryock argues that racialization should be seen as a "'moral analogy' that give[s] Arabs and Muslims a more secure place within a dominant structure of American identity politics" (2008, 98). As race represents a central element of American society from which Arab Americans often feel excluded due to their perceived racial ambiguity (e.g., Samhan 1999; Tehranian 2008), activists and emerging young scholars have adopted the racialization perspective to challenge their invisibility. Indeed, as Shryock observes, "The fact that many Arab Americans now believe antiterrorism policies have constituted them as 'a distinct racial group' says a great deal about the trauma of 9/11, the experience of marginalization and stigma, and how these are reshaping identity politics amongst Arabs and Muslims in the United States" (84).

We contend that these racialization arguments in and by themselves have become claims for the inclusion of Arab Americans within the larger American society. Furthermore, it is ironic that Arab American advocates and scholars have adopted racialization as a perspective to fight marginalization, stigma, and discrimination. Racialization lacks clarity and specificity as an analytical tool. It is at best a sensitizing concept rather than as an empirically verifiable one.

Before 9/11, the Arab community in the United States tended to be mobilized by events in the Middle East. Most scholars working in this field concur that the 1967 Arab-Israeli war was a watershed event ushering in a renewed consciousness for Arab Americans. By the end of the century, this identity had become "a matter of justice and honor to defend the Arab cause and specifically the rights of Palestinians" (Kayal 1995, 252). Yet precisely because of the conflicts in the Middle East, the *Arab American* label has not produced cohesion for Arabic-speaking peoples and their descendants in the United States. A number of Lebanese Maronites and Iraqi Chaldeans have resisted it for political and ideological reasons, especially after 9/11 (see chapter 1).[11]

Muslims consider identity as the "mother of all issues (*umm al masa'il*)" (Y. Haddad 2000, 22). Every time political or other leaders announce publicly that the United States is a Judeo-Christian nation, Muslims feel powerless and believe that the notion of separation of church and state in the U.S. Constitution is being violated (23). Muslims see contradictory behavior in American society when Christian values are encouraged by the president but efforts to build a moral and just Islamic state in the Middle East are denounced. Government support of the Jewish state, coupled with continual denunciation of Islamic states as "extremist," presents another double standard. According to Yvonne Haddad, during the last third of the twentieth century U.S. foreign policy toward Muslim nations "continue[d] to trouble and alienate the majority of Muslim citizens" in the United States (24). U.S. foreign policy in the region remains a thorny issue for Arab and Muslim Americans.

American scholars who work in the fields of immigration and ethnic and racial studies seem to have their own trends and fashions in ethnic labels and groupings. In 1980, the *Harvard Encyclopedia of American Ethnic Groups* had an entry under "Arabs" (Naff 1980), whereas the 1997 *Encyclopedia of American Immigrant Cultures* did not. The editors of the latter publication, however, provided separate entries for the Iranians, Druze, Egyptian Copts and Muslims, Jordanians, Lebanese Christians and Muslims, Palestinians, Syrians, and Yemenis. The complementary volume to the *Harvard Encyclopedia, The New Americans,* focuses on immigrants rather than ethnic groups. It includes an entry on immigrants from the Middle East and North Africa (Gold and Bozorgmehr 2007) and a separate entry for immigrants from Iran (Bozorgmehr 2007). As more Middle Eastern and South Asian scholars conduct research on their own diasporas, they are likely to draw more public attention to their previously "invisible" groups and increase the odds that their studies will be cited in mainstream literatures (see Okamoto 2005).

Notes

1. "Arab American Heritage Park Festival," *Aramica,* August 1–15, 2005, 14–15.

2. Quoted in Moustafa Bayoumi, "Arab America's September 11," *Nation,* September 25, 2006. Dean Obeidallah is reported to say, "Arabs are the new blacks" in his comedy routine (Lorraine Ali, "Television: Mid-east Humor. Seriously—'The Watch List,' Comedy Central's New Online Show, Features (Very Funny) Americans of Middle-East Descent," *Newsweek,* January 19, 2007).

3. This respondent had a green card, but it made little difference. He was very upset that his fellow passengers did not get the same treatment.

4. Brad Foss, "Arab-Looking Passengers Expect Scrutiny Now, and Try to Lessen the Embarrassment," Associated Press, August, 28, 2002.

5. Salam Al-Marayati, "Guilty of 'Flying While Muslim'?" *Los Angeles Times,* December 11, 2004.

6. See Neil MacFarquhar, "U.S. Muslims Say Terror Fears Hamper Their Right to Travel," *New York Times,* June 1, 2006, A1, A22; Jean Merl, "Muslims, Others Air Grievances to FBI: At the Agency's Town Hall Meeting, Speakers Tell of Their Frustration and Embarrassment at Being Singled Out," *Los Angeles Times,* April 9, 2006. In November 2006, six imams were asked to disembark from a U.S. Airways flight leaving Minneapolis for "unsettling" behavior, such as praying at the gate and uttering the word "Allah" on boarding the plane, reported by passengers and crew. They were returning home from a conference of North American Imams Federation (Libby Sander, "6 Imams Removed from Flight for Behavior Deemed Suspicious," *New York Times,* November 22, 2006, A18.

7. The Associated Press, "Airline Passenger Told to Conceal Arabic T-Shirt: Human Rights Activist Was Briefly Barred from JetBlue Flight to Oak-land," August 30, 2006, www.msnbc.msn.com/id/14591252/from/ET/.

8. CAIR, "Hearings on Profiling Sought after Imams Removed from MN Flight," press release, November 21, 2006, RedOrbit, www.redorbit.com/news/business/739944/hearings_on_profiling_sought_after_imams_re-moved_from_mn_flight/index.html; Sander, "6 Imams Removed"; Alexandra Marks, "In Imams' Airline Case, a Clash of Rights, Prejudice, Security," *Christian Science Monitor,* May 1, 2007, 1.

9. Type II errors are false positives, as when an African American is found guilty without evidence because of his or her race.

10. For example, on January 17, 2007, SALDEF and the Community Relations Service of the Department of Justice released a police training video. It aims to educate law enforcement officials about the cultural norms of Sikh Americans, as Sikhs have been the subject of more hate crimes since 9/11. SALDEF, "Department of Justice and SALDEF Release New Law Enforcement Roll Call Training Video," press release, January 19, 2007, www.saldef.org/content.aspx?a=1633. See also SMART, "Recommendations for Law Enforcement when Interacting with Sikh Americans," 2003, www.sikhmediawatch.org/pubs/LawEnforcementRefrCard.PDF. On November 21, 2006, SALDEF issued a press release announcing that its cooperation with DHS had

resulted in a poster on the Sikh *kirpan* that would be distributed to 8,700 federal facilities (SALDEF, "SALDEF Asks for Community's Support to Continue Awareness, Empowerment Efforts," press release, November 21, 2006, http://saldef.org/content.aspx?a=1609). See also Michelle Boorstein, "A Pointed Reminder for Security Screeners: Disputes over Sikhs' Required Daggers Prompt a Federal Poster on Respectful Procedures," *Washington Post,* November 21, 2006, A6.

11. See also Jodi Wilgoren, "Going by 'Joe,' Not 'Yussef,' but Still Feeling Like an Outcast," *New York Times,* September 11, 2002, A15.

REFLECT AND CONSIDER

- How has racism influenced the incorporation of Muslims into American society?
- How might the framing of Muslim Americans in an international context help explain some of the problems they face in the United States?

THE REALITY OF ASIAN AMERICAN OPPRESSION

BY ROSALIND CHOU AND JOE FEAGIN

White Racial Framing: Anti-Asian Imagery Today

Today whites and others still apply numerous elements of an old anti-Asian framing to Asian Americans. As we will see throughout this book, many whites hold inconsistent views of Asian Americans. They commonly view Asian Americans as high achievers and "model minorities," but will often discount the meaning of those achievements as being done by exotic "foreigners," "nerds," or social misfits. For example, some research studies show that Asian American students are often viewed positively by whites, but mainly in regard to educational or income achievements. A recent summary of research concludes that most stereotypes of Asian American students "are negative, such as non-Asians' notions that Asians 'don't speak English well,' 'have accents,' and are 'submissive,' 'sneaky,' 'stingy,' 'greedy,' etc."[1] To complicate matters, racial stereotyping is gendered and sexualized. Asian American men feel the brunt of emasculating white stereotypes that place them at the bottom of a U.S. masculinity hierarchy, while many Asian American women are exoticized as sexual objects.[2] Racism is often perpetuated through different systems of oppression in an intersectional way—thus, these differences in white-imposed constructions of Asian American men and women.

Subtle and blatant stereotyping of Asians and Asian Americans still predominates in many areas of U.S. society. Consider just a few recent examples. In November 2013, comedian and talk show host Jimmy Kimmel aired a skit on his late night show in which he led a roundtable discussion with children. The discussion topic in the roundtable was the U.S. debt to China and the punch line was delivered by one of the children suggesting that we "*kill* all the Chinese." The broadcasting of the skit demonstrates how Kimmel, and the writers and producers of the show, consider mass genocide of the Chinese as acceptable comedic content. Moreover, in February 2013, Asian American basketball player Jeremy Lin burst onto the NBA scene with "surprising" athletic prowess for the New York Knicks team. During the months of "Linsanity" where media outlets dedicated extensive coverage to the exceptionalism of Lin's play, he was also met with numerous racial taunts and slurs by fans and other athletes. Two ESPN cable channel writers used a racial slur in their headlines about Lin: a "Chink in the Armor" was used on their journalistic website. Floyd Mayweather insisted Lin was not worthy of this attention and was made a celebrity only because of his Asian heritage, not in spite of it.[3] In fall of 2013, a documentary on Jeremy Lin's journey to the NBA was released, and in an interview in the film he noted that racism has played a part in his entire athletic career.

In spring of 2011, a UCLA student, Alexandra Wallace, created an anti-Asian YouTube video titled "Asians in the Library" that went viral.[4] In it, Wallace complains of "hordes of Asians" at UCLA, of their not having "American" manners, and about their parents for "not teaching their kids to fend for themselves." She also makes a mockery of Asians who speak their native languages and minimizes the Fukushima nuclear tragedy in Japan. The university failed to address the racist rant, although Wallace did apologize and resign from the school for personal reasons.[5] She received some notoriety from the racist incident and was asked to appear on MTV. This is one of very few examples of institutional consequences for whites who engage in anti-Asian racism, and of the apparent acceptance of Wallace as a humorous figure in pop culture.

The Adidas company was challenged by civil rights groups for making shoes that had a negative caricature of a buck-toothed, slant-eyed Asian as a logo. In another case, a large pictorial cartoon concerning fund-raising investigations of Democratic Party leaders appeared on the cover of an issue of the prominent magazine *National Review*. The cover showed caricatures of then president Bill Clinton and his wife, Hillary Clinton, as slant-eyed, buck-toothed Chinese in Mao suits and Chinese hats—images suggesting old stereotyped images of Asian Americans' characteristics. Since the nineteenth century, white cartoonists, political leaders, and media commentators have portrayed Chinese and other Asian Americans in such stereotyped terms, often to express a fear of the "yellow peril." When confronted, the *National Review*'s white editor admitted these were negative Asian caricatures but refused to apologize. Such reactions, and the fact that there was little public protest of the cover other than from Asian American groups, suggest that such crude images and other associated stereotypes remain significant in a dominant racial framing of people of Asian descent.[6]

In addition, a U.S. animation company made a cartoon (*Mr. Wong*) and placed at its center an extreme caricature of a Chinese "hunchbacked, yellow-skinned, squinty-eyed character who spoke with a thick accent and starred in an interactive music video titled *Saturday Night Yellow Fever*."[7] Again Asian American and other civil rights groups protested this anti-Asian mocking, but many whites and a few Asian Americans inside and outside the entertainment industry defended such racist cartoons as "only good humor." Similarly, the makers of a puppet movie, *Team America: World Police,* portrayed a Korean political leader speaking gibberish in a mock Asian accent. One Asian American commentator noted the movie was "an hour and a half of racial mockery with an 'if you are offended, you obviously can't take a joke' tacked on at the end."[8] Moreover, in an episode of the popular television series *Desperate Housewives* a main character, played by actor Teri Hatcher, visits a physician for a medical checkup. Shocked that the doctor suggests she may be going through menopause, she replies, "Okay, before we go any further, can I check these diplomas? Just to make sure they aren't, like, from some med school in the Philippines." This racialized stereotyping was protested by many in the Asian and Pacific Islander communities.

Although sometimes played out in supposedly humorous presentations, continuing media-reproduced stereotypes of Asians and Pacific Islanders include old white-framed notions of them as odd, foreign, un-American, relatively unassimilated, or culturally inferior. Noteworthy in these accounts is the connection of more recent anti-Asian stereotyping, mostly by whites, to the old anti-Asian stereotyping of the nineteenth and early twentieth centuries. For the majority of non–Asian Americans, particularly those who control the media, certain negative images of Asians and of Asian Americans (especially Asian immigrants and their children) blend together in a common anti-Asian racial framing. The strong protests of Asian American civil rights and other organizations to all such racialized stereotyping and mocking underscore this important point.

Anti-Asian stereotypes are still frequently encountered in everyday discourse. Asian Americans, including children, often note that they face mocking language and other racially hostile words, such as these: "Ching chong Chinaman sitting on a rail, along came a white man and snipped off his tail"; "Ah so. No tickee, no washee. So sorry, so sollee"; and "Chinkee, Chink, Jap, Nip, zero, Dothead, Flip, Hindoo."[9] A disc jockey at a Toledo, Ohio, radio station called Asian restaurants and made mock Asian commentaries, such as "ching, chong, chung" and "me speakee no English." Similarly, a CBS talk show host mocked an Asian Excellence Awards ceremony by playing a fake excerpt with "Asian men" saying things like "Ching chong, ching chong, ching chong." Comedian Rosie O'Donnell also used a repeated "ching chong" to mock Chinese speech on her ABC talk show. One striking reaction to the O'Donnell comment was hundreds of blogger entries on Internet websites that defended her comments and (erroneously) asserted the comments were *not* racist.[10]

To modern ears such language mocking and other Asian mocking may seem novel, but it is actually an old part of the white racist framing of Asian Americans. White English speakers on the West Coast developed this mocking in the mid- to late nineteenth century as their way of making fun of the English-Chinese speech of Chinese workers, as well as of racializing them. An early 1900s ragtime song goes, "Ching, Chong, Oh Mister Ching Chong, You are the king of Chinatown. Ching Chong, I love your sing-song."[11]

Anthropologist Jane Hill has shown how in the United States such mocking of language links to systemic racism. In particular Hill has studied the extensive mocking of Spanish, such as the making up of fake Spanish words and phrases. Mock Spanish—common on birthday cards, on items in gift shops, and in commentaries from board rooms to the mass media—is mostly created by college-educated Americans, especially white Americans. Similar language mocking has long been directed at African Americans and Asian Americans. "Through this process, such people are endowed with gross sexual appetites, political corruption, laziness, disorders of language, and mental incapacity."[12] Language mocking is not just lighthearted commentary of no social importance, because such mocking usually is linked to racial framing and societal discrimination against the racialized "others." While native speakers of languages such as French or German do not face serious discrimination because of their accents when they speak English, Asian Americans, Latinos, and other Americans of color do often face such discrimination. As one scholar has underscored, "It is crucial to remember that it is not all foreign accents, but only accent linked to skin that isn't white, or which signals a third-world homeland, evokes such negative reactions."[13]

Model Minority Imagery: An Apparent Contradiction?

Today, frequent anti-Asian mocking and caricaturing signal the continuing presence of a strong racist framing of Asians and Americans of Asian descent. Some people, especially whites, may play down the significance of such racist framing and instead argue that a strong positive image of Asian Americans has often been asserted by whites. They note that whites, especially in the mainstream media and in politics, regularly broadcast positive reports on achievements of Asian Americans in schools and workplaces. From this point of view, one should note, an Asian American group has "succeeded" in U.S. society when its attainments on a limited number of quantitative indicators of occupation, education, and income are at least comparable to those of white Americans. A superficial reading of these indicators leads many to view virtually all Asian Americans as successful and thus as not facing significant racial barriers in this society. Such analyses may be correct in regard to a certain type of success measured by particular socioeconomic indicators for Asian American groups as a whole, but not in regard to the socioeconomic problems faced by large segments within these groups or in regard to the various forms of racial discrimination that most Asian Americans still face in their daily lives.

Take Japanese Americans, for example. Recent data indicate that Japanese Americans are more likely to hold managerial or professional jobs than their white counterparts, and their unemployment rate is less than that for whites. Median income for their families is more than for white families nationally, and a smaller percentage falls below the federal poverty line than for whites. However, Japanese American workers mostly live in the West, where there is a relatively high cost of living. We should note too that in California the difference in median incomes between Japanese American families and white families is reversed. Per capita income for Asian American groups is also generally lower than that for whites, who average smaller families. In addition, many Asian immigrants and their children, especially those from Southeast Asia and rural backgrounds, have experienced much poverty and other serious economic difficulties over the past few decades.[14]

Moreover, although Japanese Americans and certain other Asian American groups have achieved significant socioeconomic success, they still face a substantial array of subtle and overt acts of discrimination. Research studies reveal some of this picture. For example, when researchers have examined Japanese and other Asian American workers in comparison with white workers with similar jobs, educational credentials, and years of job experience, the Asian American workers are found to be paid less on average and are less likely to be promoted to managerial positions.[15] In addition, Asian American workers often face exclusion from numerous positions in business, entertainment, political, and civil service areas, regardless of their qualifications and abilities. Japanese and other Asian Americans periodically report a "glass ceiling" in corporations or exclusion from business networks. About 5 percent of the population, Asian Americans are far less than 1 percent of the members of the boards of Fortune 500 firms; one tabulation revealed that just *one* Asian American headed up a Fortune 500 firm not founded by an Asian American. White executives periodically assert that in their firms Asian Americans are best as technical workers and not as executives. Given this stereotyped view, Asian Americans are often hired as engineers, computer experts, and technicians, but no matter what their qualifications are they are rarely considered for top management positions. Moreover, given this discrimination, many younger Asian Americans have pursued scientific and technical educations and rejected the fine arts, humanities, and social sciences, areas they might have preferred. Career choices are thus influenced by both past and present discrimination. In addition, many business opportunities in corporate America remain limited by persisting anti-Asian sentiment.[16]

The "great recession" of 2008–2009 disproportionately affected Asian Americans, further challenging the "model minority" myth. According to the National Coalition for Asian-Pacific American Community Development, Asian Americans have seen a 38 percent increase in their poverty population while the general poverty population grew by 27 percent during the same time period, with the African American poverty population growing by 20 percent.[17] This poverty rate is not just affecting the newer immigrant population, for 60 percent of the net increase in Asian American/Pacific Islander poverty was in the native-born segment of that population.[18] In 2010, compared to whites, blacks, and Latinos, Asian American workers had the highest share of unemployed workers who were unemployed long term (more than half a year). Additionally, when compared to their similarly educated white counterparts, highly educated Asian Americans suffer from disproportionately higher unemployment rates. Asian Americans with bachelor's degrees are more likely to be unemployed than whites. This is especially significant because 57 percent of the Asian American labor force is in this category.[19] Oftentimes, education is seen as the "great equalizer," but we see that Asian Americans obtaining advanced degrees still face economic disadvantages. In spite of much data contradicting their commonplace view, numerous social scientists and media commentators have regularly cited the educational and economic "success" of a particular Asian American group, one typically described as the "model minority," as an indication that whites no longer create significant racial barriers for them.[20] For example, a 2012 research report of the prestigious Pew Research Center cites this socioeconomic success and asks unreflectively, "Are Asian Americans a 'Model Minority'?" The report also compares, again uncritically, the supposedly successful achievements of Asian Americans with the lesser achievements of Hispanic Americans.[21]

This continuing use of a white-named and white-framed perspective on Asian Americans is highly problematical. We can pinpoint when this model myth was likely first constructed. In the mid-1960s, largely in response to African American and Latino (especially Mexican American) protests against discrimination, white scholars, political leaders, and journalists developed the model minority myth in order to allege that all Americans of color could achieve the American dream—and not by protesting discrimination in the stores and streets as African Americans and Mexican Americans were doing, but by working as "hard and quietly" as Japanese and Chinese Americans supposedly did. This model image was created *not* by Asian Americans but by influential whites for their public ideological use.[22] One example is a 1960s *U.S. News & World Report* article entitled "Success Story of One Minority Group in U.S." This major media article praised the hard work and morality of Chinese Americans, and its analysis strongly implied that if black Americans possessed such virtues, it would not be necessary to spend "hundreds of billions to uplift" them.[23]

For decades now, prominent commentators and politicians have cited the educational or economic success of Asian Americans as proof that they are fully melded into the U.S. "melting pot," with many "ascending above exclusion" by "pulling themselves up by their bootstraps."[24] Today, variations of this model stereotype remain pervasive, and leading politicians, judges, journalists, and corporate executives assert them regularly.[25] Even other Americans of color have sometimes been conned by this model minority view and declared it to be so true that governments do not need to be concerned with the discrimination against Asian Americans. For example, black Supreme Court nominee Clarence Thomas, at his Senate confirmation hearings, asserted that Asian Americans have "transcended the ravages caused even by harsh legal and social discrimination" and should not be the beneficiaries of affirmative action because they are "overrepresented in key institutions."[26]

One of the contemporary ironies of such uninformed views is that private and government reports in recent years have shown that today educational success varies among the Asian American groups and, indeed, that many Asian Americans in numerous groups still face significant obstacles to academic success, in some cases more than in the past.[27] For example, one savvy higher education journalist noted that numerous articles in college newspapers have used Asian Americans as a point of humor, but their portrayals usually feed the "model minority" myth. Asian American students are still often seen as an "invasion" and their demeanors as "inscrutable." On these college campuses lies a "continued pattern of Asian American students being (a) the butt of such jokes, basically the punch line; (b) that the jokes are heavily laden with racial stereotypes; and (c) that these … essays reveal volumes about racial relationships, tensions, and perceptions of Asian American students as all being, in some way, the same—foreigners, math and science nerds, and all around different from the regular average college student."[28]

Notes

1. Long Le, "The Dark Side of the Asian American 'Model Student,'" August 2, 2006, http://news.newamerica-media.org/news (retrieved January 5, 2007).

2. Rosalind Chou, *Asian American Sexual Politics: The Construction of Race, Gender, and Sexuality* (Lanham, MD: Rowman and Littlefield).

3. For more, see Rosalind S. Chou's video "Linsanity: A Sociological Look," http://vimeo.com/37290995.

4. Alexandra Wallace, "Asians in the Library," last modified March 2011, www.youtube.com.

5. Associated Press, "Alexandra Wallace, Student in Anti-Asian Rant, Says She'll Leave UCLA," *Huffington Post*, March 19, 2011.

6. "Daphne Kwok, Organization of Chinese Americans, and John O'Sullivan, *National Review*, Discuss Recent Cover Story for That Magazine That Asian Americans Are Saying Is Offensive and Racist," NBC News Transcripts, March 21, 1997; Mae M. Cheng, "Magazine Cover Ripped; Coalition Calls *National Review* Illustration Racist," *Newsday*, April 11, 1997, p. A4.

7. Doris Lin, "The Death of (Icebox.com's) Mr. Wong," USAsians.net, http://us_asians.tripod.com/articles-mrwong.html (retrieved December 14, 2006).

8. Jennifer Fang, "Team America: Racism, Idiocy, and Two Men's Pursuit to Piss Off as Many People as Possible," Asian Media Watch, October 28, 2004, www.asianmediawatch.net/teamamerica/review.html (retrieved December 17, 2006). We draw here in part on Feagin and Feagin, *Racial and Ethnic Relations*, chap. 11.

9. Helen Zia, *Asian American Dreams: The Emergence of an American People* (New York: Farrar, Straus, and Giroux, 2000), pp. 134ff.

10. Steven A. Chin, "KFRC Deejay Draws Suspension for On-Air Derogatory Remarks," *San Francisco Examiner*, December 6, 1994, p. A2; "Current Affairs," *JACL News*, www.jacl.org/index.php (retrieved December 19, 2006); Media Action Network for Asian Americans, "Latest Headline News," www.manaa.org (retrieved December 18, 2006); Jennifer Fang, "Racism Abounds following Rosie," www.racialicious.com /2006/12/15/ racism-abounds-following-rosie (retrieved September 25, 2007).

11. Fang, "Racism Abounds."

12. Jane H. Hill, "Mock Spanish: A Site for the Indexical Reproduction of Racism in American English," unpublished research paper, University of Arizona, 1995.

13. Rosina Lippi-Green, *English with an Accent* (New York: Routledge, 1997), pp. 238–239.

14. Feagin and Feagin, *Racial and Ethnic Relations*, pp. 292–293.

15. Tim Wise, *Affirmative Action: Racial Preference in Black and White* (New York: Routledge, 2005), pp. 136–137.

16. Feagin and Feagin, *Racial and Ethnic Relations*, pp. 292–293.

17. The National Coalition for Asian Pacific American Community Development, "Spotlight on Asian American and Pacific Islander Poverty: A Demographic Profile," June 17, 2013, http://nationalcapacd.org/ spotlight-asian-american-and-pacific-islander-poverty-demographic-profile.

18. Ibid.

19. Marlene Kim, "Unfairly Disadvantaged? Asian Americans and Unemployment during and after the Great Recession (2007–10)," Economic Policy Institute, April 5, 2012, www.epi.org/publication/ ib323-asian-american-unemployment/.

20. See Ronald Takaki, "Is Race Surmountable? Thomas Sowell's Celebration of Japanese-American 'Success,'" in *Ethnicity and the Work Force*, ed. Winston A. Van Horne (Madison: University of Wisconsin Press, 1985), pp. 218–220.

21. Paul Taylor et al., "The Rise of Asian Americans" (Washington, DC: Pew Research Center, 2012–2013).

22. William Petersen, "Success Story, Japanese-American Style," *New York Times*, January 9, 1966, p. 21.

23. "Success Story of One Minority Group in the U.S.," *U.S. News & World Report*, December 26, 1966, pp. 73–76.

24. See J. N. Tinker, "Intermarriage and Assimilation in a Plural Society: Japanese Americans in the United States," *Marriage and Family Review* 5 (1982): 61–74; V. Nee and J. Sanders, "The Road to Parity: Determinants of the Socioeconomic Achievements of Asian-Americans," *Ethnic and Racial Studies* 8 (1985): 75–93; and D. A. Bell, "The Triumph of Asian-Americans," *New Republic*, July 15, 1982, pp. 24–31.

25. See, for example, James T. Madore, "Long-Quiet Asian Group Starts to Mobilize," *Christian Science Monitor*, May 20, 1988, p. 7.

26. Senate Judiciary Committee, "Capitol Hill Hearings," September 20, 1991.

27. Kathleen Wyer, "Beyond Myths: The Growth and Diversity of Asian American College Freshmen, 1971–2005," Research Report, Higher Education Research Institute, UCLA, 2007.

28. Sharon S. Lee, "Satire as Racial Backlash against Asian Americans," *Inside Higher Ed*, February 28, 2008, http://insidehighered.com/views/2008/02/28/lee (retrieved March 1, 2008).

REFLECT AND CONSIDER

- Why is there is so little recognition of anti-Asian discrimination?
- Is the model minority a useful or fatally flawed concept?

HIGHLIGHT

FUTURE IMMIGRATION WILL CHANGE THE FACE OF AMERICA BY 2065

BY D'VERY COHN, *PEW RESEARCH CENTER*

SUMMARY

This piece from the Pew Research Center analyzes changes in the US population up to 2065. Cohn, based on Pew Research Center projections, suggests that the total population will increase by 117 million, but that no racial or ethnic group will constitute a majority. Whites will decline to approximately 42 percent of the population, but the Latino and Asian populations will increase significantly. Overall, immigrants will constitute one third of all Americans.

EXCERPT FROM
"FUTURE IMMIGRATION WILL CHANGE THE FACE OF AMERICA BY 2065"

A snapshot of the United States in 2065 would show a nation that has 117 million more people than today, with no racial or ethnic majority group taking the place of today's white majority, according to new Pew Research Center projections. About one-in-three Americans would be an immigrant or have immigrant parents, compared with one-in-four today. These projections show that new immigrants and their descendants will drive most U.S. population growth in the coming 50 years, as they have for the past half-century. Among the projected 441 million Americans in 2065, 78 million will be immigrants and 81 million will be people born in the U.S. to immigrant parents. The projected changes in population makeup could have implications in a variety of realms, changing the face of the electorate, raising the education levels among the foreign-born population and altering the nation's birth patterns. Non-Hispanic whites will remain the largest racial or ethnic group in the overall population but will become less than a majority, the projections show. Currently 62% of the population, they will make up 46% of it in 2065. Hispanics will be 24% of the population (18% now), Asians will be 14% (6% now) and blacks will be 13% (12% now).

 READ THE REST OF THE ESSAY:

bit.ly/immigrationpew

READ, LISTEN, WATCH, INTERACT!

READ

Coming to America
Arab American National Museum.
READ AT bit.ly/arabamerican

The Tenement Museum
READ AT bit.ly/tenementresearch

LISTEN

Built By Immigrants, U.S. Catholic Churches Bolstered by Them Once Again.

Tom Gjelten and Marisa Penaloza, 9.9.2015, NPR.
LISTEN AT bit.ly/immigrantcatholic

Leaving China's North, Immigrants Redefine Chinese in New York
Hansi Lo Wang, 1.26.2016, NPR
LISTEN AT bit.ly/chinesenewyork

WATCH

30 Days: Immigration
CNN
AVAILABLE AT bit.ly/30daysimmigration

El Norte
Gregory Nava, PBS, 1983
AVAILABLE AT bit.ly/ElNorte

Sin Nombre
Cary Joji Fukunaga, 2009
AVAILABLE AT bit.ly/sinnombrefukunaga

Which Way Home
Rebecca Cammisa, 2009
AVAILABLE AT bit.ly/whichwayhomecammisa

INTERACT

Drop the I-Word [Illegal]
ColorLines: News for Action.
INTERACT AT bit.ly/dropillegal

Immigrant Nation.
Library of Congress
INTERACT AT bit.ly/immigrantnation

RACISM: THEORIES FOR UNDERSTANDING

H ave you ever gotten into an argument with someone about what is racist or what counts as racism? Do you ever censor yourself in fear that you might sound racist? Do you sometimes feel that people are just being "too sensitive" about race, or you hate when others say you are being too sensitive? We can usually agree that the person who belongs to a White supremacist group or even a person who outright refuses to hire a person of color is racist but many of us are hesitant to discuss the problems of racism any further than that. Others of us might openly talk about racism, but are not able to sufficiently support our points when questioned by others. To discuss racism, we need theories for understanding it.

This section, Racism: Theories for Understanding, provides different conceptualizations of racism. Racism does not always look the same: it can be on the individual or institutional level, it can overt or covert, it can be intentional or subconscious. As racism changes depending on context, it can be difficult to know when it is in operation and how to assess it in order to stop it.

Peter Rose, in "The Nature of Prejudice," outlines the fundamentals of how racism manifests, usually overtly, in areas such as prejudice, discrimination, and the relationship between the individual and society. In "Racism Without Racists: 'Killing Me Softly' with Color Blindness" by Eduardo Bonilla-Silva and David Embrick, we learn about color-blind racism, a contemporary ideology that supports the new racism that emerged after the Civil Rights era. Bonilla-Silva and Embrick outline the four frames of color-blind racism in order to explain how individuals use these frames to describe racialized outcomes in such a way that communities of color, rather than institutional discrimination, are falsely to blame. The next piece, "Colorstruck" by Margaret Hunter, raises the very important issue of colorism—intraracial and interracial discrimination based on skin tone and complexion. Hunter points out the benefits and costs, psychological and material, associated with light and dark skin tones. In the following reading, Hephzibah Strmic-Pawl explains that White supremacy is not solely defined by the presence of White supremacy groups, but rather is a theoretical concept that describes the systematic and systemic ways that the racial order benefits Whites. In "The White Supremacy Flower: A Model for Understanding Racism," Strmic-Pawl uses a flower as a metaphor to trace how the United States society is rooted in policies and ideologies created to benefit Whites and oppress people of color. In the last reading of this section, "Family Law, Feminist Legal Theory, and the Problem of Racial Hierarchy" by Twila L. Perry, we learn how race and racism are shaped by intersections with other identities such as gender and class. Perry's analysis is based on intersectionality, a theory that describes how individuals have a matrix of intersecting identities; for example, a White woman is not "White as a race" + "woman as a gender," rather she is a "White woman," wherein those two identities cannot be separated from one another. Intersectionality posits that hierarchies are not additive and cannot be disentangled from one another, and Perry analyzes how hierarchies of gender, class, and race intersect to shape ideas about alimony and transracial adoption. The highlight for this section, "Yes, All White People Are Racists" from *Alternet* brings our attention to implicit bias, the subconscious biases we have towards certain races. Together, these readings provide a way to understand and conceptualize how racism manifests and persists.

AS YOU READ

- Compare and contrast individual and institutional racism.
- Explain the connections among race, racism, and the racial hierarchy.
- Recognize the complexities in how racism is implemented.

THE NATURE OF PREJUDICE

BY PETER ROSE

Defining Prejudice

Prejudice—literally, prejudgment—may be defined as "a system of negative beliefs, feelings, and action-orientations regarding a group of people."[1] While prejudgments can be positive as well as negative, because of the detrimental psychic and social consequences that often result from hostile attitudes, sociologists usually concern themselves with and accentuate the negative.

The definition of group prejudice stated above incorporates the three major dimensions of all attitude systems: the *cognitive* (beliefs), the *affective* (feelings), and the *conative* (predispositions to act in particular ways, or policy orientations).[2]

The cognitive component pertains to the "intellectual" side of prejudice, for it involves knowledge, however faulty. This is expressed in stereotypical conceptions and misconceptions of various social groups by others, for example: whites who think that African Americans are shiftless, lazy, and untrustworthy, but wonderfully musical; Gentiles who imagine that Jews are avaricious, brash, and smart, but "too intelligent for their own good"; Englishmen who think of the Irish as argumentative, heavy drinkers; Irishmen who imagine Englishmen to be stuffy bores; and men of all ethnic backgrounds who think women are "the weaker sex."

Cognition refers to "cranial" reactions, that is, pictures in the mind's eye. Although the ethnocentric individual frequently generalizes about groups he knows little or nothing about, the prejudiced person generalizes about groups he thinks he knows well.

The second dimension, called "affective," refers to the way one feels about what is perceived. The emotions evoked are "visceral" in that they are often manifested in gut feelings of revulsion, fear, hate, or indignation, as illustrated by the following expressions:

"It makes me mad just thinking about my kid going to school with all those workaholic Asians. He'll never be able to keep up."

"Don't you just hate the way the Mexicans are moving in? I simply can't stand them."

"I know it's wrong, but I really shiver at the thought of rooming with a Muslim student next year."

Often emotions aroused in the prejudiced person are based upon presumptions about certain people, and thinking about or confronting members of particular groups frequently elicits thoughts about how to act.

Group prejudices involve both thoughts and feelings about people. "However false as to fact, prejudice has a certain logic, a logic not of reason but of the emotions. ... Prejudice is more than false belief; it is a structure of false belief *with a purpose,* however unconscious."[3] This is why prejudice as an attitude represents a predisposition to act (the conative dimension) in a particular way toward a social group. It is a state of readiness for action but not in itself overt behavior or discrimination.

Prejudice and Discrimination

Discrimination may be defined as the differential treatment of individuals belonging to particular groups or social categories.[4] Although frequently they are opposite sides of the same coin, prejudice and discrimination, as both analytical and concrete concepts, should not be confused. The difference between prejudice as an attitude and discrimination as overt behavior was summed up by an English judge in his comments to nine youths convicted of race rioting in the Notting Hill section of London: "Everyone, irrespective of the color of his skin, is entitled to walk through our streets in peace with their heads held erect and free from fear. ... These courts will uphold (these rights) ... *think what you like. ... But once you translate your dark thoughts into savage acts, the law will punish you, and protect your victim.*"[5]

American civil rights workers have long recognized the significance of the distinction. The late Dr. Martin Luther King Jr., in his first address to the Atlanta, Georgia, Junior Chamber of Commerce, put it bluntly: "The law may not make a man love me, but it can restrain him from lynching me, and I think that's pretty important."[6]

The prejudiced person may not actually behave outwardly the way he or she thinks or says he or she will act. Attitudes do not always lead to hostile or aggressive actions. Furthermore, many individuals discriminate against others without harboring particularly negative feelings toward the groups to which they belong. In one of several books on inter-group relations published in the mid-1950s, Dean and Rosen reported, "Conformity with the practices of segregation and discrimination is often quite unrelated to the intensity of prejudice in the individuals who conform."[7] Others have continued to corroborate the generalization, adding the following corollary: social contact itself and the conventions characteristic of the particular circumstances in which contact takes place often help to determine how an individual will act at a given time. Sometimes people may even behave toward others in direct opposition to their own predispositions. The situation itself frequently provides the cues for "appropriate" behavior. For example, for years many liberals conformed to practices of segregation when vacationing in the South, and southerners who held moderate views about the desegregation issue often remained silent on the matter in their home communities.

Merton's Typology

Nearly sixty-five years ago, comparing the presence or absence of prejudicial attitudes on the part of individuals with their willingness or reluctance to engage in discriminatory activity, Robert K. Merton described the relationship between prejudice and discrimination. The typology he devised is still useful. It includes four types of persons and their characteristic response patterns.[8]

The Unprejudiced Nondiscriminators

These "all-weather liberals," as Merton called them, sincerely believe in the American creed of freedom and equality for all, and practice it to the fullest extent. They are the vigorous champions of the underdog, take the Golden Rule literally, and cherish American egalitarian values. It would appear that liberal individuals such as these would be most able to influence others in the realm of intergroup hostility and discrimination. Yet, as Merton indicates, their effectiveness is limited by certain "fallacies."

First there is the "fallacy of group soliloquies." Liberals tend to expend their energies in seeking out one another and talking chiefly to others who share their point of view. The feeling of agreement that logically ensues by interacting mainly with those who agree leads to the second fallacy, that of "unanimity." Through discussions with like-minded individuals the liberal may feel that many more people agree with his attitudes regarding ethnic relations than do in fact. Finally, there is the "fallacy of privatized solutions," depicted by Merton as follows: "The ethnic liberal, precisely because he is at one with the American creed, may rest content with his own individual behavior and thus see no need to do anything about the problem at large. Since his own spiritual house is in order, he is not motivated by guilt or shame to work on a collective problem."[9]

The problem of the unprejudiced nondiscriminator is not one of ambivalence between attitude and action—as in the case of the two types described below—but rather it is a lack of awareness of the enormity of the problem and a clear-cut approach to those who are not so liberally inclined.

Unprejudiced Discriminators

The many homeowners throughout the urban North and Midwest long denied having any personal feelings against black people, but steadfastly tried to keep them out of their neighborhoods for fear of what others would say and do. This illustrates the case of the unprejudiced discriminator, who is, at best, a "fair-weather liberal." More pragmatic than "all-weather liberals," they discriminate when such behavior is called for, seems to be appropriate, or is in their own self-interest. Expediency is the motto; "Don't rock the boat" the guiding principle.[10] Merton suggests that the "fair-weather liberal" is frequently the victim of guilt because of the discrepancy between conduct and personal beliefs and is thus especially vulnerable to the persuasion of those more willing to press for civil and human rights and more amenable to making changes when authorities impose them.

Prejudiced Nondiscriminators

This third type might be called "timid bigots." Like so many of those who have half-facetiously been called "the gentle people of prejudice," they are not activists. They feel definite hostility toward or dislike many groups and subscribe to conventional stereotypes of their negative attributes. Yet, like "fair-weather liberals," they too react to circumstances. If the situation—as defined by law or custom—precludes open discrimination, they conform. They serve African American and other minority group customers, sit next to them on buses or trains, and send their children to school with them. Feeling they are forced to "grin and bear it," they often take the position that they are merely cogs in a big machine. "What can I do," they say, "fight the system, fight city hall?"

Although both the "fair-weather liberal" and the "fair-weather illiberal" share the theme of expedience, Merton states,

> Superficial similarity in behavior of the two in the same situation should not be permitted to cloak a basic difference in the meaning of this outwardly similar behavior, a difference which is as important for social policy as it is for social science. Whereas the timid bigot is under strain when he conforms to the creed, the timid liberal is under strain when he deviates. ... He does not accept the moral legitimacy of the creed; he conforms because he must, and will cease to conform when the pressure is removed.[11]

Prejudiced Discriminators

These are the people who embody the commonly held assumption that prejudice and discrimination are mutually dependent. Such "active bigots" neither believe in the American creed nor act in accordance with its precepts. Like the "all-weather liberal," the prejudiced discriminator conforms to a set of standards; but in this case "his ideals proclaim the right, even the duty, of discrimination."[12] He or she does not hesitate to express the basic attitude—"all whites are superior to colored people"—or to convert it into overt behavior. He or she is willing to defy law, if necessary, to protect beliefs and vested interests.

In recent years in this country we have witnessed a resurgence of organized "resistance" movements, some taking the form of citizen's militias, made up of those who would readily fit under Merton's rubric "Prejudiced Discriminators."

Each of these categories is, of course, an ideal type, a model against which reality is to be measured. Although it is rare that one finds a single individual who is all saint or all sinner, "fair-weather liberals" and "timid bigots" do exist. Several caveats should be borne in mind: although many people prejudiced against one minority, say Italians, often tend to dislike others, such as Jews and blacks,[13] prejudice toward one minority does not necessarily mean prejudice toward all. Those who are anti-black are not, ipso facto, anti-Semites—or vice versa.[14]

Nor do dominant groups have a monopoly on prejudice. Many minority group members subscribe to images of other minorities that coincide with those held by members of the dominant groups. Examples include the anti-Semitism of some blacks as well as anti-black sentiments expressed by some Jews, both of which came to light during the crisis over the community control of schools in New York City in 1968–1969,[15] during the presidential primaries of 1988 when Jesse Jackson was a Democrat contender, and in continuing debates about support for Israel.[16] Furthermore, for many racial, religious, and ethnic minorities the dominant group represents "the enemy camp."[17] Brewton Berry and Henry L. Tischler indicate that such hostility is often a direct product of socialization. They cite a story told by editor of the *Carolina Israelite*, Harry Golden, to illustrate the point—focusing on how prejudice is learned.

> My first impression of Christianity came in the home, of course. My parents brought with them the burden of the Middle Ages from the blood-soaked continent of Europe. They had come from the villages of Eastern Europe where Christians were feared with legitimate reason.
>
> When occasionally a Jewish drunk was seen in our neighborhood, our parents would say, "He's behaving like a Gentile."
>
> For in truth, our parents had often witnessed the Polish, Romanian, Hungarian, and Russian peasants gather around a barrel of whiskey on Saturday night, drink themselves into oblivion, "and beat their wives." Once in a while the rumor would spread through the tenements that a fellow had struck his wife, and on all sides we heard the inevitable, "Just like a Gentile."
>
> Oddly enough, too, our parents had us convinced that the Gentiles were noisy, boisterous, and loud—unlike the Jews. ... If we raised our voices, we were told, "Jewish boys don't shout." And this admonition covered every activity in and out of the home: "Jewish boys don't fight." "Jewish boys don't get dirty." "Jewish boys study hard."[18]

Socialization and Social Conformity

Rather than conceiving of group prejudice as an inborn tendency or a rent in one's basic personality, most sociologists today view it as a social habit. This thesis derives from the general proposition that cultural traits are learned. In the process of learning the ways of their groups—the process of socialization—individuals acquire both self-perceptions and images of others. If the teaching is effective, the individual internalizes (in substantial measure, but never fully) the sentiments and customs of his social milieu—including the "appropriate" prejudices.

As sociologists MacIver and Page once wrote, "The individual is not born with prejudices any more than he is born with sociological understanding. The way he thinks as a member of a group, especially about other groups, is at bottom the result of social indoctrination, in both its direct and its indirect forms, indoctrination that inculcates beliefs and attitudes, which easily take firm hold in his life through the process of habituation."[19]

An old southerner put it this way:

> I grew up just 19 miles from Appomattox. The teaching I received both in school and from my parents was hard-core South, with no chance of insight into the thinking and ways of other peoples. I was taught to look down upon Negroes, tolerate Jews (because we had to do business with them) and ignore Catholics.
>
> We celebrated Jefferson Davis's birthday, but ignored Lincoln's; the name Robert E. Lee was spoken with reverence and Appomattox was a shrine. The Golden Rule only applied to others who were either Methodist or Baptist, white and without a foreign-sounding name. ...[20]

The acceptance of various prejudices does not require direct contact between the learner and the members of groups held in low esteem. If the agents of socialization—parents or peers, teachers, preachers, or community leaders—are themselves prejudiced people, they are apt to be effective conveyers of group antipathies whether the objects of their attitudes are immediate neighbors or distant out-groups.

The lessons learned in this "natural" process of enculturation constitute a serious problem for those educators and other persons who attempt to make more realizable the values of the American ethos. They are competing with the home, playground, and, sometimes, the mass media, which for many people represent the normal and desirable way of life, a way of life that all too often is inconsistent with and disruptive of ideals of freedom, social equality, and unhampered opportunity. This situation is aggravated by the fact that group antipathy has been found to exist not only among individuals of high socioeconomic status but also among those in the rank and file.

Culture and Institutionalized Racism

Many contemporary writers and most militant minority group leaders consider institutionalized racism to be the principal source of prejudice against nonwhite peoples (or those treated as a "racial" group, like Jews in Nazi Germany). Their explanations find expression in many forms—from academic rhetoric to the argot of the street—but the theme remains more or less the same. The core argument is that a belief in their own superiority is deeply ingrained in the minds of those in the dominant sector (in our country this means white people) and in their social mores. They have internalized the same views as those promulgated by the early anthropologists and perpetuated by those who, for several centuries, claimed to be lifting and carrying "the white man's burden." The late Whitney M. Young put it succinctly when he wrote that "racism ... is the assumption of superiority and the arrogance that goes with it."[21]

As noted earlier, many southerners found scientific racism a justification for the exploitation of Africans during the first half of the nineteenth century, a time when the institution of slavery was being severely challenged. Increasing evidence suggests that others shared their views but, instead of putting down the blacks, they put them out, out of their minds. Joel Kovel, for example, in his psychohistory *White Racism* contends that in this country racism is still manifest in efforts to control (or what he calls the pattern of "dominative racism") or to avoid ("aversive racism").

He explains, "In general, the dominative type has been marked by heat and the aversive type by coldness. The former is clearly associated with the American South, where, of course, domination of blacks became the cornerstone of society; and the latter with the North, where blacks have so consistently come and found themselves out of place. The dominative racist, when threatened by the black, resorts to direct violence; the aversive racist, in the same situation, turns away and walls himself off."[22]

To pursue the point one step further, it is interesting to note that, like Alexis de Tocqueville long before him, Kovel asserts that aversive racists have been more intense in their reaction than their dominative countrymen. As long ago as the 1830s, Tocqueville had suggested, "The prejudice of race appears to be stronger in the states that have abolished slavery than in those where it still exists; and nowhere is it so intolerant as in those states where servitude has never been known. ..."[23] In the years following the order to end legal segregation in all regions of the United States, the observations of Tocqueville became quite apparent. White northerners who long overlooked what was happening in their midst while condemning southerners for their racial prejudice, began revealing that they were by no means immune to racism themselves.

Institutionalized racism pertains to discriminatory practices reflected in customs and laws and practices engaged in, even by those previously called "reluctant discriminators," and the rules surrounding what is required, what is expected, what is forbidden—and with whom.

Critical Race Theory

Based on an assumption that "most people understand that 'race' as it is used in our society is a social construction not a biological truth [the fact remains] that race remains with us as a compelling myth that has real consequences."[24] It is, according to law professor Richard Delgado, the sine qua non of "Critical Race Theory."[25] Delgado and other writers on the subject contend that, far more than class or region, "race" has been and remains at the very nexus of inequity in the United States and that discrimination based on assumptions about race (as socially defined) persists not only in custom but, in many places, including the Constitution, in law.

Delgado and his coauthor, Jean Stefancic, summarize the basic tenants of the approach by noting that in our society (1) "racism is ordinary, not aberrational"; (2) "white over color ascendancy serves important purposes, both psychic and material"; and (3) "race and races are products of social thought and relations."[26]

Much of the writing of those who place themselves (or are placed) in the camp of the Critical Race Theorists frames arguments in language that highlights many of the explanations of prejudice and its effects cited in the preceding sections of this chapter. For example, Delgado and Stefancic's propositions clearly reflect ideas of some of those scholars and activists we have just discussed: who hold to cultural explanations, claiming that we should worry not only about the bigots but the "gentle people of prejudice," those who are social conformists; we should understand the functions of prejudice according to those who offer both Marxian and Freudian (and other psychological) arguments relating to material advantages and psychic rewards of power over others—and the disadvantages of those whom they exploit and victimize; and be mindful of a leitmotif that appears again and again throughout this volume, the idea that race, as it is generally used, is a social construction. But the Critical Race Theorists break new ground in their emphasis on racism itself, particularly, but not exclusively, in its embeddedness within certain influential institutions, most especially the legal and educational systems.[27]

Often the words of the Critical Race Theorists seem to echo Gunnar Myrdal's observations about the very real distinctions he and his researchers noted between professed beliefs and actual conduct, between "creed" and "deed." Many go further, following one of their pioneers, the Harvard Law professor Derrick Bell, who suggested that even the creed itself is biased. He noted that our guiding document, the US Constitution, favors property over justice, reinforcing the tendency to maintain the status quo ante. He and others claim that whites, even those (or, perhaps, especially those) who are strict constitutionalists, like many liberals, rarely support efforts to redress grievances of African Americans or other minorities unless it is in their own self- or group interest to do so.

Other Critical Race Theorists such as Kimberlé Crenshaw,[28] Mari J. Matsuda,[29] and Lani Guinier[30] contend that the whole legal system must be changed in order to avoid the persisting pitfall of failing to move forward. Social policy as well as the actual structure of a representative democracy must be reformed to enhance the expansion of rights in an agenda that emphasizes the equality of outcome instead of the traditionally restrictive idea (deeply rooted in our legal philosophy) of an equality of opportunity. A common theme in their writings is that it is almost impossible for those who are handicapped at the starting gate to run an equal race. Thus, if the law is to be used as a means to fight prejudice and its effects, it must start by addressing its own inherent weaknesses.

Related to such a critique of the legal system is one that has to do with the nature of research itself. A number of Critical Race Theorists, many of whom are members of various "minority" groups, argue that much of what is written about the character of prejudice, discrimination, and racism in America comes from the pens and computers of those who have never endured the stigma of being "second class" themselves. Richard Delgado, for example, calls for far more appreciation of the perspectives of victims of oppression to fully comprehend the impact of socialization and social conformity in American society.[31]

In a way, it raises an issue that has long been both an epistemological and a political debate in the social sciences: Who is the better judge of thoughts and actions—outside "observers" or inside "members"? To this author, as argued in a paper on the subject in 1978,

> The sociological perspective calls for providing a framework within which to understand what is being studied, what is being read, the larger picture of the systems in which people live and work and play and suffer, the context in which to indicate and text the variables that relate to human affairs everywhere.
>
> I now feel very strongly that the work of the sociologist is like that of the Japanese judge in Rashomon, the one who asks various witnesses and participants to describe a particular event as seen through their own eyes. Like the judge, neither teachers of sociology nor students can be allowed to get off the hook. We must analyze the disparate pieces of evidence and then try to figure out how they fit together. ... Then perhaps we will be better able to know the troubles others have seen and be better able to understand them.[32]

Notes

1. Daniel Wilner, Rosabelle Price Walkley, and Stuart W. Cook, "Residential Proximity and Intergroup Relations in Public Housing Projects," *Journal of Social Issues,* 8:1 (1952), p. 45. For several classic discussions of the definition of prejudice, see Gordon W. Allport, *The Nature of Prejudice* (Cambridge: Addison-Wesley, 1954), pp. 3–16; Brewton Berry, *Race and Ethnic Relations* (Boston: Houghton Mifflin, 1958), pp. 363–371; John Harding et al., "Prejudice and Ethnic Relations," in Gardner Lindzey (ed.), *Handbook of Social Psychology,* Vol. II (Cambridge: Addison-Wesley, 1954), pp. 1021–1061; George Simpson and J. Milton Yinger, *Racial and Cultural Minorities,* rev. ed. (New York: Harper and Row, 1958), pp. 14–19; and Robin M. Williams Jr., *The Reduction of Intergroup Tensions* (New York: The Social Science Research Council, Bulletin No. 57, 1947), pp. 36–43.

2. See Bernard M. Kramer, "Dimensions of Prejudice," *Journal of Psychology,* 27 (April 1949), pp. 389–451.

3. Arnold M. Rose, "Anti-Semitism's Root in City Hatred," *Commentary,* 6 (October 1949), p. 374.

4. This is essentially the same definition used by Robin M. Williams Jr., op. cit., p. 39.

5. As reported in *Time* (September 29, 1958), p. 58. Italics added.

6. As reported in the *New York Times* (October 21, 1966), p. 28.

7. John P. Dean and Alex Rosen, *A Manual of Intergroup Relations* (Chicago: University of Chicago Press, 1955), p. 58.

8. Robert K. Merton, "Discrimination and the American Creed," in R. M. MacIver (ed.), *Discrimination and National Welfare* (New York: Harper and Row, 1949), pp. 99–126. The passages to follow are largely summary statements of Merton's thesis. Only direct quotations will be noted.

9. Ibid., p. 105.

10. See, for example, Robert O. Blood, "Discrimination without Prejudice," *Social Problems,* 3 (October 1955), pp. 114–117.

11. Merton, op. cit., p. 108.

12. Ibid., p. 109.

13. See Allport, op. cit., p. 68.

14. See, for example, E. Terry Prothro and John A. Jenson, "Interrelations of Religious and Ethnic Attitudes in Selected Southern Relations," *Journal of Social Psychology,* 32 (August 1950), pp. 45–49.

15. See, for example, Herbert J. Gans, "Negro-Jewish Conflict in New York," *Midstream* (March 1969).

16. See Peter I. Rose, "Blaming the Jews," *Society* (November/October 1994), pp. 35–40.

17. See, for example, Gerhard W. Ditz, "Out-Group and In-Group Prejudice among Members of Minority Groups," *Alpha Kappa Deltan* (Spring 1959), pp. 26–31; and Catton and Hong, op. cit., pp. 178–191.

18. Harry Golden, *You're Entitled* (Cleveland: World Publishing Company, 1962), p. 259.

19. Robert M. MacIver and Charles H. Page, *Society: An Introductory Analysis* (New York: Holt, Rinehart and Winston, 1949), p. 407.

20. Letter to the Editor of the *New York Times* (May 16, 1963). The letter was signed by Tom Wilcher.

21. See Whitney M. Young Jr., *Beyond Racism: An Open Society* (New York: McGrawHill, 1969).

22. Joel Kovel, *White Racism: A Psychohistory* (New York: Pantheon, 1970), pp. 31–32.

23. Alexis de Tocqueville, *Democracy in America* (New York: Vintage Books, 1945), Vol. I, p. 373.

24. From the brochure, *Only Skin Deep: Changing Visions of the American Self* (New York: International School of Photography, 2005).

25. For a synoptic view of "Critical Race Theory," see Richard Delgado and Jean Stefancic (eds.), *Critical Race Theory: An Introduction* (New York: New York University Press, 2001).

26. Ibid., p. 7.

27. See Joe F. Feagin, *Discrimination American Style: Institutional Racism and Sexism* (Englewood Cliffs, NJ: Prentice Hall, 1978).

28. Crenshaw, *Critical Race Theory*.

29. See, for example, Mari J. Matsuda and Charles R. Lawrence III, *We Won't Go Back: Making the Case for Affirmative Action* (New York: Houghton Mifflin, 1997).

30. Lani Guinier has published several books on the subject. The one in which she makes a case for proportional representation within electoral districts is *The Tyranny of the Majority: Fundamental Fairness in Representative Democracy* (New York: Simon and Schuster, 1995).

31. See Peter I. Rose, "Nobody Knows the Trouble I've Seen: Some Reflections on the Insider-Outsider Debate," The Katherine Asher Engel Lecture, Northampton, MA, Smith College. 1978. Another version of this appeared as Chapter 10, "Insiders and Outsiders," in *They and We*, 4th ed. (New York: McGraw-Hill, 1990). pp. 213–231.

32. Rose, *They and We*, pp. 230–231.

REFLECT AND CONSIDER

- How does prejudice differ from discrimination?
- Compare and contrast individual racism with institutional racism.

RACISM WITHOUT RACISTS: "KILLING ME SOFTLY" WITH COLOR BLINDNESS

BY EDUARDO BONILLA-SILVA AND DAVID G. EMBRICK

In the post-civil rights era, nothing seems "racist" in the traditional sense of the word. Even David Duke, Tom Metzger, and most members of the Ku Klux Klan and other old-fashioned white supremacist organizations claim they are not racist, just pro-white. Moreover, the "white street"[1] asserts that whites "don't see any color, just people." They assume that although the ugly face of discrimination is still around, it is no longer the central factor determining minorities' life chances. Finally, they claim to aspire, much like Dr. Martin Luther King Jr., to live in a society where "people are judged by the content of their character, not by the color of their skin."

However, regardless of whites' "sincere fictions" (Feagin et al. 1995; Feagin and Sikes 1994), racial considerations shade almost everything in America. Blacks and dark-skinned minorities lag well behind whites in virtually every area of social life; they are about three times more likely to be poor than whites, earn about 40 percent less than whites, and have about one-tenth of the net worth of whites. They also receive an inferior education compared to whites, even when they attend so-called integrated (at best, desegregated) schools (for details on all these statistics, see ch. 4 in Bonilla-Silva 2001).

How is it possible to have this tremendous degree of racial inequality in a country where most whites claim that racism is "a thing of the past"? More importantly, how do whites explain the apparent contradiction between their professed color blindness and the United States' color-coded inequality? Eduardo Bonilla-Silva refers to this as the strange enigma of "racism without racists." In his 2003 book, *Racism without Racists*, he attempts to solve this enigma by arguing that "whites," as a social collectivity, have developed a new, powerful, and effective racial ideology to account for contemporary racial matters, which he labels color-blind racism. Whereas Jim Crow racism explained minorities' standing mainly as the result of their imputed biological and moral inferiority, color-blind racism avoids such facile arguments. Instead, whites rationalize minorities' status as the product of market dynamics, naturally occurring phenomena, and their presumed cultural deficiencies. Despite its apparent "racism-lite" character, this ideology is as deadly as the one it replaces.

Before we attempt to deconstruct color-blind racism, let us explain why a new racial ideology is at play in the first place. Color-blind racism acquired cohesiveness and dominance in the late 1960s as the mechanisms and practices for keeping blacks and other racial minorities "at the bottom of the well" changed. We argue that contemporary racial inequality is reproduced through "new racism" practices that are predominantly subtle, institutional, and apparently nonracial (see Bonilla-Silva 2001, ch. 4). In contrast to the Jim Crow era, where racial inequality was enforced through overt means (e.g., signs saying "No Negroes Welcomed Here" or shotgun diplomacy at the voting booth), systemic white privilege is maintained nowadays in a "now you see it, now you don't" fashion. For example, residential segregation, which is almost as high today as it was in the past, is no longer accomplished through overtly discriminatory practices (e.g., bombs and housing covenants) (see Massey and Denton 1993). Instead, covert behaviors, such as not showing all the available units, steering minorities and whites into certain neighborhoods, quoting higher rents or prices to minority applicants, the racializing of credit scores, or not advertising units at all are the weapons of choice to maintain separate communities. New racism practices have been documented in a variety of venues: schools, jobs, banks, restaurants, and stores. Hence, as we will illustrate, the contours of color-blind racism fit quite well with the way racial inequality is reproduced these days.

Methodology

The data we use to make our case comes from two similarly structured projects: the 1997 Survey of Social Attitudes of College Students and the 1998 Detroit Area Study on White Racial Ideology. The Survey of Social Attitudes of College Students is based on a convenient sample of 627 students (of which 451 of the respondents were white) from large universities in the South and Midwest and a mid-size university on the West Coast. Of the white students who provided contact information (about 90 percent), 10 percent were randomly selected for interviews (forty-one students altogether, of which seventeen were men and twenty-four women and of which thirty-one were from middle- and upper-middle-class backgrounds and ten were from working-class backgrounds).

The 1998 Detroit Area Study is a probabilistic survey based on a representative sample of 400 black and white Detroit metropolitan area residents (323 white residents and 67 black residents). The response rate to the survey was 67.5 percent. In addition, 84 respondents (67 whites and 17 blacks) were randomly selected for in-depth interviews. The hour-long interviews were race matched, followed a structured protocol, and were conducted in the subjects' homes (for details, see Bonilla-Silva 2003).

Since ideologies are discursive, we use mostly interview data to document the major components of color-blind racism. By racial ideology, we mean *the racially based frameworks actors use to justify/oppose the racial status quo.* We operationalize the notion of racial ideology as an interpretive repertoire made up of *frames, style,* and *racial stories.* The *frames* of any dominant[2] racial ideology are *set paths for interpreting information* and *operate as cul-de-sacs* because they explain racial phenomena in a predictable manner, as if those who invoke them are getting on a one-way street without exits. Frames are not false consciousness as they provide the intellectual and moral road map whites use to navigate the always-rocky road of domination and derail nonwhites from their track to freedom and equality.[3] The four central frames of color-blind racism are abstract liberalism, naturalization, cultural racism, and minimization of racism, and we illustrate each one separately in subsequent sections.

Abstract Liberalism: Unmasking Reasonable Racism

This frame incorporates tenets associated with political and economic liberalism in an abstract and decontextualized manner. By framing race-related issues in the language of liberalism, whites can appear "reasonable" and even "moral," while opposing all practical approaches to deal with de facto racial inequality. For instance, by using the tenets of the free market ideology in the abstract, they can oppose affirmative action as a violation of the norm of equal opportunity. The following example illustrates how whites use this frame. Jim, a thirty-year-old computer software salesperson from a privileged background, explained his opposition to affirmative action as follows:

> I think it's unfair top to bottom on everybody and the whole process. It often, you know, discrimination itself is a bad word, right? But you discriminate every day. You wanna buy a beer at the store and there are six kinda beers you can get, from Natural Light to Sam Adams, right? And you look at the price and you look at the kind of beer, and you … *it's a choice.* And a lot of that you have laid out in front of you, which one you get? Now, should the government sponsor Sam Adams and make it cheaper than Natural Light because it's brewed by someone in Boston? That doesn't make much sense, right? Why would we want that or make Sam Adams eight times as expensive because we want people to buy Natural Light? And it's the same thing about getting into school or getting into some place. And universities, it's easy, and universities is a hot topic now, and I could bug you, you know, Midwestern University I don't think has a lot of racism in the admissions process. And 1 think Midwestern University would, would agree with that pretty strongly. So why not just pick people that are going to do well at Midwestern University, pick people by their merit? I think we should stop the whole idea of choosing people based on their color.

Since Jim assumes hiring decisions are like market choices (e.g., choosing between competing brands of beer), he embraces a laissez-faire position on hiring. The problem with Jim's view is that labor-market discrimination is alive and well (e.g., it affects black and Latino job applicants 30 to 50 percent), and most jobs (as much as 80 percent) are obtained through informal networks (Braddock and McPartland 1987; Royster 2003). Jim's abstract position is further cushioned by his belief that although blacks "perceive or feel" like there is a lot of discrimination, he does not see much discrimination out there.

Hence, by upholding a strict laissez-faire view on hiring and, at the same time, ignoring the significant impact of discrimination in the labor market, Jim can safely voice his opposition to affirmative action in an apparently race-neutral way. This abstract liberal frame allows whites to be unconcerned about school and residential segregation, oppose almost any kind of government intervention to ameliorate the effects of past and contemporary discrimination, and even to support their preferences for whites as partners/friends as a matter of choice.

Naturalization: Decoding the Meaning of "That's the Way It Is"

A frame that has not yet been brought to the fore by social analysts is the naturalization of race-related matters. The word "natural" and the phrase "that's the way it is" are often interjected to normalize events or actions that could otherwise be interpreted as racially motivated (residential segregation) or racist (preference for whites as friends and partners). But, as social scientists know quite well, these are not natural but socially produced outcomes. An example of how whites use this frame is Bill, a manufacturing firm manager in his fifties, who explained the limited level of school integration as follows:

> I don't think it's anybody's fault. Because people tend to group with their own people. Whether it's white or black or upper-middle class or lower class or, you know, Asians. People tend to group with their own. Doesn't mean if a black person moves into your neighborhood, they shouldn't go to your school. They should and you should mix and welcome them and everything else, but you can't force people together. If people want to be together, they should intermix more.

> [Interviewer: Okay. So the lack of mixing is really just kind of an individual lack of desire?]

> Well, individuals, it's just the way it is. You know, people group together for lots of different reasons: social, religious. Just as animals in the wild, you know. Elephants group together, cheetahs group together. You bus a cheetah into an elephant herd because they should mix? You can't force that [laughs].

Although most respondents were not as crude as Bill, they still used this frame to justify the racial status quo.

Cultural Racism: "They Don't Have It Altogether"

Pierre Andre Taguieff (2001) has argued that modern racial ideology does not portray minorities as inferior biological beings. Instead, it *biologizes* their presumed cultural practices (i.e., present them as fixed features) and uses that as the rationale for justifying racial inequality (he labels this "differentialist racism"). This cultural racism is very well established in the United States.[4] The newness of this frame resides in the centrality it has acquired in whites' contemporary justifications of minorities' standing. The essence of the frame, as William Ryan (1976) pointed out a long time ago, is "blaming the victim" by arguing that minorities' status is the product of their lack of effort, loose family organization, inappropriate values, or some combination thereof. An example of how whites use this frame is Kim, a student at Midwestern University. When asked "Many whites explain the status of blacks in this country as a result of blacks lacking motivation, not having the proper work ethic, or being lazy. What do you think?" Kim responded,

> Yeah, I totally agree with that. I don't think, you know, they're all like that, but, I mean, it's just that if it wasn't that way, why would there be so many blacks living in the projects? You know, why would there be so many poor blacks? If they worked hard, they could make it just as high as anyone else could. You know, I just think that's just, you know, they're raised that way and they see that parents are, so they assume that's the way it should be. And they just follow the roles their parents had for them and don't go anywhere.

Although not all whites were as crude as this student, most subscribed to this belief, whether in its nastiest, most direct versions or in a "compassionate conservative" manner.

Minimization of Racism: Whites' Declining Significance of Race Thesis

Most whites do not believe that the predicament of minorities today is the product of discrimination. Instead, they believe that it's because of their "culture," "class," "legacies from slavery," "Mexican/Puerto Rican backward culture," "culture of segregation," "lack of social capital," "poverty," and so on and so forth. It's "anything but racism!" An example of how whites use this frame is Sandra, a retail salesperson in her early forties, who explained her view on discrimination as follows:

> I think if you are looking for discrimination, I think it's there to be *found.* But if you make the best of any situation, and if *you don't use it as an excuse.* I think sometimes it's an excuse because people felt they deserved a job, whatever! I think if things didn't go their way, I know a lot of people have a tendency to use prejudice or racism or whatever as an *excuse.* I think in some ways, yes, there is [sic] people who are prejudiced. It's not only blacks, it's about Spanish, or women. In a lot of ways there [is] a lot of *reverse* discrimination. It's just what you wanna make of it.

This needs very little comment. Since most whites, like Sandra, believe discrimination has all but disappeared, they regard minorities' claims of discrimination as excuses or as minorities playing the infamous "race card."

The Style of Color Blindness: How to Talk Nasty about Blacks Without Sounding "Racist"

Ideologies are not just about ideas. In order for the frames of an ideology to work effectively, those who invoke them need rhetorical devices to weave arguments in all kinds of situations. In the case of color-blind racism, given the post-civil rights normative context, whites need these devices to save face and still be able to articulate their racial views. Hence, we define the *style* of a racial ideology as its peculiar *linguistic manners and rhetorical strategies* (or *race talk),* that is, the technical tools that allow users to articulate its frames and racial stories. Since a full discursive analysis of the five stylistic components of color blindness is beyond the scope of this chapter, we only illustrate three: semantic moves, projection, and rhetorical incoherence.

Semantic Moves

Semantic moves, such as phrases that protect users' moral standpoint (e.g., "I am not a racist, but … "), allow whites to express their racial views in a coded and safe way—safe because they can always go back to the safety of the disclaimers ("I didn't mean that because *I am not a racist*" and "Some of my best friends are black"). However, since moves like "I am not a racist" or "Some of my best friends are black" have become cliché and are therefore less effective, whites have developed new moves to accomplish the same goals.[5]

One such rhetorical move for stating racial views without opening yourself to the charge of racism is taking apparently all sides on an issue. We label this as the "Yes and no, but … " move. Sandra, the retail person in her forties cited above, answered the question "Are you for or against affirmative action?" in the following apparently cryptic manner:

Yes and no. I feel someone should be able to have *something,* education, job, whatever, because they've earned it, they deserve it, they have the ability to do it. You don't want to put a six-year-old as a *rocket scientist.* They don't have the ability. It doesn't matter if the kid's black or white. As far as letting one have the job over another one just because of their race or their gender, I don't believe in that.

Sandra's "yes and no" stand on affirmative action is truly a strong "no" since she does not find any reason whatsoever for affirmative action programs to be in place.

It Wasn't Me! The Role of Projection in Color-Blind Racism

Psychologists know that projection is part of our normal equipment to defend the "self." It is also an essential tool in the creation of a corporate identity ("us" versus "them"). More significantly, projection helps us "escape from guilt and responsibility and affix blame elsewhere." Thus, it was not surprising to find that whites projected racism or racial motivations onto blacks as a way of avoiding responsibility and feeling good about themselves.

The following example illustrates how whites project racial motivations onto blacks. In her answer to the interracial marriage question, Janet, a student at Southern University, projected onto people who marry across the color line:

> I would feel that in most situations they're not really thinking of the, the child. I mean, they might not really think anything of it, *but* in reality I think most of the time when the child is growing up, he's going to be picked on because he has parents from different races and it's gonna ultimately affect the child and, and the end result is they're only thinking of them. Both their own happiness, not the happiness of, of the kid.

By projecting selfishness onto those who intermarry, Janet was able to voice her otherwise problematic opposition to these marriages safely.

Rhetorical Incoherence

Finally, we want to provide one example of rhetorical incoherence. Although incoherence (e.g., grammatical mistakes, lengthy pauses, or repetition) is part of all natural speech, the level of incoherence increases noticeably when people discuss sensitive subjects. And because the new racial climate in America forbids the open expression of racially based feelings, views, and positions, when whites discuss issues that make them feel uncomfortable, they become almost incomprehensible.

For example, Ray, a Midwestern University student and a respondent who was very articulate throughout the interview, became almost incomprehensible when answering the question about whether he had been involved with minorities while in college.

Um so to answer that question, no. But I would not, I mean, I would not ever preclude a black woman from being my girlfriend on the basis that she was black. Ya' know, I mean, ya' know what I mean? If you're looking about it from, ya' know, the standpoint of just attraction, I mean, I think that, ya' know, I think, ya' know, I think, ya' know, all women are, I mean, all women have a sort of different type of beauty, if you will. And I think that, ya' know, for black women, it's somewhat different than white women. But I don't think it's, ya know, I mean, it's, it's, it's nothing that would ever stop me from like, I mean, I don't know, I mean, I don't if that's, I mean, that's just sort of been my impression. I mean, it's not like I would ever say, "No, I'll never have a black girlfriend," but it just seems to me like I'm not as attracted to black women as I am to white women, for whatever reason. It's not about prejudice, it's just sort of like, ya' know, whatever. Just sort of the way, way like I see white women as compared to black women, ya' know?

The interviewer followed up Ray's answer with the question, "Do you have any idea why that would be?" Ray replied: "I, I, I [sighs] don't really know. It's just sort of hard to describe. It's just like, ya' know, who you're more drawn to, ya' know, for whatever reason, ya' know?" Ray's answer suggests that he is not attracted to black women and has serious problems explaining why.

Conclusion

In this chapter, we suggested there is a new dominant racial ideology in town: color-blind racism. This ideology is suave but deadly, hence the line from the song by Roberta Flack, "killing me softly," in the title of our chapter. *But let's not forget that a soft, color-blind approach to racial death still leads to death!* Whites need not call minorities niggers, spies, or chinks to keep them in their new, but still subordinated, place.

Yet, at the heart of color blindness lies a myth: the idea that race has all but disappeared as a factor shaping the life chances of people in the United States. This myth is the central column supporting the house of color blindness. Remove this column from the house's foundation, and the house collapses. Removing this column, however, will not be an easy task because whites' racial views are not mere erroneous ideas to be battled in the field of rational discourse. They constitute, as we argued in this chapter, a racial ideology, that is, a loosely organized set of frames, phrases, and stories that help whites justify contemporary racial inequality. These views, then, are symbolic expressions of whites' dominance and cannot just be eradicated with "facts" because racial facts are highly contested. In the eyes of whites, evidence of racial disparity in income, wealth, and education is evidence that there is something wrong with minorities; evidence of blacks' overrepresentation in the criminal justice system or on death row is proof of blacks' criminal tendencies.

Let us now conclude by suggesting concrete things we can do to fight color-blind racism. First, we need to nurture a large cohort of antiracist whites to begin challenging color-blind nonsense from within (Feagin and O'Brien 2003). Whites' collective denial about the true nature of race relations may help them feel good, but it is also one of the greatest obstacles to doing the right thing. In racial matters, as in therapy, the admission of denial is the preamble for the beginning of recovery. Are we suggesting that all whites are color-blind racists? The answer is no. We classified 10 to 15 percent of the white respondents as "racial progressives."[6] However, the identity of these respondents may surprise some of you: young working-class women. Why would this section of the white population be more likely to be racially progressive? We suggest that it is because they experience the double-whammy (being women and workers) and can empathize with minorities' plight. It is equally important that they are more likely to share intimate social spaces (e.g., neighborhoods, jobs, schools) with minorities, which, combined with their low status, produces the kind of race contact that Gordon Allport (1958) believed would produce better race relations.

Second, researchers need to provide counterideological arguments to each of the frames of color-blind racism. We need to counter whites' abstract liberalism with concrete liberal positions based on a realistic understanding of racial matters and a concern with achieving real racial equality. Are blacks color-blind, too? The answer is that color-blind racism has a small direct, and a larger indirect, effect on them that blunts the potential all-out character of their oppositional ideology. This means that color-blind racism is a dominant ideology as it makes happy, happy, happy those at the top of the racial order and confuses those at the bottom; that is, it has become a hegemonic ideology (similar to capitalism, patriarchy, and the like).

Third, we need to undress whites' claims of color blindness. We must show in creative ways the myriad facets of contemporary whiteness: whites living in white neighborhoods, sending their kids to white schools, associating primarily with whites, and having their primary relationships with whites. And because of the subtle character of modern white supremacy, new research strategies, such as audits (e.g., Housing and Urban Development audits), mixed research designs (surveys and interviews), and racial treason (Ignatiev and Garvey 1996), will be required to unveil the mask of whiteness. Given the new demography of the United States, why the focus on the black-white dyad? To this, our answer is twofold: 1. A new research project by Bonilla-Silva and Michael Emerson is being conducted to assess the parameters of the new racial stratification order (the Latin Americanization of race relations) and can offer arguments and preliminary data on how other groups might fit into the ideological constellation. In this project, they are positing that a new racial order is emerging in the United States, characterized by a tri-racial, rather than a bi-racial, division and the increasing salience of skin tone as a stratification element (see Bonilla-Silva 2004). 2. Despite the new racial demography, we believe, like Joe Feagin (2000) and others, that the black-white paradigm still ordains the macro racial issues in the country; it is still through this prism that newcomers are assessed (close to whiteness or blackness).

Fourth, modern white supremacy must be challenged wherever it exists—in churches, neighborhoods, schools, our places of work, and even in academic organizations such as the American Educational Research Association and the American Sociological Association. Those committed to racial equality must develop a personal practice to challenge white supremacy. Is this a racial ideology or a general post-civil rights ideology? In this chapter, we described the racial ideological aspects of the larger ideological ensemble, which always includes a plurality of subjects of domination (e.g., gender, race, class). At least one analyst makes the case that post-civil rights ideology is characterized by "muted hostility"[7] (Jackman 1994).

Finally, the most important strategy for fighting "new racism" practices and the ideology of color blindness is to recreate a civil rights movement. Changes in systems of domination and their accompanying ideologies are never accomplished by racial dialogues, "Can't we all just get along?" "workshops on racism," education, or "moral reform" alone. Moral, counterideological, and educational appeals always need a social movement, in our case, a new civil rights movement that demands equality of results now! Only by demanding what seems impossible now will we be able to make genuine racial equality possible in the future.

Notes

1. We are using the notion of "white street" to refer to how "average" whites think and talk about race. The idea is similar to the way that American commentators talk and write about the "Arab street."

2. In this chapter, we only examine the dominant racial ideology. However, we would be remiss if we did not point out that not all whites spout this ideology. In fact, we document the views of white racial progressives, who make up about 10 percent of the white respondents in these samples in chapter 6 of Bonilla-Silva 2003.

3. Here, we are using the notion of ideology in the Althusserian sense, that is, of ideology as a practice that allows users to accomplish tasks.

4. Although some analysts believe that the idea of the "culture of poverty," as elaborated by Oscar Lewis in the 1960s, was the foundation of a racialized view on poverty, historians have documented the long history of this belief in America. See, for example, Michael A. Katz's *In the Shadow of the Poorhouse* (1986).

5. These moves have not disappeared completely as many respondents still used them. However, because ideologies are always in process, in construction, new and more refined moves have emerged.

6. We classify as racial progressives respondents who support affirmative action and interracial marriage and who recognize the significance of discrimination in the United States.

7. In her book *The Velvet Glove,* Jackman (1994) argues that in the post-civil rights era, gender, class, and race ideology has shifted from overt to covert, or "muted," hostility. Thus, in Jackman's estimation, men, capitalists, and whites are less likely to employ the "nasty" tropes of the past, and hit women, workers, and minorities with a "velvet glove."

References

Allport, Gordon W. 1958. *The nature of prejudice.* New York: Doubleday/Anchor Books.

Bell, Derrick. 1992. *Race, racism, and American law.* Boston, MA: Little, Brown, and Company.

Bonilla-Silva, Eduardo. 1997. Rethinking racism: Toward a structural interpretation. *American Sociological Review* 62 (3): 465–80.

———. 2001. *White supremacy and racism in the post-civil rights era.* Boulder, CO: Lynne Rienner Publishers.

———. 2003. *Racism without racists: Color-blind racism and the persistence of racial inequality in the USA.* Boulder, CO: Rowman & Littlefield.

———. 2004. From bi-racial to tri-racial: Towards new system of racial stratification in the USA. *Racial and Ethnic Studies* 27 (6) (November): 1–20.

Bonilla-Silva, Eduardo, and Amanda E. Lewis. 1999. The "new racism": Toward an analysis of the U.S. racial structure, 1960-1990s. In *Race, Nation, and Citizenship,* ed. Paul Wong, 100–50. Boulder, CO: Westview.

Braddock, Jomills, and James McPartland. 1987. How minorities continue to be excluded from equal employment opportunities: Research on labor market and institutional barriers. *Journal of Social Issues* 43 (1): 5–39.

Feagin, Joe R. 2000. *Racist America: Roots, realities, and future reparations.* New York: Routledge,

Feagin, Joe R., and Eileen O'Brian. 2003. *White men on race: Power, privilege, and the shaping of cultural consciousness.* Boston, MA: Beacon Press.

Feagin, Joe R., and Melvin Sikes. 1994. *Living with racism: The black middle class experience.* Boston: Beacon.

Feagin, Joe R., Hernan Vera, and Nikitah Imani. 1995. *The agony of education: Black students at white colleges and universities.* New York: Routledge.

Firebaugh, Glenn, and Kenneth E. Davis. 1988. Trends in antiblack prejudice, 1972–1984: Region and cohort effects. *American Journal of Sociology* 94 (2) (September): 251–72.

Ignatiev, Joel, and John Garvey. 1996. *Race traitor.* New York: Routledge.

Jackman, Mary R. 1994. *Velvet glove: Paternalism and conflict in gender, class, and race relations.* Berkeley: University of California Press.

Katz, Michael A. 1986. *In the shadow of the poorhouse: A social history of welfare in America.* New York: Basic Books.

Lewis, Oscar. 1966. The culture of poverty. *Scientific American* 215 (4): 19–25.

Massey, Douglas S., and Nancy A. Denton. 1993. *American apartheid: Segregation and the making of the underclass.* Cambridge, MA: Harvard University Press.

Royster, Deirdre A. 2003. *Race and the invisible hand: How white networks exclude black men from blue-collar jobs.* Berkeley: University of California Press.

Ryan, William. 1976. *Blaming the victim.* New York: Vintage Books.

Schuman, Howard, Charlotte Steeh, Lawrence Bobo, and Maria Krysan. 1997. *Racial attitudes in Ameiica: Trends and interpretations.* Cambridge, MA: Harvard University Press.

Sniderman, Paul M., and Thomas Piazza. 1993. *The scar of race.* Cambridge, MA: Harvard University Press.

Taguieff, Pierre-Andre. 2001. *The force of prejudice: Racism and its doubles.* Minneapolis: University of Minnesota Press.

REFLECT AND CONSIDER

- Describe how the adoption of a "color-blind" approach can actually result in the persistence of racism.
- How does color-blind racism connect to racial discrimination on the institutional level?

COLORSTRUCK

BY MARGARET HUNTER

I f you're white you're alright, if you're brown stick around, if you're
yellow you're mellow, if you're black get back! Light, bright, and
almost white. Blue-black. African. La güera. La prieta. La morena.
India. La negrita. Colorstruck.

The blacker the berry, the sweeter the juice. This saying, unlike many others,
promises an even sweeter inside for a person with dark brown skin and suggests
that darker skin is actually more desirable than light.

Most Americans are familiar with problems of racial discrimination in the
United States. African Americans and Mexican Americans have made great
progress in combating persistent racial discrimination whether encountered in
housing, education, the work place, or other areas. Hidden within the process
of racial discrimination, is the often overlooked issue of colorism. Lighter-
skinned African Americans and Mexican Americans enjoy substantial privileges that are still unattainable to their darker-skinned brothers and sisters.[1]
Colorism is a problem affecting all Americans. Although typically described

as a "black" or "Chicano" problem, colorism is practiced by whites and people of color alike. Given the opportunity, many people will hire a light-skinned person before a dark-skinned person of the same race, or choose to marry a lighter-skinned woman rather than a darker-skinned woman.[2]

Even the federal government is becoming increasingly concerned with color-based discrimination. "The Equal Employment Opportunity Commission [EEOC]... says it is handling more color-discrimination complaints pitting blacks, Hispanics, Native Americans, and others against members of their own race or ethnic group."[3] In the early 1990s, the EEOC typically received less than 500 complaints of color-bias per year. By 2002, the number had nearly tripled to 1,400 complaints of color-bias. This explosion may be related to increasing cases of discrimination, and it may also be evidence of increasing awareness that color-based discrimination is not only wrong, it's illegal.

Many cases of color-based discrimination have ended up in the courts. In 2002, the EEOC sued the owners of a Mexican restaurant in San Antonio, Texas for color-based discrimination. A white manager at the restaurant claimed that the owners directed him to hire only light-skinned staff to work in the dining room. The EEOC won the case and the restaurant was forced to pay $100,000 in fines.[4] In 2003, a dark-skinned African American won a claim of $40,000 from a national restaurant chain for color-based discrimination from a fellow black employee. The plaintiff argued that he suffered constant taunting and color-based epithets about his dark skin from lighter-skinned African American co-workers.[5] These are just two examples of how colorism affects people of color on a daily basis. Most people of color will not end up in court over color bias, but all people of color will experience or witness unfair treatment because of a person's skin tone.

Sociological research reveals that lighter-skinned African Americans and Mexican Americans earn more money, complete more years of education, live in more integrated neighborhoods, and have better mental health than do darker-skinned African Americans and Mexican Americans.[6] The long history of skin color stratification for both of these groups has its roots in their colonization and enslavement by Europeans. Europeans and white Americans created racial hierarchies to justify their subhuman treatment of the people of color they colonized and enslaved. This was the beginning of the ideology of white supremacy. The alleged superiority of whiteness, and all things approximating it including white or light skin, was the rule.

White racism is the fundamental building block of colorism, or skin color stratification, among Mexican Americans and African Americans. The maintenance of white supremacy in this country is predicated on the notion that dark skin represents savagery, irrationality, ugliness, and inferiority. White skin, and thus whiteness itself, is defined by the opposite: civility, rationality, beauty, and superiority.[7] These meanings are infused into actual body types to create the system of racism as we know it today.

> Racist ideology usually involves an esthetic appraisal of physical features, a mythology about traits of mind and personality correlated with physical features, and an almost mystical belief in the power of "blood" to elevate or to taint.[8]

Skin color and features associated with whites, such as light skin, straight noses, and long, straight hair, take on the meanings that they represent: civility, rationality, and beauty. Similarly, skin colors and features associated with Africans or Indians, such as dark skin, broad noses, and kinky hair, represent savagery, irrationality, and ugliness. The values associated with physical features set the stage for skin color stratification.

This study of color bias is further complicated by its simultaneous attention to sexism. One woman I interviewed describes her frustration with men of color and their perceptions of beauty.

> In terms of models and catalogs, there are no black women, only white women. … I guess they're [black and Latino men] attracted to white women. I think they like more long hair, light eyes, lighter complexion. I know some Latino guys say, "I don't want no indigenous looking girl." Black guys are like, "I don't really like dark girls unless they have long hair." But not a lot of dark girls are going to have long hair. That's white girls. I think they like a lighter, closer to white variety of females.

Skin color bias creates many painful experiences for women of color, especially darker-skinned women. This has led many women to try to alter their appearances through skin bleaching creams, make-up application, use of colored contact lenses, dieting, hair straightening and hair extensions, and even cosmetic surgery. Many of these procedures have the effect of whitening or Anglicizing a woman's appearance in order to make her more "beautiful."[9]

In fact, the pursuit of light skin color can be so important it can prove fatal. A Harvard Medical School researcher found outbreaks of mercury poisoning in Saudi Arabia, Pakistan, Tanzania, and the southwestern United States. He came to learn that the poisoning, found almost exclusively in women, was caused by the widespread use of skin-bleaching creams containing toxic levels of mercury.[10] Children, too, suffered—either from in utero absorption during pregnancy, or from mothers who put the bleaching cream on their children eager for them to have the benefits of light skin, the more valued complexion.

Noted social scientist Vicki Ruiz describes the pressure from inside and outside of the Mexican American community for young women to pursue beauty and to wear cosmetics.

The use of cosmetics, however, cannot be blamed entirely on Madison Avenue ad campaigns. The innumerable barrio beauty pageants, sponsored by mutualistas, patriotic societies, churches, the Mexican Chamber of Commerce, newspapers, and even progressive labor unions, encouraged young women to accentuate their physical attributes.[11]

Ruiz provides a persuasive example of the power of beauty to structure the lives of women. Her long list of Mexican organizations that support the ideology of beauty is alarming, especially because it includes organizations such as "churches" and "progressive labor unions." Her description of the pursuit of beauty, often in the name of ethnic pride (at ethnic festivals and celebrations), illustrates the inherent contradictions between racial pride and a pursuit of beauty than valorizes whiteness.

In her essay about young black women and their beauty attitudes and practices, sociologist Maxine Leeds describes the contradictory position many young black women find themselves in.

These students frequently stated that there was a beauty standard that valued lighter skin and longer and straighter hair. They distanced themselves from that standard and articulated a more inclusive idea of beauty. Yet their own taunts about skin color and hair length indicate that they, to some degree, accept a Eurocentric ideal.[12]

She describes her interview participants as able to see beauty in traditionally black identities including dark skin color and short, natural hair, but it seems as if they have not completely released the power of the white ideal of beauty.[13] They stand outside of a white cultural ideal, yet they have internalized it. When Leeds asked the young women if there was anything they would change about their appearance, most responded with wanting longer hair, lighter skin or lighter eyes—all traits associated with whites and not blacks.

Another way in which sexism interacts with racism is in its structuring of the marriage market. Women learn to compete with one another for men in the marriage marketplace. Women compete with one another over many traits including educational credentials, income, family status, and perhaps most importantly, beauty. Skin color is closely tied to the definition of beauty such that light-skinned or white women are considered more "beautiful" than darker-skinned women of color.[14] In this way, beauty works as a form of social capital for women. Beauty is capital because it is transformable into other types of capital, such as economic capital or money.[15] The amount of beauty a woman possesses may help her land a well-paying job or marry a high-status, wealthy man.

But what about the Black is Beautiful movement and the Brown Pride movement? In the 1960s and 1970s many African Americans and Mexican Americans were involved in cultural revolutions that inverted the racist norms of white beauty and celebrated brown skin, African and Indian features, and natural hair. These movements were significant and were part and parcel of the larger struggles for political and economic rights. It was common to hear young Chicanos referring to "Aztec Goddesses" and young blacks to "Nubian Princesses." But this burgeoning aesthetic, though influential, did not create a substantial permanent change in American culture. Blacks and Chicanos will forever be imprinted with the proud messages of those days, but many of those values have become more talk than reality as skin-bleaching creams continue to be used and facial cosmetic surgery is on the rise among people of color.

How are lighter and darker women affected by their skin tone in the worlds of work, education, and the marriage market? Resources are allocated unequally to light and dark-skinned women and beauty is constructed to elevate the status of light-skinned black and Mexican American women who most closely physically resemble whites. Skin color, racial, and gender hierarchies all work at the ideological level to construct beauty as a tool of patriarchy and racism. Because beauty is an ideology, its standards serve the interests of dominant social groups. In this case beauty is a hegemonic ideology and its existence serves the interests of whites in that it maintains white privilege. Beauty as an ideology also serves the interests of men because it maintains patriarchy as it divides women through competition and reduces their power.

The ideology of beauty is linked to ideologies of competence and intelligence. In a public sphere still debating racial differences in intelligence,[16] racial images that signify who "looks smart" are heavily influenced by race, gender, and skin color. People with light skin and Anglo features, usually associated with rationality and civility, are more likely to be perceived as intelligent and competent than are individuals with skin colors and features associated with Africans or Indians and thus associated with savagery, and incompetence.[17]

The status characteristics of race, color, and gender also work at the material level as they affect educational outcomes, income differences, and occupational characteristics of individuals and groups. Often through the ideological work discussed above, women are discriminated against both overtly and covertly in the worlds of work and education. For example, a light-skinned Mexican American woman is viewed by other Mexican Americans and by whites as higher status, less racially conscious (and therefore less threatening), more "respectable," and more assimilable than her darker-skinned counterparts. These perceptions give her a competitive edge in schools and job markets still tainted by racism.

On average, women, earn less money than men; people of color earn less than whites, and darker-skinned people of color earn less than lighter-skinned people of color.

Notes

1. Kathy Russell, Midge Wilson, and Ronald Hall, *The Color Complex: The Politics of Skin Color Among African Americans* (New York: Anchor Books, 1992).

2. Margaret Hunter, "Colorstruck: Skin Color Stratification in the Lives of African American Women," *Sociological Inquiry* 68, no. 4 (1998): 517–35.

3. Marjorie Valbrun, "EEOC Sees Rise in Intrarace Complaints of Color Bias," *Wall Street Journal,* August 7, 2003.

4. Valbrun.

5. Valbrun.

6. Carlos Arce, Edward Murguia, and W. Parker Frisbie, "Phenotype and Life Chances Among Chicanos," *Hispanic Journal of Behavioral Sciences* 9 (1987): 19–32. Michael Hughes and Bradley Hertel, "The Significance of Color Remains: A Study of Life Chances, Mate Selection, and Ethnic Consciousness Among Black Americans," *Social Forces* 68, no. 4 (1990): 1105–20. Verna Keith and Cedric Herring, "Skin Tone and Stratification in the Black Community," *American Journal of Sociology* 97, no. 3 (1991). Richard Seltzer and Robert C. Smith, "Color Differences in the Afro-American Community and the Differences They Make," *Journal of Black Studies* 21, no. 3 (1991): 279–286. Kendrick Brown, "Consequences of Skin Tone Bias for African Americans: Resource Attainment and Psychological and Social Functioning," *African American Research Perspectives* 4 (1998): 55–60. E. Codina and F. Montalvo, "Chicano Phenotype and Depression," *Hispanic Journal of Behavioral Sciences* 16 (1994): 296–306. F. Montalvo *Skin Color and Latinos: The Origins and Contemporary Patterns of Ethnoracial Ambiguity Among Mexican Americans and Puerto Ricans* (monograph) (San Antonio, TX: Our Lady of the Lake University, 1987). Edward Murguia and Edward Telles, "Phenotype and Schooling among Mexican Americans," *Sociology of Education* 69 (1996): 276–89. H.E. Ransford, "Skin Color, Life Chances, and Anti-White Attitude," *Social Problems* 18 (1970): 164–78. J. Relethford, P. Stern, S. P. Catskill, and H.P. Hazuda, "Social Class, Admixture, and Skin Color Variation in Mexican Americans and Anglo Americans Living in San Antonio, Texas," *American Journal of Physical Anthropology* 61 (1983): 97–102. Edward Telles and Edward Murguia, "Phenotypic Discrimination and Income Differences among Mexican Americans," *Social Science Quarterly* 71, no. 4 (1990): 682–96.

7. Toni Morrison, *Playing in the Dark: Whiteness and the Literary Imagination* (New York: Vintage Books, 1992).

8. St. Clair Drake, *Black Folk Here and There*, Vol. 1. (Los Angeles, UCLA Center for African American Studies: University of California Press, 1987), 23.

9. Ronald Hall, "The Bleaching Syndrome: African Americans' Response to Cultural Domination Vis-à-vis Skin Color," *Journal of Black Studies* 26, no. 2 (1995): 172–84.

10. S. Allen Counter, "Whitening Skin can be Deadly," *Boston Globe*, December 16, 2003.

11. Vicki Ruiz, *From Out of the Shadows: Mexican Women in Twentieth Century America* (New York: Oxford University Press, 1998), 55–56.

12. Maxine Leeds, "Young African-American Women and the Language of Beauty," in *Ideals of Feminine Beauty: Philosophical, Social, and Cultural Dimensions,* ed. Karen Callaghan (London: Greenwood Press, 1994), 6.

13. See also Selena Bond and Thomas Cash, "Black Beauty: Skin Color and Body Images Among African American College-Age Women," *Journal of Applied Social Psychology* 22 (1992): 874–88.

14. Mark E. Hill, "Skin Color and the Perception of Attractiveness Among African Americans: Does Gender Make a Difference?" *Social Psychology Quarterly* 65, no. 1 (2002): 77–91.

15. I use the term social capital here to describe a combination of Pierre Bourdieu's social and symbolic capital. See Pierre Bourdieu, *Distinction* (Cambridge, MA: Harvard University Press, 1984).

16. Richard J. Herrnstein and Charles Murray, *The Bell Curve: Intelligence and Class Structure in American Life* (New York: The Free Press, 1994).

17. St. Clair Drake, *Black Folk Here and There*, Vol. 1.

REFLECT AND CONSIDER

- Explain how colorism is a manifestation of White Supremacy.
- Describe some of the consequences of colorism on the micro and macro level.

THE WHITE SUPREMACY FLOWER: A MODEL FOR UNDERSTANDING RACISM

BY HEPHZIBAH V. STRMIC-PAWL

Understanding contemporary racial inequality requires studying the complex relationships among race, racism, and power. Scholars investigate the contours of modern racism, particularly how to recognize it and what constitutes modern racism. A branch of this investigation has led to a focus on White Privilege, the examination of the benefits that Whites receive and the power assigned to Whiteness. Another branch focuses more on the concept of White Supremacy, a critical approach to how race and racism are systemically and systematically embedded in society. The theoretical boundaries between White Privilege and White Supremacy can be confusing and unclear as they often overlap in their analyses of racial inequality. However, in this paper I integrate the two concepts into one model, the White Supremacy Flower, which outlines the foundations of racism, the evolution of racism, and the perpetuation of racism.

I first review the definitions of White Privilege and White Supremacy and draw analytical distinctions between the two concepts. Second, I provide a description and the tenets of the White Supremacy Flower. I close with the conceptual benefits of this model for understanding racism.

Hephzibah V. Strmic-Pawl. 2015. "More Than a Knapsack: The White Supremacy Flower as a New Model for Teaching Racism." *Sociology of Race and Ethnicity,* 1(1): 192-197. by SAGE Publications.

White Supremacy And White Privilege

White Privilege

The concept of 'White Privilege' became widely popular with the release of Peggy McIntosh's 1988 paper "White Privilege: Unpacking the Invisible Knapsack." Her paper analyzes the undue and unearned benefits that White people receive. To elucidate her idea of "privileges," McIntosh lists twenty-six benefits that Whites carry in a "knapsack," such as dolls and greeting cards predominantly representing Whites, and the fact that Whites are not regularly asked to speak for the entire White race. She states: "I have come to see white privilege as an invisible package of unearned assets which I can count on cashing in each day, but about which I was 'meant' to remain oblivious."

Since McIntosh's paper, the field of White Privilege scholarship has burgeoned and become a site of critical analysis. It asks scholars and laymen, alike, to question even our day-to-day practices in order to identify where unspoken privileges help Whites succeed. Paula Rothenberg (2004, 1) defines White Privilege as "the other side of racism … It is often easier to deplore racism and its effects than to take responsibility for the privileges some of us receive as a result of it." Opportunities to discuss White Privilege are now widespread. The *Knapsack Institute* hosts *The White Privilege Conference,* a multiple day conference where people gather to "challenge concepts of privilege and oppression" (see www.whiteprivilegeconference.com). People also may be familiar with White Privilege through social networking campaigns, such as BuzzFeed's (Jha and Wesely 2014) 'privilege' quiz or BuzzFeed's (Blackmon 2013) "17 Deplorable Examples of White Privilege." A city in Minnesota even ran a White Privilege campaign where they posted large billboards of faces of White people along with types of White privileges; examples of some of the privileges are: "Is White skin really fair skin" and "lucky to be the majority" (Un-Fair Campaign n.d.). White Privilege initiatives such as these do the necessary job of asking White people to reflect on the ways in which the racial hierarchy benefits them. They also bring much needed attention to seeing White as a race, rather than White fading into the background as the unraced, normal person.

White Supremacy

White Supremacy, in contrast to the term White Privilege, is a term often hard to digest as it conjures up images of White superiority groups. Yet, groups such as the Ku Klux Klan and the Aryan Brotherhood, are only a very small portion of White Supremacy. Instead, White

Supremacy is a useful theoretical concept to describe the systemic and systematic ways the racial order benefits those deemed White and operates to oppress people of color (Bonilla-Silva 2003; Feagin 2006; Marshall 2011; Smith 2005; Takaki 1993; Yancey 2008). White Supremacy is all encompassing of society and is upheld by intertwined systems, institutions, and ideologies. An example of a system is capitalism, which was strengthened with the selling of enslaved Africans and continues today through the maintained lower socioeconomic status of people of color. Examples of institutions are education, criminal justice, and health care, all of which disproportionately operate to benefit Whites. The ideologies change through time, from manifest destiny to Jim Crow to today's color-blind racism, but the central defining characteristic of these ideologies remains the same: the privileging of Whiteness as the norm, standard, and the best for society (Baptist 2014; Bonilla-Silva 2003; Feagin 2006; hooks 2000). Charles W. Mills, a leading philosopher on race, defines White Supremacy as "a multidimensional system of domination not merely encompassing the 'formally' political that is limited to the juridico-political realm of official governing bodies and laws but…extending to white domination in economic, cultural, cognitive-evaluative, somatic, and in a sense even 'metaphysical' spheres" (2003, 42). White Supremacy is not just "in" society, but it is "of" society. For example, if one were to use the metaphor of society as a box and White Supremacy were *in* the box, then to fix the problem we could take it out. However, if we understand that White Supremacy is *of* society then that means the box is composed of White Supremacy, a much harder problem to solve.

Outlining the Difference between White Privilege and White Supremacy

Both White Privilege and White Supremacy need to be a part of a racial analysis, but people often focus only on White Privilege. Leonardo (2004, 140–141) helps clarify the danger of focusing on just the White Privilege side: "The discourse on privilege comes with the psychological effect of personalizing racism rather than understanding its structural origins in interracial relations… Whites today did not participate in slavery but they surely recreate white supremacy on a daily basis." When Whites confront their privilege, they analyze their lives to see if/how/when one's Whiteness was or is a benefit. And, although that analysis is needed, it does not accurately reflect the structural facets and enduring pain of racism. Whites can and should critically reflect on their privilege, but that process does not necessarily affect the *structure* of racism, which permits the devaluing of people of color. In other words, we need to articulate White Privilege as the benefits given to Whites, but it is White Supremacy that makes those benefits possible while also providing the infrastructure for oppression of people of color. White Privilege is a subset or particular manifestation of White Supremacy. It is White Supremacy that makes the racial hierarchy a reality in the first place.

The White Supremacy Flower

The White Supremacy Flower model is an amalgamation of the theoretical contributions of many race scholars (Alexander 2010; Bonilla-Silva 2003; Hill Collins 2000; Feagin 2006; Gallagher 2003; Marshall 2012; Omi and Winant 1994; Takaki 1993); it provides a model for understanding the roots of racism, the evolution of racism, and the maintenance of racism in the U.S.

The model takes the shape of a very simple flower with a daisy like bloom and has three main components: the roots, the stem, and the bloom (see Figure 4.4.1). The flower begins with the roots. The roots represent the foundation of the U.S. with events such as Native American genocide, plantation slavery, and the creation of the Constitution. In the 1400s it is estimated there were 10 million Native Americans in what is now the U.S., but by 1900, through disease and violence, the number who survived was 300,000. Plantation slavery began in the mid 1600s by trafficking people from areas including Congo, Angola, Nigeria, Senegal, and Gambia; by 1662 life-long slavehood was formally instituted and was inherited through one's mother. During the Civil War there were approximately 4 million enslaved or 7 free people for every enslaved person. George Washington, Thomas Jefferson, and James Madison, founding fathers of the U.S. and Constitution, all had slaves. The Constitution guaranteed rights only to White male property owners (Baptist 2014; Davis 2006). The foundation, that is the roots of the U.S., is genocide and slavery of people of color coexisting alongside the rights and opportunities given to Whites.

The next part of the flower is the stem, which represents the history of the U.S. from its foundations to today. The stem includes both the events and the processes that move the nation from one point to another. Events along the stem include anti-immigrant laws, government policies, and Jim Crow laws. The Chinese Exclusion Act, instituted in 1882, put a moratorium on Chinese immigration and prevented Chinese in the U.S. from attaining citizenship. The Dawes Act of 1887 took 90 million acres from Native Americans and parceled the land out to White settlers. In 1896 *Plessy v Ferguson* instituted legal segregation between Blacks and Whites. Later policies upheld the organization of institutions, policies, and ideologies for the benefit of Whites. The GI Bill of 1944 helped many soldiers attain an education after the war, but Blacks were not permitted to attend most schools. The Federal Housing Authority program after WWII helped to finance over half of suburban housing, but 98 percent of recipients were White. Meanwhile, from 1941–1946, over 100,000 Japanese in the U.S., including citizens, were taken from their homes and put in internment camps for the nativist fear that all Japanese were war traitors (Dunbar-Ortiz 2014; Katznelson 2005; Takaki 1993). Institutional racial discrimination

FIGURE 4.4.1. The White Supremacy Flower Model

Artist credit: Ali Cohen

continued to be a hallmark during the 1900s. In the 1950s and 1960s some critical inroads were made towards eradicating racial inequality including *Brown v. Board of Education,* which in 1954 outlawed public school segregation, the Civil Rights Act of 1964, which declared racial equality, and the Voting Rights Act of 1965, which set measures to ensure equal and fair access to voting. It is largely believed that since these landmark legislations there has been consistent movement and progress towards racial equality; this point then leads to the bloom of the flower.

The bloom represents the contemporary U.S. It is often presumed that the U.S. has 'bloomed' into a nation based on equity and inclusion, yet reality does not reflect this idea. Each petal of the bloom is a different racial inequality such as residential segregation, education gaps, and the prison system. A persistent racial problem is residential segregation; sociologists use the index of dissimilarity to measure racial residential segregation where 0 represents perfect integration and 100 perfect segregation. The index of dissimilarity for Blacks and Whites reaches near perfect segregation at an index of above 80 for 8 metro areas, including the large cities of Detroit, Milwaukee, New York and Chicago. For Asian-Whites it's above 60 for 11 metro areas, and the smallest index is 26.8 (Frey and Myers 2005). The education gap also persists with a 21 point gap between Whites and Hispanics in 4th grade math and 26 points for Black and Whites in 4th grade math. The high school dropout rate of Blacks and Hispanics is twice that of Whites (Chapman et al. 2011). The criminal justice system reflects racial inequality as well with 1 in 3 Black men and 1 in 6 Latino men compared to 1 in 17 White men who face a likelihood of imprisonment. The criminal justice system has proved to be harsher towards people of color at every step of the process including surveillance, arrests, and sentencing (Alexander 2010; Bonczar 2003). The petals of this flower represent the many institutional inequalities that plague the U.S., but another important petal is White Privilege. White Privilege, as the benefits accorded to Whites, is a contemporary manifestation of White Supremacy and a strong petal of this blooming flower.

The petals of the bloom reflect the many contemporary racial inequalities across institutions. In this metaphor, petals that represent particular problems are often targeted by government policies. For example, one petal can be the racialized wealth gap where Whites have a median net worth of $141,000 while Blacks are at $11,000 and Hispanics at $13,700 (Kochhar and Fry 2014). Current attempts to alleviate that gap include food stamps and Section 8 housing, but the problem with such tactics is that they target the economic issue rather than also taking race(ism) into account. When policies fail to see how White Supremacy supports and intertwines with economic issues, then they treat the problem as just a fiscal issue rather than a racialized-fiscal issue; thus, the problem is not comprehensively addressed. Moreover, even in a theoretical scenario where food stamps did help to solve the problem of wealth inequality, only that one petal falls off the flower. Thus, continuing with the logic of this model the loss of one petal does not kill the plant.

The bloom or particular petals can also revamp or renew throughout time. For instance, Michelle Alexander (2010), in her analysis of the prison system, outlines a race relations cycle of four steps: collapse, transition, backlash, and new social control. Alexander explains that when Jim Crow segregation ended there was a transition period when society was unsure of the racial order and expectations, followed by a backlash against Blacks and their progress so that a new form of social control was instituted—the War on Drugs and the resulting prison industrial complex. In other words, according to the White Supremacy Flower model, the petal of Jim Crow segregation fell off but since the White Supremacy flower was still alive, a new petal of the War on Drugs grew in its place. The ability of the petals/bloom to re-grow and adapt accounts for how racism changes and evolves.

What does the White Supremacy Flower Teach Us?

The White Supremacy Flower model provides three particular lessons about racism: 1) how the country has a foundation in White Supremacy, 2) how racism evolves and revamps itself, and 3) how everyone, Whites and people of color alike, can participate in upholding the system.

The first lesson is that White Supremacy is the foundation, the very roots, of the United States. A main reason that people use to proclaim the end or decline of racism is that slavery, and similar horrific racist events, occurred so long ago that it appears impossible, and at least highly unlikely, that there could be contemporary racial inequalities. However, when we understand this history as the foundation of this nation, the connections between yesterday and today are clear. The nation was founded in White Supremacy and has grown from this base.

The second lesson the Flower provides is that racism continues to evolve, not dissolve. Because race in the 1800s looks very different from race in the 1900s, which then looks very different from race in the 2000s, it appears that racism has been consistently on the decline and, with a Black president, maybe even dissipating. The Flower shows how racism changes but isn't going away. As the flower matures and gets more complex so do the manifestations of racism; the bloom may look different and petals may change, but racism continues unless there is attention to the plant that feeds it.

The third and very critical lesson that the White Supremacy Flower teaches is that everyone, regardless of racial identity, can participate in White Supremacy. It is clearer how Whites participate or benefit, particularly since White Privilege is a part of White Supremacy. Yet, it is also clear that combating White Privilege alone does not accomplish much in reducing racism. Moreover, all races can uphold White Supremacy if they participate in the system. For example, skin-bleaching products support the notion that White is beautiful, and allegiance to meritocracy rationalizes racial wealth inequality. Supporting the structure of White Supremacy does not require one to be White, and being White does not mean one supports the system. To create change, people of all races must actively resist the system.

References

Alexander, Michelle. 2010. The New Jim Crow: Mass Incarceration in the Age of Colorblindness. The New Press.

Baptist, Edward E. 2014. The Half Has Never Been Told: Slavery and the Making of American Capitalism. Basic Books.

Blackmon, Michael. 2013. "17 Deplorable Examples of White Privilege. And This Isn't Even the Tip of the Iceberg." Accessed May 27, 2015. http://www.buzzfeed.com/michaelblackmon/17-harrowing-examples-of-white-privilege-9hu9#.ntJeY70jXm.

Bonilla-Silva, Eduardo. 2003. Racism without Racists: Color-Blind Racism and the Persistence of Racial Inequality in America. Lanham, Maryland: Rowman & Littlefield Publishers.

Chapman, Chris, Jennifer Laird, Nicolle Ifill, and Angelina KewalRamani. 2011. "Trends in High School Dropout and Completion Rates in the United States: 1972–2009." Washington D.C.: National Center for Education Statistics.

Davis, David Brion. 2006. Inhuman Bondage: The Rise and Fall of Slavery in the New World. Oxford: Oxford University Press.

Dunbar-Ortiz, Roxanne. 2014. An Indigenous Peoples' History of the United States. Beacon Press.

Feagin, Joe R. 2006. Systemic Racism: A Theory of Oppression. New York: Taylor & Francis.

Frey, William and Dowell Myers. 2005. "Racial Segregation in U.S. Metropolitan Areas and Cities, 1990–2000: Patterns, Trends and Explanations." University of Michigan, Institute for Social Research: Population Studies Center.

Gallagher, Charles A. 2003. "Color-Blind Privilege: The Social and Political Functions of Erasing the Color Line in Post Race America." Race, Gender & Class 10 (4): 22–37.

Hill Collins, Patricia. 2000. Black Feminist Thought: Knowledge, Consciousness, and the Politics of Empowerment. Psychology Press.

Hooks, Bell. 2000. Feminist Theory: From Margin to Center. Pluto Press.

Jha, Rega and Tommy Wesely. 2014. "How Privileged Are You? Checklist Your Privilege." Accessed May 27, 2015. http://www.buzzfeed.com/regajha/how-privileged-are-you#.gbb0254aAB

Katznelson, Ira. 2005. When Affirmative Action Was White: An Untold History of Racial Inequality in Twentieth-Century America. New York: W. W. Norton & Company.

Kochhar, Rakesh, and Richard Fry. 2015. "Wealth Inequality Has Widened along Racial, Ethnic Lines since End of Great Recession | Pew Research Center." Accessed March 14, 2015. http://www.pewresearch.org/fact-tank/2014/12/12/racial-wealth-gaps-great-recession/.

Leonardo, Zeus. 2004. "The Color of Supremacy: Beyond the Discourse of 'White Privilege.'" *Educational Philosophy & Theory* 36 (2): 137–52.

Marshall, Wende Elizabeth. 2011. *Potent Mana: Lessons in Power and Healing.* New York: SUNY Press.

McIntosh, Peggy. 1988. "White Privilege: Unpacking the Invisible Knapsack." Working Paper 189. Accessed March 15, 2015. http://files.eric.ed.gov/fulltext/ED355141.pdf#page=43)

Mills, Charles W. 2003. "White Supremacy as Sociopolitical System: A Philosophical Perspective." In *White Out: The Continuing Significance of Racism*, edited by Ashley Doane and Eduardo Bonilla-Silva, 35–48. New York: Routledge.

Omi, Michael, and Howard Winant. 1994. Racial Formation in the United States: From the 1960s to the 1990s. Psychology Press.

Smith, Andrea. 2005. *Conquest: Sexual Violence and American Indian Genocide.* Cambridge, MA: South End Press.

Rothenberg, Paula S. 2004. White Privilege: Essential Readings on the Other Side of Racism. New York: Macmillan.

Takaki, Ronald T. 1993. *A Different Mirror: A History of Multicultural America.* Boston, MA: Little, Brown & Company.

"Un-Fair Campaign." 2014. Accessed September 17, 2015. http://unfaircampaign.org/.

Yancy, George. 2008. *Black Bodies, White Gazes: The Continuing Significance of Race.* Lanham, Maryland: Rowman & Littlefield.

REFLECT AND CONSIDER

- Suppose White privilege ceased to exist. Why is this not the complete solution?
- How does the White Supremacy Flower help us understand the historical foundations of racism but also the persistence of contemporary racism?

FAMILY LAW, FEMINIST LEGAL THEORY, AND THE PROBLEM OF RACIAL HIERARCHY

BY TWILA L. PERRY

Introduction

Developing theoretical and doctrinal frameworks to improve women's lives is no easy task, made even more challenging by the tremendous diversity that exists among women. In recent years, a wide range of critical approaches including feminist legal theory, critical race theory, critical race feminism, lat-crit, and gay and lesbian legal theory has reflected the diversity of women's lives. Yet, these discourses encounter difficulties in bringing women together because of the multiple contexts in which the positions, interests, and priorities of various groups may diverge or conflict.

The existence of racial hierarchies among women is undertheorized in feminist legal theory and warrants much more attention than it presently receives. Reflected in popular culture and in cultural, political, and legal discourses, informal rankings of women by race and ethnicity are rooted in the histories of different groups; they persist as a consequence of continuing racial discrimination and unequal economic status.

As a central area of inquiry in feminist legal theory, family law has the potential to expose the reality of racial hierarchies through issue analysis. I begin this chapter briefly describing two of the movements in legal scholarship addressed to improving the lives of women—feminist legal theory and critical race feminism. I then describe my journey toward work in these areas, offering observations on the nature of hierarchies and the obstacles to their frank discussion. The chapter then addresses two family law issues—the search by family law scholars for a theory of alimony and the controversy over transracial adoption—to illustrate the existence of racial hierarchies among women. Finally, I comment briefly on the possible impact of recent demographic changes and suggest how attending to racial hierarchy can enrich a family law analysis.

Feminist Legal Theory and Critical Race Feminism

Feminist legal theory took root in the 1970s when advocates of women's rights began using the legal system to fight sex discrimination. As the number of women in law schools, practice, and the academy grew, women began challenging the very foundation of legal rules and structures impacting women. Legal academia also witnessed the emergence of a critical legal studies movement among left-oriented scholars which emphasized approaches critiquing liberalism's focus on individual autonomy and the separation of law and politics. Critical legal studies stressed skepticism toward the value of legal rights, arguing that a focus on legal rights reinforces the status quo and keeps oppressed groups politically passive (Chamallas 2003: 66–67).

Many feminists embraced critical legal studies but also developed a separate analysis of the law that was responsive to the particulars of women's lives. While there is no one definition of feminist legal theory, as an approach it describes and analyzes the law's impact on women, particularly focusing on how law subordinates women. Feminist scholarship employs various methodologies from traditional analysis to personal narrative with the goal of improving women's circumstances.

Some scholars see feminist legal theory unfolding in three stages. The first stage in the 1970s focused on legal equality—the idea that gender should not determine legal rights and obligations. The second stage, evolving during the 1980s, emphasized the difference in women and men's lives, arguing that accounting for that difference was necessary to achieve gender justice. The third stage, which unfolded rapidly in the late 1980s and early 1990s, focused on diversity, with scholars debating issues of essentialism and attending to the differences among women rather than the differences between women and men (Chamallas 2003).

In the late 1980s, the number of law professors of color substantially increased, and critical race theory emerged as some of these professors began writing about race in new ways (Crenshaw et al. 1996; Delgado and Stefancic 1999). Critical race theory was partially an outgrowth of the critical legal studies' critique of neutrality in law. However, many race crits believed that critical legal studies failed to address adequately questions involving race (Crenshaw 2002; Valdez et al. 2002). Critical race theorists wrote about issues that were the subject of litigation in the civil rights movement, like affirmative action, voting rights, employment discrimination, and segregation in housing and education. They also wrote about the societal structures that enable racism's perpetuation. Some discussions involved cases where racial implications had been ignored, minimized, or misunderstood. Concepts of cultural domination and unconscious racism, exploration of the reasons behind persisting racial subordination and racial hierarchy, and a critique of the liberal ideal of color blindness took center stage. Some critical race theorists, notably Patricia Williams, Derrick Bell, and Richard Delgado, incorporated narratives, personal experience, and autobiography into their scholarship.

Toward the end of the 1980s, more black women entered the legal academy and began examining feminist legal theory. In two influential articles, Professors Kimberle Crenshaw (1989) and Angela Harris (1990) offered critiques of white feminist legal scholarship, advancing a new approach to legal analysis insofar as it applied to black women's lives. They argued that many white feminists articulated a feminist theory lacking in relevance for most black women. They advocated an intersectionality approach that took into account the intersection of the factors of race and gender. Race and gender were not two separate factors that complicated black women's lives, but instead they formed a complex and inextricable brew.

During the 1990s, a growing group of scholars incorporated methodological approaches including intersectionality and the use of narratives into their work; they addressed various substantive concerns ranging from reproductive rights and family life to criminal, constitutional, and employment law. The output was large, and Professor Adrien Wing's compilation, *Critical Race Feminism*, first published in 1997, is now in its second edition (Wing 2003).

I began addressing issues of race and feminism in the mid-1990s, but my thinking about the intersection of race and gender evolved gradually. Growing up in a low-income black community in New York City in the late 1950s and 1960s, it was obvious to me that, in America, race powerfully impacts on an individual's circumstances and opportunities. From my vantage point, the plight of black people seemed to be the same whether they were male or female, although I did receive one very clear message about gender as I was growing up. I knew I must take care of myself economically—I could not expect a man to care for me financially. I learned that black men had a hard time in America and were often denied work opportunities that could provide economic security. Thus I understood that, for black women, marriage, motherhood, and work would likely be combined.

Only after graduating from law school did I begin thinking more deeply about gender. As an associate in a large corporate law firm, as a law clerk to a federal judge, in law practice representing the government, and in teaching law, it became clear that being a woman, independent of race, could be a professional disadvantage. At the law firm in the mid-1970s, I was exposed to the world of all-male lunch clubs on Wall Street and the vestiges of a system that relegated many women lawyers to trusts and estates work with no meaningful partnership opportunities. In my federal clerkship and in practice at the US Attorney's office, I saw that paltry numbers of women were judges or federal lawyers. During my early years in teaching law, I saw many obstacles to success for women in the academic world, challenges likely unthinkable for their male colleagues. Women professors who were mothers met the challenge of gaining tenure under a level of stress and exhaustion that was different than their male colleagues. As a professor of family law, I was able to consider the impact of gender in a systematic way. Many years later, I rarely think about gender without simultaneously thinking about race.

Much of my work examines intersections between feminist and critical race theory in the area of family law and resonates with the period of feminist theory that emphasized diversity among women. It draws upon much critical legal scholarship—especially feminist legal theory and critical race theory—and is inspired by the work of an earlier generation of black feminist intellectuals. These women played multiple roles as writers, scholars, and activists; their audiences were both academics and ordinary black women with a political bent. Women like Audre Lorde, whose pioneering work was at the intersection of feminism, race, and sexual orientation and women like Angela Davis and bell hooks have produced work enormously helpful to me.

The Problem of Racial Hierarchy

The issue of racial hierarchies among women is complex and troubling. Hierarchies reflect status and power relationships in a society, and they function in both concrete and subtle ways. In terms of the concrete, those who occupy the upper levels of a hierarchy often have the power to discriminate against and stigmatize those on the lower rungs. Those at the upper level can also accrue substantial psychological benefits from their status. Not surprisingly, those on the lower rungs often suffer economic and psychological consequences. Their employment, educational, and housing opportunities are fewer than the opportunities of the dominant group. Aware of their stigmatized and devalued status, women on the lower rungs may experience frustration and resentment. Failing to engage the issue of hierarchies is like operating without an important tool for understanding institutions, groups, and interpersonal relationships.

Hierarchies of Gender and Race

Gender hierarchy is reflected in many areas of life: in employment, in the family, in the media, and in the treatment one receives in public spaces. One of feminist legal theory's major contributions is its unmasking of the persistence of gender hierarchies even in areas where the law, on its face, is gender neutral. Gender hierarchy is a reflection of the powerful institution and ideology of patriarchy, in which dominance results from the biological status of being male.

While women occupy the lower rung of a gender hierarchy, there are also hierarchies among women. These hierarchies are based on many different factors such as class, sexual orientation, educational background, physical appearance, and immigration status. Martha Fineman (1991b) notes that society's attitudes toward women often reflect a hierarchy that judges women's worth by the standard of their relationships to men—married women at the top, widows the next rung down, divorced women another rung lower, and single mothers at the bottom. This hierarchy obviously disadvantages black women, who are disproportionately unmarried and disproportionately likely to experience marital disruption (Bramlett and Mosher 2002). Even if married, black women are more likely than white women to be widowed because black men have lower life expectancies than white men (US Census Bureau 2009: 76).

Even among women of color, there is a hierarchy. While women of color of various ethnicities are the victims of racial and ethnic stereotypes, in this country, the most degrading and vicious stereotypes are reserved for black women. Indeed, the racial hierarchy that exists among women of color may ultimately warrant an analysis as searching as the one which minority women have applied to mainstream feminism (Perry 2000).

Racial hierarchies differ from gender hierarchies. While men are dominant in the gender hierarchy, often devaluing white women and inflicting harm on them through domestic violence and workplace discrimination, white men and women are also intimates. They band together and bond to create what is perhaps society's most important social and economic unit—the family. Together they engage in what many consider life's most important enterprise—raising children. White men and women are also each others' mothers, fathers, sisters, brothers, grandparents, and cousins. Thus, despite gender hierarchy's existence, along with the issues, tensions, power struggles, and even violence that this may bring, white men and women are in many ways a team.

Although there has been a substantial increase in interracial marriages and multicultural families in recent years (US Census Bureau 2009: 52), black people and white people generally do not share family relationships. Indeed, it is rare for whites and blacks to share close, inter-connected experiences where they work toward common goals with an expectation of shared rewards. The hierarchy that exists between them is generally not softened by the intimacy and interdependency often present in the gender hierarchy between white men and women.

Discussing Hierarchies

Engaging men and women in a conversation about gender hierarchies can be complicated and fraught with emotion. Yet, it is often easier for women to talk about their differences with men than to talk about the differences between women—especially women of different races. Rarely do women engage in serious discussion about class differences between women of the same race. Discussing class origins and differences is a sensitive issue that can invoke a complicated range of feelings. While the self-made man is accorded a certain kind of status and admiration, a woman lifting herself up by her bootstraps doesn't elicit the same response.

Talking about race is even harder for women than talking about class. If they are honest, many people would agree that most conversations about race take place between people of the same race rather than of different races. Barack Obama's speech about race in the middle of the 2008 Democratic primary brought renewed attention to the fact that chasms in perspectives, understanding, and conversations about race run deep. When gender and the complex intersectionality of race and gender that are the core of many black women's experiences are added to the mix, the task is even more formidable.

Discussing race in the context of a legal issue that involves education or employment is one thing, but many family law issues can hit close to home emotionally. Thus, most of us, even those most committed to social justice, have to admit that we routinely take race into account in making some of our most important life decisions—who to date, who to marry, who to adopt. The relative position of people in the racial hierarchy is relevant in those determinations. Whether we will admit it, love, romantic or familial, is not blind when it comes to race.

Conversations about racial hierarchies can also be uncomfortable for those at the top of the hierarchy if they are not committed to trying to change the situation. It is difficult for those occupying the bottom rung of a hierarchy to listen to a person at the top acknowledge their advantaged position but act as if there is nothing to do about it. For the person on the lower rung, it is not pleasant to acknowledge a diminished status. All of this unease makes it easier for women to ignore the problem of racial hierarchies than to try to address it.

Race and Hierarchy in Family Law

The search by feminist scholars for a theory of alimony and the continuing controversy over the subject of transracial adoption are examples of family law issues that have the potential to expose the existence of racial hierarchies among women. Both areas pose problems for feminist legal theory.

The Search for a Theory of Alimony

In the late 1980s and early 1990s, family law and feminist scholars began developing a theory of alimony. This effort became necessary because developments like no-fault divorce and increased opportunities for women in the workplace caused the traditional justifications for alimony—fault and need—to lose their force. Some opponents of alimony asked, what is the theoretical basis for imposing a legal duty on one person to continue to provide financial support for another person to whom he or she no longer has a legal tie?

The need to develop a theory of alimony came about at around the same time as the emergence of the racial critique of feminist legal theory. In my own writing, I began exploring the implications of the search for a theory of alimony for those women who seemed least likely to benefit from it—black women and other women of color (Perry 1994).

The search for a theory of alimony has been largely based on a paradigm marriage. In the paradigm marriage, the wife sacrifices or slows down her career to attend to the needs and interests of her husband and children. She makes this decision believing that her marriage is for life and that in her later years she will enjoy economic security with her husband. However, if the marriage ends after she has made her sacrifice and investment but before she has "reaped her reward," the wife often finds herself in a troubling position. The husband can walk away with the most valuable asset of the marriage—a career with future earning potential. The wife finds herself with diminished economic and workplace opportunities. Family law and feminist scholars are concerned with finding ways to lessen what for many women is likely to be a hard economic fall.

Many scholars seemed to have this paradigm in mind as they developed a theory of alimony. However, the structure of marriages for most black couples often do not fit this paradigm. Most black men earn less than white men and, historically, a disproportionate number of married black women remain in the workforce compared with white women. Indeed, culturally and historically, most black women have been raised with the expectation that their future includes both mothering and working. Many black women have less of an expectation of economic compensation at the end of a marriage than a middle or upper-middle class white woman might have.

Thus, many theories proposed to justify alimony for upper-middle class white women had little relevance to the lives of most black women. Contract-based arguments premised on the concept of "expectation" that a wife's homemaker services would be rewarded over the long run seemed less relevant in a marriage where the wife was a major contributor to family finances. Theories of alimony dependent on the premise that women have "sacrificed" their careers for the well-being of their families also seemed less relevant to women who were less likely to be candidates for career trajectories leading to high status, high-paying jobs. The "law and economics" approach, justifying alimony as compensation to homemakers in marriages where spouses made the "economically rational" decision to maximize the opportunities of one spouse in the labor market, did not seem relevant to marriages where the wife worked just to make ends meet.

Moreover, alimony could be viewed as a privilege enjoyed after divorce by the most advantaged women in the society and could easily reinforce hierarchies among women based not on their own merits or achievements, but on their attachments to men. A woman economically supported by her husband was viewed as an individual deserving of financial support once she was on her own, while women without husbands whose economic needs might need to be met by the state were viewed as undeserving or even the subject of scorn. Both women may have been superb homemakers and wonderful mothers, but only one was viewed as deserving of sympathy and help. A theory of economic support for women based so closely on their attachments to men raises some troubling issues for feminist legal theory.

Many people are surprised to learn that very few divorced women are awarded or collect alimony. Thus, some feminists argue that alimony should be abolished because it misleads women into believing that the law will provide economic protection for them should their marriages end. They advocate, instead, that married women make decisions about work and family that will put them in a position to be economically independent in the event of divorce. This suggestion also has implications for the issue of racial hierarchies among women.

The problem this suggestion presents is who will care for the children of the upper-middle class women who enter the workforce to achieve financial independence? Their ability to work while simultaneously meeting responsibilities at home will depend upon household help, likely provided by poor women of color. The reality that the woman-employer has an interest in paying as little as possible for that help gives rise to an inherent conflict between the employer and the employee. Obviously, the hierarchal relationship between white women and African-American women in this context has historical roots reaching all the way back into slavery, and it is a context that has economic, psychological, and emotional dimensions (Rollins 1985).

Transracial Adoption

In recent years, transracial and international adoption have received substantial attention. Transracial adoption has been the subject of almost continuous controversy in this country since the early 1970s. During the 1990s, the number of international adoptions in this country increased substantially, and these adoptions became the frequent focus of articles in the media and law journals. Even though issues such as poverty, the economic status of women, the nature of mothering, and the relationships between women of different classes, races and ethnicities, and nations concern many feminists, there is a lack of feminist discussion or analysis of transracial and international adoption.

Very troubling is the fact that transracial adoption is usually a one-way street. Children of black women are adopted by white women; the reverse almost never occurs. The flow of children in international adoption is also one-way—the children of women of color in poorer countries are adopted typically by white women in Western nations. Though conceptualizing these adoptions as humanitarian acts is appealing, they raise serious issues for feminist theory.

Can white families raise black children to be emotionally healthy individuals with the "survival skills" necessary to survive in an often racially hostile society? Do black communities have a legitimate political interest in social policies concerning transracial adoption? Does transracial adoption represent cultural genocide or cultural imperialism? The willingness of the social welfare system to remove black children from their families rather than focusing on family preservation efforts is a central concern. Furthermore, arguing, as some advocates do, that racial considerations in adoption undermine equality and are not in children's best interests ignores the reality that, in America, race almost always matters.

In America, black mothers have been subjected to a great deal of disparagement. They are often depicted as lazy welfare cheats or emasculating matriarchs raising a future generation of criminals and non-achievers. These negative stereotypes, which devalue black mothers and reinforce the low status of black women, are significant in the transracial adoption controversy. The images appear in books, movies, and other media outlets, as well as in legal cases where white families and black mothers are at odds.

If a society values the mothering of some women more than that of others, the separation of devalued mothers from their children is less likely to be seen as cause for concern. The children of such women may be thought to receive a lucky break if they are adopted by a higher-status family. Moreover, women who know that they are devalued will likely resent a pattern of adoption that transfers children from their group to women of higher status. They may experience feelings of resentment and hostility toward the valued group. This resentment impedes the ability of women from diverse backgrounds to form coalitions beneficial to all women.

Ironically, even as black mothers have been disparaged in their mothering of black children going all the way back to slavery, they have been viewed positively as the caretakers of white children. Black women who work as nannies, especially those employed for a long period by the same family, often serve a mothering function. The nanny's job is to provide the children in her care with physical care, discipline, and affection. In many instances, a nanny effectively may raise her employer's children. There are many black women in this country who have successfully "raised" white children without occupying the status of legal mother, but they are often denigrated in the role of mothers to their own children.

Feminist theory needs to engage the issue of racial hierarchies in the context of transracial adoption. However, it is not surprising that movement in this direction has been slow; there has been little discussion of adoption generally from a feminist perspective. Outside of the surrogacy context, feminists have expended little energy on mothers who give their children up for adoption.

Racism, patriarchy, and poverty are often reasons why so many children of color end up in the adoption system, whether coercively removed or "voluntarily" placed. Mothers of color are more likely than white, privileged women to live in circumstances where it is difficult to care for children. Some women have their children taken away. Others see adoption as the only practical solution; this reality presents a problem with complex moral dimensions that invites deeper feminist exploration.

Feminist theory could offer helpful concepts and methods for analyzing transracial adoption, but not nearly enough has been done in this area. For example, feminist theory is often considered hostile to a law and economics analysis, yet some advocates of transracial adoption employ a simplistic "supply and demand" approach to transracial adoption—refusing to take their analysis beyond the assertion that there is a large supply of black children available for adoption and a large demand for them by white families. Such an analysis leaves the mothers of these children out of the equation. Feminist themes of care and connection focus attention on the one-on-one nurturing relationship between an adoptive mother and child, but this attention can gloss over the fact that the one-way street of transracial adoption raises political and moral issues.

Autonomy and choice are important concepts for feminists when examining the decision to become a parent but are rarely used to interrogate the circumstances surrounding a poor woman's "choice" to give up her child for adoption. Arguments opposing the use of wealth as a factor in child custody decisions have not led to similar arguments in the adoption context about the unequal distribution of wealth between poor women and wealthier adopting women. The narratives of white adoptive mothers are prominent in articles supporting transracial adoption, but the emotional dimensions of a poor woman's decision to give her child up for adoption or the pain of women whose children have been removed through state intervention often receive short shrift.

The Potential for Convergences

The Search for Common Ground

The search for a theory of alimony and the controversy over transracial adoption illustrate the failure of feminist approaches to account for the material circumstances of many black women's lives. Greater incorporation into family law of issues involving race is important, not only to head off claims that black women's concerns are marginalized or ignored. The failure of feminist theory to engage the intersection of race and gender results in lost opportunities for women from diverse backgrounds to engage more fully in collaborative thinking and action.

Feminist theory and critical race feminism have many reasons to find more common ground and become more mutually enriching. First, the goals of the two movements are similar. Both seek to promote the ability of women to sustain themselves economically, to care for their children and other dependent family members, and to find fulfilling personal relationships. Both movements seek justice and equality for groups that have known intentional discrimination and institutionalized inequality. Both focus on critiquing legal rules, examining institutional and societal structures and frameworks for bias, and unpacking concepts such as hierarchy and subordination. Both are more flexible than traditional legal methods and sometimes employ narratives, parables, or personal stories. Both face similar challenges in confronting questions of intersectionality, identity, essentialism, and the meaning of equality. Both have a stake in common issues such as the sustaining of affirmative action as a tool for expanding opportunities in areas where opportunities have been restricted (Perry 1994).

Exploring racial hierarchy should come naturally to feminist legal theory, since identifying and articulating harms suffered by women is an important part of that enterprise. It is not a great leap from work in the context of gender hierarchy to identifying the nature of the benefits some women receive as the consequence of a race-based hierarchy. White feminists including Peggy MacIntosh (1998) and Ruth Frankenberg (1993) have been leaders in describing the daily benefits white women receive based on their racial status, and there is more work to be done in this area.

REFLECT AND CONSIDER

- How are hierarchies of race and gender connected?
- Explain how Perry takes an intersectional approach to analyzing alimony and transracial adoption.

HIGHLIGHT

YES, ALL WHITE PEOPLE ARE RACISTS—NOW LET'S DO SOMETHING ABOUT IT

BY TIM DONOVAN, *ALTERNET*

SUMMARY

This piece from *Alternet* addresses the concept of implicit bias, a biased perception of a group that an individual may hold without realizing it. For example, Whites often have unintentional preferences for other Whites, preferences that can lead to a range of unequal outcomes in areas such as hiring, pay, and politics. Tim Donovan discusses the concept of implicit bias and reviews recent research by Harvard University, University of Washington, and University of Virginia.

EXCERPT FROM
"YES, ALL WHITE PEOPLE ARE RACISTS"

In the Implicit Bias module on race, for instance, "positive" and "negative" words are paired with computer-generated images of Black African faces and White European faces. The test instructs you to match the categories by quickly pressing a button on the left or right side of your keyboard, so that you're connecting "good" words with black faces and "bad" words with white faces — and vice versa. The test measures how quickly you're able to successfully follow the exam's instructions; if you're better at pairing "good" words with white faces than with black faces, you probably have some measure of implicit bias against black people. (As I did when I took the test.) Other modules explore one's potential gender bias, age bias, religious bias, and so forth. The results are as disturbing as they are instructive, and they're buttressed by an increasingly robust body of research. The overwhelming majority of white people who've taken the test exhibit a preference for whiteness; for blacks, respondents are split nearly down the middle, with about half favoring black faces and half favoring white faces. (Because, the study's authors speculate, the assumptions embedded in our culture that lead to this implicit bias can affect people of any race.)

READ THE REST OF THE ESSAY:

bit.ly/racismalternet

READ, LISTEN, WATCH, INTERACT!

READ

The Race Conversation Starbucks Wants You to Have
Mona Charen, 2.20.2015, National Review
READ AT bit.ly/racestarbucks

7 Reasons Why "Colorblindness" Contributes to Racism Instead of Solves It
Jon Greenberg, 2.23.2015, EverydayFeminism
READ AT bit.ly/colorblindracism

LISTEN

Can Babies Be Racist?
Michel Martin with Briggite Vittrup, 9.14.2009, NPR
LISTEN AT bit.ly/babiesracism

The Personal, Social and Economic Costs of Racism
The Diane Rehm Show, 4.30.2014
LISTEN AT bit.ly/racismcosts

WATCH

 Dark Girls

D. Channsin Berry and Bill Duke, 2013

AVAILABLE AT bit.ly/darkgirlsdoc

 White Like Me: Race, Racism & White Privilege in America

Tim Wise, 2013

AVAILABLE AT bit.ly/whiteprivilegewise

INTERACT

 Hate Map

Southern Poverty Law Center

INTERACT AT bit.ly/hatemapsplc

 Take a Test

Project Implicit.

INTERACT AT bit.ly/projectimplicittest

*Take an implicit bias test on skin-tone, Asians, Arab-Muslims, Race (Blacks and Whites), or Native Americans.

STRUCTURED RACIAL INEQUALITY

W hy do you get up and go to school and/or work every morning? Many Americans are unhappy with their jobs, yet the vast majority of us continue to work hard—why? Because we believe that if we work hard then we will be rewarded. In fact, this idea has long characterized the United States, as it has been defined as the "land of opportunity." Yet, reality stands in stark contrast to this belief. Some groups routinely enjoy greater access to resources such as income, wealth, education, healthcare, social esteem, and power than other groups, and this disparity has continued over time. Most often, people of color, notably African Americans and Latinos, remain disproportionately poor (26 percent and 25 percent, respectively, in 2014), and, on average, White Americans still display better outcomes than do people of color. For instance, Whites are much wealthier, enjoying much higher median household wealth than African Americans and Latinos. They also dominate corporate America and the American state. However, we have to be careful not to overstate the facts, as millions of White Americans are also poor.

Typically, societies need to justify persistent racial inequality and do so through the construction of legitimating ideologies. In the first selection, Heather Beth Johnson, in "The American Dream of Meritocracy," discusses the dominant American legitimating ideology: the American Dream. She argues that Whites believe that meritocracy—ability and individual effort as the main determinants of success—explains their superior economic ranking, while the structural inequities actually shaping their position within the race-class hierarchy are ignored. In this way, wealthy Whites privilege their agency over external causes in explaining their social class. In the second selection, "Racial Orders in American Political Development," King and Smith highlight the central role race plays in social stratification in the United States. They argue that there are "racial institutional orders," which they define as coalitions of political actors that use racial concepts to frame social reality and shape the behavior of rivals. In their view, American history has revolved around the conflict between a set of White supremacist political orders and a set of transformative egalitarian orders. Over time, the balance of power has shifted in favor of the latter.

To a large extent, structured racial inequality in the United States is rooted in residential segregation, because geography often determines such outcomes as school quality, the likelihood of obtaining good jobs, the probability of living in safe neighborhoods, and relative levels of wealth and income. All of these factors are highly correlated with race, since Whites are more likely to experience positive outcomes in these realms than are non-Whites. Discussing segregation in "Migration and Residential Segregation," John Iceland, in the third reading, points to these outcomes when he notes that White Americans tend to live apart from other groups. In contrast, though African Americans have become less segregated over time, they still experience notably more segregation than all other groups. Meanwhile, Asians, though less segregated than African Americans, are becoming more so because of new Asian immigrant neighborhoods.

Discrimination in the labor market strongly influences the persistence of structured racial inequality, and in the fourth reading, "White, Young, Middle Class," Yasemin Besen-Cassino illustrates how this inequality is reproduced in youth-oriented jobs in a mall. In the last reading, "Why Both Social Structure and Culture Matter in a Holistic Analysis of Inner-City Poverty," William J. Wilson offers a theory of the causes of poverty among African Americans, arguing that though the reasons are primarily structural—notably historical racism and the restructuring of the American economy—secondary behavioral (cultural) effects can also interact with these structural causes to reinforce poverty. The Highlight, "Nine Charts About Wealth Inequality in America," discusses the many sources and cumulative nature of wealth disparities.

AS YOU READ

- Consider the extent to which notions of meritocracy frame American life.
- Assess how multiple institutions reproduce racial inequality.
- Evaluate how these institutions restrict upward mobility and limit agency.

THE AMERICAN DREAM OF MERITOCRACY

BY HEATHER BETH JOHNSON

The American Dream has been continually re-invented over time, so that for each generation of Americans it has held different meanings. And since the phrase "the American Dream" could mean different things to every one of us, it might be more accurate to call it "the American Dreams." At its core, however, some aspects of the Dream (or Dreams) are consistently fundamental. Simply, the American Dream explains the logic of our country's social system. *It is a way (or perhaps the way) we are to understand how American society operates.* It is how we make sense of our particular social structure. The American Dream rests on the idea that, with hard work and personal determination anyone, regardless of background, has an equal opportunity to achieve his or her aspirations. The American Dream promises that our system functions as a meritocracy. *Within a meritocracy people get ahead or behind based on what they earn and deserve, rather than what circumstances they were born into.* This notion is central to the American Dream, and is the central logic of how our system is supposed to operate. The American Dream, in many ways, defines us and sets our system apart from others.

Given the importance of the American Dream to our national identity, and the enormity of it in shaping our core ideologies, it is curious how little attention the idea has received in academe, especially in the social sciences. Until relatively recently, no one had traced the history of its origins, meanings, or cultural impacts. In the past decade, however, groundbreaking scholarship on the American Dream has yielded important understandings. We know, for example, that the principles of the American Dream were promoted by even the very first settlers to arrive from Britain. Later, the American Dream was central to the charter of the United States when the Declaration of Independence was created. And although the phrase "the American Dream" does not appear to have been coined until around 1931, it has quickly become recognizable the world over. The American Dream is, for better or for worse, the central creed of our nation.

As a creed, the American Dream represents a basic belief in the power and capacity of the individual. Deeply embedded in this belief is a particular notion of individual agency—the idea that over the course of our own lives we are each accountable for whatever position we find ourselves in. Full collective potential for this agency, though, depends on exactly that which the dream promises: A system of opportunity, so that regardless of background each individual has an equal chance to prosper. The American Dream promises that an egalitarian system will allow individuals to advance based on their own merit. This promise resonates throughout contemporary American society telling us—through multiple variations on a theme, through school assignments and television advertisements, through song lyrics and newspaper stories—that in a meritocratic process we rise or fall self-reliantly. So, despite differences across generations and regardless we each have unique hopes and dreams, we share the American Dream of meritocracy in common: That is, we are each subject—in one way or another—to our nationalist ideology of meritocracy.

Meritocracy explains not only how our society works but how inequality exists. The idea is that what we reap—good or bad—is merited; whatever we have, whatever our status, whatever our place in the social world, we earn. A system of meritocracy does not assert equality *per se*—within any social hierarchy some individuals will inevitably be positioned higher and some lower—rather, it justifies inequality of social positioning by the meritocratic process itself. Inequality of outcomes is justified and legitimized by equality of opportunity. This meritocratic idea has roots dating back to the British colonialists' aspirations for a society founded in a "natural aristocracy." In their vision upward mobility and prominence would be merited and achieved, rather than ascribed. For those first families settling from Europe, this vision was a defiant rebellion from other forms of social structure where social rank was inherited based on such distinctions as family lineage, royalty, and caste. Although they never precisely defined how merit should be measured, it was always clear how it should not be: achievement based on individual merit is not unearned advantage; it is not inherited privilege. A meritocratic system is contingent upon a societal commitment to fair competition so that no individual or group is advantaged or disadvantaged by the positions or predicaments of their ancestors.

The American Dream of meritocracy is at once a simple idea and a complex national ethos. For some people the American Dream may simply represent owning a home, while for others it might represent striking it rich. Although those may be part of what the American Dream means for many people, as a foundational ideology it is about more than material abundance or a place with streets-paved-with-gold. It is about opportunity—not just an opportunity, but equal opportunity. It is about not just a chance, but equal chances. In her landmark book, *Facing Up to the American Dream: Race, Class, and the Soul of a Nation*, political scientist Jennifer Hochschild explicates the American Dream and identifies its main tenets. She distinguishes key premises which interlock to form its philosophical foundation. These premises include meritocracy, the notion that in our social system upward and downward mobility is based on personal achievement so that people get ahead or behind based on merit; equal opportunity, the notion that all members of society are given equal opportunity for social mobility; individualism, the notion that each individual makes it on his or her own; and the open society, the notion that the United States is a free country, the melting pot of the world, the land of opportunity for all people. As Hochschild outlines, the American Dream is a set of deeply held beliefs, a particular mind set. It is a particular way of viewing the world, and it is a particular way in which we want the world to view us. For many Americans, the American Dream is a great source of pride. But even many who question it as an accurate portrayal of social life believe strongly in the egalitarian and inclusive principles for which it stands.

As a dominant ideology the American Dream echoes throughout our nation, it carries on through generations, and can cement in crystal form in our minds. But it can also be easily taken for granted. For as central the American Dream is to our national identity, we don't consciously reflect on it often. As historian Jim Cullen has noted, the American Dream is "an idea that seems to envelop us as unmistakably as the air we breathe." We can be reminded of it, without even being aware, every time we are told that we will achieve if we work hard enough, or that we could have achieved if we had only worked harder. The American Dream can inspire great aspirations and explain great achievements, and it can depress us as we ponder our regrets. It is malleable enough to fit in almost any social situation. We can use it to justify our accomplishments: I earned it on my own. This is the result of my hard work. I deserve this. And we can feel the sting of it as we question ourselves: Should I have worked harder? Could I have gone farther? Why am I not where he is? And, we can use it to question others' social standing: Why doesn't she try harder? Doesn't he want more? Why don't they make better choices? The American Dream is all around us, and, in many ways it is in us.

Ultimately, the American Dream is an explanation for the hierarchical ordering of our class positions in our social world. It explains our relative rank as the result of solely our own doing, not as the result of social forces or the circumstances we find ourselves in. It is not surprising, then, that Americans might genuinely believe that they independently earn and deserve their class positions—the dominant ideology of our culture tells them so. This internalized sense of class positioning has been the subject of scholarly research, especially in regards to working-class and poor families. In Richard Sennett and Jonathan Cobb's pivotal book *The Hidden Injuries of Class*, for example, they discuss the "hidden injury" of the internal class conflict experienced among working-class men. They wrote that "Every question of identity as an image of social place in a hierarchy is also a question of social value. ... This is the context in which all questions of personal and social legitimacy occur." The American Dream helps to sustain these "hidden injuries" by bombarding people with the message that their social place—and their social value, their self-worth—is directly and exclusively the result of their own actions.

In their interviews for this book, people spoke in depth and at length about the American Dream, despite the fact that in the first 182 interviews the families were not even asked about it. Those parents were told that the project was to study assets and inequality, and during the interviews they were asked to speak about the communities they lived in, their children's schools, and their families' financial histories. Over and over, however, the focus of the interviews turned to beliefs in meritocracy as families repeatedly brought up the subject and wove it into the conversations. I must admit that I myself was surprised with the extent to which the interview findings were so ideological in nature. And I was even more surprised when interviews—including those interviews from the second phase which did directly ask people about their thoughts on the American Dream—revealed the depths of people's commitment to, and belief in, meritocracy as a real and valid explanation for how contemporary American society operates. People from all walks of life spoke forthrightly of their belief in meritocracy, not just as rhetoric, but as an accurate explanation of our social system.

Trying to confirm these findings has been frustrating due to the lack of qualitative studies that have asked people in-depth about their perspectives on the American Dream. Curiously, even in terms of quantitative studies, surprisingly few public opinion polls have been conducted on the subject of the American Dream. However, related social survey data that do exist reflect that Americans overwhelmingly believe that their country operates as a meritocracy. Indeed, after his review of the data political scientist Everett Carl Ladd concluded that survey research "shows Americans holding tenaciously and distinctively to the central elements of their founding ideology." He found Americans' belief in the American Dream to be more intense, pervasive, and firmly entrenched than generally recognized. Very recent qualitative research on post-civil rights views also finds that in in-depth interviews people are remarkably insistent in their beliefs that the playing field is level, that meritocracy is real. While these findings are definitely in line with my own, perhaps the most compelling affirmation for me has been to discover that other sociologists doing in-depth interviewing on subjects not explicitly focused on the American Dream are finding, as I have, that respondents consistently evoke the American Dream—specifically the notion of meritocracy—as their own theme in interviews. In the 200 interviews conducted for this study, what families said, their views, their decisions, and their experiences, were explicitly framed by their belief in meritocracy. These families' perspectives give a vivid account of the place and significance of the American Dream in contemporary life.

The reality of wealth in America though—the way it is acquired, distributed, and the way it is used—is a direct contradiction to these fundamental ideas. In interviews with American families we have seen a way how that plays out. Examining school decision-making (just one arena wherein families potentially experience the ramifications of wealth inequality), those parents from backgrounds of even moderate wealth had a significant advantage over parents with family histories of wealth poverty. Disproportionately white, wealth-holding parents used the financial assistance, intergenerational transfers, and security of their family wealth to help access schools for their own children that were viewed as advantageous by all of the parents. Meanwhile, parents without family wealth to rely upon, who were disproportionately black, were navigating the same arena unaided, with relatively limited resources and constrained capacities. *A central incongruity surfaces when families' school decisions are considered in the context of the American Dream: the assets that the wealth-holding families had owned, relied upon, and utilized in choosing schools had most often originated from non-merit sources.* Inherited wealth and the security of family wealth were critical advantages being passed along to the next generation—advantages often unearned by the parents themselves, and always unearned by their children.

A foundational conflict exists between the meritocratic values of the American Dream and the structure of intergenerational wealth inequality. Simply, advantageous resources inherited and passed along in families are not attained through individual achievement. Although wealth can, of course, be earned by an individual entirely independently, in the case of the families we spoke with it had not. This is the aspect of family wealth that concerns us here. Family wealth generates unearned advantages for those who have it. It is a form of privilege. In light of their beliefs in the American Dream, how do those families who present the most transparent contradiction to the idea of meritocracy—families with wealth privilege—understand their positioning and the unearned advantages they pass along to their children?

We could presume that as with other forms of privilege (such as race privilege or gender privilege) wealth privilege would generally appear invisible and be taken for granted by those who have it. However, one of the most striking aspects of the interviews was the acknowledgement of wealth privilege on the part of wealth-holding families. The parents who had benefited from family wealth acknowledged a structure of wealth inequality that grants privilege to some families and disadvantage to others, and they acknowledged the advantages they were passing along to the next generation through the schools that they chose.

Acknowledging Advantage: A Structure of Wealth Inequality

Given the fact that these families had so vehemently expressed their beliefs in the legitimacy of the American Dream, it was startling to hear them so openly discuss the reality of structured wealth inequality in American society. Not only did parents talk openly about this, they expressed specific views concerning the advantages conferred by wealth. Wealth-holding families thought of wealth as a distinctive resource to be used in particular ways, and even asset-poor families had concrete opinions about how they would use wealth—as opposed to income—if they had it. *Regardless of whether a family had a lot, a little, or none, wealth was thought of as a special form of money, different from income.* Wealth was perceived as a vehicle to provide opportunities, experiences, and material things, as well as a source to provide other less tangible advantages that were harder to articulate but no less important (a sense of security, or confidence about the future, for example). *As a whole, families' perspectives on the advantages of family wealth centered around two notions: wealth as a push and wealth as a safety net.* While families across the board alluded to these ideas, they were especially prevalent among the wealthier families, who emphasized them repeatedly. The first notion—a "push"—or an "edge" as some referred to it, was used by parents to explain how family wealth put some people "ahead" of others right from the start and "paved the way" for them over time.

Int: Do you believe that you would have achieved the same social and economic situation that you have today if you weren't given the same financial support from your parents?

James: I would say no, because I feel what it has given me is the edge today. But for us today—for what I am, where I work, my abilities as well as my level of education—I feel without that I don't think I would be where I am today. Because the son would not have been successful without his father doing this—

Pamela: Paving the way for him—

James: [Nods] So, his father paved the way for him to start off and climb up the ladder to be what he is right now. Each kid has the potential, aspiration, a dream. And with wealth you can guide them, you can steer them that way. And you can help them, smooth the way for them, open up doors which they had never seen before.

Pamela and James Gordon, just as the other parents from backgrounds of family wealth, had experienced how that wealth had given them a push and believed it had made a positive difference in the trajectory of their life course. And they believed that this same push they were now giving their own children would make a difference for them too down the road.

Some of the wealth-holding families interviewed were more resistant than others to explicitly conceptualize that "push" they referred to, or those differences "down the road," as concrete "advantage." Joel, for example, asserted right away that wealth passed on to children is "not advantage." He did, however, believe that "it helps." While he described the wealth passed along in families as "a pushing factor," he was careful to not suggest that this translated into actual advantage.

> Int: Does the financial help in terms of wealth that some people receive from their families give them certain advantages?
>
> Joel: Not advantage, but it helps. It will help.
>
> Int: Do you think it's significant?
>
> Joel: Depends on what kind of financial help you're talking about.
>
> Int: I'm not talking about billionaires. I'm talking, like, giving a kid after he graduates a $45,000 car. Or giving him, like, $30,000 for his wedding gift.
>
> Joel: That helps, yeah, that does help. Yeah, the normal help that the parents give to the children, that is a pushing factor. Just puts you ahead a little bit.
>
> Int: Do you believe those without stable economic situations have a harder time achieving success?
>
> Joel: Yes, I do. That's the rule of life. I mean if you have the money you have peace of mind. So you probably can make better decisions. If you're under pressure for lack of money you could go wrong, you could make wrong decisions, definitely.

Here we see a tension between the ideology of meritocracy and the reality of structured wealth inequality in the nuances of how Joel Conrad talked about, perceived, and made sense of family wealth. While a few other parents expressed similar resistance to acknowledging that the "push" of family wealth was a form of privilege, most families did not. Victoria and Abraham Keenan, for example, conceptualized what they were doing for their own children as "absolutely" giving them advantages. While they were careful to point out that they were not "multi-millionaires" like other people they knew, they did fully believe, and acknowledge, that their family wealth was giving their children "a better chance of becoming successful." Implicit in the way they discussed the passing along of their wealth was their acknowledgement that by doing so they were passing along advantage.

Family wealth was believed to give children a push that, as Abraham said, "gives them a better chance of becoming successful." Some families, of course, can give bigger pushes than others, but even small pushes are clearly advantageous. Children who get the pushes of family wealth benefit from advantages they did nothing to individually earn. The acknowledgement of this on the part of the families who were passing advantages along is an important part of their perspectives on wealth privilege and an important insight to how they think about inequality. The second major way that parents depicted the advantages of family wealth was that it acted as a "safety net" for them in important decisions and throughout their lives. Parents from wealth-holding families repeatedly articulated their sense that family wealth was a "safety net" that gave them tremendous "peace of mind." The Barrys, a white couple whose families on both sides had given them significant financial assets over the years, described their wealth-holdings, and the family wealth they believed they could rely upon in the future, as "a sense of economic security." When asked what that sense of security provides for them, Briggette answered:

> Briggette: Sleep at night. It's very non-tangible things. Being able to give my children a sense of peace. Being able to live worry free. It's really non-tangible things. Knowing that I will probably never have the income that my parents had, but still being comfortable with that and being able to provide for my children what they need.

Another parent who explicitly described her family's wealth as a "safety net," went on to explain, "Well, I think just having, um, the assets, just gives us a certain freedom. … You know? You're more freer and more comfortable." The sense of security parents felt from the safety net of family wealth, their desire to re-establish that safety net for their own children, and their ability to rely on it and expand on it in investing in their children's futures cannot be overemphasized. This was a major way that individuals we interviewed—for example Cynthia and Paul Perkins, a white middle-class couple with three children in Boston—acknowledged the power of wealth and wealth's associated privileges.

When a "safety net" of wealth—or, "a cushion for the future"—could not be relied upon, families without it felt the insecurity of having nothing on which to fall back. This is where the difference between wealth and income is perhaps the clearest. As Lenore Meehan, a young black mother from Boston explained it: "You know, if you look on paper, I make a lot of money, but it doesn't feel like it. … I mean, I don't feel like I'm economically secure at all." While she was up-front about the fact that she felt she made quite a lot of money working as a dispatcher for the police force, Lenore's income simply could not provide the sense of security that family wealth was granting to other parents who had it. The families interviewed from all race and class backgrounds made a clear distinction between wealth and income and had concrete understandings of the kinds of advantages that family wealth can provide. Their conceptualization of the "push" and the "safety net" that wealth affords for families and children (and that lack-of-wealth prohibits) reveals their intrinsic awareness and understanding of the power of wealth. *Their acknowledgement of the role of wealth in shaping opportunities, life trajectories, and future chances reveals their awareness and understanding of a structure of wealth inequality.*

References

Hochschild, Jennifer. 1995. *Facing Up to the American Dream: Race, Class, and the Soul of a Nation.* Princeton, NJ: Princeton University Press.

_____. 1981. *What's Fair? American Beliefs about Distributive Justice.* Cambridge, MA: Harvard University Press.

Schwartz, John E. 1997. *Illusions of Opportunity: the American Dream in Question.* New York: W. W. Norton.

Sennett, Richard & Cobb, Jonathan. 1972. *The Hidden Injuries of Class.* New York: W. W. Norton.

REFLECT AND CONSIDER

- What are the implications of the American dream for poor people?
- Why is wealth a good measure of social inequality?

RACIAL ORDERS IN AMERICAN POLITICAL DEVELOPMENT

BY DESMOND S. KING AND ROGERS M. SMITH

W hether race is *the* "American Dilemma," racial inequities have been and remain confounding features of U.S. experience. Has racial injustice been a great aberration within a fundamentally democratic, rights-respecting regime? Has the United States instead been an intrinsically racist society? Has racial discrimination been the spawn of psychological or cultural pathologies, or a tool of class exploitation, or a political "card" to be played in power games, or something else?

One might expect political science in the United States to be the center of debates, if not answers, on such questions. But American political scientists have historically not been much more successful than America itself in addressing racial issues. We seek to do so by connecting theoretical frameworks emerging in the subfield of American political development, including King (1995), Lieberman (2002), Orren and Skowronek (1994, 1996, 1999, 2002), and Smith (1993, 1997), with insights from scholars of race in other areas of political science and other disciplines (e.g., Omi and Winant 1994; Dawson and Cohen 2002; Wacquant 2002). We argue that American politics has historically been constituted, in part, by two evolving but linked "racial institutional orders:" a set of "white supremacist" orders and a competing set of "transformative egalitarian" orders. Each of these orders has had distinct phases, and someday the United States may transcend them entirely—though that prospect is not in sight.

This "racial orders" thesis rejects claims that racial injustices are aberrations in America, for it elaborates how the nation has been pervasively constituted by systems of racial hierarchy since its inception. Yet more than many approaches, it also captures how those injustices have been contested by those they have injured and by other political institutions and actors. It does not deny that the nation's "white supremacist" racial orders have often served vicious economic exploitation or that their persistence reveals psychological and cultural pathologies. Instead it provides a framework to organize empirical evidence of the extent and manner in which structures of racial inequalities have been interwoven with economic as well as gender and religious hierarchies and social institutions.

But more than many scholars, our approach analyzes the "political economy" of American racial systems by stressing the "political," not the "economy." We see all political institutional orders as *coalitions of state institutions and other political actors and organizations that seek to secure and exercise governing power in demographically, economically, and ideologically structured contexts that define the range of opportunities open to political actors.* "Institutional orders" are thus more diversely constituted and loosely bound than state agencies; but they are also more institutionalized, authoritatively empowered, and enduring than many political movements. *Racial* institutional orders are ones in which political actors have adopted (and often adapted) racial concepts, commitments, and aims in order to help bind together their coalitions and structure governing institutions that express and serve the interests of their architects. As in any coalition, the members of a racial order support it out of varied motives. Economic aims are central for many, but others seek political power for its own sake, or to quiet social anxieties, or to further ideological goals. Leaders hold them together by gaining broad agreement on the desirability of certain publicly authorized arrangements that predictably distribute power, status, and resources along what are seen as racial lines. Hence these alliances necessarily combine what scholars have often treated as distinct "ideational" and "institutional" orders (cf., e.g., Smith 1997; Lieberman 2002; Orren and Skowronek 2004). And though the racial institutions they create at least seem to serve many members' economic interests, their coalitional nature means that their unifying aim must be power for many purposes, not just profits (cf. Goldfield 1997: 30–31, 91).

By presenting racial orders as political coalitions, we build on Omi and Winant's (1994: 53–76) depiction of "racial formation" as a product of many elite led "racial projects." But in their account, political actors or "intellectuals" attacking or defending the dominant racial ideology drive racial transformations (86). Like many other scholars of American political development, we treat political entrepreneurs *and* the preexisting institutional orders in which they operate as the key independent variables shaping all political change, including racial development. We also disagree that, despite some forces working at cross purposes, the American state has preserved "an overall unity" as a "racial state," granting "no political legitimacy" to "oppositional racial ideologies" or "competing racially defined political projects" (80, 84). Instead, we see the American state as comprised of multiple institutional orders, including competing racial orders with conflicting ideologies. Though the rival orders have always had unequal power, to understand change we must recognize both that competing racial orders have long existed and that all have included some governing institutions. No American racial "project" has gone far without aid from some such institutions, and no racial conflict can be grasped without seeing how these institutions have shaped the sincere aims of the actors involved and their strategic calculations. Rather than seeing racial change as many sociologists do, as "the product of the interaction of racially based social movements and the state" (Omi and Winant 1994: 88; Wacquant 2002: 52), we see it as the product of the interaction of opposing racial orders, as well as other political orders, all of which include some state institutions and some nonstate political actors and organizations.

The balance of power in those interactions has shifted over time in part because, like most politically constructed coalitions, America's racial orders have been complex and breakable. Most political actors possess partly conflicting identities and interests, and there are always many goals they might like to pursue. But because preexisting contexts define the problems and options actors face, politics usually involves choosing sides among two or three major approaches to what are widely seen as the dominant issues of the day, even if the prevailing approaches and issues do not express one's concerns fully. To accomplish much at all, American political actors have generally felt compelled to join either their current form of white supremacist order or its more egalitarian opponent. This means, however, that the competing racial orders have always included some members whose alignment was tentative and alterable, while others in each era have at least sought to remain unaligned or to forge a third direction. Because of the limits of politics, the latter choices have usually meant effectively aiding one order more than the other, or becoming politically unimportant, until exceptional circumstances have opened up new coalitional options and policy directions.

In the antebellum era, for example, many supported institutions of white supremacy as buttresses to African-American chattel slavery and the acquisition of Native American lands. Others simply wanted institutional protections against aggrieved nonwhites, or a socially recognized superior status, while some displayed psychological aversions, even genocidal impulses, toward people "of color." Though most of these white supremacists sided with slavery when it was the issue of the day, some did so reluctantly, and others opposed it, temporarily allying with advocates of an egalitarianism they did not share. Given these internal tensions and changing demographic contexts, in order to sustain a coalition powerful enough to control key governing institutions, antebellum white supremacists sometimes had to modify prevailing legal definitions of "whiteness," "blackness," and other racial categories. They slowly concluded that they had to label all with any African ancestry "black" and accept the Irish and many other immigrants as "white" (Jacobson 1998; Williamson 1984, 17–21). Yet they remained largely unified around the goal of maintaining the U.S. as a "white man's nation."

The internal tensions among those championing egalitarian changes over the content of egalitarian goals and the means for pursuing them have been greater still. American discourses and institutions promising equal rights burgeoned in opposition to British aristocracy. Initially few British colonists thought them inconsistent with African slavery. But from the start, many black and some white Americans did; and some who opposed slavery favored full racial equality. Yet they worked in alliance with many more who were antislavery advocates of less extreme forms of white supremacy, such as "tutelary" status or colonization for nonwhites. And throughout history, many who have rejected all versions of white supremacy still have differed on whether priority should be given to seeking economic equity, equal political status, or cultural recognition. Hence even when they were allied on issues such as ending slavery or segregation, advocates of racial change have disagreed over whether their ultimate goal should be full integration or some form of more egalitarian racial pluralism. Over time there have been major shifts in the degree and kinds of egalitarianism that have predominated among reformist institutions and actors, defining the phases of the nation's transformative egalitarian racial orders.

Changes have occurred in part because individuals positioned on the margins of racial orders, in relation either to the aims or to the power structures of those orders, have sometimes switched their dominant allegiances at critical junctures. Such was true of Andrew Johnson, who was ardently antislavery but otherwise did not favor altering systems of white supremacy; and Harry Truman, who had never been a strong racial egalitarian but who concluded for domestic, international, and personal reasons that it was wiser to ally with antisegregationist northern Democrats than white supremacist southerners (Klinkner with Smith 1999: 77–9, 206–24).

Despite these complexities, in particular settings it is not hard to discern what were commonly seen as the main proposals on the nation's agenda that promised to increase or decrease racial equality of conditions in the near term. Scholars can recognize that issues such as slavery, Jim Crow segregation, and racially targeted aid programs have at different times been the central disputes around which political battle lines have formed. Hence in each era scholars can identify empirically the main institutions and actors allied to sustain the then-dominant forms of white supremacy, thereby comprising that period's "white supremacist" order, and the leading institutions and actors working for more egalitarian racial conditions, its "transformative egalitarian" order. The existence and analytical utility of these racial orders are not discredited by the presence of internal tensions in the orders, including marginal and "dual" members who may change sides, by some who seek to stay unaligned, or by the fact that the orders modify their goals and members over time. Rather, these features add to their explanatory force. The processes of change wrought by the problems leaders face in sustaining these orders amidst internal tensions, by the conflicts of the orders with each other, by the defection of actors and institutions from one order to its rival, and by their interactions with other actors and institutions comprising American life, all have been engines of significant political development.

The "racial orders" approach is a theoretical framework that can enable empirical studies of racial systems to falsify hypotheses. If a racial order works against the economic interests of many participants, as antebellum laws banning free blacks in Old Northwest states arguably did for many employers and even white workers, as Jim Crow laws clearly did for transportation companies, and as race-based immigration restrictions probably did for many wealthy supporters, it is hard to claim their economic aims drove that order. And if the systems of economic and political inequality sanctioned by a racial order come to be greatly modified, as in the shattering of the interweaving of white supremacy and slavery before the rise of de jure segregation systems, it is implausible to deny that the order has undergone true development. Thus this approach can also help scholars map the stages and extent of the nation's real but incomplete progress toward racial equity and the political contests through which progress has come. And insofar as our framework can unify and strengthen empirical findings on racial developments, it can also vindicate the claim that these contests have been fundamentally political.

Useful as this framework is for making sense of racial development, our main claim here is that a "racial institutional orders" approach helps explain many features of American politics that may appear *unrelated* to race, such as congressional organization and bureaucratic autonomy. We conclude that the internal developments, clashes, and broader impacts of American racial orders have been and remain so central that all scholars of American politics ought always to consider how far "racial order" variables affect the phenomena they examine. Analysts should inquire whether the activities of institutions and actors chiefly concerned either to protect or to erode white supremacist arrangements help to account for the behavior and changes in the nation's political institutions, coalitions, and contests they study. Any choice not to consider racial dimensions requires explicit justification.

This is so precisely because racial orders have been constitutively interwoven with many other highly significant institutional orders, including gender and class hierarchies. Still, we recognize that African Americans, Asian Americans, Latinos, and Native Americans, like all others, have had political concerns that are best captured by stressing their membership in other such orders, not their racial positioning (Reed 2003). We hope that the framework we advance here will aid the study of all these political orders, providing us with ways to identify and measure their profound intersections with racial institutions and conflicts. We suspect that these intersections will show how the unusual prominence of racial orders in America's development has also given distinctive shape to its gender and class systems.

Conclusion

Today, racially inflected contests in courts, legislatures, electoral campaigns, and popular discussions over affirmative action; school and residential segregation; felon disfranchisement; majority-minority districts; racial profiling; the disparate racial impact of incarcerations and the death penalty; hate crimes; reparations for slavery; Native American rights; immigration policies; bilingualism; multiculturalism; "model minority" stereotyping; and racial discrimination in housing, auto, and credit markets, and in hiring and promotions, all still roil American political waters. Many putatively nonracial issues, such as restraints on free speech, vouchers for private schools, the revival of federalism, and disputes over public health, environmental, and social assistance policies, all continue to be shaped by race-related struggles. Few of these issues, or the wider developments with which they are linked, can be understood without exploring the enduring tensions between and within the nation's racial orders.

Our argument has not been that race explains everything in American politics, or even that race is always important for every dimension of American political development. Many of the apparently nonracial issues just listed, and many more, are indeed heavily shaped by other concerns. But we maintain that the internal dynamics of American racial orders, and their interactions with each other and with other aspects of American political life, have so often been so important that the question of what role race may be playing should always be part of political science inquiries. The failure of political scientists to deal adequately with race in their scholarship has been all too much a part of the failure of Americans to deal adequately with race in their common lives. That is why this failure is one that our discipline has a special need, and a special duty, to rectify.

Bibliography

Primary sources

Court cases
Buchanan v. Warley (1919) 245 U.S. 60

Gratz v. Bollinger (2003) 439 U.S. 249

Plessy v. Ferguson (1896) 163 U.S. 537

Rogers v. Alabama (1904) 192 U.S. 226

U.S. v. Wong Kim Ark (1898) 169 U.S. 649

Study

NAACP (1913) "Segregation in the Government Departments in Washington," Washington DC: NAACP.

References and secondary sources

Almaguer, T. 1994. *Racial Fault Lines: The Historical Origins of White Supremacy in California*. Berkeley: University of California Press.

Balfour, L. 2003. "Unreconstructed Democracy: W. E. B. Du Bois and the Case for Reparations." *American Political Science Review*, 97: 33–44.

Bates, B.T. (2001) *Pullman Porters and the Rise of Protest Politics in Black America 1925–1945*. Chapel Hill: University of North Carolina Press.

Bay, M. (2000) *The White Image in the Black Mind*. New York: Oxford University Press.

Bensel, R.F. (1984) *Sectionalism and American Political Development, 1880–1980*, Madison: University of Wisconsin Press.

Berlin, I. (1974) *Slaves Without Masters: The Free Negro in the Antebellum South*, New York: Pantheon.

Berwanger, E.H. (1967). *The Frontier Against Slavery: Western Anti-Negro Prejudice and the Slavery Extension Controversy*, Urbana: University of Illinois Press.

Carpenter, D.P. (2001) *The Forging of Bureaucratic Autonomy: Reputations, Networks and Policy Innovation in Executive Agencies 1862–1928*, Princeton, NJ: Princeton University Press.

Carter, D.T. (1996) *From George Wallace to Newt Gingrich: Race in the Conservative Counterrevolution, 1963–1994*, Baton Rouge: Louisiana State University Press.

Cohen, C.J. (1999) *The Boundaries of Blackness: AIDS and the Breakdown of Black Politics*, Chicago: University of Chicago Press.

Cronon, E.D. (ed.) (1963) *The Cabinet Diaries of Josephus Daniels 1913–1921*, Lincoln: University of Nebraska Press.

— ([1955] 1969) *Black Moses: The Story of Marcus Garvey and the Universal Negro Improvement Association*, Madison: University of Wisconsin Press.

Dawson, M.C. (1994) *Behind the Mule*, Princeton, NJ: Princeton University Press.

— (2001) *Black Visions: The Roots of Contemporary African American Political Ideologies*, Chicago: University of Chicago Press.

Dawson, M.C. and Cathy C. (2002) "Problems in the Study of the Politics of Race." In I. Katznelson and H.V. Milner (eds) *Political Science: The State of the Discipline*, New York: W. W. Norton, 488–510.

Du Bois, W. E. B. ([1935] 1992) *Black Reconstruction in America*, New York: Atheneum.

Dudziak, M.L. (2000) *Cold War Civil Rights: Race and the Image of American Democracy*, Princeton, NJ: Princeton University Press.

Ellis, J.J. (2000) *Founding Brothers*, New York: Alfred Knopf.

Ericson, D.F. (1999) "Dew, Fitzhugh, and Proslavery Liberalism." In D. F. Ericson and L. B. Green (eds) *The Liberal Tradition in American Politics: Reassessing the Legacy of American Liberalism*, New York: Routledge.

— (2000) *The Debate over Slavery: Antislavery and Proslavery Liberalism in Antebellum America*, New York: New York University Press.

Foner, E. (1988) *Reconstruction: America's Unfinished Revolution, 1863–1877*, New York: Harper and Row.

Frankenberg, E., Lee, C., and Orfield, G. (2003) "A Multiracial Society with Segregated Schools: Are We Losing the Dream?" The Civil Rights Project, Harvard University. Online. Available: <http://www.civilrightsproject.harvard.edu/research/reseg03/Are-WeLosingtheDream.pdf.> (accessed April 18, 2004).

Franklin, J.H. and Moss, Jr., A.A. (1988) *From Slavery to Freedom: A History of Negro Americans*, 6th edn, New York: Alfred A. Knopf.

Fuchs, L.H. (1990) *The American Kaleidoscope: Race, Ethnicity, and the Civic Culture*. Hanover, NH: University Press of New England.

Gilens, M. (1999) *Why Americans Hate Welfare*. Chicago: University of Chicago Press.

Gillette, W. (1979) *Retreat From Reconstruction 1869–1879*, Baton Rouge: Louisiana State University Press.

Goldfield, M. (1997) *The Color of Politics: Race and the Mainsprings of American Politics*, New York: New Press.

Greenstone, J.D. (1986) "Political Culture and American Political Development: Liberty, Union, and the Liberal Bipolarity." *Studies in American Political Development*, 1: 1–49.

— (1993) *The Lincoln Persuasion: Remaking American Liberalism*. Princeton, NJ: Princeton University Press.

Hartz, L. (1955) *The Liberal Tradition in America: An Interpretation of American Political Thought Since the Revolution*, New York: Harcourt, Beace.

Horsman, R. (1981) *Race and Manifest Destiny*, Cambridge, MA: Harvard University Press.

Hoxie, F.E. (1984) *A Final Promise: The Campaign to Assimilate the Indians, 1880–1920*, Lincoln: University of Nebraska Press.

Hutchinson, E.P. (1981) *Legislative History of American Immigration Policy, 1798–1965*, Philadelphia: University of Pennsylvania Press.

Jacobson, M.F. (1998) *Whiteness of a Different Color: European Immigrants and the Alchemy of Race*, Cambridge, MA: Harvard University Press.

Katznelson, I., Geiger, K., and Kryder D. (1993) "Limiting Liberalism: The Southern Veto in Congress 1933–1950," *Political Science Quarterly*, 108: 283–306.

Kelley, R.R.D. (1994) *Race Rebels*, New York: Free Press.

Kennedy, S. (1959) *Jim Crow Guide: The Way It Was*, Boca Raton: Florida Atlantic University Press.

Kesler, C.R. (1998) "The Promise of American Citizenship," in N. Pickus (ed.) *Immigration and Citizenship in the Twenty-First Century*, Boston: Rowman and Littlefield.

Kinder, D.R. and Sanders, L. (1996) *Divided by Color*, Chicago: University of Chicago Press.

King, D. (1995) *Separate and Unequal: Black Americans and the U.S. Federal Government*, Oxford: Oxford University Press.

Klinkner, P.A. with Smith, R.M. (1999) *The Unsteady March: The Rise and Decline of Racial Equality in America*, Chicago: University of Chicago Press.

Kousser, J.M. (1974) *The Shaping of Southern Politics: Suffrage Restriction and the Establishment of the One-Party South, 1880–1910*, New Haven, CT: Yale University Press.

Kryder, D. (2000) *Divided Arsenal*, New York: Cambridge University Press.

Lieberman, R. (1998) *Shifting the Color Line*, Cambridge, MA: Harvard University Press.

— (2002) "Ideas, Institutions, and Political Order: Explaining Political Change," *American Political Science Review*, 96: 697–712.

Litwack, L.F. (1961) *North of Slavery: The Negro in the Free States, 1790–1860*, Chicago: University of Chicago Press.

Logan, R.W. ([1954] 1965) *The Betrayal of the Negro from Rutherford B. Hayes to Woodrow Wilson*, New York: Collier Books.

McAdam, D. (1984) *Political Process and the Development of Black Insurgency*. Chicago: University of Chicago Press.

McFeely, W.S. (1991) *Frederick Douglass*, New York: W.W. Norton.

McMahon, K.J. (2003) *Reconsidering Roosevelt on Race: How the Presidency Paved the Road to Brown*, Chicago: University of Chicago Press.

Meier, A. and Rudwick, E. (1976) "The Origins of Nonviolent Direct Action in Afro-American Protest: A Note on Historical Discontinuities," in A. Meier and E. Rudwick (eds) *Along the Color Line: Exploring the Black Experience*, Urbana: University of Illinois Press, 314–32.

Mendelberg, T. (2001) *The Race Card: Campaign Strategy, Implicit Messages, and the Norm of Equality*, Princeton, NJ: Princeton University Press.

Morris, T.D. (1974) *Free Men All: The Personal Liberty Laws of the North*, Baltimore, MD: Johns Hopkins University Press.

Nelson, W.E. (1988) *The Fourteenth Amendment: From Political Principle to Judicial Doctrine*, Cambridge, MA: Harvard University Press.

Ngai, M.M. (1999) "The Architecture of American Immigration Law: A Reexamination of the Immigration Act of 1924," *Journal of American History* 86: 67–92.

Nieman, D.G. (1991) *Promises to Keep: African Americans and the Constitutional Order, 1776 to the Present*, New York: Oxford University Press.

Omi, M. and Winant, H. (1994) *Racial Formation in the United States: From the 1960s to the 1990s*, 2nd edn, New York: Routledge.

O'Reilly, K. (1995) *Nixon's Piano: Presidents and Racial Politics from Washington to Clinton*, New York: Free Press.

Orren, K. and Skowronek, S. (1986) "Editor's preface," *Studies in American Political Development*, 1: vii–viii.

— (1994) "Beyond the Iconography of Order: Notes for a 'New Institutionalism.'" in L.C. Dodd and C. Jillson (eds) *The Dynamics of American Politics: Approaches and Interpretations*, Boulder, CO: Westview Press, 311–30.

— (1996) "Institutions and Intercurrence: Theory Building in the Fullness of Time," in I. Shapiro and R. Hardin (eds) *Nomos XXXVIII: Political Order*, New York: New York University Press: 111–46.

— (1999) "In Search of Political Development," in D.F. Ericson and L.E. Bertch Green, (eds) *The Liberal Tradition in American Politics: Reassessing the Legacy of American Liberalism*, New York: Routledge, 29–41.

— (2002) "The Study of American Political Development," in I. Katznelson and H. V. Milner (eds) *Political Science: The State of the Discipline*, New York: W.W. Norton: 722–54.

— (2004) *The Search for American Political Development*, Cambridge, UK: Cambridge University Press.

Oshinsky, D.M. (1996) *Worse Than Slavery: Parchman Farm and the Ordeal of Jim Crow Justice*, New York: Free Press.

Pierson, P. and Skocpol, T. (2002) "Historical Institutionalism in Contemporary Political Science," in I. Katznelson and H. V. Milner (eds) *Political Science: The State of the Discipline*, New York: W.W. Norton: 693–721.

Quadagno, J. (1994) *The Color of Welfare: How Racism Undermined the War on Poverty*, New York: Oxford University Press.

Reed, A. (1999) *Stirrings in the Jug: Black Politics in the Post-Segregation Era*, Minneapolis: University of Minnesota Press.

— (2003) "The Study of Black Politics and the Practice of Black Politics: Their Historical Relation and Evolution," Paper presented at the Yale Conference on Problems and Methods in the Study of Politics, December 2003. Online. Available: <http://www.yale.edu/probmeth/main> (accessed September 21, 2007).

Schickler, E. (2001) *Disjointed Pluralism: Institutional Innovation and the Development of the U.S. Congress*, Princeton, NJ: Princeton University Press.

Skocpol, T. (1979) *States and Social Revolutions*, New York: Cambridge University Press.

Skowronek, S. (1982) *Building a New American State*, Cambridge: Cambridge University Press.

Skrentny, J.D. (2002) *The Minority Rights Revolution*, Cambridge, MA: Belknap Press.

Smelser, N.J., Wilson, W.J., and Mitchell, F. (eds) (2001) *America Becoming*, Washington, DC: National Academy of Sciences.

Smith, R.M. (1993) "Beyond Toncqueville, Myndal and Hartz: The Multiple Traditions in America," *American Political Science Review*, 87: 549–66.

— (1997) *Civic Ideals: Conflicting Visions of Citizenship in U.S. History*, New Haven, CT: Yale University Press.

Sniderman, P.M. and Piazza, T. (1993) *The Scar of Race*, Cambridge, MA: Harvard University Press.

Swain, C.M. (2002) *The New White Nationalism in America: Its Challenge to Integration*, New York: Cambridge University Press.

Takaki, R. (1993) *A Different Mirror: A History of Multicultural America*, Boston: Little, Brown.

Valelly, R.M. (1995) "National Parties and Racial Disfranchisement," in P. E. Peterson (ed.) *Classifying by Race*, Princeton, NJ: Princeton University Press.

Wacquant, L. (2002) "From Slavery to Mass Incarceration: Rethinking the 'Race Question' in the U.S." *New Left Review*, 13: 41–60.

Waters, M. (2001) *Black Identities: West Indian Immigrant Dreams and American Realities*, Cambridge, MA: Harvard University Press.

Weiss, N.J. (1969) "The Negro and the New Freedom: Fighting Wilsonian Segregation" *Political Science Quarterly*, 84: 61–79.

Wiecek, W.M. (1977) *The Sources of Antislavery Constitutionalism in America, 1760–1860*, Ithaca, NY: Cornell University Press.

Williams, W.L. (1980) "United States Indian Policy and the Debate over Philippine Annexation: Implications for the Origins of American Imperialism," *Journal of American History*, 66: 810–31.

Williamson, J. (1984) *New People: Miscegenation and Mulattoes in the United States*, New York: Free Press.

Yu, H. (2001) *Thinking Orientals: Migration, Contact and Exoticism in Modern America*, New York: Oxford University Press.

Zangrando, R.L. (1980) *The NAACP Crusade Against Lynching 1909–1950*, Philadelphia, PA: Temple University Press.

Zilversmit, A. (1967) *The First Emancipation*, Chicago: University of Chicago Press.

REFLECT AND CONSIDER

- What is the American dilemma?
- How does conflict between progressive forces and those that are hostile to people of color affect how racial and ethnic groups interact with each other?

MIGRATION AND RESIDENTIAL SEGREGATION

BY JOHN ICELAND

Racial and Ethnic Residential Segregation

Many social scientists have examined the residential patterns of immigrants and minority groups over the years. In 1925, sociologist Ernest Burgess described how new immigrants tended to settle in central city ethnic enclaves close to employment opportunities but would often then move to farther, less dense residential areas as they became more familiar with their surroundings and their incomes rose.[1] Many other studies have also documented the very high levels of black-white segregation. The black-white color line has been a very rigid one, reinforced by discrimination and sometimes violence directed toward blacks.[2] Since the 1980s interest in the residential patterns of other groups—mainly Asians and Hispanics—has grown following the increase in immigration from non-European countries in recent decades.

Focusing on this more recent period, figures 5.3.1 and 5.3.2 show trends in racial/ethnic residential segregation for whites, blacks, Hispanics, and Asians

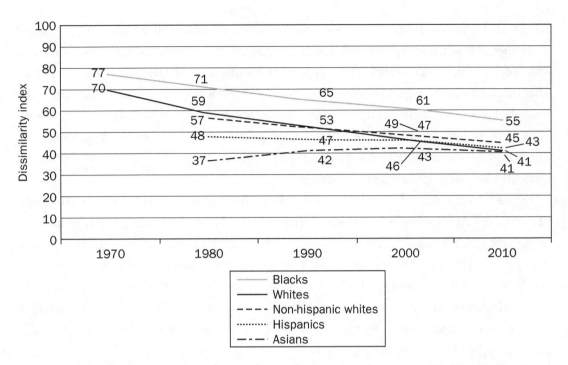

FIGURE 5.3.1 Mean dissimilarity by group, 1970–2010. Note: The reference group is all nongroup members, according to the definition of the group used. Segregation calculations are weighted by the size of the group population of interest and include only those metros with at least 1,000 members of the group of interest. Sources: 1980–2010 numbers from Iceland and Sharp 2013; 1970 numbers from Iceland et al. 2010.

from all who were not group members over the 1970 to 2010 period averaged across all metropolitan areas. Figure 5.3.1 employs the *dissimilarity index,* the most commonly used measure of segregation, which indicates the evenness in the distribution of people across neighborhoods in a metropolitan area. If the metropolitan area is, for example, 20 percent black, then each neighborhood should be 20 percent black if that metropolitan area were considered to exhibit no segregation of blacks. The index varies from 0 to 100, with higher numbers indicating more segregation. Figure 5.3.2 uses the *isolation index,* which is a measure of exposure of one group to others. This index also ranges from 0 to 100, with 100 indicating the highest level of isolation. It measures the average percentage of group members in the neighborhood where the typical group member lives. Holding other factors equal, larger ethnic groups will be more isolated than smaller ones simply because of the presence of more co-ethnics with whom to share neighborhoods.

Figure 5.3.1 indicates that white and black dissimilarity from others not of their own group has continuously declined over the 1970 to 2010 period. Among blacks, the drop was from 77 to 55, and among whites, it was from 70 to 41. A common rule of thumb is that dissimilarity scores over 60 are high, those from 30 to 60 are moderate, and those below 30 are low. Thus, black and white segregation fell from very high levels to more moderate ones. Nevertheless, black and white segregation remains very high in some midwestern and northeastern metropolitan areas, where racial divisions are more entrenched than in growing Sun Belt metropolitan areas. For example, black-white dissimilarity scores in Detroit, Milwaukee, New York, and Chicago range from 76 to 80 (this is indicative of extreme segregation), while those in Las Vegas, Phoenix, Charleston, South Carolina, and Raleigh all range between 36 and 41.[3] Low-income blacks in particular face very high levels of segregation.[4]

Figure 5.3.1 also shows that Hispanic dissimilarity declined slightly from 1980 to 2010 (from 48 to 43), and Asian segregation increased slightly (from 37 to 41). Findings from other studies suggest that the relative stability of Hispanic and Asian segregation is a function of new immigrants fortifying ethnic enclaves even as longer-term immigrants and their children seek out more integrated environments.[5] One notable finding is that by 2010, levels of segregation of whites, Hispanics, and Asians from those who were not group members had nearly converged to the 41 to 44 range. Black segregation remains higher, though it nevertheless declined significantly over the 1970 to 2010 period.

Figure 5.3.2 shows trends using the isolation index. Here we see a bit of a different story, with whites standing out as being considerably more isolated than any other group. The isolation index of 79 for all whites in 2010 indicates that the typical white individual lived in a neighborhood that was 79 percent white. This figure is down from 94 percent in 1970, indicating that whites live in more diverse neighborhoods than they used to, which in turn reflects the growing diversity in the nation as a whole.[6]

Among other groups, we see that black isolation steadily declined over the period, from 66 in 1970 to 46 in 2010, even though the relative size of the black population in the United States has not changed much. This indicates that the typical African American individual no longer lives in a neighborhood that is majority black. It should be noted that declines in black isolation are in large part a function of blacks living in neighborhoods with other minorities, such as Hispanics, as blacks are only modestly more likely to live in neighborhoods with whites than they used to be.[7] Black isolation levels have nearly converged with Hispanic isolation levels, in part reflecting the similarity in the size of the two groups. Asian isolation has increased steadily but remains below that of other groups, reflecting this group's relatively small, though growing, population. Isolation of each group tends to be highest in areas with the high concentrations of that group, such as Altoona, Pennsylvania, and Parkersburg, West Virginia, for whites; Detroit and Memphis for blacks; Laredo and McAllen, Texas, for Hispanics (both of these metropolitan areas are located along the U.S.-Mexico border); and Honolulu and San Jose for Asians.[8]

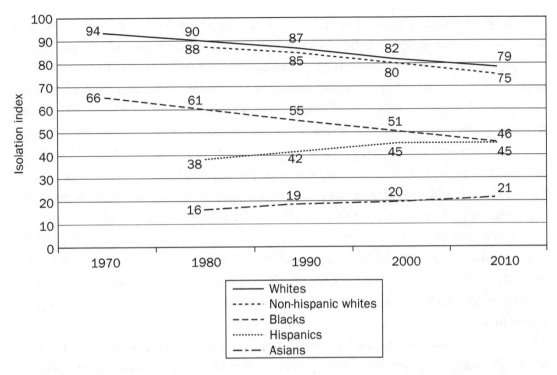

FIGURE 5.3.2 Mean isolation, by group, 1970–2010. Note: The reference group is all nongroup members, according to the definition of the group used. Segregation calculations are weighted by the size of the group population of interest and include only those metros with at least 1,000 members of the group of interest. Sources: 1980– 2010 numbers from Iceland and Sharp 2013; 1970 numbers from Iceland et al. 2010.

Economic Residential Segregation

Economic segregation in modern America can be traced in part to increases in suburbanization through the twentieth century, described above. In the nineteenth century the urban poor generally lived in areas and alleyways near the homes of the affluent, as people of all classes typically lived in the central city, where jobs were located.[9] Class segregation in northern cities began increasing in the first decades of the twentieth century with the growth in black population and with improvements in transportation and the rise of the automobile industry, which allowed the construction and growth of accessible suburban neighborhoods. Suburbanization surged dramatically after World War II, and suburbanites were overwhelming white and middle class.[10]

By the 1960s and 1970s there was growing discussion about the increase in "ghetto" poverty, which referred specifically to black poverty in inner cities and to "concentrated" poverty (a racially more neutral term), commonly defined as neighborhoods with poverty rates of 40 percent or more. Research indicated a rapid increase in concentrated poverty during this time period and lasting until about 1990.[11] The popular press also described the growth of the urban "underclass," referring to the non-normative behaviors of those living in high-poverty dysfunctional neighborhoods, such as dropping out of school, having children out of wedlock, receiving welfare, having low attachment to the labor force, and abusing drugs and alcohol.[12]

Interest and research on concentrated poverty waned somewhat after the mid-1990s, in part because the number of people living in high-poverty neighborhoods declined substantially in the 1990s. The 1990s were a decade of declining poverty more generally, as well as the depopulation of inner cities and the growing suburbanization of blacks and other minority groups of all income levels.[13] Nevertheless, in the wake of growing income inequality and the economic downturn in the 2000s, concentrated poverty once again appears to have increased in the 2000s. Those living in high-poverty neighborhoods were more racially diverse than in the past, suggesting that concentrated poverty is less of an inner-city black phenomenon than it used to be.[14]

While the studies above focused on concentrated poverty—the proportion of people living in neighborhoods with very high poverty rates—others have focused on income segregation more generally. In one study, researchers Sean Reardon and Kendra Bischoff divided families along the income distribution into six groups. They then measured how segregated they were

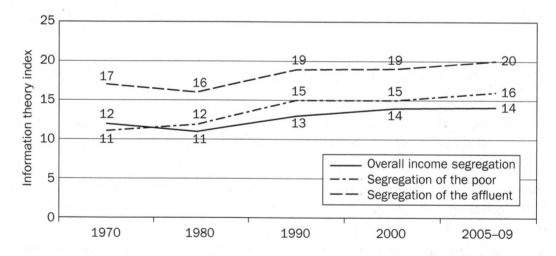

FIGURE 5.3.3 Average family income segregation and segregation of poverty and affluence, 1970–2009. Note: The analysis includes 117 metro areas with populations greater than 500,000. Income segregation is based on a six-category income variable. The poor are defined as families with incomes in the lowest income decile, and the affluent are families in the highest income decile. Source: Reardon and Bischoff 2011, 28.

from one another using the information theory index, which, like the dissimilarity index, measures how evenly different groups are distributed across neighborhoods. It varies from 0 to 100, with 100 indicating the highest level of segregation.[15] Figure 5.3.3 shows income segregation averaged over 117 metropolitan areas from 1970 to 2005–9 for all groups together and also for the poor and the affluent families in particular (i.e., those in the bottom and top deciles of the income distribution, respectively). It indicates that income segregation generally increased over the period, with the largest increases occurring in the 1980s but with some stability since. Residential segregation by income was particularly pronounced among African American families in both the 1980s and the 2000s and among Hispanic families in the 2000s (not shown in the figure). Among the most segregated metropolitan areas by income are Bridgeport, Connecticut, New York City, Philadelphia, Newark, and Dallas—all metro areas with large affluent populations who often live in expensive housing enclaves that poorer families cannot afford.[16]

Notes

1. Burgess 1925.
2. Burgess 1928; Massey and Denton 1993; Taeuber and Taeuber 1965; Myrdal 1996.
3. Logan and Stults 2011; Iceland, Sharp, and Timberlake 2013.
4. Iceland and Wilkes 2006.
5. Iceland 2009; Iceland and Scopilliti 2008.
6. Isolation is a little lower for non-Hispanic whites than for whites in general because of the relative size of the two white groups. (Holding other factors constant, larger groups tend to be more isolated.)
7. Logan and Stults 2011.
8. Sharp et al. 2010; Marsh et al. 2010; Sanchez et al. 2010; Hall et al. 2010.
9. Sugrue 1993, 92–93.
10. Massey and Denton 1993, 26–59.
11. Jargowsky 1997, 38–43.
12. Auletta 1982.
13. Frey 2011, 1.
14. Kneebone, Nadeau, and Berube 2011, 1–16.
15. It should be noted that a score of 50 when using dissimilarity is not indicative of the same level of segregation as a score of 50 when using the information theory index.
16. Reardon and Bischoff 2011, 14–18.

REFLECT AND CONSIDER

- How might immigration simultaneously increase diversity and also the segregation of some groups?
- Considering trends over time, should we be optimistic about the segregation of African Americans or pessimistic over their continuing high levels of segregation from White Americans?

"WHITE, YOUNG, MIDDLE CLASS": AESTHETIC LABOR, RACE AND CLASS IN THE YOUTH LABOR FORCE

BY YASEMIN BESEN-CASSINO

A typical Coffee Bean employee is usually a stuck-up Caucasian teenager who was spoiled by their parents.

—Aaron, twenty-two-year-old male

People in the long line of customers who visited the Coffee Bean daily often noticed the young and vibrant composition of the workforce at the coffee shop. Linda, a middle-age regular customer, told me she really enjoyed the cool, hip, and young atmosphere of the coffee shop. Despite patronizing the coffee shop on a daily basis, many customers failed to also recognize the racial and ethnic composition of the contemporary workforce. Yet the majority of the young people I spoke with were well-aware of the racial and economic inequalities that plague the youth labor force. Bobby, a twenty-year-old male liberal arts major, described the current composition of the Coffee Bean's staff as predominantly affluent and white. He believed that "a typical Coffee Bean employee would probably be Caucasian. He or she would probably be a high school or college student working part-time from middle to upper class." Similarly, Brianna, a nineteen-year-old fellow female student, described the current composition of the coffee shop as "white, young, middle class." Such racial and socioeconomic inequalities are not limited to the coffee shop, but are typical of many desirable jobs. To outside observers, these youth jobs may all appear to be identical. Like objectivist researchers, all people see is that these youth jobs offer low pay, no benefits, and odd hours, rendering them all about the same. However, the lived experience of these jobs from the perspectives of the young actors is vastly different. Where young people choose to work does not just reflect taste or choice but becomes an important social marker. As Pierre Bourdieu (1984) argues in *Distinction*, consumption habits, tastes, and lifestyle choices often reflect socioeconomic and class inequality. Similarly, in the context of youth jobs, we see a similar reflection of racial and socioeconomic inequality in choice of jobs. Jules remembered that at the popular high-end clothing store where she worked part-time while still in school, all her co-workers were from the "same background, they came from a very high socioeconomic class, no one was considered poor." Working at this particular clothing store was considered a prestigious job in her peer group, and being from a higher socioeconomic class gave her an advantage in getting the job. She perceived that the employees had a certain look: The majority of her co-workers looked very fit and athletic, with straight teeth and fashionable clothes. Working there was an important marker of social status, confirming the outward appearance of affluence. Many times, after the store closed, Jules would hang out with her co-workers and go to parties. After the store closed for the day, she remembered turning the music on, getting some free pretzels from other friends working at the pretzel place, and just hanging out. Working at the store gave her social cachet, and so long as she was at the mall, she retained it; once she went home, she was no different from anyone else. The hierarchy of jobs and shares creases layers of inequality surrounding workplace choice. I explore the socioeconomic and racial inequalities that surround youth jobs. In particular, I focus on socioeconomic and racial inequality's influence on getting jobs, showing that less-affluent and minority youth have difficulty entering the labor force. Furthermore, many who do find jobs find them in undesirable locations or in stores with less social appeal. Because part-time jobs create opportunities for socializing and confer social status upon young people, I show that youth from lower socioeconomic backgrounds and minority youth have difficulty finding desirable jobs. I show that such inequalities are justified and perpetuated by employers through notions of aesthetic labor. As Jules remembered, all the workers at her clothing store conformed to the look of the store athletic builds, fit bodies, shiny hair, and gleaming straight teeth. Such physical attributes are covert markers of socioeconomic status and social class. Therefore, more-affluent youth have an advantage in getting these more desirable jobs. Furthermore, class inequality is reflected in the ability to purchase goods sold in the store. Every week at the clothing store, Jules told me, the staff were required to wear a different color polo shirt, and only the affluent youth—those who were able to afford spending their whole paycheck on high-end clothing—were able to keep up with the requirements. Jules later regretted having worked at the clothing store because of the amount of money she spent on the clothes. Even though the pay was low and the hours were limited, the opportunity to use her employee discount and keep up with her peers resulted in a great financial burden. Using similar in-depth interviews, I discuss the costs and social implications of such inequalities in the labor force.

The Affluent Youth: Socioeconomic Inequality in the Youth Labor Force

Many of the young people who worked at the Coffee Bean admitted that they did not do it for the money. For them, the prestige of working for a desirable brand was one of the attractions. This is not to say that they did not understand that other people working there may have needed the money, but the workers I interviewed held that these disadvantaged youth were in the minority. A number of interviewees said that disadvantaged young people could not get jobs in better places and were stuck in less desirable positions, such as fast-food jobs. The hierarchy among jobs is one that is known to many. Amy, a twenty-one-year-old student, differentiated among youth jobs and observed how lower income youth got stuck in fast-food jobs: "The typical [fast-food] employee tends to be someone of lower educational background, who works there out of necessity. [These individuals] … also tend to come from a family of lower socioeconomic status."

The sorting of teens into jobs was evident to almost everyone I spoke with. Greg, a nineteen-year-old male, similarly identified the young workers of the coffee shop as middle- and upper-class youth who did not have to work: "A Coffee Bean employee is generally a young and spirited person from the middle to upper class of society. … They have a good future ahead of them and are just doing this as a part-time job."

What was really striking was that these affluent young people were happy to work and monetary gratifications seemed secondary. Work fulfilled a specific, current function for these young people, but they were not there for the long term: They were "just doing this as a part-time job," and they would move onto bigger and better things in the future. However, as a result of the fun environments and the social benefits, the more prestigious and better jobs are often taken up by more affluent youth. Even if less affluent youth were to apply for these more desirable jobs, the young people I spoke with agreed that it would be very difficult for them to be hired. As we see by the way corporations market these jobs, more affluent youth are preferred.

Also surprising in young people's description of the typical Coffee Bean employee and fast-food-chain employees was the immediate association of work with personality, social and political affiliation, and lifestyle choices: "A typical Coffee Bean employee would be stuck up. They would probably be more Republican than a fast-food employee. Because of the difference in price of the product and the income of the customers, Coffee Bean branches are located in richer areas than fast-food chains are" (Charlene, eighteen-year-old female).

Even though many of them acknowledged the central role that economic background played in finding desirable jobs, the choice of workplace still resulted in inferences about personal, social, and political choices and personality traits. Instead of seeing this economic inequality as a structural issue, many young workers reduced economic, social, and racial barriers to differences in personality. It was not that the less affluent youth could not find work at certain stores, but that they were not the kind of people who would work there. These youth who worked for less desirable brands were just different, socially, politically, and personally. Like lifestyle branding, where consuming a product signifies a particular lifestyle, working for certain corporations has a similar effect. Because a student works for a less desirable fast-food franchise, he or she is considered personally inferior rather than a person who is funneled into a work choice as a result of structural barriers. Such a view was prevalent in the interviews I conducted. As twenty-one-year-old Stephanie observed, "[Coffee Bean employees] are preppy people. They sit huddled around as they wait to make coffee and … they make jokes … [At fast-food chains] they are young people that are not usually too happy about the fact that they are working in a place that is not too friendly, and the people are usually of a different quality."

The social element of the job—hanging out with their friends and meeting new people—is central to young people. Work provides not only a central space for young people to socialize but also a common vocabulary for that socialization. Because the products are geared toward a higher SES audience, young people take these jobs to be associated with the cool brands. Mostly, it is about the atmosphere that the workplace creates. The atmosphere of the coffee chain might have been designed to attract customers, but it also attracted employees. As Jules remembered, the high-end clothing store was like a party full of cool people. She wanted to work there because it was the most fashionable place and the place to be seen. Because less affluent youth do not have the right look, it would be very difficult for them to find these jobs; just as they would not be invited to that party, they would not fit in at the store.

This is not to say that wages play no role in work decisions. However, the young people I interviewed agreed that "it's different." According to Dylan, a nineteen-year-old male student, workers at the Coffee Bean did not use their earnings for necessities or immediate needs.

Their earnings went to what be called "elite expenses": "The typical Coffee Bean employee is probably a college student trying to pay off [elite] expenses like car notes or phone bills. ... The typical fast-food employee is probably a high school student or a high school dropout. The student is probably just trying to pay off his or her expenses ... or just trying to make ends meet." Others who were not so lucky as to find these desirable jobs were the ones paying for school or helping their families. Sean, a twenty-year-old college student, said that employees of the Coffee Bean were not supporting families or using their earnings for necessities, whereas typical fast-food workers needed their paychecks for more immediate financial needs.

Overall, in the discourse of young people, we can see how seemingly similar jobs actually hide enormous inequalities. The desirable jobs are reserved for more affluent youth, who have the right look and image. The more economically disadvantaged youth, who need these jobs to survive, are often left with the less desirable fast-food jobs. Such inequalities are typically normalized through looks, appearance, and aesthetic labor.

Racial Differences in the Workforce

In addition to more attractive jobs being dominated by more affluent youth, we also see a racial component in the descriptions of youth who take those jobs. Many young people I spoke with described these desirable jobs as "white jobs." Just as economically disadvantaged youth find it more difficult to get jobs, nonwhite youth, especially African American youth, also find it much harder to get these jobs. Mason was an African American full-time college student at a state university. During his college education, he had been working part-time. He told me about the difficulties he had had finding a job. Because he lived in a predominantly African American, working-class town, he believed that his place of residence was associated with crime and poverty. He said that once he put his address down on applications, he reduced his chances of getting a callback. In his experience, high-end malls in particular did not like applicants from his neighborhood, because potential employers feared their brands would become associated with low-income consumers. He also remembered being asked whether his friends from the neighborhood would be coming to the store to hang out or ask for discounts and free merchandise. Often times, he provided the address of his grandmother—who is in a more acceptable area—or his school address when applying for jobs. Many times, the higher-status and better employers turned him down, telling him he just did not have the right look or that his look did not fit the image of the brand. Carter, another African American college senior, worked at a high-end clothing store and told me that he noticed that many African American youth were utilized in stock-room positions rather than at the front of the store. According to Carter, it was not clear whether this was due to their race or socioeconomic status, both of which were highly correlated. Many African American youth, according to Carter's observations, had ended up in the less visible back of the store because they did not have the means to keep up with the business's appearance requirements. Mason and Carter agreed that, although the inequality inside the store in terms of positions and job requirements was important, a bigger form of inequality lay in the barriers against entry into the jobs to begin with.

The stories these young people told are reflected in the larger data. Typically, there are marked racial and ethnic differences in the youth labor force. Before the economic recession, 64 percent of white youth between ages fourteen and fifteen were employed while still in school. However, the labor-force participation rates of African American and Hispanic youth remained at 43 and 41 percent, respectively. As teenagers get older, their labor-force participation rates increase for every racial and ethnic category, but the racial differences remain consistent. Even among youth employed in freelance jobs, we see a marked racial difference: 48.3 percent of white fourteen- to fifteen-year-olds are employed in freelance jobs, whereas freelance labor-force participation rates for African American and Hispanic youth are only 33.1 percent and 30.1 percent, respectively (Herman 2000). With older youth, we still see the persistence of racial inequality. According to the U.S. Bureau of Labor Statistics (Herman 2000), among white youth between ages sixteen and nineteen, the employment rate in 2010 was 36.8 percent, while it was only 24.9 percent among African American youth. Especially when we compare unemployment rates, we see markedly higher unemployment rates for African American youth, which tells us that they are actively looking for jobs but are unable to find them. Even as young people age, we see that the racial and ethnic differences are sustained. Among fifteen- to seventeen-year-olds, the unemployment rate—the number of people looking for work who cannot find it—is 35 percent for African American youth and 30 percent for Hispanic youth, but it is only 17 percent for white youth (Herman 2000). Unemployment inequality still persists among older youth. The U.S. Bureau of Labor Statistics (Herman 2000) finds that among white sixteen- to nineteen-year-olds, the unemployment rate is only 21.7 percent, while among African American youth in the same age bracket, the unemployment rate is 41.3 percent.

Since the recession, youth labor-force participation has declined considerably. According to the U.S. Bureau of Labor Statistics (Herman 2000), approximately one-third of all youth are employed while still in school. A limited number of jobs means that when affluent youth take positions to secure social benefits, there are real consequences for others—youth who really need the money, or adults forced into these less desirable jobs—who are not able to get the jobs the affluent youth are taking. This increased competition also means that employers can be more selective about whom they hire and can afford to reject candidates who do not perfectly match the stores' preferred images. Mason remembered preparing for one interview by shopping at the store and wearing the most recent clothes from the store to the interview; even so, in some high-end clothing stores, he and his friends were told they did not have the right look. Racial inequality within jobs, such as African American workers' being assigned to different tasks, has received ample attention in the literature, but here we are seeing a different kind of inequality, one in which African American youth are left out of the labor market entirely or are pushed into lower-status workplaces. Moreover, just as we shall see with the role of gender in youth employment, many of the reasons often given for the different statuses of African Americans and whites in the labor force simply do not apply to the youth labor market. It is difficult for employers to argue that there are differences in positions based on race because of qualifications or experience when almost none of the prospective employees, African American or white, has any experience at all.

Costs and Social Consequences

Being left out of the labor force has important consequences. First, there are economic repercussions. Youth, especially ones from more economically disadvantaged backgrounds, often need the income they would have derived from working. This lost income will inevitably have adverse effects on their lives, ranging from inability to contribute to the family's pooled income to inability to cover school-related expenses. However, the negative effects of unemployment are not limited to economic repercussions. Working while still in school, especially fewer hours of employment in nonintensive sectors, can be beneficial in other ways, such as emotional development or work habit formation.

All told, better jobs are dominated by association with a more affluent white look, while lower-income and minority youth are left with less desirable jobs or are often left out of the workforce. What is more troubling is the fact that such decisions are normalized and perpetuated with considerations of aesthetic labor: Nonwhite and nonaffluent youth simply do not have the right look.

REFLECT AND CONSIDER

- Is "lookism" a form of racism?
- How is racial inequality reproduced in the workplace?

WHY BOTH SOCIAL STRUCTURE AND CULTURE MATTER IN A HOLISTIC ANALYSIS OF INNER-CITY POVERTY

BY WILLIAM JULIUS WILSON

In recent decades, discussions of race, inequality, and family hardship have consolidated around two opposing perspectives—the one held by those who would support a mainly structural explanation for chronic hardship versus that of those who espouse cultural explanations. This article is an attempt to demonstrate the importance of understanding not only the independent contributions of social structure and culture, but also how they interact to shape different group outcomes that embody racial inequality.

We should be clear about what we mean by these two important concepts of social structure and culture. *Social structure* refers to the way social positions, social roles, and networks of social relationships are arranged in our institutions, such as the economy, polity, education, and the organization of the family. A social structure could be a labor market that offers financial incentives and threatens financial punishments to compel individuals to work; or it could be a "role" associated with a particular social position in an organization such as a church, family, or university (e.g., pastor, head of a household, or professor) that carries certain power, privilege, and influence external to the individuals who occupy that role (Alexander and Thompson 2008).

When we talk about the impact of social structures, we are making explicit references to the forces they set in motion, given specific social circumstances, that affect human behavior. Basically, two types of structural forces contribute directly to racial group outcomes such as differences in poverty and employment rates: social acts and social processes. The term *social acts* refers to the behavior of individuals who occupy particular positions within society. Examples of social acts are stereotyping; stigmatization; discrimination in hiring, job promotions, housing, and admission to educational institutions; and exclusion from unions, employers' associations, and clubs when any of these are the acts of individuals or groups exercising power over others.

Social processes refers to the "machinery" of society that exists to promote ongoing relations between members of the larger group. Examples of social processes that contribute directly to racial group outcomes include laws, policies, and institutional practices that exclude people on the basis of race or ethnicity. These range from explicit arrangements, such as Jim Crow segregation laws and voting restrictions, to more subtle institutional processes, such as school tracking that purports to be academic but often reproduces traditional segregation, racial profiling by police that purports to be about public safety but focuses solely on minorities, and redlining by banks that purports to be about sound fiscal policy but results in the exclusion of blacks from home ownership. In all of these cases, ideologies about group differences are embedded in organizational arrangements.

Many social observers who are sensitive to and often outraged by the direct forces of racism, such as discrimination and segregation, have paid far less attention to those political and economic forces that *indirectly* contribute to racial in equality.[1] I have in mind political actions that have an impact on racial group outcomes even though they are not explicitly designed or publicly discussed as matters involving race, as well as impersonal economic forces that reinforce long standing forms of racial inequality. These structural forces are classified as indirect because they are mediated by racial groups' position in the system of social stratification (the extent to which the members of a group occupy positions of power, influence, privilege, and prestige). In other words, economic changes and political decisions may have a greater adverse impact on some groups than on others simply because the former are more vulnerable as a consequence of their position in the social stratification system. These indirect structural forces are often so massive in their impact on the social position and experiences of people of color that they deserve full consideration in an attempt to understand the factors leading to differential outcomes along racial lines.

Culture, on the other hand, refers to the sharing of outlooks and modes of behavior among individuals who face similar place-based circumstances (such as poor segregated neighborhoods). Therefore, when individuals act according to their culture, they are following inclinations developed from their exposure to the particular traditions, practices, and beliefs among those who live and interact in the same physical and social environment (Hannerz 1969). This definition is not limited to conceptions of culture defined in the simple and traditional terms of group norms, values, and attitudes toward family and work. It also includes cultural repertoires (habits, styles, and skills) and the micro-level processes of meaning making and decision making—that is, the way that individuals in particular groups, communities, or societies develop an understanding of how the world works and make decisions based on that understanding.[2] The processes of meaning making and decision making are reflected in cultural frames (shared group constructions of reality). In this article I will use the generic concept of *cultural traits* to refer to one or more of these different but related components of culture.

There are two types of cultural traits relevant to the study of race and urban poverty: one represents national views and beliefs on race and the other embodies patterns of intragroup interaction in settings created by discrimination and segregation and that reflect collective experiences within those settings. When we talk about the impact of cultural traits, we are also making explicit references to the forces they set in motion, given specific social circumstances, that affect human behavior.

Racism has historically been one of the most prominent American cultural frames and has played a major role in determining how whites perceive and act toward blacks. At its core, racism is an ideology of racial domination with two key features: (1) beliefs that one race is either biologically or culturally inferior to another and (2) the use of such beliefs to rationalize or prescribe the way that members of the "inferior" race should be treated in this society as well as to explain their social position as a group and their collective accomplishments. In the United States today, there is no question that the more categorical forms of racist ideology—in particular, those that assert the biogenetic inferiority of blacks—have declined significantly, even though they still may be embedded in institutional norms and practices. An example would be school tracking, the practice of grouping students of similar capability for instruction, which not only tends to segregate African American students but often results in placing some black students in lower-level classes even though they have the cultural capital—requisite skills for learning—to compete with students in higher-level classes.[3]

However, there has emerged a form of what Lawrence Bobo and his colleagues refer to as "laissez-faire racism," a perception that blacks are responsible for their own economic predicament and are therefore undeserving of special government support (Bobo, Kluegel, and Smith 1997). The idea that the federal government "has a special obligation to help improve the living standards of blacks" because they "have been discriminated against for so long" was supported by only one-fifth of whites in 2001 and never has been supported by more than one-quarter of whites since 1975. Significantly, the lack of white support for this idea is not related to background factors such as level of education and age (Bobo, Kluegel, and Smith 1997).

The vast majority of social scientists agree that, as a national cultural frame, racism in its various forms has had harmful effects on African Americans as a group. Indeed, considerable research has been devoted to the effects of racism in American society. However, there is little research and far less awareness of the impact of emerging cultural traits in the inner city on the social and economic outcomes of poor blacks. Note that distinct cultural traits in the inner city have not only been shaped by race and poverty but, in turn, often shape responses to poverty, including, as we shall soon see, responses that may contribute to the perpetuation of poverty.

Nonetheless, although culture matters, from a historical perspective it is hard to overstate the cumulative impact of structural impediments on black inner-city neighborhoods. We have to consider, of course, the racialist structural factors such as the enduring effects of slavery, Jim Crow segregation, public school segregation, legalized discrimination, residential segregation, the Federal Housing Administration's redlining of black neighborhoods in the 1940s and 1950s, the construction of public housing projects in poor black urban neighborhoods, employer discrimination, and other racial acts and processes. But we also have to take into account the impact of political, economic, and policy decisions that were at least partly influenced by race, as well as those that are nonracial, such as the effect of impersonal changes in the economy on poverty and joblessness in the inner city (Wilson 2009).

Nonetheless, despite the obvious fact that structural changes have adversely affected inner-city neighborhoods, there is a widespread notion in America that the problems plaguing people in the inner city have little to do with racial discrimination or the effects of living in segregated poverty. For many Americans, it is the individual and the family who bear the main responsibility for their low social and economic achievement in society. If unchallenged, this view may suggest that cultural traits are at the root of problems experienced by the ghetto poor, because most Americans tend to focus on the outlooks and modes of behavior shared by many inner-city residents.

Culture provides tools (habits, skills, and styles) and creates constraints (restrictions or limits on outlooks and behavior) in patterns of social interaction. These constraints include cultural frames (shared group constructions of reality) developed over time through the processes of *meaning making* (shared views of how the world works) and *decision making* (choices that reflect shared definitions of how the world works). For example, in the inner-city ghetto, cultural frames define issues of trust—street smarts and "acting black" and "acting white"—that lead to observable group characteristics.[4]

One of the effects of living in a racially segregated, poor neighborhood is the exposure to cultural traits that may not be conducive to facilitating social mobility. For example, some social scientists have discussed the negative effects of a "cool-pose culture" that has emerged among young black men in the inner city, which includes sexual conquests, hanging out on the street after school, party drugs, and hip-hop music. These patterns of behavior are seen as a hindrance to social mobility in the larger society (Majors and Billson 1992; Patterson 2000, 2006).

The use of a cultural argument, however, is not without peril. Anyone who wishes to understand American society must be aware that explanations focusing on the cultural traits of inner-city residents are likely to draw far more attention from policy makers and the general public than structural explanations will. It is an unavoidable fact that Americans tend to de-emphasize the structural origins and social significance of poverty and welfare. In other words, the popular view is that people are poor or on welfare because of their own personal shortcomings. Perhaps this tendency is rooted in our tradition of "rugged individualism." If, in America, you can grow up to be anything you want to be, then any destiny—even poverty—can be viewed through the lens of personal achievement or failure. Certainly it is true that most Americans have little direct knowledge or understanding of the complex nature of race and poverty in the inner city, and therefore broad-based explanations that focus on the cultural traits of individuals and families are more likely to gain acceptance.

Toward a Holistic Social Policy Approach

Policy makers dedicated to combating the problems of race and poverty and who recognize the importance of structural inequities face a major challenge: how to generate political support from Americans, who tend to place far more emphasis on cultural traits and individual behavior than on structural inequities in explaining social and economic outcomes. After all, beliefs that attribute joblessness and poverty to individual shortcomings, including those that represent cultural traits, do not engender strong support for social programs to end inequality. But in addressing the problem of structural impediments, it would not be wise to leave the impression in public discussions that cultural problems do not matter. Even though more weight should be given to structural causes of inequality because they continue to play a far greater role in the subjugation of black Americans and other people of color, proposals to address racial inequality should reflect awareness of the inextricable link between aspects of structure and culture.

Given the foregoing analysis, I think that the problems of race and urban poverty can be most effectively addressed with a holistic approach—an approach that recognizes the complex web of structural and cultural factors that create and reinforce racial inequality.

Notes

1. I first discussed the concepts of indirect and direct forces of racial inequality in my contribution to a co-authored introduction to the volume *America Becoming: Racial Trends and Their Consequences* (Smelser, Wilson, and Mitchell 2001).

2. My discussion in this section on the concept of "culture" owes a great deal to the work of Lamont and Small (2008).

3. For a review of the literature on school tracking, see Jane Free (2004).

4. There is mixed evidence for the outcomes of "acting white" as it applies to education. One of the best-known studies of this concept is Fordham and Ogbu (1986). They studied African American students at a high school in Washington, D.C., and concluded that the fear of acting white was one of the major factors undermining student achievement. In contrast, Prudence Carter's (2003, 2005) studies have not supported the idea that students who avoided "acting white" held lower educational aspirations. Roland Fryer (2006) presents yet another perspective. He found that a high grade point average (GPA) presents a social disadvantage for Hispanics and blacks in public, integrated schools, but he saw no such effect in schools that were segregated (80 percent or more black) or private. He also noticed a marked difference in this effect among black boys and black girls; black boys in public, integrated schools were particularly susceptible to social ostracism as their GPAs increased and were penalized seven times more than black students (including both genders) overall.

References

Alexander, Jeffrey C., and Kenneth Thompson. 2008. *A contemporary introduction to sociology: Culture and society in transition*. Saint Paul, MN: Paradigm.

Bobo, Lawrence, James R. Kluegel, and Ryan A. Smith. 1997. Laissez faire racism: The crystallization of a kinder, gentler, antiblack ideology. In *Racial attitudes in the 1990s*, ed. Steven A. Tuch and Jack K. Martin. Westport, CT: Praeger.

Bobo, Lawrence, and Ryan A. Smith. 1994. Antipoverty politics, affirmative action, and racial attitudes. In *Confronting poverty: Prescriptions for change*, ed. Sheldon H. Danziger, Gary D. Sandefur, and Daniel H. Weinberg, 365–95. Cambridge, MA: Harvard University Press.

Brazelton, T. Berry. 1992. *Touchpoints: Your child's emotional and behavioral development*. Reading, MA: Perseus Books.

Carter, Prudence L. 2003. "Black" cultural capital, status positioning, and schooling conflicts for low-income African American youth. *Social Problems* 50:136–55.

Carter, Prudence L. 2005. *Keepin' it real: School success beyond black and white.* New York: Oxford University Press.

Clampet-Lundquist, Susan, and Douglas S. Massey. 2008. Neighborhood effects on economic self-sufficiency: A reconstruction of the Moving to Opportunity experiment. *American Journal of Sociology* 114:109–45.

Commission of the European Communities. 1990. *The perception of poverty in Europe: Poverty 3* Eurobarometer Brussels series.

Commission of the European Communities. 2007. Poverty and exclusion. *Eurobarometer*, Brussels.

DeLuca, Stefanie. 2007. All over the map: Explaining educational outcomes in the Moving to Opportunity program. *Education Next* 7 (4): 28–36.

Dobbie, Will, and Roland G. Fryer, Jr. 2009. Are high quality schools enough to close the achievement gap? Evidence from a social experiment in Harlem. http://www.economics.harvard.edu/faculty/fryer/papers_fryer.

Evans, William N., Wallace E. Oates, and Robert M. Schwab. 1992. Measuring peer group effects: A study of teenage behavior. *Journal of Political Economy* 100 (5): 966–91.

Fordham, Signithia, and John Ogbu. 1986. Black students' school success: Coping with the "burden of 'acting white.'" *Urban Journal* 18 (3): 176–206.

Free, Jane. 2004. Race and school tracking: From a social psychological perspective. Paper presented at the annual meeting of the American Sociological Association, San Francisco, August 14.

Fryer, Roland G. 2006. "Acting white": The social price paid by the best and brightest minority students. *Education Next*, 6 winter: 53–59.

Hannerz, Ulf. 1969. *Soulside: Inquiries into ghetto culture and community.* New York: Columbia University Press.

Jargowsky, Paul. 1997. *Poverty and place: Ghettos, barrios, and the American city.* New York: Russell Sage Foundation.

Jargowsky, Paul. 2003. *Stunning progress, hidden problems: The dramatic decline of concentrated poverty in the 1990s.* Washington, DC: Brookings Institution.

Kaufman, J. E., and J. Rosenbaum. 1992. The education and employment of low-income black youth in white suburbs. *Educational Evaluation & Policy Analysis* 14 (3): 229–40.

Keels, Micere, Greg J. Duncan, Stefanie DeLuca, Ruby Mendall, and James Rosenbaum. 2006. Fifteen years later: Can residential mobility programs provide a long-term escape from neighborhood segregation, crime and poverty? *Demography* 42:51–73.

Kling, Jeffrey R., Jeffrey B. Lieberman, Lawrence F. Katz, and Lisa Sanbonmatsu. 2004. Moving to Opportunities and tranquility: Neighborhood effects on adult economic self-sufficiency and health from a randomized housing voucher experiment. Princeton IRS Working Paper 481, Princeton University.

Kluegel, James R., and Eliot R. Smith. 1986. *Beliefs about inequality: Americans' views of what is and what ought to be*. New York: Aldine de Gruyter.

Lamont, Michèle, and Mario Luis Small. 2008. How culture matters for the understanding of poverty: Enriching our understanding. In *The color of poverty: Why racial and ethnic disparities exist*, ed. David Harris and Ann Lin. New York: Russell Sage Foundation.

Majors, Richard, and Janet Billson. 1992. *Cool pose*. Lexington, MA: Heath.

Patterson, Orlando. 2000. Taking culture seriously. In *Culture matters: How values shape human progress*, ed. Lawrence E. Harrison and Samuel P. Huntington. New York: Basic Books.

Patterson, Orlando. 2006. A poverty of the mind. *New York Times*, March 26.

Pew Research Center. 2007. *Optimism about black progress declines: Blacks see growing values gap between poor and middle class*. Washington, DC: Pew Research Center.

Plotnick, Robert, and Saul Hoffman. 1993. Using sister pairs to estimate how neighborhoods affect young adult outcomes. Working Papers in Public Policy Analysis and Management, no. 93–8. Graduate School of Public Affairs, University of Washington, Seattle.

Quigley, John, and Steven Raphael. 2007. Neighborhoods, economic self-sufficiency, and the MTO. The Brookings-Wharton Papers on Urban Economics Affairs, vol. 8. Washington, DC: Brookings Institution. Rosenbaum, James, S. DeLuca, and T. Tuck. 2001. Moving and changing: How places change people who move into them. IPR Working Paper, WP–02–09, Institute for Policy Research, Northwestern University, Evanston, IL.

Rosenbaum, James E., and Susan J. Popkin. 1990. *Economic and social impacts of housing integration: A report to the Charles Stewart Mott Foundation*. Evanston, IL: Institute for Policy Research, Northwestern University.

Rosenbaum, James E., and Susan J. Popkin. 1991. Employment and earnings of low-income blacks who move to middle-class suburbs. In *The urban underclass*, ed. Christopher Jencks and Paul E. Peterson, 342–56. Washington, DC: Brookings Institution.

Rosenbaum, James, S. Popkin, J. Kaufman, and J. Rusin. 1991. Social integration of low-income black adults in white middle-class suburbs. *Social Problems* 38 (4): 448–61.

Sampson, Robert J. 2008. Moving to inequality: Neighborhood effects and experiments meet social structure. *American Journal of Sociology* 114 (July): 191–233.

Sampson, Robert J., Patrick Sharkey, and Stephen W. Raudenbush. 2008. Durable effects of concentrated disadvantage on verbal ability among African-American children. *Proceedings of the National Academy of Sciences of the United States of America* 105:845–52.

Sharkey, Patrick. 2008. The intergenerational transmission of context. *American Journal of Sociology* 113 (January): 931–69.

Small, Mario L., and Kathryn K. Newman. 2001. Urban poverty after *The Truly Disadvantaged*: The rediscovery of the family, the neighborhood, and culture. *Annual Review of Sociology* 27 (1): 23–45.

Smelser, Neil J., William Julius Wilson, and Faith Mitchell, eds. 2001. *America becoming: Racial trends and their consequences*. Vol. 1. Washington, DC: National Academy Press.

Tough, Paul. 2008. *Whatever it takes: Geoffrey Canada's quest to change Harlem and America*. New York: Houghton Mifflin Harcourt.

Wilson, William Julius. 2009. *More than just race: Being black and poor in the inner city*. New York: Norton.

REFLECT AND CONSIDER

- How do structure, culture and poverty fit together in Wilson's argument?
- How does Wilson's argument compare to the culture of poverty argument?

HIGHLIGHT

NINE CHARTS ABOUT WEALTH INEQUALITY IN AMERICA

BY THE URBAN INSTITUTE

SUMMARY

This article summarizes the reasons for wealth inequality in America, especially as measured across race and ethnicity. It argues that wealth inequality results from a combination of inequality in incomes, inequality in cumulative lifetime earnings, disparities in rates of home ownership, less savings, a greater debt load for people of color versus Whites, and the failure of the federal government to promote asset building by lower-income families. All these factors result in an increase in wealth inequality as Americans get older.

EXCERPT FROM
"NINE CHARTS ABOUT WEALTH INEQUALITY IN AMERICA"

Why hasn't wealth inequality improved over the past 50 years? And why, in particular, has the racial wealth gap not closed? These nine charts illustrate how income inequality, earnings gaps, homeownership rates, retirement savings, student loan debt, and lopsided asset-building subsidies have contributed to these growing wealth disparities. Average wealth has increased over the past 50 years, but it has not grown equally for all groups. Between 1963 and 2013,

- families near the bottom of the wealth distribution (those at the 10th percentile) went from having no wealth on average to being about $2,000 in debt,
- those in the middle roughly doubled their wealth—mostly between 1963 and 1983,
- families near the top (at the 90th percentile) saw their wealth quadruple,
- and the wealth of those at the 99th percentile—in other words, those wealthier than 99 percent of all families—grew sixfold.

These changes have increased wealth inequality significantly. In 1963, families near the top had six times the wealth (or, $6 for every $1) of families in the middle. By 2013, they had 12 times the wealth of families in the middle.

READ THE REST OF THE ESSAY:

bit.ly/wealthurban

READ, LISTEN, WATCH, INTERACT!

READ

Fighting Voter Suppression

Civil Liberties Union (ACLU)
READ AT bit.ly/fightvotersuppression

Investigation of the Ferguson Police Department

United States Department of Justice, Civil Rights Division, 2015
READ AT bit.ly/fergusoninvestigation

LISTEN

Historian Says Don't 'Sanitize' How Our Government Created Ghettos

Fresh Air, 5.14.2015,NPR
LISTEN AT bit.ly/governmentghettos

New Efforts to Revamp Police Procedures Among Charges of Racism

The Diane Rehm Show, 12.8.2014
LISTEN AT bit.ly/revamppolice

Segregation: Six Decades Dead in Court, But Still Alive in Many Schools

Claudio Sanchez, 4.16.2014, NPR
LISTEN AT bit.ly/segregationlives

WATCH

The Interrupters
Steve James and Alex Kotlowitz, 2012
AVAILABLE AT http://bit.ly/interruptersjames

Unnatural Causes (4 part series)
Larry Adelman, 2008
AVAILABLE AT bit.ly/unnaturalcauses

INTERACT

A More Perfect Union: A Virtual Exhibit of Barack Obama's Race Speech at the Constitution Center on March 18, 2008.
National Constitution Center
INTERACT AT bit.ly/obamaracespeech

Racial Residential Segregation Measurement Project
Population Studies Center, University of Michigan
INTERACT AT bit.ly/racesegregation

RACISM IN POPULAR CULTURE

How many hours do you spend watching television shows? On your phone? On Facebook, Twitter, Instagram, Snapchat, or other apps? You and likely almost everyone you know has a television, a smartphone, and maybe even a computer or tablet. As never witnessed before in US history, today's society is wrapped up in technology and popular culture. This high-level and easily accessible engagement with a range of media means that it is increasingly important to understand how race and racism permeate popular culture.

Popular culture includes a wide spectrum of media, from classical outlets such as television, movies, and books, to more contemporary forms of media found on the Internet, but it also includes our engagement with popular activities such as sports. Critical media theorists have long realized that media is much more than entertainment, as consumption of images is connected to our perceptions of social groups. Certainly, as consumers we have agency in which media we consume and/or how we choose to feel about that media; in other words, just because one might enjoy playing *Grand Theft Auto* doesn't mean that one wants to start stealing cars. Yet, the reality is that there are clear correlations between popular culture and the status of racial groups in society. Sociological studies look at how racial groups are represented and/or misrepresented, how the meanings attached to race and racial groups are constructed, and how racial stratification is maintained through the structure and organization of media outlets.

In the first reading of this section, "The Revolution Will Not Be Available on iTunes" by Dustin Kidd, an overview is given of which racial groups are represented in television, movies, music, and books. Kidd finds that some groups are highly overrepresented, while other groups are missing both on the production side and in their representation. The next reading moves to discuss race in the virtual realm; Rebecca West and Bhoomi Thakore analyze how participants in online discussion forums, even though they cannot see each other, still reproduce racist ideologies. Group members are more likely to value White members of the group, and White members are more likely to dismiss conversations about race as unpleasant and irrelevant. The following two readings look into how sports construct popular understandings of racial groups; Ben Carrington addresses Blacks, and Krystal Beamon addresses Native Americans. Carrington takes a particularly critical eye in analyzing the "racial signification of sport" and in examining how the body acts as "a metaphor of social relationships." Carrington argues that sports are much more than entertainment or even about making money as sports create and maintain racialized meanings that then support the racial hierarchy. In Beamon's look at sports, the focus is on Native American mascots and the ways in which tribes continue to resist the use of such degrading imagery. These mascots represent Native Americans as "savage warriors," which has serious, deleterious effects on Native communities that can be seen through the high suicide rates among Native American youth. However, popular culture can also be used for good and affect social movements; the Highlight "Pop Culture's Black Lives Matter Moment Couldn't Come at a Better Time" examines the connections between the rise of positive images of Blackness and the rise of the Black Lives Matter movement.

AS YOU READ

- Evaluate how race is embedded in both the production side and the consumption side of popular culture.
- Examine the connections between media and the racial hierarchy.
- Assess how the media could be a tool for advancing positive racial relationships and challenging the racial hierarchy.

THE REVOLUTION WILL NOT BE AVAILABLE ON iTUNES: RACIAL PERSPECTIVES

BY DUSTIN KIDD

Racial Demographics in Popular Culture

In popular culture, whose stories are told the most, whose are told the least, and whose stories are missing? When we compare the demographics of representation to the demographics of the social world, who is represented accurately, who is overrepresented, who is underrepresented, and who is invisible?

In film, white characters have dominated screens since the beginning of the industry, but nonwhite characters have always been very important as well, especially considering film's fascination with race and racial hierarchy, which dates back to 1915's *The Birth of a Nation* (Griffith). This film caused significant controversy when it was released, because it celebrates the role of the Ku Klux Klan in the Reconstruction era and also portrays black characters as violent, sexual, and insidious. It was a divisive film that is important for both American film history and American race relations.

The best analysis of racial representation in film today is found in Stacy Smith and Marc Choueiti's study of the one hundred top-grossing films of 2008 (Smith and Choueiti 2009). They find that whites constitute 71.2 percent of speaking and/or named characters. So whites are heavily overrepresented. Blacks are also overrepresented, but not by much, constituting 13.2 percent of roles, compared to 12.6 percent of the US population. Asians are overrepresented as well. Making up 4.8 percent of the US population, Asians have 7.1 percent of speaking or named roles in the one hundred top-grossing films of 2008.

So if Asians, blacks, and whites are all overrepresented, who is getting pushed out? The answer is Hispanics, the second largest and fastest growing racial group in the United States. Hispanics make up 16.3 percent of the population, yet they only have 4.9 percent of roles in films. That is a massive underrepresentation. [...] Smith and Choueiti do not count Native American characters.

Turning to television, one scholar who has devoted particular attention to the relationship between race and television is sociologist Darnell Hunt. He conducted a content analysis of prime time television in the 2002 new fall season, counting characters by their racial identity (Hunt 2003). He found that whites accounted for 74.3 percent of roles, which makes them over-represented in comparison to their proportion of the American population at the time, 69.1 percent.

Perhaps surprisingly, blacks were also overrepresented. At the time they accounted for 12.1 percent of the population, but made up 15.9 percent of prime time roles. The over-representation of whites and blacks was made possible yet again by the underrepresentation of Hispanics. Hispanics comprised 12.5 percent of the population, but only 3.2 percent of prime time roles. Asians made up 2.7 percent of roles, which approaches their portion of the population at the time of 3.6 percent. Native Americans were completely absent from prime time television that year.

To update this information, I conducted my own analysis of the 2010–2011 television season. I coded characters by their race, gender, sexuality, and disability status, following pro-tocols established in similar research, such as Hunt's methods for coding race in the report just described. [...] In the area of race, I found patterns that are only slightly different. White overrepresentation not only persists, it has increased. I found that whites accounted for 81.8 percent of prime time roles in 2010–2011. Representation of whites in prime time has increased during a period when the white proportion of the population has decreased, to 63.7 percent. The increase in white representation is largely explained by the decline of black representation, which is down to just 9.6 percent. Over a period of eight years, blacks went from being over-represented to being underrepresented. The reasons for this decline may be varied, but certainly the merger of UPN, a network that was known to feature black characters, with the WB, into a new network, the CW, explains much of the change. The CW targets white teenagers and has none of the black-themed shows that once appeared on UPN. But one network alone cannot explain such a dramatic decline. During the years between the two studies, the black proportion of the population increased slightly, from 12.3 to 12.6 percent.

Underrepresentation of Hispanics persists, even as the Hispanic population grows. Only 3.5 percent of prime time characters in 2010-2011 were Hispanic, compared to a population proportion of 16.3 percent. Although Hispanic roles are increasing in prime time, even as black roles are shrinking, the gap between the number of roles and the proportion of the population makes Hispanics the most underrepresented group on television. Representation of Asians has increased to 3.4 percent of roles, as the Asian demographic in America has increased to 4.8 percent. Native Americans, who comprise 0.9 percent of the population, are completely invisible on TV.

Hunt's study (2003) also includes an analysis of the types of roles played by different racial groups. He finds that Asians are more likely than all other groups to appear as criminals; Asians and whites are more likely than other groups to appear as doctors; blacks are more likely than whites to appear as lawyers (but Latinos and Asians did not appear as lawyers at all in the year of his analysis); Latinos are more likely than all other groups to appear as students; and blacks and Latinos are more likely than other groups to appear as police officers. All racial groups are more likely to appear in dramas than sitcoms—dramas have larger casts and account for more programming—but a larger proportion of blacks and Hispanics had roles in sitcoms than whites or Asians.

Few demographic racial analyses have been conducted for music, which is odd, because it is quite easy to obtain annual lists of the Top 100 for various genres and for all genres. I conducted a simple coding of the performers of the Top 100 songs, across all genres, for 2010, using a list provided on *Billboard's* website.[1] The performers were placed in the same racial codes that the census uses. If the song was performed by a pair or a group, then the first determination I made was whether the performers were racially homogenous. If so, then that song was placed under the racial category of those performers. If they were not racially homogenous, then the song was coded as mixed/other, meaning that the performers were a mixture of racial representations. I also placed one individual artist under mixed/other, who represented two of the songs on the chart (both Top 10). That artist is Taio Cruz, born in London to a Nigerian mother and Brazilian father. Cruz does not fit neatly into American census categories. […]After I coded all one hundred songs, an interesting story emerged. White artists were responsible for forty-five of the songs, making them underrepresented. Black artists were responsible for thirty-six of the songs, making them significantly overrepresented. Hispanics produced only two of the songs, and Asians only one. Native Americans were not represented in the Top 100 songs of 2010. Sixteen of the songs fell into the mixed/other category. Some of these songs were made by racially mixed groups like the Black Eyed Peas. Many of the songs were made by a pairing of a white singer with a black rapper, or a white DJ (such as David Guetta) with a black rapper or singer.

These numbers, which I quickly tabulated on my computer, actually offer a window into a much broader story about the role of race in American music. The American recording industry has a long history of relying on black musicians to produce much of its output. Johnny Cash discusses this openly in his autobiography, *Cash* (1997). He points to the important role played by Sam Phillips, the founder of Sun Records in Memphis, Tennessee, who discovered not only Johnny Cash but also Elvis Presley, Jerry Lee Lewis, and many others: "Sam Phillips was a man of genuine vision. He saw the big picture, which was that the white youth of the 1950s would go crazy for music that incorporated the rhythms and style of the 'race' records he produced for artists like Howlin' Wolf, Bobby Bland, B. B. King, Little Milton, James Cotton, Rufus Thomas, Junior Parker, and others" (Cash 1997, 79). From Cash's perspective, Phillips was a visionary, but he was also motivated by economic realities. Black performers could be paid much less than whites and, more important for American popular and country music, black songs could be purchased very cheaply to be recorded by white performers.

What of racial representations in literature? One of the best studies of children's books examines the inclusion of black characters throughout the twentieth century. Bernice A. Pescosolido, Elizabeth Grauerholz, and Melissa A. Milkie (1997) conducted a content analysis of children's picture books from 1937 to 1993. They divide these books into three types: (1) all winners of the prestigious Caldecott Medal (or Caldecott Honor), which are relatively expensive; (2) a sample of books listed in the *Children's Catalog*, a resource used mostly by children's librarians; and (3) all books in the Little Golden Books series, which are comparatively inexpensive. In total, the authors analyzed 2,448 children's picture books. Quantitatively, they calculated the percentage of books in each year that included at least one black character, as well as the percentage that featured only black characters. Qualitatively, they examined the prominence of the black characters, the types of roles they play, and the nature of their interactions with white characters. Their strongest finding is that black characters are shockingly underrepresented across the board. Across all years and all three types of books, only 15.1 percent of books had at least one black character, and only 3.3 percent had only black characters. Of course, many books have no human characters whatsoever, so the authors also calculated the percentages after subtracting the books that had no humans in them. In the resulting sample of 1,967 books, 18.4 percent had at least one black character, and 3.9 percent had only black characters.

The authors find that black representation has shifted in response to racial politics and does not reflect linear progress throughout the century. They divide the period of their analysis into four key epochs. The early years, 1937 through the mid-1950s, are marked by modest levels of black representation (between 10 and 20 percent of books in any given year included one or more black characters), confined mostly to surface contact interactions with whites (based on social roles, not relationships) or the inclusion of black characters in depictions of "all god's children," to use a phrase suggested by the authors. The late-1950s through the mid-1960s are characterized by significantly declining black representations. During this period, in any given year, only 5 percent or less of books included one or more black characters. Importantly, these were the years of the civil rights movement and of the highest levels of racial conflict in the United States, according to the authors' analysis of accounts in the *New York Times*. So it seems that the publishing industry was responding to racial conflict by removing black characters from children's books. The third period the authors identify, the mid-1960s through the mid-1970s, is characterized by a rapid increase in black characters, reaching a height of 30 percent of books having at least one black character. This increase would seem to mark the success of the civil rights movement. However, the quality of black representations during this period varies greatly. Many of the black characters in this time period are placed in African settings, which the authors refer to as safe and distant. The period following 1975 is identified as a stabilizing period, with higher levels of black representations than before, but still relatively few.

The comparison among the three types of books—Caldecott Medal books, *Children's Catalog* books, and Little Golden books—allows the authors to examine the important role played by **gatekeepers,** who are cultural leaders and institutions that mediate between cultural objects and their audiences. A DJ is a gatekeeper in the music world, just as a movie critic is a gatekeeper in the film world. Gatekeepers make careful selections from the range of cultural objects to curate a particular cultural experience. The three types of books that the authors examined reflect three different types of gatekeepers, with the Caldecott Award being the most prestigious and selective of the three. The Caldecott winners are most likely to feature black characters and to place them in American, not African, settings. The Caldecott books continued to increase in black representations, even during the period when representation was otherwise stabilizing for children's books overall in the 1980s.

The misrepresentation that we see today in the mass media is an extension of misrepresentations that date back at least to the early twentieth century. Sociologist Steven Dubin collected and analyzed mass culture objects that feature black characters such Aunt Jemima and Uncle Mose. Drawing on Pierre Bourdieu and Jean-Claude Passeron's (1977) concept of **symbolic violence,** Dubin (1987) refers to these objects as "symbolic slavery," arguing that they place black characters in positions of subservient work while juxtaposing humor and violence. Dubin's examples include a beanbag game that involved throwing bags at a board full of black faces, trying to get the bag through the mouth of a face. He also discusses "Niggerhead" golf tees, which came in a pack decorated with a black man's head that is pierced by a golf tee.

These images, taken as a whole, constitute a profound world of imagery that attempts to render racial minorities powerless.

Race In Production

What are the racial demographics of the labor force that produces popular culture? Who are the directors, writers, producers, editors, publishers, and so forth? We begin with film. Smith and Choueiti (2009) find that only six of the one hundred top-grossing films of 2008 had a black director, with one of those directors—Tyler Perry—working on two of the films. Only one of the black directors in the list of films is female: Gina Prince-Bythewood, who directed *The Secret Life of Bees.*

Does the race of the director matter for the content of the film? It does. Films with a black director have much higher black representation on-screen. In the six films that Smith and Choueiti identified with a black director, 62.6 percent of the roles were played by blacks, compared to 10.9 percent in films without a black director (Smith and Choueiti 2009). This is further evidence that diversity in the labor force of the cultural industries is the most important way to generate diversity in on-screen representations.

The 1987 film *Hollywood Shuffle* offers a humorous but striking account of the way Hollywood treats black actors and the roles they play on-screen (Townsend 1987). Although the film is decades old, it still captures the relationship between race and film fairly accurately. The film was directed by Robert Townsend, a black filmmaker who also served as a writer and producer on the film, and as its star. Townsend plays Bobby Taylor, a young aspiring actor who is quickly dismayed by his prospects in Hollywood. In one scene, Bobby meets another actor, named Jesse Wilson, at an audition. Jesse warns Bobby not to "sell out" by accepting a role that is demeaning to black people: "The only role they gonna let us do is a slave, a butler, or some street hood or something." But when the casting agent calls Jesse's name, he changes his tune and even his speaking style and hurries off to audition. Bobby then has a fantasy about a black acting school where white instructors offer to teach black people how to talk jive and walk black and to play "TV pimps, movie muggers, and street punks."

In his book *Channeling Blackness,* Darnell Hunt examines the racial dynamics of the behind-the-scenes world of television, which he describes as follows: "Network television continues to be defined by a highly insular industry in which White decision makers typically reproduce themselves by hiring other Whites who share similar experiences and tastes" (Hunt 2005, 17). As evidence for this claim, Hunt examines various aspects of the storytelling process. He starts by looking at the "showrunner" position—the executive producers who are most in charge of what we actually see on television. The number of black showrunners in any given year can be counted on one hand, with the highest being five in 1990 (his analysis stopped with 2003).

In a review of the 2000–2001 television season, Hunt finds that minorities accounted for only 6 percent of directors on prime time television: 3 percent black, 2 percent Hispanic, and 1 percent Asian. Hunt then looks at the demographics of TV writers for 2002 and finds that only 13 percent were minorities. Many of these writers were working for the now-defunct UPN network. Most surprisingly, even on shows that targeted minority audiences, the majority of writers were white.

One issue that people often take for granted is the ownership of local television stations. Working at, and owning, local television stations is an important way that Americans participate in television production, especially given that so many television shows are made in southern California. The local television station makes TV more local and familiar than it would be otherwise. There are 1,349 television stations across America. A report from 2006 finds that minorities own only 3.26 percent of local television stations, compared to the 76.58 percent of stations owned by whites. Most of the remaining stations were owned by groups, with no one person maintaining a controlling interest. Hispanics, the second largest population in the United States, own just 1.11 percent of television stations. Blacks own 1.30 percent, Asians 0.44 percent, and Native Americans 0.37 percent (Turner and Cooper 2006).

These studies show again and again that racial minorities are significantly underrepresented in the production of popular culture, so it should come as little surprise that they are under-represented in much of the content of popular culture. *In fact, minorities are actually better represented in popular culture content than they are in the production process.*

Note

1. http://www.billboard.com/charts/year-end/2010/hot-100-songs.

REFLECT AND CONSIDER

- Why is it important to pay attention to the representation of racial groups in media outlets such as television programs and music?
- Apply the concept of "symbolic violence" to the representation of people of color in popular culture.

RACIAL EXCLUSION IN THE ONLINE WORLD

BY REBECCA J. WEST AND BHOOMI THAKORE

Introduction

"Hi, TansyTen! Welcome to the Playhouse … You should look around for Sandrine10 and MskratMlly. I think that they will be good friends for you!"

In most online communities, moderators have the responsibility of both welcoming people and controlling the environment of the online space. These two tasks are often accomplished simultaneously. In the message above, a moderator has suggested that TansyTen, a new member of this community, reach out to two more established members. On the surface, this is a very welcoming gesture, in that it helps the new member make connections with other users. However, a little context reveals a more complex situation: In her introduction to the forum, TansyTen identified herself as a Black woman. The two members suggested by the moderator are also Black. As TansyTen said later during a one-on-one interview,

> "It's like, here I am, and I said I was Black in my profile…and (the moderator) thought I'd be friends with these other people, but we

don't have anything in common except we're Black ... I mean, really, I mean, it's hard to find Black people on the internet but I can find them on my own. Like, am I not supposed to talk to the white people?"

The opening interaction took place in an online forum where adult women come together to discuss the collecting of American Girl dolls, is a consciously multi-ethnic and multi-racial product line. In the forum the role of race in the success or failure of these products is a frequent topic of conversation. Through these public conversations, other racial processes come to the forefront. Thus, this forum provides a rich site to examine the power of race in the virtual world.

The actions seen in the case above are an example of boundary policing in virtual spaces. It is well known that the internet remains segregated both in access and within the interactions. What is of deeper sociological interest is the question of *why* this segregation occurs. By examining the interactions within a specific virtual community, we can begin to understand how participants in online spaces create and maintain racial boundaries. We argue that this segregation is maintained by both active and passive means, resulting in a space where discussions of race presuppose a social order in which white identity is idealized and normalized.

As the World Wide Web continues to develop, so too does the ease in accessing information online. Today, more and more people participate in multiple forms of virtual communities. Forums, message boards, and social networking sites are part of the social fabric around the world. People participate in these types of forums for many reasons: information seeking, problem solving, professional obligations, and, of course, for social contact. These online worlds provide a place for their users to join with others who share a common interest, regardless of social or geographic location. Additionally, these worlds provide another "socially manifest" space wherein users may consume, create, and define the texts that shape their interests. For fans, this is particularly salient[1]. As Kozinets has pointed out, these virtual social groups have a tangible influence on the people who participate in them, and their participation influences many aspects of their behavior both on and off line[2]. As spaces of significant social interaction and information transmission, the extent to which online interactions shape ideologies must be examined.

In this paper, we take a deep look at how online patterns of discussions create racialized boundaries, and discuss how these boundaries reproduce some of the inherent problems with inter-racial interactions in the offline world. Through the use of virtual ethnographic observation, survey data, and interviews, we will identify those exclusionary practices that are alive and well in the supposedly egalitarian and utopian space of the online world. We identify two types of boundaries and define them as *exclusionary* and *essentializing*.

In our analysis, we present the ways in which some of the interactions in this online forum correspond to the established sociological concepts of racial perceptions, racialized interactions, and colorblind racism. We conclude with the takeaway points of our findings and discuss how these data provide a new understanding of how racialized social processes operate online.

American Girl

"American Girl" (AG) refers collectively to a line of eighteen inch vinyl play dolls, appropriately scaled accessories, and books aimed at girls aged eight to eleven. Diamond *et al.* described the company as a "$436 million doll empire" that gains its appeal by combining immersive retail and catalog environments[3]. American Girl sells not only specific representations of "girlhood," but promotes the values and cultural norms associated with middle-class white American culture.

The company debuted in 1986 with a line of three "historical" dolls, all white, each with a distinctive story. As the years have progressed, the company has expanded that line to twelve historical dolls covering two hundred and fifty years from Kaya, the Nez Perce girl from 1754, to Julie, the white latchkey daughter of a divorced mother in 1974. These dolls have explicit racial and ethnic identities, ranging from American Indian to Swedish to African American. Each of these dolls comes with a series of books that construct a historically and culturally appropriate narrative. The girl consumer can purchase accessories that illustrate events and items in the stories (such as clothes, furniture, dishes and sports equipment).

In addition to this historical line, the company has two other product lines that are relevant to our study: the "MyAG" line of contemporary dolls, and a "Limited Edition" series, also of contemporary girlhood. Within the "MyAG" line, the consumer is invited to choose a doll from a range of options in terms of physical appearance, including the shape of the face, skin tone, hair color and texture, and eye color. Unlike the historical line, these dolls do not have a set narrative; the girl consumer is invited to create her own narrative. That narrative can be expanded on by purchasing various accessories—everything from horses to barbecue grills.

We stated in the introduction that American Girl is "consciously multi-racial and multi-ethnic." This fact is particularly demonstrated in the company's third line of products, the "Girl of the Year" (GotY) series of dolls. This line combines the contemporary focus of the MyAG line with the narrative element of the historical line. As limited edition collectibles, these dolls come with small collections of accessories and furniture that correspond with elements of their stories. Each doll also has some unique aspect in terms of physical appearance: a different hair style, color of eye, or even a completely new head shape. At the time of writing, American Girl has created eleven GotY dolls, three of which have had explicitly non-white racial and ethnic identities. The remaining characters have been, presumably, white. It should be noted that while race and ethnicity are explicitly discussed within the text of the books for the non-white dolls, race is never mentioned for the other seven.

In the collecting forum, members have made a variety of comments that exemplify this practice of assuming whiteness as the unmarked, normative category. For example, the original face sculpt (mold) introduced by American Girl in 1986 was then and is now only available in the lighter shades of vinyl. This face is referred to by collectors as the "classic mold." The other face molds introduced later are referred to by either the name of the character or the race that the face represents (*i.e.*, the "Addy" or "African-American mold"). Again, whiteness is implied, while non-whiteness is explicit and Othered. American Girl's selections of historical and modern images that are memorialized in doll form construct a narrative of the fulfillment of the American dream: assimilation, middle-class achievements, and symbolic diversity[4]. Although there are minority, lower-class, and immigrant characters, the ultimate goal (of the dolls) is to reach a higher level of achievement within the system, rather than to challenge it.

While American Girl is a set of toys aimed at preteen girls, it is important to note that children's consumption is mediated through their family structure. Generally, parents and other caregivers must provide the opportunity and means for children to consume any item. The significance of parents' beliefs in the selection of children's toys is often overlooked, not only in the analysis of the American Girls collection, but also in the analysis of the consumer toy market[5]. In guiding their children's consumption, parents have the opportunity to challenge or reinforce pre-existing ideologies about girlhood, America, and race.

American Girls are not "just dolls;" they are a specific set of consumer goods that are both produced by and productive of American ideology[6]. Consumers' interactions with American Girl are significant for the study of race because the products themselves are explicitly racialized. This racialization is not merely that the dolls fit particular stereotyped expectations of appearance; it is also expressed specifically by the literature produced by the American Girl company[7]. Because of this, these products invite discussions of race without outside provocation—that is, because race is made explicit in the products themselves, the social space for a discussion of these issues is created. This condition of possibility is where new social forms may emerge or old ones may be reified[8]. In this study, we have chosen to examine adults who collect these products. In addition to purchasing these products for their children, these collectors interact with these products for their own entertainment and use them as the means towards forming friendships with others. Although women are recognized as a consuming group—85% of all consumer purchases are made by women—the interpersonal meaning of their leisure activities remains under studied[9]. With this analysis, we are seeking to examine the intersections of leisure-time consumption, women's social networks, and racial ideology.

Methods

Our project focused on members of a specific online forum, which we have identified as "The Playhouse." This forum was established in 2006 and has more than 4000 registered members. Of these, an average of 300 members log in daily, with an average of 497 new comments posted on a daily basis. Between November 2009 and January 2010, the members of this forum were offered a survey that asked for demographic information and personal collecting and online forum behavior. Of the 297 members who began the survey, 285 members completed at least 75% of the questions. Overall, they establish that the forum was predominately women (95%), almost entirely white (91%), and had a median income in the $40,000–$59,999 range.

The Playhouse group is what Kozinets would classify as an "electronic bulletin board"[10], in that it focused on a specific product. In fact, 93.4% of members reported that they used the forum specifically to find out information about new American Girl products. The Playhouse does have some features of a "chat room", but discussions there were limited to related American Girl products. Additionally, the relationships in the Playhouse are much more tangible to members—30.7% of the members reported that they view the other members of the forum as either casual or close friends.

In addition to the survey, we used virtual ethnography to examine the actual interactions between the members. This observation period extended from 2009 to 2011, and included an in-depth review of the community archives that date back to spring of 2006. In particular, we analyzed the "Introductions" section of the forum in order to establish the racial demographics of regular users. One of the authors (West) had established membership in 2007 and actively participated in the community. This long-term membership contributed to rapport between researcher and the subjects, and also helped contribute to the excellent survey response rate. As well as including observations of the public interactions on the forum, we also include analysis from interpersonal messages shared with us by members.

For the purposes of this research, the archives of the community were treated as transcripts. As in traditional ethnography, intervention of the researcher can unintentionally alter virtual community interactions. Thus, our analysis of the public forum interactions only includes those threads where the researchers were not participants. Virtual ethnography was a particularly appropriate method for this study not just because it took place online, but because it allowed us access to a group that may have been otherwise unreachable [2]. But, this location is not a convenience sample—as an online gathering of fans of American Girl, the Playhouse board becomes a socially manifest space, one with no physical location [1]. The only way to investigate this arena is to engage in participant-observational methods inside the community.

While the internet is often viewed as public space and therefore not subject to privacy considerations, the fact that this forum required participants to register with the moderator and gain approval for membership suggests that the members may have held a different view of the space. Accordingly, we sought permission from the forum moderators to conduct our research. When this was granted, members of the forum were offered the opportunity to opt out of having their forum contributions included in this study. (No members took advantage of this offer). The name of the forum, the usernames of the participants, and any identifiable information has been altered to protect anonymity, following the practices suggested by Hines[11]. All other standard practices for anonymity were followed as well. All research methods were approved by the Institutional Review Board of Loyola University Chicago.

Finally, interviews were conducted with survey respondents who volunteered for further contact. Twenty-three interviews were conducted in all. Two of these interviews were with community moderators, while the rest were with members who had participated in the community for at least six months. Sixteen of the interviewees were white; four were African-American; two were Asian-American; and one was Native American. Both moderators that were interviewed were white women.

It should be noticed that children (or explicitly, girls) as consumers of American Girl products do not necessarily recognize or discuss the racial questions present in these objects. Acosta-Alzuru noted in her dissertation that while the girls' mothers emphasize the importance of the books and historical narratives that accompany American Girl dolls, the girl consumers rarely enact these storylines or even read the books[12]. Our study population is focused on adult women—50.9% of whom are mothers—and they also emphasized the importance of the American Girl narratives. About 40% of our survey population indicated that their enjoyment of the story that came with a doll was "somewhat important" when they chose to purchase the doll, while 55.6% said that looks of the doll were "not important at all." While a slight difference, our respondents do appear to emphasize the importance of the stories over the appearance of the dolls. The narrative aspect of American Girl was also noted as something that justified the high price point of the products. While 61.9% of respondents said that the prices were "high" and 12.7% said the prices are "very high," 94.1% of respondents offered a comment that the quality of the products, especially their educational aspects, justified the prices. (Perhaps unsurprisingly, none of the collectors felt the prices were either "low" or "too low.")

From Integration to Segregation: A Timeline

It can be difficult to establish the racial diversity of an online space, particularly a "general" one such as The Playhouse where members are not expected to be of any particular background. While our survey data established that 18.1% of the members of the forum identified as non-white, this number does not provide much insight into people's actual participation. After further investigating the "Introductions" forum, we established that 27% of those who posted descriptions of themselves identified as explicitly non-white. Using this information, we were able to trace the pattern of participation by racial minorities over time.

When the forum was created in spring of 2006, many of the original members had been members of other online communities, creating a core group of members who were already generally familiar with each other's identities and interests. Excluding the creator of the community and the three people named as moderators, there were 35 original or core members. Many of these original members used the same user names they were known by in the previous communities. Even though these core members already knew each other, they wrote introductory posts as a courtesy to new members. The racial composition of the community at that point in time was very similar to what it was at the time we conducted our survey, with a slightly higher percentage of members identifying as non-white in their introductions (six out of the 35 "core" members, or 17.2%). The forum has had at different times between four and seventeen moderators that have had different responsibilities, including directing discussions, organizing the various sections of the boards, arranging offline activities for members, and directly enforcing the rules of the forum. For this analysis we have focused on the actions of the four moderators of the general discussion forum. These moderators were all women; three of them identified their race as white, while the remaining moderator chose not to disclose her racial identity.

In December of 2006, this changed. At this point, another American Girl collecting forum changed its membership requirements and rules for participation. As a result, many members of this second community were either banned or chose to leave, and moved to The Playhouse as an alternative. While the actions in the other community are not part of our analysis (consent to conduct research in this second community was sought in 2009, but the request was refused), many of these new members expressed their feelings of being targeted by the rule changes as racial, religious, and sexual minorities in that community, and turned to The Playhouse as a more "liberal" or inclusive forum. At this point, the number of self-identified racial minorities increased slightly, with 22.5% of the members indicating their non-white racial identity in their introductions.

However, the Introductions only tell one part of the story of community activity. Posting an introduction to the board is how a member moves from a "lurker" (non-participating member) to an active status. Lurking is a common and expected internet behavior where a hopeful member may observe without contributing until they are familiar with the community norms and introduce themselves when they have some confidence that they will not break a norm[13]. However, a member who introduces themselves does not always become an active participant and, as we later discuss, active participants may also drop out of participation.

Having determined members' racial identities, we investigated their patterns of participation throughout their membership in the community. There can be many reasons why a member will choose to stop participating in a community—including life events, loss of interest in the topic, or moving to a new forum. But when race is considered, it became clear that active non-white members were more likely than active white members to end their participation in this forum. For example, at the time of writing, only two of the original core non-white members of the community were still participating, whereas 18 of the 29 white members were. Further, while 26% of the white members who joined after problems with the second community participated beyond their first introductory post to The Playhouse, only 7% of the non-white members participated at the same level. It is apparent that these discrepancies are based on the exclusionary practices by white members toward non-white members.

The non-white members of the Playhouse did not end their interest in American Girl collecting or their allegiance to online communities focused on their hobby. Instead, they moved on to create other forums in other venues, such as through personal blogs, Facebook groups, or self-created Wikis. Unlike the Playhouse, these new communities are not known as central hubs of activity for American Girl. As TansyTen, the moderator of one of the new groups that is discussed later in this paper, these new groups are places for those who had explicitly been excluded from and discriminated against in the Playhouse.

Racialized Identification and Friendship "Steering"

As Nakamura has extensively discussed, the establishment of an individual's racial identity in an online space is determined by two factors: how much an individual chooses to share, and the interpretation of that information by their audience [14,15]. Both of these aspects are at play in the Playhouse forum. When a person joins the community, they are expected to make a post that will serve as their introduction to the community. These posts share many common themes: the individual will mention how they first became interested in American Girl, discuss why they sought out the forum, and provide some personalizing details such as geographic location, their profession, or their marital status.

Racial and ethnic identity is one of the personalizing details that members sometimes include, as in the example below,

> "Hey guys! I'm sure many of you have seen me around the board already, but I figured I'd make a 'formal' introduction. I'm Anju, short for Anjana, although I also go by Anu (it's my 'daknam', or informal name at home). I am Indian-American, (…) I was born in (New England) but I grew up (…) about a half an hour away from Williamsburg, VA (Felicity's hometown!) (Posted June 2007)"

After reviewing the introductory posts on the forum, a clear pattern emerged. The only members who mentioned their race were those who are non-white. To be clear, not every non-white member discussed their racial identity in their introduction, but absolutely no white members thought this information was important enough to establish who they were in the forum. Introductions from white people were more likely to resemble this example,

> "I have a 2 year old daughter and ever since I knew she was a girl (about 5 months into my pregnancy) I have been collecting AG dolls. I wish they had had these dolls when I was young, I had Barbies but these dolls are so much cooler and I love the books. I am hoping to start making clothes for them, too. I can't wait until my daughter gets a little older so she can play with them with me! (My family thinks I'm nuts, but I'm used to that!) (Posted December 2006)"

This pattern is hardly surprising. White people often do not consider themselves to have any race at all. This follows directly on the idea of whiteness as a default racial identity [8,41]. In fact, this pattern echoes American Girl's own practices of identifying the race of their characters. The introductions posted on this forum serve as more than an individual's entree in to a community—they become the basis for how others, particularly moderators, interacted with the individual. As our introductory respondent TansyTen explained, the mention of race in her profile led moderators to steer her toward the other Black women on the forum, without any knowledge of other similar interests or collecting choices.

Given that these introductory posts are short, there could be an argument that the "steering" of people is a result of the moderators having to work with the few details they have. However, the introductory posts are not the only information that the moderators (and others on the boards) have about the members. They are also aware of what dolls the person collects and what discussions the member is more likely to participate in. TansyTen's collecting interests were on the contemporary line of dolls, and she felt strongly that she would only purchase dolls that represented Blackness to her. The two members she was referred to both preferred the historical dolls, and had repeatedly noted that they had a preference for the dolls with white features. In other words, while TansyTen and these other members are both interested in American Girl, they have radically different preferences for the various products.

Unfortunately, the opportunity to ask a moderator about how they chose to suggest friends for new members did not present itself. Whatever the specific motivation of the moderators was, it is important to note that only the members of color who were interviewed mentioned receiving such introductory messages—white respondents did not. Regardless of how the moderators intended their actions, the non-white members of the community perceived them as racist and exclusionary.

Community Discussion and Essentializing

American Girl as a company has consciously created an impression of racial and ethnic diversity, but the actual product line-up does not support this image. While the average consumer may not be aware of the intricacies of the company's history, the collectors are. They have dedicated much time to their hobby, and thus recognize what the company has done and has failed to do.

One such failure is the fact that American Girl has not yet created a GotY character who is African-American. An oversight obvious enough to have received attention in the popular press, this "missing" representation is discussed regularly every year within the community. The discussions about this oversight generally begin in the summer, when members look to see if book covers have been made available to retailers, or if there are leaked products available on eBay. The discussion generally reaches its peak in the fall when American Girl releases some early information on its website or to the national press. The conversation subsides when the new doll is released in January, and the pattern repeats. These discussions in the forum center on the questions of whether an African-American character would be economically viable for the company. The members of the community overwhelmingly expressed a desire for a Black GotY doll in their forum posts, a desire that was also reflected in responses to the survey of members—almost 90% of survey respondents expressed the hope that American Girl would release a Black limited edition doll in the near future.

The fact that this discussion happens on an annual basis is surprising because the majority of forum members surveyed did not participate in the discussions. In the survey, 86.7% said they read the discussions centered on race, only 36.6% said they participated. This was supported with the analysis of the forum archives, which showed that the conversation about racial representation in American Girl was maintained by a core group of participants.

However, the explanation of the choice to not participate, and the perception of these discussions, reveal a distinctly racialized pattern. White community members repeatedly expressed a feeling that discussions about race were unpleasant, uncomfortable, or something that was irrelevant to the topic of doll collecting and should be stopped. As these white members stated in their survey comments,

> "I find (the discussions) shallow. While I am all for racial equality among people, I will not buy a doll with features I do not find attractive just to prove that I'm not a racist."
> "They're fucking annoying. Seriously. I'm all for more diversity, but a lot of time I feel like the Addy love is solely countering racism, and sometime the arguments seem racist against white collectors."
> "I just want them to shut up. There's a new thread every few days about race and it makes me want to leave."

On the other hand, non-white survey respondents had a different interpretation. While they also said that these conversations could be uncomfortable, they also stated that they enjoyed the conversations because they allowed them a chance to discuss issues they saw as problems. As some of these non-white members said in their survey comments,

> "They tend to be very frustrating. Usually someone says something cluelessly insensitive and continue to be clueless throughout, and nobody really stops them."
> "I seem to most often post only to correct others' misinterpretations of a race or culture."
> "I participate. And often people don't like my opinions b/c I am not white washing anything making it all peaches and cream."

In addition to these different perceptions of the conversation, non-white survey respondents were more likely to state that they used to participate in the racial discussions but have since stopped. While 45% of non-white respondents reported no longer participating in these discussions, only 15% of white respondents stopped participating. As one non-white respondent said,

> "Not anymore! Not since I was told my own ethnic identity does not exist … It was just one person but they were pretty offensive in their complete cluelessness…"

The survey data provide an interesting look at the overall attitude toward racial discussions in the Playhouse community. When the responses are viewed without controlling for race, there is a generally negative attitude about racial discussions, and an overall wish that the discussions would stop. The actions of the community moderators tend to reflect this wish. While moderators maintained a rather hands-off approach in most topic threads, rarely stepping in to guide the discussion, they became more involved in those threads where the discussion centered on race. Discussions where race was introduced were often moved from the main discussion area to an "off topic" section (where participation was less active and threads tended to end). Members were often told to look for past discussions on the topic that have been "merged" (combined with similar threads) and "archived" (placed in an area of the board were further discussion is not permitted). Most telling was the frequency of warnings from moderators about content—present in only 3% of general topics, but 97% of race topics.

However, as our analysis shows, the opposition to discussions of race is not equally shared among members of the community. When the race of the respondents is considered, it is clear that the opposition to discussions of race comes primarily from the white community members. In responding to this community wish, the moderators are indeed responding to a majority—however, that majority is explicitly white. By maintaining the perspective of the white members only, non-white members are not permitted in the discussion and excluded as a result.

Notes

1. Sandvoss, C. *Fans: The Mirror of Consumption*; Polity Press: Cambridge, UK, 2005.

2. Kozinets, R.V. The field behind the screen: Using netnography for marketing research in online communities. *J. Mark. Res., 39*, 61–72.

3. Diamond, N.; Sherry, J.F.; Muniz, A.M.; McGrath, M.A.; Kozinets, R.V.; Borghini, S. American Girl and the brand gestalt: Closing the loop on sociocultural branding research. *J. Mark., 73*, 118–132.

4. Acosta-Alzuru, C.; Lester Roushanzamir, E. Everything we do is a celebration of you! Pleasant Company constructs American girlhood. *Commun. Rev., 6*, 45–69.

5. Acosta-Alzuru, C.; Kreshel, P.J. I'm an American girl...whatever that means: Girls consuming Pleasant Company's American Girl identity. *J. Commun., 52*, 139–161.

6. Medina, V.E. And that's What I Think Being an American Girl is all about! Girls' Reflections on American Girl and Contemporary American Girlhood. Ph.D. Thesis, University of Missouri, Columbia, MO, USA, 2012.

7. Marshall, E. Consuming girlhood: Young women, femininities, and American Girl. *Girlhood Stud., 2*, 94–111.

8. Stalp, M.C.; Williams, R.; Lynch, A.; Radina, M.E. Conspicuously consuming: The Red Hat society and midlife women's identity. *J. Contemp. Ethnogr.*, *38*, 225–253.

9. Rafaeli, S.; Ravid, G.; Soroka, V. De-Lurking in Virtual Communities: A Social Communication Network Approach to Measuring the Effects of Social and Cultural Capital. In Proceedings of the Annual Hawaii International Conference on System Sciences, Big Island, HI, USA, 5–8 January 2004. Available online: http://www.unhas.ac.id/~rhiza/arsip/jarkomsos/lurkers.pdf (accessed on 22 January 2013).

10. Hines, C. Virtual Ethnography: Modes, Varieties, Affordances. In *The SAGE Handbook of Online Research Methods*; Fielding, N., Lee, R.M., Blank, G., Eds.; SAGE: London, UK, 2008.

11. Acosta-Alzuru, M.C. The American Girl Dolls: Constructing American Girlhood through Representation, Identity, and Consumption. Ph.D. Thesis, University of Georgia, Athens, GA, USA, 1999.

12. Nakamura, L. *Cybertypes: Race and Ethnicity on the Internet*; Routledge: New York, NY, USA, 2002.

13. Nakamura, L. *Digitizing Race: Visual Cultures of the Internet*; University of Minnesota Press: Minneapolis, MN, USA, 2007.

14. Bobo, L.; Sidanius, J.; Sears, D.O. *Racialized Politics: The Debate about Racism in America*; University of Chicago Press: Chicago, IL, USA, 2000.

15. Miller, K.D.; Fabian, F.; Lin, S. Strategies for online communities. *Strat. Manag. J.*, *30*, 305–322.

REFLECT AND CONSIDER

- Compare and contrast racial discrimination in visual media versus online virtual spaces.
- Explain the racialized patterns that exist in the online forums.

FEAR OF A BLACK ATHLETE: MASCULINITY, POLITICS AND THE BODY

BY BEN CARRINGTON

There is one expression that through time has become singularly eroticized: the black athlete

Frantz Fanon, *Black Skin, White Masks*

At the start of the twenty-first century the salience of 'race' appears at once both opaque and ubiquitous. The facts of blackness, or the lived experiences of being black in the new century, are no longer marked by an invisibility within the public sphere that once so clearly expressed black peoples' lack of social power. Official discourse within the West readily promotes and even minimally endorses the mantras of 'equal opportunities', 'diversity' and 'multiculturalism' as unmistakable public goods. Mainstream media culture too is dominated by black faces and bodies, from the sports fields and fashion catwalks, to our cinematic screens and music video channels, and even (occasionally) within the cultural spaces of award ceremonies for novelistic and avant-garde artistic production. Consumers can now enjoy the spectacle of blackness in a way which is no longer threatening by its mere presence, for those who now actively desire a taste for 'a bit of the other'. Yet alongside the rush to embrace this putative post-race utopia, the material and ideological effects of racial inequality, discrimination and violence continue to brutally manifest themselves within the public and private spheres of Western liberal democracies. The spectacle of 'hyperblackness' itself unwittingly reveals the psychic investments that such racialised identifications produce in projecting colonial discourses about the racial Other forwards into the post/colonial present.

This article maps some of these ambivalent tendencies by tracing the continuities of racial ideologies as they are articulated within aspects of contemporary media culture. It is suggested that historical colonial fantasies about the excesses of black sexuality continue to exercise a hegemonic role in the representation of blackness. It is also argued that the black (male) body has come to occupy a central metonymic site through which notions of 'athleticism' and 'animalism' operate, and that the athletic black body in particular remains deeply inscribed into the psychic imaginary of the West. These tropes of blackness provide the discursive boundaries within which the black subject is still framed. The argument proceeds via a reading of cultural texts within present-day media culture. It examines their effects in reinforcing racial hierarchies, and the distinctive corporeal patterns of identification they generate. The essay ends by tracing the implications of the contemporary commodification of the black body for transformative subaltern politics and the extent to which black vernacular cultures can still offer modes of resistance.

The Politics of Representation

The body now occupies a central position within both social theory and contemporary media culture.[1] Attention to representation allows us to map dominant ideologies as they circulate through culture and reproduce themselves as sites for the interpellation of individuals into specific gendered, classed, and racialised subjectivities. By examining 'the symbolic significance of the body as a metaphor of social relationships'[2] we can trace the meanings embedded within cultural representations of particular bodies, and how these operate to sustain specific power relationships between groups and therefore influence lived cultures. As Stuart Hall notes, 'cultural meanings are not only "in the head". They organise and regulate social practices, influence our conduct and consequently have real, practical effects'.[3] Exposing and exploring the representation of certain types of bodies enables us to understand the inherently political process of representation itself. This is particularly the case with social groups that battle over the way they are perceived by others—in trying to break free from, or challenge, stereotypes—and how they are then able to perceive themselves. As Richard Dyer points out, how particular social groupings are portrayed within cultural representation 'is part and parcel of how they are treated in life, that poverty, harassment, self-hate and discrimination (in housing, jobs, educational opportunity and so on) are shored up and instituted by representation'.[4] Dyer continues by suggesting that how we are seen as subjects 'determines in part how we are treated; how we treat others is based on how we see them; such seeing comes from representation'.[5] We can understand stereotyping as an effect of power—as a discursive strategy that attempts to establish particular subject positions as fixed, often degenerate types, as a way of legitimating social hierarchies and inequalities. It is important then to view the process of representation as a primary site for the construction and constitution of identities, collective and individual, rather than merely being a secondary reflection of already formed social identities. It is therefore also a point at which the attempt to secure dominant relations may be resisted and challenged,

The Racial Signification of Sport

bell hooks suggests that historically, 'competition between black and white males has been highlighted in the sports arena'.[6] This is not surprising given that sport is one of the few arenas for public displays of open competition, domination and control. Many accounts of the historical development and significance of sports during the nineteenth and early twentieth centuries within the United States of America, Canada and Western Europe have suggested that sport acted as a key social institution whereby 'manly virtues and competencies' could be both learned and displayed as a way of avoiding wider social, political and economic processes of 'feminisation'.[7] The rapid growth of organised sports during this period is seen 'as the creation of a homosocial institution which served to counter men's fears of féminisation in the new industrial society'[8] and helped to 'naturalise', by its overt emphasis on the 'obvious' fact of biological difference, men's collective power in society.

Although it is a homosocial space, mainstream competitive sport is of course profoundly homophobic. This apparent contradiction is resolved by the formation of explicit and implicit rules governing the degree of intimate bodily contact within sports that disavows the inherently homoerotic possibilities of sports contests (with its codes of domination and penetration) even as the participants engage in activities that outside of the sports arena are prohibited by dominant heterosexual masculinity. As Brian Pronger notes, despite sport's 'inner libidinal logic', homoeroticism is controlled 'as an excess to the system by a comprehensive, unwritten but well-known and closely adhered-to set of rules' that can be seen to govern and restrict 'the nature of caresses, hugs, and kisses on the playing field, not to mention the display of erections, erotic massage, masturbation, fellatio, and buggery in locker rooms, showers, washrooms, sleeping accommodation, or at team socials'.[9] Thus the potentially disruptive challenge to normative gender codes are resolved by the governance of inter-male desire, meaning that 'sportsmen (and boys) can play with each other's bodies in highly erotic and intimate ways without that desire becoming other to the system of masculinist hetero-normativity that sport produces'.[10] Thus the ideological values of sport constructed a homosocial space within which femininity was degraded, women excluded and heterosexist norms embedded. Given this, sport's symbolic space offered opportunities for those marginalised by hegemonic masculinity to challenge dominant projections of white, middle-class, male heterosexuality—even as male power was being consolidated in formal economic and political life—and became a highly charged regulatory social space.

Sports are also, of course, a context in which black bodies can be gazed upon, safe in the knowledge that the circumscribed arena of the sports field provides a legitimate space for such racialised homosocial encounters.[11] It is evident that colonial myths about black power have been most clearly expressed in the discourse of the 'tough' black athlete making the *athletic black body* a key repository for contemporary white male desires and fears about blackness.[12] Sport can be viewed as a mechanism for the production of temporally bounded space that is delimited by desire itself.

What we might term the 'racial signification of sport' means that sports contests are more than just significant sporting events. Rather, they act as a key signifier for wider questions about identity within racially demarcated societies in which narratives about the self and society are read both *into* and *from* sporting contests involving racial competition. Though this is rarely publicly acknowledged, the racial signification of sport means that success by black athletes has profound effects on the white male imaginary. Black male achievement in two of the most prized sports, the men's Olympic 100 metres in athletics and the World Heavyweight Championship in boxing, clearly poses a threat to white hegemonic masculinity. The perennial search for the 'Great White Hope' first emerged as a term after Jack Johnson's successes at the beginning of the twentieth century. That this phrase is still part of common sports lore reveals the almost desperate longing for *any* white man to reclaim the mantle of masculinity that the Heavyweight Champion of the World is meant to bestow, and also the pain caused to the white male psyche of black success in sport.

Occasionally however the hidden racialised meanings of competitive sport are revealed. American basketball player, Dennis Rodman, for example, has said 'when you talk about race in basketball, the whole thing is simple: *a black player knows he can* go out on the court and *kick a white player's ass*. He can beat him, and he knows it. It's that simple, and it shouldn't surprise anyone. The black player feels it every time. He knows it from the inside'.[13] And witness also the earlier, unguarded, remarks by the white British boxer Alan Minter before his comprehensive defeat at the hands of Marvin Hagler, when he remarked, 'I have spent many years reaching the world title. I have no intention of letting a black man take it from me'.[14] When challenged about his comments, Minter made the somewhat spurious defence that he had, of course, been misquoted and what he had actually said was that he would never allow *this particular* black man to beat him.[15]

The sports media in particular have played a central role in biologising black performance via their constant use of animalistic similes to describe black athletes. Black athletes—female and male—are invariably described as being strong, powerful and quick but with unpredictable and 'wild' moments when they supposedly lack the cognitive capabilities—unlike their white peers—to have 'composure' at critical moments. Previous sports journalists were less circumspect than their modern equivalents in their use of language in which heroic qualities which would otherwise enhance the *human* capacities of the athlete are instead read as intrinsic reflexes of the unthinking black body. Paul Gallico, the *New York Times* sports editor, described Joe Louis, before one fight, as, 'the magnificent animal ... He eats. He sleeps. He fights ... Is he all instinct, all animal? Or have a hundred million years left a fold upon his brain? I see in this colored man something so cold, so hard, so cruel that I wonder as to his bravery. Courage in the animal is desperation. Courage in the human is something incalculable and divine'.[16]

This colonial discourse still has a contemporary resonance in framing 'deviant' aspects of black masculinity. When, in June 1997, Mike Tyson engaged in the wrong sort of violence in biting his opponent Evander Hollyfteld's ear during their Heavyweight Championship clash, the British print media went into a frenzy in projecting discourses of bestial animalism onto Tyson. The incident was deemed of such international and political importance that it dominated not only the sports leaders but the front pages of nearly all the British broadsheet and tabloid papers, most with colour photographs of a missing lobe of Hollyfield's ear, complete with blood, and a snarling Tyson. The *Mirror* headline proclaimed 'Ban Beast' Tyson', whilst the *Independent's* Sport section counterpoised a jubilant 'all- white' Tim Henman against the black robed Tyson, under the caption 'Beauty and the beast: Britain's Tim Henman brings a smile to Centre Court while Mike Tyson descends to new levels of savagery'. The *Express* avoided any ambiguity and simply called Tyson a 'Monster' in its Sports Special. Whilst the paper actually lead with the headline 'Savage' on its main front page. Lest we be unsure of how Tyson should be viewed the opening paragraph to the lead story read, 'When Mike Tyson's career started it carried the mark of greatness. Effectively, it has ended with that of the beast'.

It is interesting, given the arguments presented here concerning the intersection of 'race', gender and sexuality in the maintenance of racial typologies, that Frantz Fanon himself demonstrates the centrality of sport, and the black athlete in particular, as a discursive field where these fantasies are most clearly projected. When Fanon gives his white patients a word association test, it is significant to note how often his respondents mention either sports, or prominent black athletes of the period, Fanon informs us that the word, 'Negro brought forth biology, penis, strong, athletic, potent, boxer, Joe Louis, Jesse Owens, Senegalese troops, savage, animal, devil, sin'.[17] For Fanon, the black male was the repository of white fears, fantasies and desires, and of all of these constructions, there was one figure above all others that held a central place within the colonial imaginary: 'There is one expression that through time has become singularly eroticized: the black athlete'.[18]

From Subhuman to Superhuman

Given the myths generated by European colonialism that continue to inform contemporary white views about black men and the central iconic place of the black male torso, various Western media's use of black athleticism and animalism should not be surprising. The black male is seen to be the embodiment of hyper-masculinity—ultra violent and the ultimate manifestation of phallic power, whose 'hyperbolic virility' signifies black masculinity as a *surplus* and therefore a threat to the 'white male corporeal ego'.[19] As argued earlier, one of the central components to the emasculating discourses of white racism is an attempt to simultaneously dehumanise and sexualise the black male body. As Fanon argued, the black man is thus reduced to his biological essence: 'The Negro symbolizes the biological'.[20] The logical conclusion to this sexualised discourse is that, via the processes of objectification, the black man is effectively reduced to the phallus: 'one is no longer aware of the Negro but only of a penis; the Negro is eclipsed. He is turned into a penis. He *is* a penis'.[21]

The black athlete assumes the pre-eminent position as a 'penis-symbol' and becomes a phantasmatic site through which anxieties concerning the fragility of Western sexuality are played out. The black athlete is thus positioned as a site for voyeuristic admiration—the black male athlete is idolised for his sheer (super-human) physicality but also controlled by a complex process of objectification and sexualisation that once again renders the dangerous black male threat controllable to white patriarchy. The fear of the black athlete as a commodity-sign is thus appropriated and consumed by its use within contemporary consumer society and its attendant media culture. As bell hooks argues, 'it has taken contemporary commodification of blackness to teach the world that this perceived threat, whether real or symbolic, can be diffused by a process of fetishization that renders the black masculine "menace" feminine through a process of patriarchal objectification'.[22]

Within the post/colonial present, the binary structure of contemporary stereotypes means that the black body becomes either *sub*-human or *super*-human—never just common, never ordinary, never defined by its unspectacular *humanity*. In the 1996 Atlanta Olympics, as Michael Johnson broke the world 200 metre record (and the last remaining track record held by a white male athlete), the BBC sports commentator David Coleman repeatedly screamed to viewers, 'This man, surely, is not human!' The 'super-human' achievements of white athletes, such as five times gold medal winning Olympian Steve Redgrave, are rarely labelled as such. White athletes' humanity is already grounded in their whiteness, making their achievements all the more remarkable. Black sporting success is something that is praised, but in a way that divorces black athletes' achievements from their (universal) humanity. Black people become, in effect, almost freaks of *nature* in their extraordinarily brilliant performances requiring implausible explanations of black physicality that ultimately serve to devalue their feats.[23] We are told that Michael Jordan can actually 'hang in the air' longer than real humans, or that the parameters of the sports themselves must be changed to prevent unfair advantages to these super-human athletes—such as the course designs that are now deemed 'necessary' to hold back Tiger Woods. The colonial discourses that once denied black peoples' humanity re-emerge now to mark the same shift in lifting the black body upwards and beyond the realm of the human once again. As Gilroy argues, the celebrated aspects of physicality that black athletes enjoy means that 'in moving from the infrahuman to the superhuman', they are carried 'beyond the human altogether'.[24]

Notes

1. For a review of the place of the body within social theory and the problematic role of 'embodiment', see Chris Shilling, 'The Embodied Foundations of Social Theory', in G. Ritzer, and B. Smart (eds), *Handbook of Social Theory*, London, Sage, 2001. Cheryl Cole provides a useful summary of sport sociology approaches to the body in 'Body Studies in the Sociology of Sport: A review of the field', in J. Coakley and E. Dunning, (eds), *Handbook of Sports Studies*, London, Sage, 2000.

2. Bryan Turner, 'Preface', in P. Falk, *The Consuming Body*, London, Sage, 1994, pviii.

3. Stuart Hall, 'Introduction', in S. Hall (ed), *Representation: Cultural representations and signifying practices*, London, Sage, 1997, P3.

4. Richard Dyer, *The Matter of Images: Essays on representations*, London, Routledge, 1993, pi.

5. Ibid.

6. bell hooks, *Outlaw Culture: Resisting representations*, London, Routledge, 1994, p31. It is important to remember though that most of the major American sports remained segregated until the 1960s. In Britain too, black boxers were prohibited from fighting for British titles until 1948.

7. For sociological analyses on the historical development of sport see Eric Dunning, *Sport Matters: Sociological studies of sport violence and civilisation*, London, Routledge, 1999; Rick Gruneau, *Class, Sports and Social*

Development, Leeds, Human Kinetics, 1999, 2nd ed; and John Hargreaves, *Sport, Power and Culture*, Cambridge, Polity Press, 1986. For an account that remains more attuned to the specifically *gendered* nature of sport's position as a 'male preserve' see Jenny Hargreaves, *Sporting Females: Critical issues in the history and sociology of women's sports*, London, Roudedge, 1994. As yet no sufficiently theorised account of sport's historical role in reproducing racialised forms of identification and racial inequality has been written.

8. Michael Messner, *Power of Play: Sports and the problem of masculinity*, Boston, Beacon, 1992, p14.

9. Brian Pronger, 'Homosexuality and Sport: Who's winning?', in J. McKay, M. Messner, and D. Sabo (eds), *Masculinities, Gender Relations, and Sport*, London, Sage, 2000, pp236–7. For a historical account of the erotic in sport see Allen Guttmann, *The Erotic in Sports*, New York, Columbia University Press, 1996. For a more sophisticated theoretical explication of these issues see Toby Miller's *Sportsex*, Philadelphia, Temple University Press, 2001.

10. Pronger, ibid., p237. Notions of phallocentric anxiety are also pursued in Toby Miller's suggestive essay, A Short History of the Penis', in *Technologies of Truth: Cultural citizenship and the popular media*, London, University of Minnesota Press, 1998.

11. On the role of the basketball court as a hypergendered space of transcendence, see Elizabeth Alexander's analysis of the popular film *White Men Can't Jump*, "'We're Gonna Deconstruct Your Life!'": The making and un-making of the black bourgeois patriarch in *Ricochet'*, in M. Blount and G. Cunningham (eds), *Representing Black Men*, London, Routledge, 1996.

12. The use of the term 'white male' refers to the totalising discourses that produce such subject positions; or as Mercer notes, 'the political problem of power represented by straight white males is a problem not about persons but about ideological subject-positions that reproduce relations of oppression', in Kobena Mercer, 'Fear of a Black Penis', *Artforum*, VoL 32, April, 1994, p81. On the racialised nature of masculine contestation see, Paul Hoch, *White Hero, Black Beast: Racism, sexism and the mask of masculinity*, London, Pluto Press, 1979. See also Tony Jefferson, 'Muscle, 'Hard Men' and 'Iron' Mike Tyson: Reflections on desire, anxiety and the embodiment of masculinity', *Body and Society*, 4, 1 (March 1998), pp77–98.

13. Dennis Rodman, *Bad As I Wanna Be*, New York, Delacorte Press, 1996, p129.

14. *London Evening News*, 21.08.80, quoted in Ellis Cashmore, *Black Sportsmen*, London, Routledge, 1982, p182.

15. Cited in Funmilago Kolaru, *Real Men Wear Black: The socio-legal significance of black male athletes in the West*, unpublished Masters Thesis, University of Kent at Canterbury, 1995.

16. Quoted in Jay Coakley, *Sport in Society: Issues and controversies*, London, McGraw-Hill, 1998, p258.

17. Frantz Fanon, *Black Skin, White Masks*, London, Pluto Press, 1986[1952], p166.

18. Ibid, p158.

19. Kaja Silverman, *The Threshold of the Visible World*, London, Routledge 1996, p 31.

20. Fanon, *Black Skin, White Masks*, op. cit., p167.

21. Ibid., p170.

22. hooks, *Feminism Inside*, op. cit., p131.

23. See Ella Shohat and Robert Stam, *Unthinking Eurocentrism: Multiculturalism and the media*, London, Routledge, 1994, p21. The stereotype of the naturally athletic black body is of course an 'impossible object'. Hence, despite being unable to find the non-existent 'running/jumping gene(s)' that are supposed to be lurking within the skins of Kenyan long distance runners, or 'West African descendant' sprinters, sport scientists still yearn for the magic piece of genetic machinery that will one day prove their fantasies of biological racial difference.

24. Gilroy, *Between Camps*, op. cit, p 348–9. There is a strange and contradictory shift within the racialised regime of representation that posits black bodies as super-human machines until we reach prison/police cells, where disproportionate numbers of black males have died at the hands of police and prison officers.

REFLECT AND CONSIDER

- Explain how sport is an institution where racial ideologies are created and maintained.
- How is the "black athletic body" both praised and dehumanized?

THE NATIVE AMERICAN EXPERIENCE: RACISM AND MASCOTS IN PROFESSIONAL SPORTS

BY KRYSTAL BEAMON

Contemporary Racism in Sports: Native American Symbols as Mascots

Native American mascots have remained a common fixture in the world of athletics at all levels from peewee leagues to professional teams. The Washington Redskin has been the mascot of one of the most popular NFL teams, located in our nation's capital, since 1932. The term is considered a disparaging reference to many Native American people. According to Stapleton (2001), "redskin" is a term with a 400-year history and first emerged in sport during a time when the American government actively sought to assimilate Native Americans. In his book *Skull Wars*, Thomas (2000) writes,

> There is today no single word more offensive to Indian people than the term "redskins," a racial epithet that conjures up the American legacy of bounty hunters bringing in wagon loads of Indian skulls and

corpses—literally the bloody dead bodies were known as "redskins"—to collect their payments.

(p. 204)

Although many Native Americans are offended by the term, 88 percent of Americans surveyed oppose a name change for the team (Sigelman 2001).

In a survey of the top 10 most common team mascots, most were birds or beasts of prey, with the exception of two: "Warriors" and "Indians" (Franks 1982). The only two nickname categories that are not predatory animals refer to Native Americans. Many would ask, what's the problem? Are we not honoring indigenous people for being such fierce warriors?

To perceive Native Americans through the eyes of mascots and sports nicknames creates a myopic and inaccurate version of the rich traditions, culture, history, and contemporary existence of the population. Native American mascots are based on the stereotypical "Cowboy and Indian" Wild West images of America's indigenous peoples, with no regard for the diverse cultures and religious beliefs of tribal groups. This manner of stereotyping Native Americans began very early upon European contact. Colonizers portrayed "Indians" as "barbaric," "wild," "bestial," and most of all "savage" (Berkhofer 1978). In fact, Americans' view of "Indians" as predatory beasts has been ingrained from the inception of our nation. George Washington wrote that "Indians" were "wolves and beasts who deserve nothing from whites but total ruin," and President Andrew Jackson stated that troops should seek out "Indians" to "root them out of their dens and kill Indian women and their whelps" (Stannard 1992: 240–41). Racist and dehumanizing descriptions produced mass fear of Native Americans as an entire race or category of people. This fear negates the concept of "honoring" tribes as the basis for naming teams as fierce warriors or other Native American-derived images.

As America grew, these stereotypes were used to justify the systematic genocide of Native Americans, as they were seen as a threat to the safety of colonizers. These images remain a part of American culture, as many Americans continue to visualize the image of a "savage warrior" with feathers and war paint when thinking of Native Americans. One can go into any costume shop and find a Native American costume complete with tomahawk and a feathered headdress. These images have become embraced by **popular culture** and controlled by the **dominant group** instead of Native Americans themselves.

Activism around Native American Imagery

Native American mascots and the use of Native American imagery in advertising and branding (i.e., Land O'Lakes butter, Sue Bee honey, Jeep Cherokee, Crazy Horse Malt Liquor, Winnebagos) grew during the era of racial segregation and legalized discrimination in America (Meerskin

2012). The use of Native American peoples as mascots ranges from generic titles such as Indians, Braves, Warriors, or Savages to specific tribal designations such as Seminoles, Apaches, or Illini. These have been prevalent since the turn of the century, at a time when Little Black Sambo, Frito Bandito, and other racially insensitive branding was commonplace in "less enlightened times" (Graham 1993: 35). While Little Black Sambo and Uncle Rastus have long since been abandoned, the equally insensitive **Chief Wahoo** remains. These images exaggerate physical and cultural aspects of Native Americans and reduce them to one stereotypical representation: savage warrior.

The fight to remove the stereotypical images of Native American mascots and nicknames in sport has been active for nearly four decades. It occurred alongside the **civil rights movement** of the 1960s as the **National Congress of American Indians (NCAI)** began to challenge the use of stereotypical imagery in print and other forms of media (Staurowsky and Baca 2004). The use of Native American mascots also fell under attack when this campaign was launched in 1968. NCAI contended that the use of Native American imagery was not only racist but further reproduced the perception of Native American peoples as sub-human. By 1969 universities began to respond, as Dartmouth College changed its nickname from "the Indians" to "Big Green." Many followed suit, including the universities of Oklahoma, Marquette, and Syracuse, which all dropped Indian nicknames in the 1970s. Currently, an estimated 1,000 academic institutions have relinquished use of Native American mascots or nicknames.

Other institutions have resisted and remain invested in retaining their racist mascots. Close to 1,400 high schools and 70 colleges and universities have refused to cede to calls for change (Staurowsky and Baca 2004). Although Native Americans protest at every home opener with signs that read "We are human beings, not Mascots," MLB's Cleveland Indians maintain the use of the caricatured Chief Wahoo. The Washington Redskins have lost trademark protection, but continue to fight through litigation to maintain the use of the team's mascot. The University of Illinois Fighting Illini fought to maintain their mascot, **Chief Illiniwek**, amid major controversy for over a decade before finally retiring the chief in 2007. The Florida State Seminoles also maintain the use of their Native American imagery, citing an endorsement from the Seminole tribe as justification. All argue that they are honoring the history of Native Americans by using them as mascots. For example, the Cleveland Indians proclaim that the team's designation was chosen to honor the first Native American to play professional baseball, Louis Francis Sockalexis. The University of Illinois argued that their mascot was an honor to the extinct tribe that once inhabited the state. Although Florida State University has been given "permission" to maintain the use of its mascot and nickname by the Seminole tribe and its chief, "there are American Indians protesting outside every Florida State game, including some Seminole people. They say the mascot looks like a Lakota who got lost in an Apache dressing room riding a Nez Perce horse" (Spindel 2002: 16).

Many organizations using Native American designations argue that some Native American individuals and tribal groups have no issue with the use of the mascots and indeed feel a sense of pride. And many fans of these teams agree. In his study of local public opinion, Callais (2010) found that supporters of retaining Native American mascots base their position on maintaining tradition and promoting a color-blind society through a tribute to Native Americans.

While some individual tribes and persons may approve of this practice, all major Native American organizations have denounced it and called for a cessation of the use of their images as mascots, nicknames, and in the branding of products. Mascots are "manufactured images" of Native Americans, and their continued promotion results in a loss of power to control use of those images.

> Indigenous mascots exhibit either idealized or comical facial features and "native" dress, ranging from body-length feathered (usually turkey) headdresses to more subtle fake buckskin attire or skimpy loincloths. Some teams and supporters display counterfeit Indigenous paraphernalia, including tomahawks, feathers, face paints, and symbolic drums and pipes. They also use mock Indigenous behaviors such as the tomahawk chop, dances, chants, drumbeats, war-whooping, and symbolic scalping.
>
> (Pewewardy 1999: 2)

These images were manufactured by their respective schools, universities, and teams. They were created in the minds of those who established them during a time of racial hatred, stereotyping, and when Native Americans were seen as a threat (Callais 2010). The "costumes" of the mascots are derived from stereotypical and widely oversimplified views of a diverse group of people. In reality, each feather and bead, the facial paint, and especially the dances have a distinct, significant, deeply spiritual, and religious meaning to each tribal group. Particular dances mark "the passage of time, the changing of the seasons, a new status in a person's life" and "dancing expresses and consolidates a sense of belonging" (Spindel 2002: 189). In the eyes of many Native Americans, to put on the "costume" and perform a "war dance" at halftime is to mock their religion. How would it go over to have a team designated the "Black Warriors" with a mascot named Chief Watutsi dressed in a loincloth dancing around with a spear? While this mascot would not probably last a single day, Native Americans have been unable to have the use of their images stopped, despite a 40-year struggle to do so.

All in Fun?

Charlene Teters, the Native American activist who called national attention to the University of Illinois fighting Illini, describes how her children reacted when they first witnessed Chief Illiniwek in the documentary *In Whose Honor* (Rosenstein 1997). She describes her son sinking into his chair as he tried to become "invisible." One of the primary arguments against the use of Native American mascots is how it affects children of all races, but especially Native American children. The flippant and inaccurate depiction of Native American culture and identity "causes many young indigenous people to feel shame about who they are as human beings" (Pewewardy 1999: 342). These feelings become a part of the identity and self-image of Native American children, working together with the objective experiences of poverty and deprivation to create low self-esteem and high rates of depression (Pewewardy 1999). One in five Native American youth attempts suicide before the age of 20. In fact, suicide is the second leading cause of death for Native American youth between the ages of 15 and 24 (Center for Native American Youth 2012). This is two and a half times higher than the national average. While there are many factors that contribute to this statistic, such as poverty and drug and alcohol abuse, the use of Native American mascots further damages the self-image of Native American youth. Mascots dehumanize Native Americans and present images, sacred rituals, and other symbols in a way that negates the reverence instilled in Native children, thus negatively impacting their self-esteem. In fact, the American Psychological Association (2001) states emphatically that the use of Native American mascots perpetuates stigmatization of the group and has negative implications for perceptions of self among Native American children and adolescents.

For non-indigenous children, the use of Native American stereotypes as mascots perpetuates the mythical "Cowboys and Indians" view of the group. In a study conducted by Children Now, most of the children studied were found to perceive Native Americans as disconnected from their own way of life (Children Now 1999). Debbie Reese, a Nambe' Pueblo who travels across the country educating children and teachers concerning Native American stereotypes, recounts the many times that children described native people as "exotic," "mythical," or "extinct" and asked if she drove cars or rode horses (Spindel 2002: 224). Most Americans do not come into meaningful contact with traditional Native Americans very often, if at all. Thus, these stereotypical images of mascots and mythical beings are how we learn about Native American culture. Unfortunately, they disallow Americans from visualizing "Indians" as real people, but encourage viewing them as fierce warriors or even clowns dancing around with tomahawks, war paint, and feathered headdresses.

Children and adults alike are profoundly influenced by stereotypical images. The **stereotype threat** is a popular social psychological theory that has been researched empirically since introduced to the literature in 1995 (Steele and Aronson 1995). Claude Steele, a Stanford University professor of social psychology, defines a stereotype threat as "the pressure that a person can feel when she is at risk of confirming, or being seen to confirm a negative stereotype about her group" (Steele and Davies 2003: 311). For instance, when women are reminded that they are women, they perform poorly on math tests due to the stereotype that women are not good at math (Spencer, Steele, and Quinn 1999). Applied to the stereotypical images of Native Americans perpetuated through mascots, these violent and trivialized images may be associated with the lowered self-images of Native youth or the current statistic in which violence accounts for 75 percent of deaths among Native Americans between the ages of 12 and 20 (Center for Native American Youth 2012).

The use of Native American mascots is an example of institutional discrimination. Chief Wahoo and other such images have become as American as baseball itself. They are ingrained into the interworking of our society and its institutions. Major societal institutions such as the economy, sports, and education discriminate against Native Americans by continuing to denigrate living human beings through mascots and team designations. Perhaps if the elite levels of sport (professional and intercollegiate) terminated their use of Native American mascots and raised awareness on the issue, K–12 schools would follow suit. This could serve as an instructional piece for schools as they confront the issue of stereotyping, a process that begins early in one's childhood.

The U.S. Civil Rights Commission released a statement in 2001 condemning the use of Native American mascots. In fact, the National Congress of American Indians, American Indian Movement, National Education Association, National Association for the Advancement of Colored People (NAACP), countless state and local school boards, and the American Psychological Association have all issued similar resolutions. Such images and symbols have been found to perpetuate stereotypes and stigmatization, and negatively affect the mental health and behaviors of Native American people (American Psychological Association 2001). As stated by Native American activist Dennis Banks, "what part of ouch do they not understand?" (Rosenstein 1997).

Conclusion

The issues that Native Americans currently experience in sport—underrepresentation and stereotyping—bring us back to the image of sport as contested terrain. While many believe that the use of Native American mascots is a way of paying tribute, many Native Americans themselves battle to gain more control over the portrayal of their own identity. Athletes are often portrayed as "savages" and "animals," images that Native Americans have fought hard to be disassociated from. And while universities and professional teams generate millions of dollars from the sale of merchandise using Native American imagery, "real" Native Americans remain one of the most impoverished racial groups in society. With a group that experiences disproportionately high rates of dropout, obesity, and suicide, perhaps more effort should be spent on encouraging Native American youth athletics participation, which may help reduce these very problems. Furthermore, their heightened level of participation in sport could also result in society adopting a more positive outlook and understanding of Native Americans, an identification that goes beyond equating Native Americans and sports with mascots.

REFLECT AND CONSIDER

- Explain how images of Native Americans, even though praised, are denigrating to the history and contemporary experiences of Native Americans.
- How does mascot imagery affect the psychological health of Native Americans?

HIGHLIGHT

POP CULTURE'S BLACK LIVES MATTER MOMENT COULDN'T COME AT A BETTER TIME

BY STEVEN W. THRASHER, *THE GUARDIAN*

SUMMARY

The Black Lives Matter movement has successfully brought conversations about racial oppression, particularly police brutality, to the forefront. In this article, Thrasher reviews some of the major events around the Black Lives Matter movement, but also brings attention to the many ways in which Blackness is being celebrated in the media. From Black Marvel superheroes to Oscar-winning Ejiofor and the replacement of Jon Stewart with Trevor Noah, there recently have been multiple positive representations of Blacks in popular culture.

EXCERPT FROM
"POP CULTURE'S BLACK LIVES MATTER MOMENT COULDN'T COME AT A BETTER TIME"

Heading into this summer we need black heroes and black superheroes, in art and in real life, more than ever. And lucky for us, they're turning up worldwide in comic books, on movie and TV screens, splashed across canvasses, and shimmying up flagpoles just when we need them. The castings of Michael B Jordan and Chiwetel Ejiofor in Marvel movies might sound disconnected from the Black Lives Matter movement or the toppling of the Confederate flag, but they're not.

 READ THE REST OF THE ESSAY:

bit.ly/cultureguardian

READ, LISTEN, WATCH, INTERACT!

READ

Anti-Defamation and Mascots

National Congress of American Indians

READ AT bit.ly/indianmascot

FAIR—Fairness and Accuracy in Reporting: Race and Racism

FAIR

READ AT http://bit.ly/fairrace

LISTEN

Are Smartphone Apps Making It Easier to Racially Profile?

All Things Considered, 10.15.2015, NPR

LISTEN AT bit.ly/techracism

In Beta Release, Apple Introduces New, Racially Diverse Emojis.

Eyder Peralta, 2.23.2015, NPR

LISTEN AT bit.ly/racialemojis

Matchmakers—Babies Buying Babies

This American Life, 1.18.2008

LISTEN AT bit.ly/babiesrace

WATCH

 Reel Injun
Neil Diamond, Catherine Bainbridge, 2009
AVAILABLE AT bit.ly/ReelInjun

 The Slanted Screen: Asian Men in Film and Television
Jeff Adachi, 2006
AVAILABLE AT bit.ly/slantedscreen

 Reel Bad Arabs: How Hollywood Vilifies a People
Sut Jhally, 2006
AVAILABLE AT bit.ly/reelbadarabs

INTERACT

 Jim Crow Museum of Racist Memorabilia
INTERACT AT bit.ly/jimcrowmuseum

 The Critical Media Project
INTERACT AT bit.ly/criticalmediaproject

CONTEMPORARY SYSTEMS OF OPPRESSION

Many of America's historical racial atrocities are in the past: plantation slavery, Jim Crow segregation, the Chinese Exclusion Act, and Japanese internment. So although at this point of the book you recognize that racism persists in American society, you might also assume that the most severe of oppressive systems are at least behind us. Unfortunately, that is not correct. There are still systems that are created, organized, and structured in ways that specifically provide opportunities and resources to Whites while also managing policies that specifically oppress people of color.

In the previous two book sections, Structured Racial Inequality and Racism in Popular Culture, the readings address the many ways in which people of color face institutional discrimination. From jobs, politics, and housing to movies, Internet, and sports, people of color have to navigate racist ideologies and discriminatory actions. However, in addition to the ways in which institutions are racially biased, there are also systems that are coordinated not only to help Whites but also hurt people of color. In Contemporary Systems of Oppression, the readings examine the systemic and systematic ways that education, imprisonment/deportation, and environmental racism operate to oppress people of color.

In the first piece, Terence Fitzgerald discusses "The State of Our Education," and the achievement gap among Whites, Blacks, and Latinos. Schools that are predominantly attended by Whites are higher achieving due to their greater resources and safer environments, while schools with predominantly Black and Latino students are more likely to fail. In addition, there is a high correlation between the stricter discipline enforced in schools with Black and Latino students and their likelihood to be imprisoned later—what has come to be known as the "school-to-prison" pipeline. Education, which is supposed to be a system to create equal opportunities, is in actuality a system that privileges Whites and disproportionately prepares Blacks and Latinos for the judicial system. In fact, the criminal justice system is so racially and economically biased that it has been labeled the "prison industrial complex." Blacks and Latinos are overrepresented in prison populations, and there are increasingly more private prisons—companies that make profit from imprisoning people. Tanya Golash-Boza, in "The Immigration Industrial Complex," makes a decisive argument that the prison industrial complex is able to continue its corruption because of the ways in which it capitalizes on society's fear of crime, and likewise the immigration industrial complex is able to operate based on fear of foreigners. Policy makers suggest anti-immigrant policies are about making the United States politically and economically safe, while certain labor sectors, deportation centers, and private prisons continue to make massive profits by taking advantage of immigrants and anti-immigrant policies. This type of systemic and systematic oppression is also observed in "green harm," the macro and micro ways in which people of color disproportionately suffer the consequences of environmental degradation. Emily Gaarder, in "Evading Responsibility for Green Harm," analyzes some manifestations of green harm, including negligent corporation policies, the disposal of trash and toxic waste, and poor water quality. Solutions to green harm usually place the blame on individuals, but Gaarder argues that public policies and corporate responsibility must be at the center of plans to address environmental inequality. The Highlight in this section, "5 Links Between Higher Education and the Prison Industry," illustrates the disturbing connections between the two systems of education and prison, which result in oppression, not freedom.

AS YOU READ

- Compare and contrast old systems of oppression with contemporary systems of oppression.
- Chart the democratic goals of these systems and the racially biased outcomes that are produced in reality.
- Analyze how these systems of oppression are connected with one another.

THE STATE OF OUR EDUCATION

BY TERENCE FITZGERALD

To Whom It May Concern ... Keep This Nigger-Boy Running.

—Ralph Ellison

The Coalition of Schools Educating Boys of Color (COSEBOC) in 2007 stated that Black men suffer from the largest achievement gap of any racial or ethnic group in the United States.[1] Twice as many Black women receive college and university degrees than Black men.[2] The COSEBOC in 2009 went on to state that Black young men were twice as likely as their White counterparts to drop out of high school.[3] And the achievements of Black males while in school are far below those of other demographics.

There has been a lot of speculation about the causes of these achievement disparities. Some have speculated that the academic gap between students of color and White students is primarily due to socioeconomic factors, not racial disparities.[4] But studies show that this is not the case. A case study in 2009 looked at the performance of both White and Black male students who were eligible for free and reduced lunches at school because of their low socioeconomic status (SES). Among these SES-matched students, Black male students academically performed twenty points lower than their White counterparts. The study also compared White and Black males who did not receive free and reduced lunches; in this cohort, Black students performed eleven points lower than their White counterparts. Other studies show these same discrepancies in middle-class and affluent populations. Blacks from affluent suburban areas suffer from the same concerns as poor urban students. And Black and Latino students from middle-class homes ranked last in comparison with White and Asian students of equivalent SES backgrounds.[5]

Clearly there is more than SES at work here. All of these studies indicate that low Black and Latino achievement is linked to something more than just the financial status of individual families. Something corrosive is occurring within public education and affecting the development and achievement of people of color, particularly Black males, regardless of social class, resources, funding, and educational opportunities within their immediate environment.

Black Male Underachievement: The Quiet Crisis

Education has been the subject of intense scrutiny in the last decade or so. Government efforts such as the No Child Left Behind Act of 2001 (NCLB) and the Race to the Top program have been followed by extensive media coverage and debate. But while education in general has received great attention, the greatest crisis in education—the underachievement of young Black men—has been almost entirely absent from the debate. A review of the major publishing outlets in the US in the last thirty years—such as *Time* magazine, *Newsweek*, and the *New York Times*—showed only a handful of articles specifically dealing with the plight of Black males in education. One such article was "Native Son" in *Time* magazine, which drew on a comparison between Richard Wright's fictional character Bigger Thomas and the generations of Black males in the 1980s. But such articles are rare and are often written by the same handful of authors.

One of the few outlets to touch on the subject has been Black-oriented and -produced art. In 1993, the film *Menace II Society* was a revelation to young Black men like me who felt a powerful identification with the movie's depiction of a racially insensitive and intolerant White American education system, Black-male-on-Black-male violence, and the consequences of urban poverty. The theme was repeated in hip-hop songs, Black TV shows, and films throughout the 1990s. Although this attention faded as the new century went on, these artistic expressions of a society-wide problem left a profound mark on me and other young Black men of the time.

The Role of School Discipline in Black Underachievement

The difficulties of Black young men in school are based on more than simply test grades or attendance, however. Central to the Black male experience in school is the issue of discipline. During their middle and high school years, Black males are disciplined, suspended, and expelled more frequently than all other demographic groups. This trend is amplified when the student is not only a young man of color but also poor.[6] Most of these suspensions are due to non-violent acts such as abusive language, not attending assigned classes, truancy, and tardiness.[7]

This trend is consistent across the country. In Palm Beach in 2006, Black males were suspended at a 53 percent rate while White males were suspended at a 6 percent rate.[8] During the same year, in places like Milwaukee, San Antonio, and Miami-Dade, Florida, Black males were suspended at rates of 52 percent, 42 percent, and 41 percent, respectively, rates far above the rates of their White peers. In Washington, DC, administrators blame the dismal 41 percent graduation rate of Black males on the extremely high rate of suspensions.[9]

It's important to remember that suspensions and expulsions are not awarded on objective criteria. It's easy to think that such disciplinary measures are earned, but this is often not the case. While writing this chapter, I was confronted with the truth of this when my quiet twelve-year-old nephew was suspended from middle school. My nephew and a fellow student, a White girl, had been involved in horse play that started when she first hit him. In normal, childlike retaliation, he hit her back and she reported him to the teacher. Soon after he was called to the assistant principal's office and told that he was being suspended. But the White girl who initiated the hitting received no such discipline.

When I heard of my nephew's suspension I drove to his house and asked him to get in the car. We were both quiet until I pulled into the local police station. "They are waiting on you," I said. "Go in and make yourself at home." He was visibly shaken, but I wanted to convey to him the seriousness of even minor physical altercations. He then let the whole story spill out, admitting his own fault but emphasizing that the girl had started it and had not been punished at all. "She got away with hitting me. The rules are not fair."

"There is no such thing as fair," I told him. "The public school system, like so much of the world, is not fair and wasn't built to be. The quicker you learn this fact, the easier it will be for you to navigate the potholes waiting for you. If you continue to be blind to the ways of the world, this [pointing to the police station] is where this country will send you. And the effects will follow you all the days of your little life."

It pained me to talk to him this way. As one of the few male role models in his life, I had tried to protect him as long as possible from the racial realities of American life. But a pre-teen ready to become a young man sat before me now. I no longer could afford such indulgences. I tried to let him know that the world was his to conquer, but also that he had to understand and navigate the pitfalls of oppression in order to thrive as I knew he could.

Underachievement, Discipline, and the Prison Pipeline

The academic underachievement of young Black males and the systematic overdiscipline in the school system has lifelong consequences for many young men. Educational attainment obviously has a direct effect on the financial, social, and political livelihood of individuals. But for young Black men, their educational experience has an additional consequence: entanglement with the prison system.

Researchers have shown how the chronically guided pathway traveled by incarcerated Black males can be predicted as early as their middle school years.[10] A 2003 study tracked 400 Black males who were incarcerated during their freshman year in high school in a major northwest US city. The author concluded that the young men most likely to end up in the prison system were those who were struggling academically in middle school. These young men attended class only about 58 percent of the school year. They were categorized as reading at a sixth-grade level at the beginning of their ninth grade of school. And they were suspended at least once within their eighth-grade year of school. This study showed more clearly than ever the strong correlation between educational underachievement and eventual imprisonment. And it raised the question: If one could be addressed, could not the other be avoided?

School-sanctioned punishment is an area that harshly affects the state of Black males in education. This area of punishment has ominous effects on the condition of Black males within the criminal justice system. Instead of simply viewing the plight of them in the classroom, one could trace the same area of concern inside local, state, and federal prisons across the country.

"Where does discipline end?" asked Francois Mauriac (1885–1970). "Where does cruelty begin? Somewhere between these, thousands of children inhabit a voiceless hell." Scholars such as Daniel Losen, senior education law and policy associate of the esteemed Civil Rights Project at UCLA, and Russell Skiba, director of the Equity Project, Center for Evaluation and Education Policy at Indiana University, in conjunction with the Southern Poverty Law Center, answered just that question in their report "Suspended Education: Urban Middle Schools in Crisis."[11] The report focused on the racial and socioeconomic inequities in middle school discipline in the US. Overall, the report states, Blacks and Latinos are disproportionately suspended in comparison with their White peers. Zero-tolerance policies have been shown to do more harm than good in relation to these populations. In fact, the implementation of the zero-tolerance policies since the 1970s has been ineffective and racially unfair.[12] The American Civil Liberties Union (ACLU) has gone as far to state that within the US, there exists "a disturbing national trend wherein children are funneled out of public schools and into the juvenile and criminal justice systems."[13] They argue that the creation and increasing use of zero-tolerance discipline policies has created a growing rate of school-based arrests and that placing students in disciplinary alternative schools has impacted students with a history of poverty, neglect, and disabilities.[14]

In the end, policies such as these have marginalized those most at risk while denying them access to education. Even though zero-tolerance policies have had consequential effects on all races, those males who are poor, Black, and Latino are the populations affected the most.[15] The Black male population has been shown to have an increased rate for involvement with the criminal justice system.

Education, Prison, and the New Jim Crow

In 2011, the NAACP reported on six US cities in state and federal prison jurisdictions in a publication titled *Misplaced Priorities: Over Incarcerate, Under Educate*.[16] The report indicated that, over the past thirty years, these six cities had invested more in the incarceration of Blacks and Latinos than in the system that was supposed to educate them. The report simply confirms what researchers and scholars have time and time again shown: the ludicrous and dangerous manner in which the country responds to the social, academic, and mental issues of people of color (specifically males). But this report in particular highlights that the plummeting resources dedicated to public education are matched by the skyrocketing resources dedicated to prisons.[17] In addition, there exists a connection between monies spent and low-performing schools that are located in neighborhoods with high incarceration trends.

For large numbers of Black and Latino males who fall short in surviving the warring confines of public and higher education, the prison system is placed within our society to catch and utilize their attributes. In 1994, 678,300 Black males were locked up in federal, state, and local prisons, for which our country spent $10 billion,[18] whereas 549,600 Black males were enrolled in college during the same year, costing $2.8 billion.[19]

In 2011, 1,598,780 prisoners were incarcerated under state and federal jurisdictions.[20] Of these, 93 percent were male, and 555,300, 331,500, and 465,100 were Black, Latino, and White males, respectively.[21] Some 63 percent of the Black and 69 percent of the Latino incarcerated population are below the age of 39 and thus are imprisoned at a significantly higher rate than White males.[22]

This commitment by the US to imprison Black males is nothing new. Scholars in fields ranging from sociology to education have discussed this topic for decades.[23] Many contend that the US prison system is a modern-day example of a once-thought-dead system in which people of color were permanently forced into a minority caste. From birth on within this designated social placement, individuals guilty of no crime other than being the delegated "other" are seen as inferior.[24] In fact, being a part of a Black minority caste comes with a foundation set in a negative ideology that dictates a set of behaviors, actions, procedures, and policies directed by non-Blacks toward people of color. Operations are increasingly explicit toward Blacks within major institutions such as the judicial system and public and higher education settings. For instance, Black males are used for cheap labor in the context of the prison industrial complex. From the end of the Civil War until World War II, they were subject to involuntary slavery in states such as Alabama, Florida, Mississippi, Louisiana, and Georgia through human labor trafficking for companies involved in pine tar production, coal mines, road construction, timber mills, farm labor, and ditch digging.[25]

The racial caste system many thought was destroyed at the end of the Jim Crow era was in actuality cleaned, redesigned, and made to fit a new time in US history. In order to control those within the Black caste, the criminal justice system came to serve the function of control previously exerted through the operation of Jim Crow. I would propose that this redesign is also seen within public schools since the end of legal segregation. [...]

In terms of education attained by those incarcerated, 41 percent did not receive a high school diploma before entering a correctional facility (68 percent in state prisons).[26] Allen J. Beck and Thomas P. Bonczar in 1997 produced a report called *Lifetime Likelihood of Going to State or Federal Prison* that noted that, within their lifetime, they statistically had a one in four (25 percent) chance of having some personal connection within the prison system.[27] In contrast, Whites and Hispanics/Latinos, respectively, had a one in twenty-three (5.9 percent) and one in six (17.2 percent) likelihood of some involvement with the prison system. In 2001 Bonczar estimated that more than 5.6 million US adults had served a varying amount of time in either state or federal prison systems.

A variance between White and Black males has also been observed from 1974 to 2001.[28] For example, the number of White males incarcerated in state and federal facilities increased from 1.4 percent to 1.9 percent to 2.6 percent in 1974, 1991, and 2001, respectively. In contrast, Black males increased their rate of incarceration from 8.7 percent to 12.0 percent to 16.6 percent in those same years. This amplification would be expected when taking into account that one in every four Black children born in the year 1990 had a parent in prison.[29] Black children born in 1978 had a one in seven chance of having a father "doing time" in prison by their fourteenth year of life.[30] In 1990, the likelihood increased to one in four. Over a twelve-year period from 1978 to 1990, these numbers represented a growth rate of 80 percent. This speaks to a 50 percent rate of growth in comparison with the rates for Black males born in 1945–1949 to 1965–1969.[31] White children, during the same periods of 1978 and 1990, were estimated at one in forty and one in twenty-five, respectively.

Angela Davis argued, "Imprisonment has become the response of first resort to far too many of the social problems that burden people who are ensconced in poverty. These problems often are veiled by being conveniently grouped together under the category of 'crime' and by the automatic attribution of criminal behavior to people of color. Homelessness, unemployment, drug addiction, mental illness, and illiteracy are only a few of the problems that disappear from public view when the human beings contending with them are relegated to cages."[32] I would add that the plight of Black and Brown males in the many correctional facilities across the country is not only a sign of an unwillingness to address social problems but the betrayal of a trusted institutional entity; public education has a dynamic that creates barriers for people of color, specifically Black males, and this dynamic continues for those who later walk upon the college and university campuses.

Notes

1. The Coalition of Schools Educating Boys of Color, "Standards and Promising Practices for Schools Educating Boys of Color: Executive Summary," available at http://coseboc.org/pdfs/Executive_Summary_Standards.pdf.

2. The National Center for Education Statistics, *Status and Trends in Education of Racial and Ethnic Minorities 2008*, available at http://nces.ed.gov/pubs2010/2010015/chapter6.asp.

3. Sharon Lewis, Candace Simon, Renata Uzzell, Amanda Horwitz, and Michael Casserly, *A Call for Change: The Social and Educational Factors Contributing to the Outcomes of Black Males in Urban Schools 2010*, available at http://dl.dropbox.com/u/3273936/A%20Call%20For%20Change-%20Revised.pdf, 22.

4. In general, all non-Whites would be considered people of color. But for the purpose of this book, Blacks, Latinos, and specific Southeast Asian groups are referred to as people of color.

5. John U. Ogbu, *Black American Students in an Affluent Suburb: A Study of Academic Disengagement* (Sociocultural, Political, and Historical Studies in Education) (Mahwah, NJ: Lawrence Erlbaum, 2008). See also Christopher Jencks and Meredith Phillips, *The Black-White Test Score Gap* (Washington, DC: Brookings Institute, 1998).

6. Daniel J. Losen and Russell Skiba, "Suspended Education: Urban Middle Schools in Crisis," available at http://www.splcenter.org/sites/default/files/downloads/publication/Suspended_Education.pdf, 4.

7. Linda M. Raffaele Mendez, "Predictors of Suspension and Negative School Outcomes: A Longitudinal Investigation," in *Deconstructing the School to Prison Pipeline,* ed. Johanna Wald and Daniel J. Losen (San Francisco: Jossey-Bass, 2003), 27.

8. Mendez, "Predictors of Suspension," 6.

9. Kavitha Cardoza, "Report: D.C. Schools Still Struggling to Produce Black Male H.S. Grads," available at http://www.nbcwashington.com/news/local/Report__D_C__Schools_Still_Struggling_to_Produce_Black_Male_H_S__Grads-100965584.html.

10. Losen and Skiba, "Suspended Education," 3.

11. Losen and Skiba, "Suspended Education."

12. Losen and Skiba, "Suspended Education." Zero tolerance relates to school discipline policies that impose removal from school for violent to truancy school violations. This can also be applied to dress code violations.

13. American Civil Liberties Union, *School-to-Prison Pipeline*, available at http://www.aclu.org/racial-justice/school-prison-pipeline.

14. American Civil Liberties Union, *School to Prison Pipeline: Talking Points*, available at http://www.aclu.org/racial-justice/school-prison-pipeline-talking-points.

15. American Civil Liberties Union, *School to Prison Pipeline*, 2–3.

16. National Association for the Advancement of Colored People, "Misplaced Priorities: Over Incarcerate, Under Educate," April 2011, available at http://naacp.3cdn.net/01d6f368edbe135234_bq0m68x5h.pdf.

17. National Association for the Advancement of Colored People, "Misplaced Priorities," 2–3.

18. Tom Mortenson, "Black Males in College or Behind Bars in the US, 1980 to 1994," *Post Secondary Opportunity* 45 (1996): 212.

19. Mortenson, "Black Males in College or Behind Bars."

20. E. Ann Carson and William J. Sabol, *Prisoners in 2011*, available at http://bjs.gov/index.cfm?ty=pbdetail&iid=4559, 2.

21. Carson and Sabol, *Prisoners in 2011*, 26.

22. Carson and Sabol, *Prisoners in 2011*, 27.

23. Thomas P. Bonczar, *Prevalence of Imprisonment in the U.S. Population, 1974–2001*, U.S. Bureau of Justice Statistics, 2003, available at bjs.ojp.usdoj.gov/content/pub/pdf/piusp01.pdf.

24. Michelle Alexander, *The New Jim Crow: Mass Incarceration in the Age of Colorblindness* (New York: New Press, 2010); John U. Ogbu, *Minority Education and Caste: The American System in Cross-Cultural Perspective* (New York: Academic Press, 1978).

25. Alan Whyte and Jamie Baker, "Prison Labor on the Rise in US," available at http://www.wsws.org/articles/2000/may2000/pris-m08.shtml.

26. Caroline Wolf Harlow, *Education and Correctional Populations*, U.S. Bureau of Justice Statistics, 2003, available at bjs.ojp.usdoj.gov/content/pub/pdf/ecp.pdf.

27. Allen J. Beck and Thomas P. Bonczar, *Lifetime Likelihood of Going to State or Federal Prison*, U.S. Bureau of Justice Statistics, 1997, available at http://bjs.ojp.usdoj.gov/index.cfm?ty=pbdetail&iid=1042.

28. Bonczar, *Prevalence of Imprisonment*.

29. Christopher Wildeman, "Parental Imprisonment, the Prison Boom, and the Concentration of Childhood Disadvantage," *Demography* 46 (2009): 265.

30. Wildeman, "Parental Imprisonment," 270–71.

31. Wildeman, "Parental Imprisonment," 271.

32. Angela Davis, *Masked Racism: Reflections on the Prison Industrial Complex*, available at http://colorlines.com/archives/1998/09/masked_racism_reflections_on_the_prison_industrial_complex.html.

REFLECT AND CONSIDER

- How do school policies create a culture of seeing Black men as deviants?
- Can Black and Latino students improve their academic performance within the educational system as it is currently constituted or does this require a structural change in the system?

THE IMMIGRATION INDUSTRIAL COMPLEX

BY TANYA GOLASH-BOZA

The Failure of Crime-Prevention Policy

The parallels between crime-prevention and immigration policies are striking. Despite substantial evidence that being tough on crime does not lead to safer communities, policies have hardly changed in response to this research.[1] In 1998, Angela Davis pointed out that, "Mass incarceration is not a solution to unemployment, nor is it a solution to the vast array of social problems that are hidden away in a rapidly growing network of prisons and jails. However, the great majority of people have been tricked into believing in the efficacy of imprisonment, even though the historical record clearly demonstrates that prisons do not work" (Davis 1998: 3).

The United States has many more people in prison and much longer sentence terms than other Western countries. In the United States, nearly 1 in every 100 people is in prison, which is six to twelve times more than the rates in other Western democracies (Tonry 1999)[2]. This is despite the fact that victimization surveys show that violent and property crime rates are about the same as in other countries. The only sort of crime for which the United States has a higher rate than other countries is gun violence (Tonry 1999). The high rates of incarceration in the United States are not due to higher rates of crime, but to policies designed to "get tough" on crime and drugs. These policies do not serve to reduce crime; rather, they represent "a shift toward a more exclusionary and punitive approach to the regulation of social marginality" (Beckett and Western 2001:55). Moreover, despite the fact that crime rates have declined in recent years, incarceration rates have continued to increase (Mauer 2001).

Incarceration has a limited impact on crime rates. First, it is just one of many factors that influence crime rates; changes in the economy, fluctuations in the drug market, and community-level responses often have more pronounced effects on crime rates. Second, there are diminishing returns to incarceration; incarcerating repeat violent offenders takes these people off the street and thus reduces crime on the streets, whereas incarcerating nonviolent offenders has a minimal effect on crime rates[3] (King, Mauer, and Young 2005). Despite this, the incarceration of nonviolent offenders has skyrocketed in recent decades.

Notwithstanding the low efficacy of imprisoning nonviolent offenders, this is the segment of the prison population that has grown the fastest. Between 1970 and 2000, incarceration rates in the United States increased fivefold. Much of this increase was due to legislation designed to fight drugs. As such, drug offenders represent "the most substantial source of growth in incarceration in recent decades, rising from 40,000 persons in prison and jail in 1980 to 450,000 today" (King, Mauer, and Young 2005: 6). The irony of this is that the incarceration of drug offenders is a highly ineffective way to reduce the number of illegal drugs sold in the United States. When street-level drug sellers are incarcerated, they are quickly replaced by other sellers, because what drives the drug market is demand for drugs (King, Mauer, and Young 2005).

One can also gather evidence from large-scale trends to show that increased incarceration does not decrease crime rates. Between 1998 and 2003, some states greatly increased the number of people they sent to prison, whereas other states did not. The average decrease in crime rates in these states, however, was similar. The states with higher increases in incarceration did not experience more substantial declines in their crime rates (King, Mauer, and Young 2005). Despite the lack of evidence that increased incarceration rates lead to decreased crimes (Lynch 1999), we continue to build prisons and imprison more people (Gilmore 2007). Politicians who invest money in the criminal justice system can claim to their constituents that they are serious about law enforcement. This strategy creates the impression that they have crime victims' interests at heart and has become essential for winning electoral campaigns (Simon 2007). In a similar fashion, politicians who vote in favor of immigration law enforcement can allege that they are in favor of efforts to improve national security.

Immigration Industrial Complex: Fear, Interests, and Other-ization

The discord between rhetoric and reality when it comes to immigration policy points to the importance of using a framework similar to that of the prison and the military industrial complexes to understand the immigration industrial complex. The MIC relies on a fear of war; the PIC relies on a fear of crime; and the immigration industrial complex relies on a fear of foreigners. These respective complexes share three major features:

1. A rhetoric of fear
2. The confluence of powerful interests
3. A discourse of other-ization

Media pundits target undocumented migrants to promote fear, whereas industries such as meatpacking profit from the presence of a marginalized and temporary workforce. Politicians play on fear of immigration to win votes, while voting on immigration policy that is profitable for certain interests in the private sector. This confluence of interests in turn explains why the United States has yet to come up with a viable solution to the "problem" of undocumented migration just as we have yet to solve the drug "problem."

The Media and Fear-Mongering

A key element of the PIC is fear of crime, which is exacerbated by media reports on crime. This fear of crime creates a situation where communities accept the militarization of their neighborhoods, and citizens vote for candidates who promise to be tough on crime. Local news outlets often focus on local violent crimes to attract viewers who want to see sensationalist news (Chermak 1994). This focus on local crime gives the false impression that violent crime is endemic; people who watch local news are more likely to be fearful of crime (Romer, Jamieson, and Aday 2003). In a similar fashion, national news networks have homed in on illegal immigration to attract viewers and have spread misinformation in the process.

News reporters, media pundits, and outspoken "anti-illegal" advocates instill fear in the hearts of people in the United States that our country is being overrun by "hordes" of "invaders" who wish to carry out the "*reconquista*" of the Southwest United States (Buchanan 2006; Huntington 2004). This fear in turn creates a situation in which people accept the increased militarization of both the border and the interior of the United States.

The Media Matters Action Network published a report on the representation of undocumented immigrants on cable news networks, appropriately titled: *Fear and Loathing in Prime Time: Immigration Myths and Cable News*. This report revealed that three shows—*The O'Reilly Factor, Lou Dobbs Tonight,* and *Glenn Beck*—consistently propagate myths about undocumented immigrants. These myths include the alleged criminality of undocumented immigrants, the falsehood that undocumented immigrants don't pay taxes, and the myth that Mexicans plan to carry out a *reconquista* of the United States (Waldman et al. 2008).

All these myths have been addressed by scholarly research. Extensive research by Rubén Rumbaut and his colleagues has demonstrated that immigrants are less likely to commit crimes than the native born; the incarceration rate of the native born was four times the rate of the foreign born in 2006 (Rumbaut et al. 2006). More than half of undocumented workers pay payroll taxes, and everyone pays property and sales taxes (White House 2005). The idea of a *reconquista* is perhaps the domain of a marginalized few, but certainly not the sentiment of most Mexican-Americans (Chavez 2006).

Lou Dobbs in particular is obsessed with the topic of illegal immigration; 70 percent of his shows in 2007 involved a discussion of illegal immigration. With these three shows—*The O'Reilly Factor, Lou Dobbs Tonight,* and *Glenn Beck*—on the air, viewers are consistently exposed to myths about illegal immigration. In the three shows combined, 402 of the shows in 2007 discussed illegal immigration, an average of more than one per day (Waldman et al. 2008).

Perhaps most controversial is these three shows' sensationalist discussion of crime. Discussion of crime took place in 189 of their shows in 2007, an average of more than once every other day. What's more, these hosts misrepresent the criminality of undocumented people. For example, on October 5, 2006, Lou Dobbs said, "Just about a third of the prison population in this country is estimated to be illegal aliens." This is a gross misrepresentation of the reality; less than 6 percent of prisoners are foreign-born, and only some of those are undocumented immigrants. The remaining are naturalized citizens, permanent legal residents, and other visa holders. Glenn Beck put flame to this fire by saying on his show on September 4, 2007, "Every undocumented worker is an illegal immigrant, a criminal, and a drain on our dwindling resources" (Waldman et al. 2008).

The constant propagation of hate-filled rhetoric dehumanizes undocumented migrants and renders them appropriate targets for law enforcement activities. One way this can be seen is in polls Lou Dobbs conducts on his show. On his March 5, 2007, show, Dobbs reported, "Ninety-eight percent of you [viewers] voted that illegal immigration, failed border security, and sanctuary laws are contributing to the rise in gang violence in this country" (Waldman et al. 2008). By consistently presenting undocumented migrants as criminals and dehumanizing them by referring to them as "illegals," these popular media pundits make viewers more likely to favor police action to rid the country of undocumented migrants.

Industry Profits from Undocumented Workers and Immigration Law Enforcement

The presence of undocumented migrants provides media pundits with a target for social discontent. Yet, undocumented workers provide a vital labor force in the United States. Moreover, certain sectors of the labor market depend heavily on undocumented migrants for labor. The undocumented labor force constitutes nearly 5 percent of the civilian labor force in the United States. This includes 29 percent of all agricultural workers, 29 percent of all roofers, 22 percent of all maids and housekeepers, and 27 percent of all people working in food processing (Passel 2006). This high concentration of undocumented migrants in certain sectors means that removing large numbers of undocumented migrants would lead to severe labor shortages in these industries. There is already some evidence that the rise in deportations and increase in border enforcement have negatively affected farm owners across the country. Severe labor shortages have led to the loss of crops, as well as the transfer of production to Mexico.[4] This loss of production, in turn, has ripple costs across the rest of the economy.

Nicholas de Genova (2005) argues that immigration policy in the United States is not designed to deter immigration, but serves to create a deportable migrant labor force. De Genova introduces the concept of "deportability" to describe the condition of undocumented migrants—deportability ensures that some migrants will be deported, but the overwhelming majority will remain, albeit in a socially marginal and vulnerable state (2005). Gilberto Rosas (2006) expands upon the arguments made by De Genova and introduces the concept of "policeability." By this, he means that the militarization of the border has created subjects that are deemed "worthy of dying in the treacherous geographies of the border, or subject to militarized policing, or vigilante actions, or daily forms of surveillance" (413). These concepts of policeability and deportability are useful for understanding the migrant condition and for exploring how the creation of disposable and marginal workers is not only detrimental to migrants, but also advantageous to employers. Punitive immigration policies not only create marginalized subjects, but also are beneficial to employers in certain sectors of the labor market insofar as they create a disposable workforce. The meatpacking industry is a prime example of this.

A quarter of all workers in food processing are undocumented migrants. Over the past two decades, the industry itself has evolved to accommodate a transient, marginalized workforce. A brief discussion of the way that meat is processed in the United States will make it clear that an undocumented workforce is the best suited for work in meatpacking plants in the Midwest.

Furthermore, it is evident there is a benefit to the owners of meatpacking plants that undocumented workers are not eligible for legalization in the United States.

As depicted in Upton Sinclair's *The Jungle* (1985 [1906]), the meatpacking industry has been characterized by grueling conditions for at least a century and has historically used immigrants as its primary source of labor. These two characteristics have changed little in the past hundred years. What *has* changed is that, starting in the 1980s, meatpacking companies began to move their plants away from urban centers and closer to rural areas where livestock abound, especially near small towns in Kansas, Nebraska, Texas, and Colorado. Along with this move, meatpackers changed the way they cut meats. Whereas previously skilled and semi-skilled butchers would cut up the cattle, now the carcasses are moved along a powered chain where each worker is responsible for a specific operation on the carcasses. This new way of processing meat has resulted in a deskilling of the workforce as well as an increase in the rate of production. Plants now process much more meat at a much faster rate than they did just twenty years ago. This efficiency has also led to extremely high rates of turnover and injury in the meatpacking industry. Turnover rates are as high as 100 percent in some plants, and incidences of carpal tunnel syndrome increased 264 percent between 1980 and 1988 (Gabriel 2006; Champlin and Hake 2006).

When Human Rights Watch conducted a study of the meatpacking industry, they found that workers who tried to form trade unions and bargain collectively were "spied on, harassed, pressured, threatened, suspended, fired, deported, or otherwise victimized for their exercise of the right to freedom of association."[5] They also found that many companies took advantage of workers' immigration status and lack of knowledge of their rights as workers in the United States to deny them these rights. Overall, they found the meatpacking industry to be characterized by unsafe working conditions, high rates of injury, and constant abuses from superiors. The changes in the way meat is processed have generated great profits for the largest meat processing firms, while putting smaller firms out of business. It may seem odd that the large meat processing companies moved out of cities with relatively high rates of unemployment to small towns with low unemployment, even given the advantages of being closer to the raw materials—the cattle. From a supply and demand perspective, it would seem that companies would have to pay higher wages to attract workers to areas with low levels of unemployment. The solution to this potential problem is that meat processing is designed in such a manner that workers can be easily trained to process meat at high rates of speed. This in turn causes high rates of injury and turnover. Thus, the meatpacking companies do not need a large, stable workforce, but rather a temporary workforce that is mobile and is willing to work for a few months and then move on. Temporary undocumented migrants are in fact an ideal workforce.

The town of Lexington, Nebraska, provides an example of this trend. Iowa Beef Processors (IBP) opened a large meat processing factory in Lexington in 1990, when the local unemployment rate was about 3 percent. When IBP opened its doors, 81 percent of the people hired were non-Hispanic, and Lexington and the surrounding areas had a low Hispanic population. Two years later, 57 percent of the new hires were Hispanic. Nearly all of these new hires had come from other states to work at IBP. The turnover rate at IBP was about 12 percent per month during its first four years, meaning that the entire workforce was replaced every nine months. While the average length of employment at IBP was eight months, the average employment at Cornland, a smaller plant in Lexington that was put out of business by the competition from IBP, had been thirty-three months (Gouveia and Stull 1997). The exceedingly high turnover rates and harsh working conditions make marginalized undocumented workers an ideal workforce for meatpacking plants. Undocumented migrants are ideal candidates for jobs with high turnover rates, because they are less likely to stay in the community once they are no longer employed there. Also, the marginalization of undocumented workers makes it difficult for them to fight for better working conditions.

Meatpacking industries profit from the *presence* of undocumented workers, insofar as they constitute a vulnerable workforce. A wide range of government contractors, however, directly benefit from immigration law *enforcement* through the profit potential. One sector that has profited from increased immigration enforcement has been the business of privately run immigrant detention centers.

The Corrections Corporation of America (CCA) is one of the main beneficiaries of the increase in immigrant detainees. CCA has a long history of profiting off of incarceration. It won its first government contract in 1984 to run an immigrant detention center in Houston. The company was inching along for the next decade, when it finally began to see substantial profits in the late 1990s. Its annual revenue shot up from $50 million in the early 1990s to $462 million in 1997. By 1998, its stock prices hit $44.00. CCA was doing so well that, at the end of the twentieth century, the company began to build speculative prisons—"excess prison space for inmates who did not yet exist" (Wood 2007: 232). These prisons were built with the expectation that the prison population would continue to grow. When rates of incarceration leveled off at the beginning of the twenty-first century, CCA faced serious problems. Its stock values fell from $44 dollars in 1998 to a mere 18 cents in December 2000. By 2001, CCA had 8,500 empty beds and was more than a billion dollars in debt (Wood 2007). Its rival, Wackenhut, also saw its stock lose a third of its value between 1998 and 2001 (Berestein 2008).

At the end of the twentieth century, the two leading private prison companies—CCA and Wackenhut—faced serious financial troubles. They had reinvested their immense profits in new prisons that were now sitting empty. The increased need for prison beds for immigrant detainees became their saving grace. On the verge of bankruptcy in 2000, CCA was awarded two contracts that allowed it to fill two empty prisons it had built speculatively—one in California City and another in Cibola County, New Mexico (Mattera, Khan, and Nathan 2003). It filled those prisons with immigrant detainees.

With these new contracts, CCA has been able to regain its financial footing. Its stock prices have fluctuated substantially but have generally improved since its low point at the end of 2000. CCA stock reached a new high of $32.40 in May 2007 and stood at about 27 dollars in May 2008. According to financial expert Eric Cheshier (2008), spring 2008 was a good time to buy CCA stock because their prospects for growth were quite positive. As of this writing, in April 2011, Google finance reports CCA stocks to be at $24.01 a share.

Many of CCA's earlier troubles stemmed from their inability to manage higher security prisons and from states cutting back funding for prisons. Thus, CCA began to set its sights on the federal government. By 2002, 32 percent of CCA's revenues came from federal agencies (Mattera, Khan, and Nathan 2003). In the post-9/11 context, the Federal Bureau of Prisons is giving even more contracts to private prison companies. Whereas there were about 15,000 federal inmates in private prisons in 2000, by 2004, there were 24,768 (Wood 2007: 233).

Much of the success of CCA is due to its lobbying efforts and political connections, combined with increased rates of detention for immigrants. Its federal lobbying expenses increased from $410,000 to $3 million between 2000 and 2004, and these efforts appear to have paid off both in terms of CCA filling its beds and gaining contracts to build new prisons (Berestein 2008). In 2007, CCA spent almost $2.5 million to lobby on legislations and regulations related to the private prison industry, and it spent $2 million in 2009.[6] At the beginning of 2000, CCA was awarded a contract to house 1,000 detainees at the CCA-owned San Diego Correctional Facility. CCA was to be paid $89.50 per day for each detainee it held. This was the beginning of a comeback for CCA. In July 2007, CCA announced that it was building a new 1,688 bed correctional facility in Adams County Mississippi, at a cost of $105 million. CCA built this facility without a management contract, because the company did not foresee difficulties in finding people to fill those prison beds. In fact, CCA had plans for 4,500 additional beds in 2007.[7] With the constantly expanding detention of immigrants, CCA could fully expect to fill those beds.

In 2009, CCA was awarded a Federal Bureau of Prisons contract for the facility. By that time, they had expanded the capacity to 2,232 beds. In addition, CCA was constructing a 3,060-bed facility in Eloy, Arizona, that would house immigrant detainees, and a 2,040-bed facility in Trousdale County, Tennessee. And, in 2008, CCA was awarded a contract from the Office of Federal Detention Trustees to build and manage a new correctional facility in Pahrump, Nevada, to house detainees as well as inmates. Business has been booming for CCA.[8]

CCA has been able to obtain favorable government contracts in part because of its ties to current and former elected officials. The former head of the Federal Bureau of Prisons, J. Michael Quinlan, is one of CCA's top executives. Both the CCA and the Geo Group have dominated the private prison sector because of their political influence. "Both benefit from extensive and intimate connections with state and local politics and the public corrections sector as well as from the usual interlocking directorships with other corporations in prison services, construction, the media, and finance" (Wood 2007: 231).

The private prison industry is just one example of how private companies benefit from the increased surveillance and punishment of immigrants. Telephone companies such as MCI and Evercom have significant contracts inside immigrant detention centers, where they charge exponentially more for phone calls than they do at phones not in prisons (Fernandes 2006: 198). Overall, DHS awards billions of dollars of contracts each year. Many of the names are familiar: Lockheed Martin, Northrop Grumman, Boeing, IBM, Unisys and, not surprisingly, Halliburton. In January 2006, the DHS awarded a $385 million contingency contract to Halliburton subsidiary, KBR, to build facilities to temporarily house immigrant detainees (Scott 2006). In many ways, the increased surveillance of the foreign born in the United States has turned out handsome profits for well-connected corporations. This is in large part because "DHS was conceived and created in a way that made it possible for private industry to become the driving force behind much of its operations. DHS was born with a massive budget, and those who were present at its creation undoubtedly saw the huge revenue potential for big business" (Fernandes 2006: 172–173).

In Whose Interest?

The failure of immigration policy has created profits for government contractors, given fodder to politicians, and made undocumented migrants the targets of mass media talk show hosts, while creating a climate of dependency on migrants for certain sectors, such as food processing. The combination of fear, political maneuvers, and corporate profits has created a confluence of interests in the militarization of immigration enforcement, despite the negative consequences and limited efficacy of these actions. Although border militarization and interior immigration law enforcement are unlikely to alleviate any of the challenges associated with the presence of a large undocumented population in the United States, they have created new social problems.

There are many reasons to be opposed to having a large undocumented population in the United States. They present a security risk insofar as there are too many people who are unaccounted for, who are fundamentally disenfranchised, and who have no investment in a nation that chooses to ignore their contributions to society. The practical solution is not to try to remove all of them or to scare them away, but to encourage them to come out of the shadows by offering them an incentive to do so.

Increased militarization of the border will lead to handsome profits for certain corporations as well as increased funding for the DHS. It will not, however, lead to a reduction in the flow of migrants. Unfortunately, it is likely to increase the death toll at the border. The solution, however, is not to make more use of tactics destined to fail, but to encourage people to request permission to enter the United States by making the process less cumbersome and rendering the quotas more in line with actual labor needs in the United States. The growth of the immigration industrial complex, however, has ensured that practical solutions are unlikely to be enacted. As long as powerful companies, politicians, and media conglomerates stand to gain from the growth of the immigration industrial complex, it will be nearly impossible to enact viable reforms.

Notes

1. The reversal of the 100-to-1 sentencing disparity between crack and powder cocaine is one example of a policy that did change, in response to research and pressure. This change, however, took more than twenty years, despite abundant evidence that the logic behind the policy was flawed.

2. Bureau of Justice Prison Statistics. June 2008. http://www.ojp.usdoj.gov/bjs/prisons.htm. Accessed October 20, 2009.

3. This is partly related to the fact that it is impossible to incarcerate all nonviolent offenders. Most people who commit nonviolent crimes such as illegal drug use, petty theft, and forgery are never caught. Increasing the numbers of people who are caught and prosecuted thus has little effect on the rates of crime.

4. Introduction of S. 1038. Dianne Feinstein. Congressional Record. http://thomas.loc.gov/cgi-bin/query/F?r111:1:./temp/~r111DtvtZW:e24262. Accessed May 11, 2011.

5. "Blood, Sweat and Fear." http://www.hrw.org/reports/2005/usa0105/1.htm#_Toc88546710, page 1. Accessed September 1, 2010.

6. "CCA Released Q4 Lobbying Numbers." Private Prison Watch. http://private-prisonwatch.net/2010/03/26/cca-releases-q4-lobbying-numbers.aspx. Accessed April 6, 2010.

7. "Corrections Corporation of America Commences Construction of a New Prison and an Expansion of an Existing Prison." July 2, 2007. Press release. CCA Website. http://investor.shareholder.com/cxw/releasedetail.cfm?ReleaseID=252246. Accessed July 22, 2009.

8. CCA Quarterly Report to the SEC. August 4, 2008. http://apps.shareholder.com/sec/viewerContent.aspx?companyid=CXW&docid=6086086. Accessed July 22, 2009.

REFLECT AND CONSIDER

- Explain the connections between the Military Industrial Complex, the Prison Industrial Complex, and the Immigration Industrial Complex.
- How does anti-immigration ideology fuel the profits of detention centers?

EVADING RESPONSIBILITY FOR GREEN HARM: STATE CORPORATE EXPLOITATION OF RACE, CLASS, AND GENDER INEQUALITY

BY EMILY GAARDER

Green harm and green criminology

Green harms take many forms, including the exploitation of the environment, the abuse of non-human animals, the human health consequences of toxic contamination, and the monopolization of natural resources by powerful nations. Green harms range from ordinary, everyday practices to exceptional acts (Beirne and South 2007; Brisman 2011). The branch of criminology that concerns itself with green harm is generally referred to as green criminology. Green criminology is the study of harms against humanity, the environment, and non-human animals. It is concerned with harms "committed both by powerful institutions (e.g., governments, transnational corporations, military apparatuses) and also by ordinary people" (Beirne and South 2007: xiii).

Engaging in green criminology broadens our view of harm, getting at the social questions of how and why some acts become labeled "crime." Green criminology also intersects with critical victimology, by questioning who is granted the status of victim and who benefits from the dominant view of which crimes and victims matter (Williams 1998). The inclusion of green criminology within the criminology curriculum helps students grapple with a wide range of social problems and develop critical thinking skills regarding how definitions of harm, crime, offenders, and victims are formed. Green criminology provides an excellent frame to explore such issues, as it works to "uncover relevant sources and forms of power, including the state's willingness or reluctance to construct certain forms of harm as crimes, as well as social inequalities and their ill effects" (Beirne and South 2007: xiv).

In 1990, Michael Lynch published the first discussion of green criminology, situating it within radical criminology. Lynch (1990) argued that green criminology should be built on European Green political theories that view environmental destruction as an outcome of modem industrial capitalist production and consumption (see also South 1998). Recent work by Lynch and Stretesky (2003) argues that green criminology should draw their definition of "green" from environmental justice considerations rather than corporate actors. This move would align green criminology with a more expansive analysis of power, as environmental justice is concerned with how intersecting forms of inequality (race, class, and gender) affect the social construction of environmental law, crime, and decision-making. For instance, the environmental justice perspective has highlighted the importance of race and class in the location of toxic waste facilities. Communities of colour, the poor, and residents of the Global South disproportionately experience the human cost of environmental degradation (see Brisman 2002; Bullard 1994; Shiva 2000).

Environmental movements in the Global South that emphasize the crushing impact of economic globalization and transnational corporations on poor countries should also provide direction to a green criminology research agenda. Activists and scholars in the Global South highlight the ways that Western financial organizations such as the World Bank and the International Monetary Fund (IMF) leave poor countries dependent on rich nations and vulnerable to corporate exploitation of their natural resources (Shiva 2000; Tandon 2008).

Green criminologists have already interrogated topics such as state corporate criminality and food (Walters 2004; 2006; 2007), water (White 2003), abuse of non-human animals (Beirne 2007), government response to noncompliance with environmental law (Hauck 2007), the role of masculinity in crimes against the environment (Groombridge 1998), and media depictions of environmental harm and responsibility (Brisman and South in press; Fitzgerald and Baralt 2010). These examples demonstrate the important contributions that criminologists can make to the documentation and analysis of green harms, only some of which are currently regarded as crimes.

State-corporate crime and the social construction of green harm

This chapter utilizes two related concepts in criminology: state-corporate crime and the social construction of crime. State-corporate crime is defined as "illegal or socially injurious actions that occur when one or more institutions of political governance pursue a goal in direct cooperation with one or more institutions of economic production and distribution" (Kramer and Michalowski 1993: 174). Corporations depend on the state to reduce costs and increase profits, which might include reducing tax burdens, controlling labor costs, setting low environmental standards, and minimally enforcing environmental or labor laws. In turn, governments rely on corporations to supply necessary goods and services and to provide tax revenue through worker salaries and corporate profit. Politicians and political parties rely on corporate donors to finance their campaigns; in exchange, they support public policy that benefits their donors. This political economy approach stresses the interdependence of corporations and government under capitalism.

State-corporate crime is distinguished from state crimes or corporate crimes because it involves a public-private partnership. Analyses of state-corporate crime can expose a wider range of criminal negotiations and activities that are largely hidden from public view. For example, Aulette and Michalowski (1993) examined a fire in a chicken processing plant in Hamlet, North Carolina where 25 workers died. They found a pattern of regulatory failure by several state and federal agencies that allowed the company to continue violating basic safety regulations to facilitate corporate profit. Kauzlarich and Kramer's (1993) study of nuclear and atomic weapons manufacturing demonstrated how the relationship between the U.S. government and private, multinational corporations resulted in massive dumping of radioactive and hazardous waste. Government and corporate interest in profit and capitalist expansion guided this institutional arrangement, which resulted in grave environmental consequences.

The concept of state-corporate crime is intertwined with the concept of crime as social construction. Kramer, Michalowski and Kauzlarich (2006: 266) explain that "[a]s a political economy of crime, [the concept of state-corporate crime] recognizes that the social process of naming crime is significantly shaped by those who enjoyed the economic and political power to ensure that the naming of crime in most instances will reflect, or at least not seriously threaten, their worldview and interests".

The development of theory and research on state-corporate crime was influenced by Richard Quinney's contributions to the study of corporate crime and the sociology of law, crime, and justice (Kramer et al. 2002). Quinney (1970) advanced the idea that law and crime are social constructions that reflect power relations. Those who benefit from systems of domination and inequality pacify or thwart resistance by the repressed through governing the consciousness of the population. Those in power maintain power by controlling the message. As such, the corporations and states seek to control information about green harm and its impact on people, non-human animals, and ecosystems. Certain environmental harms or acts against non-human animals are illegal; others are not. The state governs whether harm is a problem (e.g., a criminal act), whether there are victims, who should be held responsible, and what the remedy should be.

Utilizing this framework, I first analyze how corporations and states use existing gender, race, and class inequalities to hide the impact of green harm on the environment, non-human animals, and humans. I then discuss how individual actors are blamed for green harm and how responsibility for avoiding green harm is placed on individuals.

From a distance: making green harm invisible

One of the ways that state-corporate harm is made less visible to the public is by concentrating the harm on marginalized populations who lack the political and economic power to fight green harm. In the U.S., toxic waste disposals are placed in poor regions with high populations of people of colour (Brisman 2002; Bullard 1994; Geddicks 1993). Wealthy industrialized nations like the U.S. outsource polluting factories and waste to the Global South (Center for investigative Reporting 1990). The connection between toxic waste locations and poor communities of colour is more than mere correlation. It is a deliberate policy of nation-states and multinational corporations. This was made exceedingly clear in 1991, when a confidential memorandum by then-chief economist of the World Bank, Lawrence Summers, was leaked. Summers wrote: "Dirty Industries: Just between you and me, shouldn't the World Bank be encouraging *more* migration of the dirty industries to the LDCs [Least Developed Countries]?" (quoted in Greenpeace 1993: 1-2). Summers was later appointed U.S. Secretary of the Treasury under the Clinton Administration and chosen by President Barack Obama to be Director of the White House National Economic Council.

Within the U.S., large-scale agricultural operations and factory farms are sites of human oppression, where poorly paid workers and the surrounding residents are exposed to a variety of environmental toxins (Cuomo 1998). Eighty to ninety percent of hired farmworkers are people of colour, predominantly Latino and African-American. Migrant workers experience the highest rates of toxic chemical injuries of any group of workers in the United States; an estimated 300,000 farmworkers suffer acute pesticide poisoning each year (U.S. General Accounting Office

1992). Female farmworkers and the children of farmworkers face additional risks due to their smaller size and because the harmful effects of pesticides may be passed on to the fetus of a pregnant woman or to her baby through nursing (Ontiveros 2002). Children are also exposed to pesticides either by their presence in the fields or through residue that their parents bring home; they are particularly susceptible because of their immature immune system, physical size, and lack of protective clothing.

Exposure to environmental health hazards from Confined Animal Feeding Operations (CAFOs) is also racially and economically disproportionated. For example, studies of North Carolina's confined swine feeding operations found decreased health and quality of life among residents in nearby areas, including "increased occurrences of headaches, runny nose, sore throat, excessive coughing, diarrhea and burning eyes" (Wing and Wolf 2000). Mirabelli and colleagues (2006) report that North Carolina schools with higher rates of students of colour and lower socioeconomic backgrounds were more likely to be located within three miles of a confined swine feeding operation. This results in greater exposure to air pollution, putting them at risk for asthma and other related health problems.

Thus far, I have focused on the ways that state and corporate actors direct green harm onto human populations already disadvantaged by racism and poverty. Their toxic spills, air pollutants, and water and soil contamination go largely undetected in communities where residents already face a dizzying array of struggles and little political clout. The instrumental use and abuse of non-human animals by governments and corporations also goes unnoticed; non human animals lack a political constituency.

Corporations use a variety of techniques to make harm done to non-human animals less visible. The majority of Americans procure meat and dairy products from a grocery store or restaurant, where animal products are neatly packaged and named in ways that disguise or distance us from their origins. Behind every meal of meat is an absence: the life and death of the animal. Adams (1990) calls this the "absent referent"—that which separates the meat eater from the animal, and the animal from the end product (a meal). The function of the absent referent is to distance the consumer/eater from the process that brought a meal to one's plate. In the case of most animals raised for human consumption, this process involved confinement, hormones to promote growth modification, injections of antibiotics to deal with the diseases that result from intense confinement and unnatural diets, and eventually, slaughter. These processes are largely hidden from public view.

Advertisements for meat often use humor to distance the consumer/eater from any harm involved in the creation of animal-based products. Much of this humor is based on gender and racial stereotypes. Adams (2003) demonstrates how men of colour and women of all races are compared to animals and meat, in common jokes and language, product advertisements, and pornographic materials. Sexism and racism are embedded in animal comparisons. Advertisements make the process seem innocent. Grauerholz (2007: 350) describes a Burger King commercial for Whoppers featuring women dressed as sandwich parts, singing lyrics such as "Yes we're tasty and eye-popping," and "Ask away, we're always willing." The double entendres, puns, and visual substitutions are just fun advertisements—the humor of the dominant culture. Men are encouraged to purchase and eat meat through advertisements that portray women's bodies as "meat"—consumable products. Meat is advertised as a "masculine" food—strong and robust. Men should consume red meat; women should eat salad.

In light of growing public concern over animal welfare and the environmental consequences of factory farms, corporations continually seek new ways to hide the conditions of confinement and slaughter of animals. In 2011, legislators in Minnesota attempted to pass a bill that would make it illegal to make audio or video recordings at an animal facility without permission. Similar bills were introduced in Florida, Iowa and New York. Livestock and crop operations, hatcheries, research facilities and kennels are among the facilities covered by these bills. The legislation was aimed at preventing whistle-blowers and animal advocates from exposing conditions of animal cruelty. One of the Minnesota bill's sponsors, State Representative Rod Hamilton, also serves as the director of communications for Christensen Family Farms, the third largest pork producer in the U.S. (Danielson 2011)—yet another example of state-corporate collusion in the interest of profit.

Conclusion

As growing numbers of citizens show concern over issues of environmental sustainability, food security, animal treatment, and related issues, criminologists can and should respond to the need for documentation and analysis of these green harms. Using the conceptual frameworks of state-corporate crime and the social construction of crime, this chapter has described the ways that state-corporate actors exploit existing race, class, and gender inequalities to evade responsibility for green harm. This chapter has also demonstrated how human inequalities, animal abuse, and environmental harm are framed as the work of individual perpetrators instead of profit-driven partnerships between corporations and governments. These tangled financial interests shift the prevention and treatment of health problems away from state-corporate accountability for toxins and toward individual citizens, who are expected to manage their risk of acquiring cancer with a dizzying array of behaviors and environments to avoid. Given that in the U.S. alone, millions of pounds of toxic chemicals are released into air, water, and soil each year, this is a tall order indeed.

This chapter's objective is to re-politicize environmental and animal issues by recasting the experiences of marginalized populations affected by "green harm" as injuries and injustices instead of inevitabilities or avoidable risks (Williams 1998). The majority of green harm is a result of corporate-political relationships in pursuit of profit, not just a few individuals making harmful choices. This chapter has explained how state-corporate actors make green harm less visible by concentrating the harm on marginalized populations. They avoid responsibility for harm by placing the blame on individual offenders, while responsibility for avoiding harm is pushed onto individual citizens. Our solutions to green harm, then, should be similarly focused. We must concentrate efforts on documenting and publicizing the impact of green harm on marginalized groups, both human and non-human. We must advocate public policy and collective action that go beyond the individual level of responsibility for green harm. Finally, we should remain vigilant in exposing the ever-widening state-corporate collusion that threatens sustainability of people and the planet.

References

Adams, C.J. 1990. *The Sexual Politics of Meat*. New York: Continuum.

————.2003. *The Pornography of Meat*. New York: Continuum.

Ascione, F.R. 1998. "Battered Women's Reports of Their Partners' and Their Children's Cruelty to Animals," *Journal of Emotional Abuse*, 1: 119–33.

Aulette, J.R. and Michalowski, R. 1993. "Fire in Hamlet: A Case Study of State-Corporate Crime," in K. Tunnell (ed.) *Political Crime in Contemporary America: A Critical Approach*, pp. 171–206. New York: Garland.

Batt, S. 1994. *Patient No More: The Politics of Breast Cancer*. Charlottetown, P.E.I. Canada: Gynergy Books.

Batt. S. and Gross, L. 1999. "They Make the Chemicals, They Run the Treatment Centers, and They're Still Looking for The Cure': No Wonder They Won't Tell You About Breast Cancer Prevention," *Sierra Magazine*, Sept/Oct.

Beirne, P. 2007. "Animal Rights, Animal Abuse and Green Criminology," in P. Beime and N. South (eds) *Issues in Green Criminology: Confronting Harms Against Environments, Humanity and Other Animals*. Collumpton: Willan.

Beirne, P. and South, N. 2007. "Introduction: Approaching Green Criminology," in P. Bieme and N. South (eds) *Issues in Green Criminology: Confronting Harms Against Environments, Humanity and Other Animals*. Collumpton: Willan.

Brisman, A, 2002. "EPA's Disproportionate Impact Methodologies—RJBA and COATCEM—and the Draft Recipient Guidance and Draft Revised Investigation Guidance in Light of *Alexander v. Sandoval*," *Connecticut Law Review*, 34(3): 1065–108.

————.2011. "'Green Harms' as Art Crime, Art Criticism as Environmental Dissent," *Journal of Contemporary Criminal Justice*, 27(4): 465–99.

Brisman, A. and South, N. in press. "A Green-Cultural Criminology: An Exploration Outline," *Crime Media Culture*.

Brown, P. and Ferguson, F.T. 1995. "'Making a Big Stink': Women's Work, Women's Relationships, and Toxic Waste Activism," *Gender and Society*, 9: 145–72.

Bryson, L., McPhillips, K. and Robinson, K. 2001. "Turning Public Issues Into Private Troubles: Lead Contamination, Domestic Labor, and the Exploitation of Women's Unpaid Labor in Australia," *Gender and Society*, 15: 755–72.

Bullard, D. 1994. *Dumping in Dixie: Race, Class and Environmental Quality*. Boulder, CO: Westview Press.

Center for Investigative Reporting. 1990. *Global Dumping Ground: The International Traffic in Hazardous Waste*. Washington, DC: Seven Locks Press.

Christie, N. 1977. "Conflicts as Property," *The British Journal of Criminology*, 17: 1–15.

Cuomo, C. 1998. *Feminism and Ecological Communities: An Ethic of Flourishing*. New York: Roudedge.

Danielson, S. 2011. "Why Don't Minnesota Lawmakers Want to Talk About Proposed Law Against Videotaping Inside Animal Facilities?" Online blog. Available at: www.simplegoodandtasty.com/2011/04/28/proposed-minnesota-law-against-videos-inside-animal-containment-facilities-gets-big-ag (accessed 27 June 2011).

Environmental Working Group, 2011. Environmental Working Group web site. Available at: www.ewg. org (accessed 29 June 2011).

Fitzgerald, A. and Baralt, L.B. 2010. "Media Constructions of Responsibility for the Production and Mitigation of Environmental Harms: The Case of Mercury-Contaminated Fish," *Canadian Journal of Criminology and Criminal Justice*, 52: 341–68.

Flynn, C.P. 2000. "Woman's Best Friend: Pet Abuse and the Role of Companion Animals in the Lives of Battered Women," *Violence Against Women*, 6: 162–77.

Gaarder, E. 2011. *Women and the Animal Rights Movement*. Piscataway, NJ: Rutgers University Press.

Geddicks, A. 1993. *The New Resource Wars: Native and Environmental Struggles Against Multi-National Corporations*. Boston, MA: South End Press.

Grauerholz, L. 2007. "Cute Enough to Eat: The Transformation of Animals Into Meat for Human Consumption in Commercialized Images," *Humanity and Society*, 31: 334-54.

Gray, J. (ed.) 2010. *State of the Evidence: What is the Connection Between the Environment and Breast Cancer?* San Francisco, CA: Breast Cancer Fund. Available at: www.breastcancerfund.org (accessed 28 June 2011).

Greenpeace. 1993. *The Case for a Ban on All Hazardous Waste Shipment from the United States and Other OECD Member States to Non-OECD States*. Washington, DC: Greenpeace USA.

Groombridge, N. 1998. "Masculinities and Crimes Against the Environment," *Theoretical Criminology*, 2: 249–67.

Gruen, L, 1993. "Dismantling Oppression: An Analysis of the Connection Between Women and Animals," in G. Gaard (ed.) *Ecofeminism: Women, Animals, Nature*. Philadelphia, PA: Temple University Press.

Hauck, M. 2007. "Non-Compliance in Small-Scale Fisheries: A Threat to Security?" in P. Beime and N. South (eds) *Issues in Green Criminology: Confivnting Hams Against Environments, Humanity and Other Animals*. Collumpton: Willan.

Hawthorne, M. 2010. "Got Cruelty? New Investigation Exposes Dairy Farm Practices." Online blog. Available at: http://strikingattheroots.wordpress.com/2010/01/26/got-cruelty-new-investigation-exposes-dairy-farm-practices/ (accessed 28 June 2011).

Kauzlarich, D. and Kramer, R.C, 1993. "State-Corporate Crime in the US Nuclear Weapons Production Complex," *Journal of Human Justice*, 5: 4–28.

Kramer, R.C. and Michalowski, R.J. 1993. "State-Corporate Crime," in K. Tunnell (ed.) *Political Crime in Contemporary America: A Critical Approach*. New York: Garland.

Kramer, R.C., Michalowski, R.J, and Kauzlarich, D. 2002. "The Origins and Development of the Concept and Theory of State-Corporate Crime," *Crime and Delinquency*, 48: 263–82.

Lynch, M.J. 1990. "The Greening of Criminology: A Perspective for the 1990s," *The Critical Criminologist*, 2: 11–12.

Lynch, M.J. and Stretesky, P.B. 2003. "The Meaning of Green: Contrasting Criminological Perspectives," *Theoretical Criminology*, 7: 217–38.

Mirabelli, M.C., Wing, S., Marshall, S.W. and Wilcosky, T.C. 2006. "Race, Poverty, and Potential Exposure of Middle-School Students to Air Emissions From Confined Swine Operations," *Environmental Health Perspectives*, 114: 591–96.

Ontiveros, M.L. 2002. "Lessons from the Fields: Female Farmworkers and the Law," *Maine Law Review*, 55: 157–89.

Quinney, R. 1970. *The Social Reality of Crime*. Boston, MA: Little, Brown.

———.1974. *Critique of Legal Order*. Boston, MA: Little, Brown, and Company.

Shiva, V. 2000. *Stolen Harvest: The Hijacking of the Global Food Supply*. Cambridge: South End Press.

South, N. 1998. "A Green Field for Criminology? A Proposal for a Perspective," *Theoretical Criminology* 2: 211–33.

Steingraber, S. 2010. *Living Downstream: An Ecologist's Personal Investigation of Cancer and the Environment*, 2nd edn. Cambridge, MA: Da Capo Press.

Tandon, Y. 2008. *Ending Aid Dependence*, 2nd edn. Nairobi and Oxford: Fahumu Books; Geneva: South Centre.

Tjaden, P. and Thoennes, N. 2000. *Extent, Nature and Consequences of Intimate Partner Violence*. Washington, DC: The Centers for Disease Control and Prevention and The National Institute of Justice, US Department of Justice.

US General Accounting Office. 1992. *Hired Farmworkers Health and Well-being at Risk: Report to Congressional Requesters*. Washington, DC: US General Accounting Office.

Walters, R. 2004. "Criminology and Genetically Modified Food," *British Journal of Criminology*, 44: 151–67.

———.2006. "Crime, Bio-Agriculture and the Exploitation of Hunger," *British Journal of Criminology*, 46:26–45.

———.2007. "Food Crime, Regulation and the Biotech Harvest," *European Journal of Criminology*, 4: 217–35.

White, R. 2003. "Environmental Issues and the Criminological Imagination," *Theoretical Criminology*, 7: 483–506.

Williams, C. 1998. "An Environmental Victimology," in C. Williams (ed.) *Environmental Victims: New Risks, New Injustice*. London: Earthscan Publications.

Wing, S. and Wolf, S. 2000. "Intensive Livestock Operations, Health, and Quality Of Life Among Eastern North Carolina Residents," *Environmental Health Perspectives*, 108: 233–38.

Zilney, L.A., McGurrin, D. and Zahran, S. 2006. "Environmental Justice and the Role of Criminology: An Analytical Review of 33 Years of Environmental Justice Research," *Criminal Justice Review*, 31: 47–62.

REFLECT AND CONSIDER

- How is green harm connected to racism?
- How is green harm a systematic process and one supported by corporate practices?

HIGHLIGHT

5 LINKS BETWEEN HIGHER EDUCATION AND THE PRISON INDUSTRY

BY HANNAH K. GOLD, *ROLLING STONE*

SUMMARY

The institutions of education and criminal justice have been shown to have serious racial bias and are structured in such a way that they help Whites while also restricting opportunities for people of color. In this article, Gold also illustrates the destructive ways that education and incarceration are intimately linked. Private prisons, college applications, boards of trustees, campus security, and funding of university research all share people, money, and/or policies—resulting in the support of private prison companies.

EXCERPT FROM
"5 LINKS BETWEEN HIGHER EDUCATION AND THE PRISON INDUSTRY"

American universities do a fine job of selling themselves as pathways to opportunity and knowledge. But follow the traffic of money and policies through these academic institutions and you'll often wind up at the barbed wire gates of Corrections Corporation of America (CCA) and GEO Group, the two largest private prison operators in the United States. In the last two decades the private prison industry has exploded, growing 784 percent at the federal level, and helping the United States to achieve the highest incarceration rate in the world. CCA operates 69 facilities throughout the United States, GEO operates 55; both typically mandate that 90 percent of their beds be filled at all times. In the last two years alone CCA has defended itself against charges of fraudulent understaffing of its facilities, medical neglect and abuse of inmates.

READ THE REST OF THE ESSAY:

bit.ly/prisonrollingstone

READ, LISTEN, WATCH, INTERACT!

READ

The Speed Kills You: The Voice of Nebraska's Meatpacking Workers

Nebraska Appleseed, 2009

READ AT bit.ly/meatpackingwork

Stop and Frisk: NYPD's 'Broken Windows' Policing 'Criminalizes' Young Black Men

Daniel A Medina, The Guardian

READ AT bit.ly/stopandfrisknypd

The Sentencing Project

READ AT bit.ly/sentencingprojectracism

LISTEN

Legal Scholar: Jim Crow Still Exists in America

Fresh Air with Michelle Alexander, 1.16.2012, NPR

LISTEN AT bit.ly/newjimcrowalexander

Three Miles

This American Life, 3.13.2015.

LISTEN AT bit.ly/threemiles

WATCH

American Drug War: The Last White Hope

Kevin Booth, 2007

AVAILABLE AT bit.ly/americandrugwarbooth

Interviews with Dr. Robert Bullard on Environmental Justice

AVAILABLE AT bit.ly/environmentalracism

Lost in Detention

Frontline, 10.18.2011, PBS

AVAILABLE AT bit.ly/lostindetentionfrontline

The House I Live In

Eugene Jarecki, 2012

AVAILABLE AT bit.ly/houseiliveinjarecki

INTERACT

Environmental Justice Atlas

EJ Atlas.

INTERACT AT bit.ly/environmentalatlas

Immigration Detention Map and Statistics

CIVIC: Community Initiatives for Visiting Immigrants in Confinement

INTERACT AT bit.ly/immigrationdetentionmap

The Counted: People Killed by Police in the U.S.

The Guardian

INTERACT AT bit.ly/countedpolice

THE FUTURE OF RACE

How far have we come in combating racial inequality? What will the United States look like in fifty years? One hundred years? Will a course like this one still be necessary for your children, grandchildren, or great grandchildren? US society has made great strides in racial progress. Plantation slavery, as one of the greatest stains on American history, ended over 150 years ago, and the first Black president was elected to two terms in office. Other racial groups have also had representational success, with many Asian ethnicities occupying the highest socioeconomic strata, a Hispanic woman appointed to the Supreme Court, and those who identify as multiracial as some of today's most popular celebrities. The question is, then, what is the future of race and racism?

Generally speaking, the reality is that though there have been important successes, racial inequality persists. As sociologists of race, we have to take a critical look at how race and racism are employed in contemporary society. We can acknowledge and celebrate racial advancements while still criticizing society for the barriers that remain. The readings in this section represent this balanced approach.

The first reading, "Liminality in the Multiracial Experience" by David Brunsma, Daniel Delgado, and Kerry Ann Rockquemore, analyzes how multiracials, people who identify with more than one race, experience racial identity as a matrix—"the intersection of different forms of Multiracial identities and experiences." Multiracials, by virtue of occupying more than one racial identity, challenge traditional notions of race and racial identity, and this article points to the complex ways in which multiracials navigate structure and agency. In the following reading, "Race and the New Bio-Citizen," Dorothy Roberts reveals the complicated ways in which race is being re-introduced as a biological concept. Roberts reviews the significant advances that science has made in areas such as medicine, reproductive technologies, and genetic ancestry testing, but also the ways in which this science dangerously places race at the center of these discoveries and thereby suggests that race has a genetic basis. In other words, the fight against race and racism continues in almost every institution of society, including presumable "fact-based, neutral" institutions such as science.

Many thought the beginning of the twenty-first century would be marked by post-racialism, the idea that society has moved to a point where race is no longer a central organizing principle, but that point clearly has not been reached. In the reading from Kathleen Fitzgerald's "A Post-Racial Society," the theoretical changes in race and the racial hierarchy are summarized. Millennials, those born after 1980, are the most racially diverse generation, but even they do not believe racism has come to an end. The hierarchy isn't going away but it might change shape, with more emphasis placed on skin tone, and less emphasis placed upon specific racial categories; in this instance, Whites and those with lighter complexions will be at the top of the hierarchy, and those with darker complexions will be at the bottom. The Highlight for this section, "Choose Your Own Identity," discusses the racial identity options for multiracials.

AS YOU READ

- Assess how multiracialism challenges traditional notions of race but is also still confined by racial ideologies.
- Debate the pros and cons of the scientific research that addresses race.
- Formulate an opinion on the progress made and the barriers still in place in dismantling racism.

LIMINALITY IN THE MULTIRACIAL EXPERIENCE: TOWARDS A CONCEPT OF IDENTITY MATRIX

BY DAVID L. BRUNSMA, DANIEL J. DELGADO, AND KERRY ANN ROCKQUEMORE

Scholarly work on Multiracial identity in the past three decades has focused on how Multiracial people form their racial identity. This body of research has found that the racial identities of Multiracial people are socially structured and that these identities are multifaceted and somewhat predictable. Multiracial research has covered interactionally negotiated racialised experiences (Rockquemore and Brunsma 2002a); familial and institutional experiences (Renn 2003, Brunsma 2005, Miville *et al.* 2005); racialised experiences across space and place (Wijeyesinghe 2001, Harris and Sim 2002, Rockquemore and Brunsma 2002b); phenotype and linguistic systems (Brown 1995, Brunsma and Rockquemore 2001, Bailey 2006); and dynamics across the life course (Hitlin *et al.* 2006). After these decades of research, Multiracial identity appears as a constant process of 'doing race' (Lewis 2003)—racial identity is both active and directed work.

Yet, an interesting pattern has emerged that limits the field's understanding of identity, race and social experience for Multiracials. This pattern is the heavy focus, especially in the work on Multiracials in the United States, on Multiracials' *racial* identities and *racial* self-understandings. We argue that this focus on racial experiences has left our understanding of Multiracial identities, in general, and black-white Multiracial identities, specifically, incomplete. Though the racial experiences of Multiracials are important—offering insight into central social processes of hybridity, double-consciousness, racialisation, marginality and identity work—racial experiences are not the *only* descriptor and locator of Multiracials' identity experiences—perhaps not even the primary ones. A Multiracial who identifies as 'Black' or 'Biracial' during one time or in one place, may not deploy this racial identity equally or consistently across all areas of social life (see Campbell 2007). Identities are more complex, fully integrating social, material, cultural, political, physical and institutional components. Recognising that individuals exist in these complex spaces requires an equally multifaceted notion of identity as a *matrix*.

Borrowing from Patricia Hill Collins' critical insights (2000), we use the idea of a 'matrix' to import her understanding of interlocking oppressions (also see Crenshaw 1991) into a heuristic discussion here of Multiracial identity. An *identity matrix* illustrates the complex interplay of various selves that form a black-white Multiracial experience. Just as intersecting oppressions affect how a black, working-class woman gains access to material resources, an identity matrix affects the availability of Multiracial self-deployments within interlocking social contexts. This grounding can be understood through strategic and agentic processes in interactional, political, cultural, physical (embodiment) and institutional social spaces.

Thinking about Multiracial identities as a matrix sheds light on the intersection of different forms of Multiracial identities and experiences. It also accounts for a contextual fluidity in how individuals deploy and understand this subjectivity. For example, in certain instances, a black-white Multiracial person's experience as a black person depends on the interplay of many other selves that are contextually available (Campbell 2007). His or her racial identity can shift into a liminal space (Turner 1964) and is neither white nor black nor Biracial. An identity matrix helps reveal such shifts as well as how Multiracial individuals use a variety of racial identity options depending on the discursive context.

With this aim in mind, we begin the work here of conceptualising and developing the identity matrix from insightful data on 231 black-white Multiracial young adults and 24 in-depth interviews from some of our original work (Brunsma and Rockquemore 2001, Rockquemore and Brunsma 2002b) in order to both rethink that original work and to push forward into potentially fruitful theoretical domains in the study of Multiraciality. In doing so, we wish to move beyond a simplistic notion of Multiracial identity towards a complex interpretation of the *identities of Multiracial people.* This is done through a theoretical development of the notion of an 'identity matrix' and an exploratory empirical glimpse at such matrices.

Qualitative results

Black-White Multiracial embodied/physical identity

Physical identity, the experience of embodied Multiraciality, is largely *felt* (Hochschild 1983), which means that the respondents described 'how [they] experience the body as lived' (Shilling 1993). One interviewee, Joshua, captures this experience, 'I mean *you* can look at me and tell I'm not Black … *you* can tell I'm not White, but *you* don't know what I am'. Joshua recognises his liminality based on the (mis)perceptions of his body by others. As Joshua feels these (mis) perceptions, he occupies a 'third space'; not black, nor white or even Biracial but liminal with regard to each. Black-White Multiracial bodies are liminally directed on the basis of their ex-periences of in-betweenness, representing the 'unknowable existence' in the racialised social structure of the United States.

Often their physicality remains unclear, until other racialised phenotypic practices are deployed in interactional space. This complexity underscores a contextual break from the normative interpretations of race as always black, white or Biracial and becomes contextually dependent as highlighted by Tiara, 'I think I look Biracial, but … people think I look Black, then they hear me talk … and they're like "uh huh" [she isn't black]'. Bodily Tiara may be perceived as black yet when she speaks, a liminal space emerges. For her, being in-between is tied to being perceived as both black (phenotypically) and white (linguistically). Madeline reiterates this embodied in-between-ness with the simple statement of, 'Physical, *you* can tell I'm mixed'. The phrase 'mixed' underscores that physicality cannot highlight an agreement about what or who is Biracial, but can only signal a break from the normative interpretations of race as black *or* white and even, as Biracial.

Across these cases we see that the respondents' understandings of physical identity are rooted in a contextually bound discourse. Tiara is black according to the US racial structure (Bonilla-Silva 1997), yet her practices (utterances) reveal a complication of these structures—a friction (Tsing 2005). Joshua, similarly, contends that his Multiracial physicality enables him to move between both black and white spaces. The salience of either his white or black 'at-tributes' depends on the racial discourse of the interactional space he is negotiating and all the respondents are aware that their skin tone is malleable, black, white, Multiracial, or, generally speaking, liminally othered.

Black-White Multiracial social identity

In this component of the identity matrix we are interested in how racial identities are deployed in social interactions, and how social spaces enable individuals to differentially negotiate and construct who they are to others. Across the interview data, an array of Multiracial social identities arise. For these individuals, the physical and the social become somewhat welded together in their contextual deployment, as illustrated by Dierdra. She describes how she deploys a Multiracial social identity when asked, on the basis of her physical appearance, about her race. 'You don't look Black. You don't look White. What are you?' In this case, the physical is a trigger for deploying a social identity. These statements—'what are you?'—highlight the contextual boundedness of these two identities.

Because the physical appearance of black-white Multiracials blurs the racial hierarchy, their agency looks different from most individuals who 'fit in'. Interaction is initially directed by discourses about physical characteristics (stereotypes) that constitute blackness, whiteness and Multiracialness; however, as the physical and the social come together, individuals are given room to negotiate physicality through their own socially defined discursive constructions of Multiraciality. To accomplish this, individuals deploy various social repertoires that circumvent, divide and complicate racial hierarchies. Tiffany illustrates this as she states, 'Um, its pretty much a day to day thing. I'm gonna be a little bit more Black today. I'm gonna be a little more White today or proper or not proper'—describing a social repertoire that is rooted in her social identity, as it is constructed around her physical identity, a repertoire that she uses to negotiate the social spaces of black and white. Rather than the physical directing the social, it provides a malleable springboard for deploying a socially appropriate racial identity. The social element of the matrix clearly highlights the importance of a liminal experience, as these respondents have shown, their racial selves reorient racial hierarchies.

Black-White Multiracial cultural identity

There is no doubt that a significant and influential component of any identity matrix is cultural. Many respondents were especially conscious about their cultural identity. It was regularly discussed through food, clothing and music. We recognise that a liminal identity matrix is facilitated by the cultural practices associated with contemporary understandings of blackness, whiteness and black-white Multiracial identities (Nedelcheva 2006).

Joshua identifies his as a black identity that he locates in his connection with a black church that he attends: 'You Know, my church is Black. And so, everything around me, culturally, the way I experience God—and all that—has been Black'. We see that for his cultural identity, Joshua locates his cultural racial self in cultural Blackness. After previously mentioning his physical identity as being somewhere in-between or 'you don't know what I am', this is a major element of recognising the liminality of identity matrices as they are contingent upon disparate racial selves, but, ultimately comprise a multifaceted racialised self.

Angelique also places her cultural identity in a different space, one that is both French and black. She says, 'I have the French and then I have the Black', going on to describe eating practices that represent her entrenchment in French culture. However, only offhandedly does she mention that she is culturally black, despite her physicality conveying a more liminal physical and social identity. Multiracials purposefully construct their cultural identity. This can mean that their cultural practices, such as church or food, are prominent indications of how they understand their cultural selves. Consistent with Nedelcheva (2006), a cultural identity clearly depends on many cultural practices, which amounts to a readily shifted cultural identity for black-white Multiracials. This means that because of their racial liminality, Multiracials' cultural identities are easily moved in and out of, from black churches to French cuisine.

Black-White Multiracial political identity

Most research on the political looks at behaviours, attitude formation, as well as socialisation and identity formation. Our notion of political identity refers to identity as it is influenced by the political structure of the United States and the immediate social and cultural conditions in which it is deployed. In particular, black-white Multiracials deploy a complex set of political identifications on the basis of both the structural underpinnings of the American political context and the varying availability of political subject positions in this context.

One interviewee, Dierdra, illustrates this liminality: 'I don't like to get into Democrat/Republican—I'm an issue person'—maintaining a Biracial identity in her political and other identities (except formal). She is able to be an 'issue person' exactly because of the liminality of being Multiracial (see Rockquemore and Brunsma 2002a, b). In this case, Dierdra is able to skirt the discursive and structural confines typically associated with black and white politics, and instead lives in a liminal political subject location. By stating she is an 'issue person', Dierdra is directly avoiding the deeply racialised climate of American politics. This 'skirting' directly enables Dierdra to exist in a liminal political third space (Brunsma and Delgado 2009). This liminal third space illustrates how the agency available to black-white Multiracials differs significantly from individuals who are often described as 'clearly' placed in the racial hierarchy of the United States.

Angelique, another respondent who described her political identity as white negotiates the political climate in an equally complex manner. Being Biracial, she must contend with a specific context of reception for her political identity. Yet, at the same time, the agency afforded by her Multiraciality enables a seemingly contradictory choice of aligning with white conservatives. 'Rush Limbaugh, I really like him, but a lot of Black people don't … he speaks his mind [and] I agree with him on some points'. Angelique is able to both identify as Biracial yet, fluidly move into predominantly white-only occupied political spaces because of the liminality afforded by her racial and political identity. She, like Joshua, can have a conversation and agree with anyone, whether white or black and she can vote like anyone, whether white or black. The normative rules of racial politics and racial hierarchies have shifted and become more malleable for individuals with liminal identities.

Black-White Multiracial formal identity

The importance of a formal identity is best highlighted by the changes made in the 2000 US Census: 'check all that apply'. Feeling 'cornered', Multiracial individuals described how it felt to be forced to pick something, and usually it was suggested that they pick 'Black'. In this instance, the liminal space that Multiracials occupy is curtailed under their formal identity and is directed by the US white-black racial hierarchy.

Yet, being 'cornered' also creates opportunity for agency, which is often manifested in the resistance strategy of 'picking at people'. 'Picking at people' is a form of resistance against the dominant discourse. It is a direct response to the white-black racial structure in the United States, wherein black-white Multiracials push back against problematic ideas that often invoke 'one-drop' rules, blood quantum and assumptions about subject locations on the basis of phenotype, as these ideas state that they should just 'mark Black'. They push back by resisting the dominant racial structures.

Desmond did this when he marked 'Biracial' on all of the survey questions. Joshua explicitly describes this as 'picking' and in response to a question that asks why he deploys a Biracial identity on all forms he responds 'I do that just to pick at people'. Joshua and Desmond show how agency provides fluidity with regard to formal identification as they are able to choose the third space of liminality as resistance to dominant racial hierarchies. Desmond's later makes a statement that confirms this agency. In his discussion of formal identity, he remarks that he felt that the survey 'wasn't an important form'. His statements imply that were it a state or federal form, he might have filled it out differently, ultimately underscoring the fluidity of his racial self. Desmond's response is congruent with the agency that is afforded to many black-white Multiracials as context, rather than macro-racial hierarchies determine his identity deployment. Multiracials can and do resist formal categorisations in ways that other racialised people cannot.

Discussion and conclusion: a Multiracial identity matrix?

In 1987, Anzaldua famously asserted that Multiracial people have 'plural personalities'. More than a decade later, Rodriguez (2000) noted that her Latino respondents used, as do all people, a plurality of selves that were deployed differently, or float buoyantly, depending on the social situation. Continued research on Multiracial people has used similar theoretical lenses to understand the identities of Multiracials; however, prior research has not completely embraced such notions, either theoretically or empirically. We believe that the notion of an 'identity matrix' begins to more fully embrace the complexity of Multiracial, and indeed all identities.

The purpose of this article was by no means singular in its attempt to define, categorise or create boundaries around Multiracial identity. Instead, it begins laying out the contours of a heuristic concept, an 'identity matrix', and empirically plays with the idea using the SBE data (Rockquemore and Brunsma 2002b), as a means to conceptualise Multiracial identity in a more nuanced and complex manner than was previously done in both our own work and the work of others currently investigating Multiraciality. The initial forays in this article show that Multiraciality as an experienced, located identity is far more difficult, complex and divergent than has been previously conceptualised. Although the concept of a matrix from which individuals draw is not a new idea, it becomes more useful when understood in conjunction with Multiracial identities, and in particular, as a multiplicity of repertoires emerge as the fields and discourses shift, which they almost incessantly do.

Multiracial identity should be understood as both structurally and agentically mandated. The context of reception serves as both the space of deployment and the dictation of that identity deployment. Yet, at the same time, the agency that is afforded to Multiracials is a particularly interesting one, such that the liminality of their physical, political, social, cultural and formal identities enables a more multifaceted toolkit for deployment (see also Mahtani 2002). If we conceptualise this uniqueness relative to the toolkits available to other racial minorities, it becomes obvious that Multiracials exist in both a privileged and a subordinate position. While one cannot change their dark skin to white skin, they often can use their other identities to gain access to spaces which individuals who identify only as black or white typically cannot. This is highlighted by many responses we see in the qualitative data where Multiracials were able to enter and leave interactions despite racial determinants dictating the space. This means that in many contexts, Multiracials have a palatable opportunity to strategically deploy their identities.

These experiences, as we have shown, vary, and a person who identifies as Multiracial does not draw from a singular Multiracial experience. We have shown that the Multiracial experience, while similar among those in our sample, depends on how a person's identity matrix is configured. The configuration can follow several directions and manifest itself in numerous combinations. Because of this multiplicity of Multiracial experience, it is difficult to pin down an identifiable, solidified 'Multiracial consciousness'. Instead, the experience of liminality itself is much closer to a consciousness than that of Multiraciality itself. Understanding Multiracial identity as liminal opens up the utility of identity matrices in the study of other liminal groups (transgendered identities, class complexities, multicultural positions, etc.) and moves our focus to a myriad of identity projects.

Although racial identity is often described as an either/or choice, our insights from this theoretical and empirical thought exercise on identity matrices, point to the possibility that racial identity is *itself* multifaceted and that studying racial identity through the concept of the 'identity matrix' is closer to the strategic and agentic formation, maintenance and navigation of an identity for Multiracials. Identity matrices allow us to begin to understand the potential of interracial or cross-racial interactions, friendships, intimacies and, indeed, solidarities. It provides the crucial identity link needed to more effectively do intersectional work that aligns structure and agency. By allowing the variation in racial identity to emerge more clearly, we can better understand interaction on both a micro level and macro level. The matrices reflect the flexibility in Multiracial identity, whereas Multiracial identity seems static and fixed, the many layers that make-up our subjectivity providing explanations for variations in experience while also allowing for 'hooks' that bring out our similarities.

Scholars must begin, as we attempt to do in this article, to think about Multiraciality beyond a monolithic approach. A moving beyond studying the Multiracial identity to studying the *identities of Multiracials*. The concept of an 'identity matrix' helps begin this work.

Acknowledgements

The authors thank the following people for their assistance in thinking through the concepts in this work: Melinda Mills, Charles Jaret, Annamaria Csizmadia, Crystal Kroner, William Force, Dave Overfelt, Steve Kehnel, James Michael Thomas and Derek Evans.

References

Abrams, D. and Hogg, M.A., 1990. Social identification, self categorization and social influence. *European Review of Social Psychology*, 1, 195–228.

Anzaldua, G., 1987. *Borderlands/La Frontera: the new Mestiza*. San Francisco, CA: Spinsters/Aunt Lute Foundation.

Bailey, B., 2006. Black and Latino: Dominican Americans negotiate racial worlds. *In*: D. Brunsma, ed. *Mixed messages: multiracial identities in the 'Color-Blind' era*. Boulder, CO: Lynne Rienner Press.

Blumer, H., 1969. *Symbolic interactionism: perspective and method*. New York: Prentice Hall.

Bonilla-Silva, Eduardo, 1997. Rethinking racism: toward a structural interpretation. *American Sociological Review*, 62, 465–480.

Brown, U., 1995. Black/White interracial young adults: quest for racial identity. *American Journal of Orthopsychiatry*, 65, 125–130.

Brunsma, D., 2005. Interracial families and the racial identification of mixed-race children: evidence from the early childhood longitudinal study. *Social Forces*, 84 (2), 1129–1155.

Brunsma, D., ed., 2006a. *Mixed messages: multiracial identities in the 'Color-Blind' era*. Boulder, CO: Lynne Rienner Press.

Brunsma, D., 2006b. Public categories, private identities: exploring regional differences in the biracial experience. *Social Science Research*, 35 (5), 555–576.

Brunsma, D. and Delgado, D., 2009. Occupying the third space: hybridity and identity in the multiracial experience. *In*: K. Iyall Smith and P. Leavy, eds. *Hybrid identities: theoretical and empirical examinations*. Leben: Brill publishers.

Brunsma, D. and Rockquemore, K.A., 2001. The new color complex: phenotype, appearances, and (Bi) racial identity. *Identity*, 1 (3), 225–246.

Burke, P.J. and Reitzes, D.C., 1981. The link between identity and role performance. *Social Psychology Quarterly*, 44, 83–92.

Campbell, M.E., 2007. Thinking outside the (Black) box: measuring black and multiracial. Identification on surveys. *Social Science Research*, 36, 921–944.

Collins, P.H., 2000. *Black feminist thought: knowledge, consciousness, and the politics of empowerment*. New York: Routledge.

Cote, J.E., 1996. Sociological perspectives on identity formation: the culture-identity link and identity capital. *Journal of Adolescence*, 19, 417–428.

Cote, J.E., 1997. An empirical test of the identity capital model. *Journal of Adolescence*, 20, 577–597.

Crenshaw, K., 1991. Mapping the margins: intersectionality, identity politics, and violence against women of color. *Stanford Law Review*, 43, 1241–1299.

Csizmadia, A., 2011. The role of racial identification, social acceptance/rejection, social cognition, and racial socialization in multiracial youth's positive development. *Sociology Compass*, 5 (11), 995–1004.

Goffman, E., 1959. *The presentation of self in everyday life*. New York: Doubleday.

Harris, D.R. and Sim, J.J., 2002. Who is Multiracial? Assessing the complexity of lived race. *American Sociological Review*, 67 (4), 614–627.

Hitlin, S.J., Brown, S., and Elder Jr, G.H., 2006. Racial self-categorization in adolescence: multiracial development and social pathways. *Child Development*, 77 (5), 1298–1308.

Hochschild, A.R., 1983. *The managed heart: commercialization of human feeling.* Berkeley: University of California Press.

Lewis, A., 2003. Everyday race-making: navigating racial boundaries in schools. *American Behavioral Scientist*, 47 (3), 283–305.

Mahtani, M., 2002. What's in a name? Exploring the employment of 'mixed-race' as an identification. *Ethnicities*, 2 (4), 469–490.

Mead, G.H., 1934. *Mind, self and society.* New York: Doubleday.

Miville, M.L., *et al.*, 2005. Chameleon changes: an exploration of racial identity themes of Multiracial people. *Journal of Counseling Psychology*, 52 (4), 507–516.

Nedelcheva, T., 2006. Cultural identity as an everyday life and ideal. *Sociological Problems*, 38, 76–88.

Park, R.E., 1928. Human migration and the marginal man. *The American Journal of Sociology*, 33 (6), 881–893.

Renn, K.A., 2003. Understanding the identities of mixed-race college students through a developmental ecology lens. *Journal of College Student Development*, 44, 383–403.

Rockquemore, K.A., 1999. Between Black and White: understanding the 'Biracial' experience. *Race and Society*, 1 (2), 192–212.

Rockquemore, K.A., 2004. Negotiating the color line: the gendered process of racial identity construction among Black/White Biracial women. *Gender & Society*, 16 (4), 484–503.

Rockquemore, K.A. and Brunsma, D.L., 2002a. Socially embedded identities: theories, typologies, and processes of racial identity among Biracials. *The Sociological Quarterly*, 43 (3), 335–356.

Rockquemore, K.A. and Brunsma, D.L., 2002b. *Beyond Black: Biracial identity in America.* Thousands Oaks, CA: Sage Publication.

Rockquemore, K.A. and Brunsma, D.L., 2008. *Beyond Black: Biracial identity in America.* 2nd ed. New York: Rowman & Littlefield.

Rodriguez, C., 2000. *Changing race: Latinos, the census, and the history of ethnicity in the United States, Critical America.* New York University Press.

Root, M.P., 1990. Resolving 'other' status: identity development of Biracial individuals. *Women and Therapy*, 9, 185–205.

Shilling, C., 1993. *The body and social theory.* London: Sage Publications.

Stryker, S., 1968. Identity salience and role performance: the relevance of symbolic interaction theory for family. *Journal of Marriage and the Family*, 30, 558–564.

Tajfel, H. and Turner, J.C. 1979. An integrative theory of intergroup conflict. In: W.G. Austin and S. Worchel, eds. *The social psychology of intergroup relations.* Monterey, CA: Brooks-Cole, 33, 47.

Tsing, A.L., 2005. *Friction: an ethnography of global connection.* Princeton, NJ: Princeton University Press.

Turner, V., 1964. *The forest of symbols: aspects of Ndembu ritual.* Ithaca, NY: Cornell University Press.

Turner, V., 1969. *The ritual process: structure and anti-structure*. Ithaca, NY: Cornell University Press.

Wijeyesinghe, C.L., 2001. Racial identity in Multiracial people: an alternative paradigm. *In*: C.L. Wijeyesinghe and B.W. Jackson, III, eds. *New perspectives on racial identity development: a theoretical and practical anthology*. New York University Press, 129–152.

REFLECT AND CONSIDER

- How does multiraciality challenge traditional classifications and experiences of race?
- Why is it beneficial to understand multiracial identity as a matrix?

RACE AND THE NEW BIO-CITIZEN

BY DOROTHY ROBERTS

The Expansion of Race-Based Biotechnology

The emergence of biocitizenship is occurring at the same time as we are witnessing a resurgence in scientific and commercial interest in genetic differences among "races" (Duster 2005). After World War II, the rejection of eugenics, which had supported sterilization laws and other destructive programs in the United States, generated a compelling critique of the biological basis of race. The classification of human beings into distinct biological races is a system of governance that arose out of European conquest, enslavement, and colonization of people in Africa and Asia. Biocitizenship did not really originate in the twenty-first century. Race has always been a form of biocitizenship: its function is to include or exclude residents from full citizenship according to their assignment to a political hierarchy based on invented biological demarcations and justifications.

Social scientists' conclusion that race is socially, politically, and legally constructed was confirmed by genomic studies of human variation, including the

Human Genome Project. These studies showed high levels of genetic similarity within the human species. Genetic differences among human beings are "clinally distributed" —they appear gradually across geographic space; they do not fall into sharply demarcated groupings (Bolnick 2008, 72). On June 26, 2000, when President Bill Clinton unveiled the results of the Human Genome Project, he proclaimed that "human beings, regardless of race, are 99.9 percent the same." Most genetic variation occurs within populations, not between them. Some scholars believed that the science of human genetic diversity would replace race as the preeminent means of grouping people for scientific purposes.

In his manifesto against racial thinking, *Against Race*, sociologist Paul Gilroy (2000, 37) predicted that advances in genomic research would eventually discredit the idea of "specifically *racial* differences" by rendering race a useless way of classifying people. Similarly, Aravinda Chakravarti (2009, 380) wrote, in a recent issue of *Nature*, that "each of us has around 6.7 billion relatives. … The global picture of relatedness that is emerging from DNA studies stands to shatter many of our beliefs about ourselves." Chakravarti is hopeful that by shifting the focus of genomewide studies from populations to individuals, "we could test once and for all whether genetic race is a credible concept" (Chakravarti 2009, 381).

Reports of the demise of race as biological fact were premature. Attention quickly shifted from the 99.9 percent genetic similarity to the 0.1 percent genetic difference, and that difference was presumed to encompass race. One of the first sites for resuscitating race was also an important aspect of biological citizenship: personalized medicine. By prescribing therapeutics that match each individual's genetic predisposition to disease and response to drugs, scientists will enable people to manage and advocate for their own health more effectively. Key to the National Institutes of Health Pharmacogenetics Research Network, which studies how genes affect people's response to drugs, is the belief that "it is important to understand the 0.1 percent difference because it can help explain why one person is more susceptible to a disease or responds differently to a drug or an environmental factor than another person" (National Human Genome Resource Institute 2005). Some researchers see race as a critical first step to producing personalized medicine because it can serve as a proxy for individual genetic difference (Tate and Goldstein 2004).

The Raw Materials of Pharmacogenomic Research

In her ethnographic study of two biopharmaceutical labs, medical anthropologist Duana Fullwiley (2008) discovered that race served as an unquestioned organizing principle for the collection, analysis, and reporting of genetic data. During a six-month fieldwork stay at the University of California, San Francisco, Department of Biopharmaceutical Sciences, Fullwiley interviewed researchers investigating the pharmacogenetics of cell membrane transporters, molecules that are vital to drug delivery. The human genomic DNA that provided the raw material for their research entered the lab already classified by race. The researchers purchased DNA from the Coriell Institutes for Medical Research Cell Repository, which identified samples according to self-reported race. Unsatisfied, they also sought a grant to build a genetic database specifically for their project that collected more "racially pure" DNA by "excluding anyone who reported racial mixing in their genealogies for the past three generations" (Fullwiley 2008, 159).

The researchers not only assumed that African American and Caucasian DNA samples would have significantly different haplotype frequencies, but they also perceived each as the other's "*opposite* race" (Fullwiley 2008, 162). When researchers found results that were inconsistent with their perception of racial categorization, instead of rethinking their presumptions about racial sameness and difference, they usually reacted against the data. So when African American genetic frequencies were too similar to Caucasian ones, the scientists concluded that the racially labeled samples must have been contaminated. The organizing principle of race has marked the very raw materials that go into creating the new biocitizen and shape the scientific conclusions researchers draw from them.

Race at the Frontier of Personalized Medicine

The promise of personalized medicine, matching drugs to each individual's unique genome, hinges on race. Until pharmacogenomics can live up to this promise, race stands in as a surrogate for individual genetic variation. In June 2005, the Food and Drug Administration (FDA) approved the first race-based pharmaceutical, BiDil, to treat heart failure specifically in African American patients. BiDil was not designed only for black people. Jay Cohn, the University of Minnesota cardiologist who patented BiDil, combined two generic drugs that have been prescribed to patients regardless of race for decades and originally intended to market it to all suitable patients. Cohn and the biotech start-up firm Nitromed repackaged BiDil as a race-specific drug as a way to get marketing approval from the FDA and to extend the patent (Kahn 2004). What is more, the clinical trial that tested BiDil involved only African Americans. Because there was no comparison group, the researchers never showed that BiDil functions only or even better in black patients than in others. Yet the FDA permitted Nitromed to market BiDil as a drug for black people.

Why do heart patients need a race-specific therapy? One theory supporting this need is that the reason for higher mortality rates among black heart patients lies in their genetic difference, either in the reason for getting heart disease or the reason for responding differently to medications for it. In its March 2001 press releases, Nitromed explained that BiDil's efficacy stemmed from "a pathophysiology found primarily in black patients." "Observed racial disparities in mortality and therapeutic response rates in black patients may be due in part to ethnic differences in the underlying pathophysiology of heart failure," the company asserted (Kahn 2003, 474). The FDA similarly explained its decision to approve BiDil specifically for African American patients in a January 2007 article in *Annals of Internal Medicine*. "We hope that further research elucidates the genetic or other factors that predict the usefulness of hydralazine hydrochloride-isosorbide dinitrate [the ingredients in BiDil]," the authors wrote. "Until then, we are pleased that one defined group has access to a dramatically life-prolonging therapy" (Temple and Stockbridge 2007, 61).

In the past, the FDA has had no problem generalizing clinical trials involving white people to approve drugs for everyone. White bodies function like human bodies. But with BiDil, a clinical trial involving all African Americans could only serve as proof of how the drug works in blacks. By approving BiDil only for use in black patients, the FDA emphasized the supposed distinctive—and substandard—quality of black bodies (Bowser 2004).

BiDil is only one example of the growing trend toward what law professor Jonathan Kahn (2006, 1349) calls "the strategic use of race as a genetic category to obtain patent protection and drug approval." The emergence of race-based biomedicine means that the pharmaceutical and biotech industries see blacks and other racialized groups as profitable markets and test populations, as companies are searching for new moneymaking drugs and as the expansion of biotechnologies increases demand for human subjects and sources of human tissue. Race is a key channel through which scientists and corporations convert biomedical research into biocapital. In this way, powerful market forces help to construct the new biocitizen along racial lines.

Extending Reprogenetics to Women of Color

Genetic science is empowering biocitizens to manage and manipulate their own health through another form of personalized medicine. At the turn of the twenty-first century, advanced reproductive technologies that combine assisted conception with genetic selection, or *reprogenetics*, increasingly allow individuals to reduce genetic risk itself by determining some parts of their children's genetic makeup (Parens and Knowles 2007; Spar 2006). With preimplantation genetic diagnosis (PGD), clinicians can biopsy a single cell from an early embryo, diagnose it for the chance of having hundreds of genetic conditions, and select for implantation only those embryos at low risk of having these conditions. As Reprogenetics, LLC, a New Jersey–based genetics laboratory that specializes in PGD, puts it, this technique allows for the "replacement to the patient of those embryos classified by genetic diagnosis as normal."[1]

In my prior work, I used to place white, affluent women who had access to high-tech reproduction and women of color who were targets of population control policies at opposite ends of a reproductive hierarchy (Roberts 1997). But the recent expansion of both reproductive genetic screening and race-based biomedicine signals a dramatic change in the racial politics of reproductive technologies. First, the important role of genetic screening in the new biopolitics that gives individual citizens the responsibility for ensuring good health by reducing genetic risk may support the wider incorporation of certain reprogenetic technologies into the health care system. Second, companies that market race-based biotechnologies now promise to extend the benefits of genetic research to people of color, and reproductive technologies are no exception.

Media promoting genetic technologies prominently feature people of color in images representing the new genetic age, in contrast to prior portrayals, which emphasized whiteness as the exclusive standard of genetic fitness. Moreover, some clinics that offer high-tech reproductive services, including PGD, explicitly appeal to clients of color.[2] Women of color are now part of the market and cultural imaginary of the new reprogenetics. As with personalized medicine, race is an essential component of reprogenetics, as clients who buy and sell eggs are grouped according to race (Fogg-Davis 2001). The price of eggs is determined by a racial supply and demand system, and customer satisfaction hinges on racial results. A Dominican woman and her white husband sued a New York fertility clinic when their daughter came out too dark (Williams 2007).

Numerous advertisements on craigslist explicitly solicit egg donors of color. For example, a posting by Beverly Hills Egg Donation notes, "ALL ETHNICITIES WELCOME!"[3] F. Williams Donor Services's listing states, "Ethnic Diverse Egg Donors Needed," and includes a photo of an Asian, a white, and a black woman.[4] Happy Beginnings, LLC, advertises, "EGG DONORS WANTED ALL ETHNIC BACKGROUNDS," specifying, "WE HAVE A VERY HIGH DEMAND FOR JEWISH, EAST INDIAN, MIDDLE EASTERN, ASIAN, ITALIAN, AND BLONDE DONORS."[5] Similarly, Pacific Fertility Center boasts that it "maintains a diverse egg donor database including Jewish egg donors, Asian egg donors, and a variety of backgrounds and ethnicities."

Although Reproductive Health Specialists, Ltd., in Illinois, displays a photograph of a large group of white couples holding white babies, captioned "Baby Picnic," its Web site contains a photograph of a smiling black man and woman and a drawing of a pregnant black woman attended to by a black male partner and a female physician.[6] Likewise, Houston IVF's Web site shows a beaming black couple holding a black baby.[7] The Illinois-based Karande and Associates, S.C., takes a very multicultural approach, using a photo of a pregnant East Asian woman for scheduling an appointment, a black woman and child for its link to donor egg information, and a South Asian man and child for the insurance information link.[8]

Some fertility clinic Web sites not only market their reprogenetic services to people of color; they also perform race-based genetic testing as part of those services. Pacific Fertility Center's Web site includes the statement, "Genetic screening is also recommended, based on ethnic background."[9] Reproductive Genetics Institute, in Chicago, similarly includes race in the factors it takes into account in its genetic testing: "Screening Results and Accuracy: By combining the results of the ultrasound and blood test along with the age, race and weight of the mother, a number can be generated by computer which represents the risk of the pregnancy being affected by Down syndrome or another chromosome problem."[10] Granted there are some rare genetic problems that are so highly concentrated in an ethnic group that is arguably defensible to segregate testing for these conditions, but most genetic mutations are not linked to race. This race-based testing reinforces the myth that races are genetically distinct from one another and that our genetic profile is determined by our race. It also reinforces the importance of race to the genetic technologies that empower biocitizens.

Genetic Ancestry Testing and Racialized Identity

African Americans have joined the growing ranks of Americans who use commercially available technologies to determine their ancestry and genealogy, one of the most popular hobbies in the United States. A cottage industry of online businesses employ techniques developed in forensic genetics and human genomic research to provide customers information about their genetic lineage. An increasing segment of this business is devoted to identifying not only genetic ancestry, but also *racial* identity. By submitting a sample of DNA and paying a fee, customers of these companies can trace their roots to particular racialized population groups (Nelson 2008).

AncestryByDNA, for example, promises to determine customers' genetic heritage by assigning percentages of ancestry from the "four anthropological groups": Native American, East Asian, sub-Saharan African, and European, described in contemporary terms as "anthropological lineages that extend back in time tens of thousands of years." Other companies attempt to restore the genealogical histories irreparably broken by the slave trade. African Ancestry, established by University of Chicago geneticist Rick Kittles, offers DNA testing to African Americans to trace their ancestry to more than 160 ethnic groups in Africa. Riding the popularity of his PBS specials, *African American Lives*, parts 1 and 2, and his book, *Finding Oprah's Roots*, Henry Louis Gates launched his own ancestry testing service, African DNA.

While the interest of many people in tracking their genetic lineage stems from curiosity about their *family* tree, African Americans are using genetic technologies to learn more about and to reconfigure their *group* identity. The companies that specialize in recovering black people's African roots cannot possibly identify customers' individual ancestors who lived in regions of Africa prior to their capture by slave traders; rather, these companies match black customers with groups of people living in Africa today based on their shared genetic traits. Ancestry testing will not reveal the identity of a black customer's great, great, great, great grandmother, but it may tell a black customer that "her mt-DNA traces to the current Mende people of Sierra Leone" (Nelson 2008, 254). Alondra Nelson (2008, 254) describes these genetic tools as "ethnic lineage instruments through which undifferentiated racial identity is translated into African ethnicity and kinship." Distinct from family-focused genealogical projects, these provide the sources for "constituting new forms of diasporic affiliation and identification" (Nelson 2008, 254).

Not only does ancestry testing help to fortify black Americans' identification with ethnic groups on the African continent; it is also a way to cement black community ties here in the United States, as it becomes incorporated into traditional black institutions and customs. For example, African Ancestry partnered with Mt. Ennon Baptist Church, a large Black church outside Washington, D.C., for a whole series of genetic events during the month of February 2008.[11] The pastor and his wife launched the program by revealing their ancestral roots during church service. Then "Where Are You From?" workshops were held during Bible study and in the chapel following each service during the month. The campaign culminated with a "Community Testing Day," when the entire congregation was offered ancestry testing at a special price and were provided a room to get their cheeks swabbed in the church building. The following Sunday, African Ancestry invited them to "receive your ancestry results and connect with your friends and family in a whole new way during the Church Anniversary Celebration."

For his part, Gates is developing an ancestry-based curriculum for public school children that centers on studying their own DNA: "My plan," he announced, "is to revolutionize the way we teach history and science to inner-city black and minority kids" (Horowitz 2007). Gates envisions a six-week unit focused on tracing students' ancestry that will be incorporated in history class. Students will initially collect family stories and records, but would turn to genetic testing when historical archives are exhausted. "We' ll swab their cheeks, and this is where the science class comes in. We'll teach them how DNA works, how ancestry tracing is possible through the analysis of their DNA" (von Zastrow 2008). Gates sees students' fascination with their own genealogies as a hook for getting black children more involved in learning, to reverse their alarming high school dropout rates. He also relates the ancestry curriculum to blacks' citizenship: "I think that any time you get kids interested in the history of the country—in this case, through the history of themselves or their extended selves, their families—it is performing a civic function" (von Zastrow 2008).

Black Americans are at the cutting edge of using genetic technologies to map not only their individual genomes, but their biosociality—and their citizenship. This is not a separate citizenship that revolves around health issues, but rather, one that incorporates new genomic research into racial identities and everyday institutions. Nelson (2008, 258–259) emphasizes that blacks use ancestry testing as part of a cultural project that seeks to reconcile the destructive legacy of slavery; rather than base their identity solely on genetic data, they treat test results as a resource that they incorporate into a more complicated process of "affiliative self-fashioning." The role genetic genealogy plays in identity making depends on black people's desire to be affiliated with Africa and on cultural understandings of kinship. The work of constructing an identity rooted in African ethnicity starts with the "Certificate of Ancestry"; it is not determined by it. Yet despite its extragenetic dimensions, treating genetic genealogy as the linchpin of identification and affiliation helps to reinforce the emerging understanding of citizenship rooted in biological sameness and difference.

There are also companies that market DNA testing specifically to Native American tribes to decide questions of enrollment (TallBear 2008). These companies use genetics either to trace an individual's recent ancestry to tribal members or to determine an individual's percentage of Native American "biogeographical ancestry." Kimberly TallBear (2008, 238) notes that DNA testing to confirm tribal membership reflects "a linear-descendency understanding of kinship and race that is focused on relationships between individuals," rather than on traditional notions of belonging based on social relationships with other tribal members. "The molecular knowledge produced by DNA tests does not account well for group kinship that is central to tribes," writes TallBear (2008, 238). Kinship is a social, legal, and cultural concept of relatedness that need not entail genetics at all; yet some ancestry testing companies reduce kinship exclusively to a genetic determination (Nash 2004).

Moreover, some ancestry testing services that claim to confirm unique Native American genetic patterns replace notions of community based on tribal relatedness with race as the source of Native American identity. These companies assume that there is a pure Native American biogeographical ancestry reflected in the genome and that genetic testing can therefore reveal whether someone is authentically Native American. Thus, these technologies promote a kind of racial identification that depends more on common genetic makeup than on common sociopolitical experiences and solidarity around the struggle against racial oppression.

References

Barr, Donald A. 2008. *Health disparities in the United States: Social class, race, ethnicity and health.* Baltimore: Johns Hopkins University Press.

Bolnick, Deborah A. 2008. Individual ancestry inference and the reification of race as a biological phenomenon. In *Revisiting race in a genomic age*, ed. Barbara A. Keonig, Sandra Soo-Jin Lee, and Sarah S. Richardson. Piscataway, NJ: Rutgers University Press, 70–85.

Bonilla-Silva, Eduardo. 2003. *Racism without racists: Color-blind racism and the persistence of racial inequality in the United States.* Lanham, MD: Rowman and Littlefield.

Bowser, Renee. 2004. Race as a proxy for drug response: The dangers and challenges of ethnic drugs. *De Paul Law Review* 53: 1111–1126.

Chakravarti, Aravinda. 2009. Kinship: Race relations. *Nature* 457: 380–381.

Collins, Jane, Micaela diLeonardo, and Brett Williams. 2008. *New landscapes of inequality.* Santa Fe, NM: School of American Research Press.

Davis, Angela Y. 2003. *Are prisons obsolete?* New York: Seven Stories Press.

Duster, Troy. 2005. Race and reification in science. *Science* 307: 1050–1051.

Entine, Jon. 2007. 10 questions for Jon Entine, Gene Expression Weblog. http://www.gnxp.com/blog/2007/10/10-questions-for-jon-entine.php.

Epstein, Steven. 2007. *Inclusion: The politics of difference in medical research.* Chicago: University of Chicago Press.

Ferdinand, Keith. 2008. Fixed-dose isosorbide dinitrate-hydralazine: Race-based cardiovascular medicine benefit or mirage? *Journal of Law, Medicine, and Ethics* 36: 458–463.

Fogg-Davis, Hawley. 2001. Navigating race in the market for human gametes. *Hastings Center Report* 31: 13–21.

Franklin, Sarah, and Celia Roberts. 2006. *Born and made: An ethnography of preimplantation genetic diagnosis.* Princeton, NJ: Princeton University Press.

Fullwiley, Duana. 2008. The molecularization of race: U.S. health institutions, pharmacogenetics practice, and public science after the genome. In *Revisiting race in a genomic age*, ed. Barbara A. Keonig, Sandra Soo-Jin Lee, and Sarah S. Richardson. Piscataway, NJ: Rutgers University Press, 149–171.

Garland, David. 2001. Introduction: The meaning of mass imprisonment. In *Mass imprisonment: Social causes and consequences*, ed. David Garland. Thousand Oaks, CA: Sage, 1–3.

Gilroy, Paul. 2000. *Against race: Imagining political culture beyond the color line.* Cambridge, MA: Harvard University Press.

Harmon, Amy. 2008a. Gene map becomes a luxury item. *New York Times*, March 4.

Harmon, Amy. 2008b. Taking a peek at the experts' genetic secrets. *New York Times*, October 19.

Harvey, David. 2005. *A brief history of neoliberalism*. New York: Oxford University Press.

Horowitz, Mark. 2007. The 2007 Rave Awards: Henry Louis Gates Jr./ancestry-based curriculum. http://www.wired.com/culture/lifestyle/multimedia/2007/04/ss_raves?slide=3.

Kahn, Jonathan. 2003. Getting the numbers right: Statistical mischief and racial profiling in heart failure research. *Perspectives in Biology and Medicine* 46: 473–483.

Kahn, Jonathan. 2004. How a drug becomes "ethnic": Law, commerce, and the production of racial categories in medicine. *Yale Journal of Health Policy, Law, and Ethics* 4: 1–46.

Kahn, Jonathan. 2006. Patenting race. *Nature Biotechnology* 24: 1349–1351.

Liptak, Adam. 2008. Inmate count in U.S. dwarfs other nations. *New York Times*, April 23.

Mykitiuk, Roxanne. 2000. The new genetics in the post-Keynesian state. Unpublished paper. http://www.cwhn.ca/groups/biotech/availdocs/15-mykitiuk.pdf.

Nakashima, Ellen. 2008. Genome database will link genes, traits in public view. *Washington Post*, October 18.

Nash, Catherine. 2004. Genetic kinship. *Cultural Studies* 18: 1–33.

National Human Genome Resource Institute. 2005. International consortium completes map of human genetic variation. National Institutes of Health News. October. http://www/genome.gov/17015412.

Nelson, Alondra. 2008. The factness of diaspora: The social sources of genetic genealogy. In *Revisiting race in a genomic age*, ed. Barbara A. Keonig, Sandra Soo-Jin Lee, and Sarah S. Richardson. Piscataway, NJ: Rutgers University Press, 253–268.

Parens, Erik, and Lori P. Knowles. 2007. Reprogenetics and public policy: reflections and recommendations. In *Reprogenetics: Law, policy, and ethical issues*, ed. Lori P. Knowles and Gregory E. Kaebnick. Baltimore: Johns Hopkins University Press, 253–294.

Pollack, Andrew. 2008. Congress near deal on genetic test bias bill. *New York Times*, April 23.

Puckrein, Gary. 2006. BiDil: From another vantage point. *Health Affairs* 25: w368–w374.

Rabinow, Paul. 1996. *Essays on the anthropology of reason*. Princeton, NJ: Princeton University Press.

Reverby, Susan. 2008. "Special treatment": BiDil, Tuskegee, and the logic of race. *Journal of Law, Medicine, and Ethics* 36: 478–484.

Roberts, Dorothy. 1997. *Killing the black body: Race, reproduction and the meaning of liberty*. New York: Pantheon

Rose, Nikolas. 2007. *The politics of life itself: Biomedicine, power, and subjectivity in the twenty-first century*. Princeton, NJ: Princeton University Press.

Salkin, Allen. 2008. When in doubt, spit it out. *New York Times*, September 12.

Satel, Sally. 2002. I am a racially profiling doctor. *New York Times*, May 5.

Satel, Sally. 2005. Race and medicine can mix without prejudice: How the story of BiDil illuminates the future of medicine. http://www.medicalprogresstoday.com/spotlight/spotlight_indarchive.php?id=449.

Spar, Debora L. 2006. *The baby business: How money, science and politics drive the commerce of conception.* Boston: Harvard Business School Press.

TallBear, Kimberly. 2008. Native-American-DNA.com: In search of Native American race and tribe. In *Revisiting race in a genomic age*, ed. Barbara A. Keonig, Sandra Soo-Jin Lee, and Sarah S. Richardson. Piscataway, NJ: Rutgers University Press, 235–252.

Tate, Sarah K., and David B. Goldstein. 2004. Will tomorrow's medicines work for everyone? *Nature Genetics* 36: S34–S42.

Temple, Robert, and Norman L. Stockbridge. 2007. BiDil for heart failure in black patients: The U.S. Food and Drug Administration perspective. *Annals of Internal Medicine* 146: 57–62.

Von Zastrow, Claus. 2008. Mounting a curricular revolution: An interview with Henry Louis Gates, Jr. Public School Insights Weblog. http://www.publicschoolinsights.org/node/2144.

Wagner, Peter. 2005. Incarceration is not an equal opportunity punishment. Prison Policy Initiative. http://www.prisonpolicy.org/articles/notequal.html.

Weiss, Rick. 2008. Genetic testing gets personal. *Washington Post*, March 25.

Williams, Patricia J. 2007. Colorstruck. *The Nation*, April 23.

Notes

1. See the Reprogenetics Web site at http://reprogenetics.com/.

2. See the Pacific Fertility Center's appeal to prospective donors at http://www.donateyoureggs.com and information about egg donation at http://www.pacificfertilitycenter.com/treat/agency_donation.php.

3. See Beverly Hills Egg Donation, advertisement, Los Angeles craigslist, SF Valley, etcetera jobs, November 22, 2008.

4. See F. Williams Donor Services, advertisement, Inland Empire craigslist, etcetera jobs, November 24, 2008.

5. See Happy Beginnings, LLC, advertisement, Reno craigslist, etcetera jobs, November 13, 2008.

6. See the Pacific Fertility Center's appeal to prospective donors at http://www.donateyoureggs.com.

7. See the Reproductive Health Specialists Web site at http://ivfplus.com/baby_party.htm; http://ivfplus.com/treatments.htm; http://ivfplus.com/patients_only.htm.

8. See the Houston IVF Web site at http://www.houstonivf.net/houstonivf/OurServices/OurServices.asp.

9. For images from the Karande and Associates Web site, see http://www.karandeivf.com.

10. See the Pacific Fertility Center's Web site at http://www.pacificfertilitycenter.com/treat/agency_donation.php.

11. See the Reproductive Genetics Institute's Web page on first-trimester screening at http://www.reproductivegenetics.com/first_trimester.html.

12. African Ancestry advertised the "Community Testing Day" during February 2008 on its Web site at http://www.AfricanAncestry.com.

REFLECT AND CONSIDER

- In what ways is race being re-introduced and discussed as biological?
- How are scientific advancements co-opted to suggest race is biological?

A POST-RACIAL SOCIETY?

BY KATHLEEN FITZGERALD

Sociological Perspectives on the Future of Race

This book began with the argument that race is a social construction, meaning that the concept of race changes across time and place. Groups categorized as racial minorities in 1840 (for example, Irish Americans) are very different than groups categorized as racial minorities in 1980 (for example, Mexican Americans). How race is defined in Brazil differs substantially from US racial categorization systems, as they have five official categories: *branco* (white), *pardo* (brown), *preto* (black), *amarelo* (yellow), and indigenous. With that knowledge, it should come as no surprise that sociologists make the argument that in the future, "race" will look different than it does today. This means that groups that are currently racialized may not be, and some groups that are not currently racialized may be. Our census will count "racial" groups differently than it does today. While no one can say for sure what groups will be racialized and what groups will become white, this chapter explores some predictions sociologists offer on what the future may hold. All sociologists do not agree on what the racial future looks like specifically, but there is consensus that we are not now, nor are we likely to be in the near future, a "postracial" society.

In Chapter 1, we challenged the media interpretation of PEW Research Center data that declared whites will be a "minority" by 2050. One of the reasons this assumption is unlikely to prove true is because sociologists predict that the definition of who is "white" will change (Yancey 2003). Similarly to Irish, Jewish, and Italian Americans in the past, some groups that are currently defined as "non-white" today will become white.

Becoming White in the Twenty-First Century

Sociologist George Yancey (2003) argues that the groups likely to become white in the next forty years are Latinos and Asian Americans. His argument is based on the recognition that African Americans face a greater degree of alienation than other racial groups. Latinos without African features and Asian Americans do not face the same degree of alienation in the United States as African Americans do, despite the fact that they undeniably face prejudice and racism.

In addition to his argument that Latinos and Asian Americans face less alienation than black Americans, Yancey argues that they are more likely to become white for several reasons. The first is that Latinos have some European heritage, which likely results in more social acceptance of them. There has also been a long trend toward **exogamy** among Latinos, marrying outside of their group. An additional argument can be made that Latinos are of value to the dominant group due to their sheer size alone. Whites may actually encourage the assimilation of Latinos, like they did the Irish in the mid-1800s, because it is in the political interest of whites to assimilate them rather than having them remain a sizable minority group. Certainly becoming white is alluring to minority groups because of the privileges attached to it, but it can also be beneficial to the dominant group in securing their power. This argument should not be taken to imply that all minority groups desire to distance themselves from their culture and "become white," just that the privileges associated with whiteness can be alluring.

Asian Americans are similar to Southern/Eastern Europeans that were incorporated into an expanded definition of whiteness in the past, according to Yancey (2003). One of the similarities is that the bulk of Asian Americans have entered the United States during roughly the same era, the post-1965 period, making their experience with racism similar to one another rather than having their experiences span multiple generations. Other arguments look to the high interracial marriage rates among Asian Americans, particularly Asian American women, and their model minority status as explanations for their likelihood to become white.

Triracial Stratification System

Sociologist Eduardo Bonilla-Silva (2010) makes a different argument for the future of race in America than the previous one offered by sociologist George Yancey, one he refers to as the **Latin Americanization thesis**. This thesis argues that the United States is shifting from a binary white/non-white racial system to a triracial stratification system, similar to that which is found in many Latin American and Caribbean countries. In this **triracial stratification system**, a stratification system refers to a status hierarchy, in this case a racial status hierarchy where instead of a binary with whites at the top and nonwhites at the bottom, Bonilla-Silva argues that whites will be at the top of the racial hierarchy; an intermediary group of "honorary whites," in the middle; and a nonwhite group, at the bottom. Unlike Yancey, Bonilla-Silva argues that some Latinos and Asian Americans are more likely to assimilate into whiteness, but not all people and groups that fall under those umbrella categories will be classified as white.

In Bonilla-Silva's triracial stratification system, the white group will be composed of traditional whites, any new white immigrants, and some Latinos; specifically those that are totally assimilated. Also included in this category are lighter-skinned multiracial individuals. The honorary whites will comprise most light-skinned Latinos, Japanese Americans, Korean Americans, Asian Indians, Chinese Americans, and most Middle-Eastern Americans. The bottom rung of the racial hierarchy will be composed of blacks, dark-skinned Latinos with visible African ancestry, Vietnamese, Cambodians, Filipinos, and Laotians (Table 8.3.1).

TABLE 8.3.1. Preliminary Map of Triracial Order in the USA

"WHITES"	"HONORARY WHITES"	"COLLECTIVE BLACK/ NON-WHITE"
whites	Light-skinned Latinos	Vietnamese Americans
new whites (Russians, Albanians, etc.)	Japanese Americans	Filipino Americans
	Korean Americans	Hmong Americans
assimilated white Latinos	Asian Indians	Laotian Americans
some multiracials	Chinese Americans	Dark-skinned Latinos
assimilated (urban) Native Americans	Middle Eastern Americans	Blacks
		New West Indians
a few Asian-origin people	most multiracials	African immigrants
		Reservation-bound Native Americans

Source: Bonilla-Silva, Eduardo. 2010. *Racism Without Racists: Color-Blind Racism & Racial Inequality in Contemporary American*, 3rd Edition. Rowman and Littlefield: Lanham, MA. (p. 180).

Some of the reasons Bonilla-Silva gives for his Latin Americanization thesis are that Latin America has a long history of race mixing that coexists with rather than supplants white supremacy. In other words, throughout Latin America, white supremacy still exists despite the very different attitudes toward miscegenation. In Brazil, someone who is fair skinned and has European features generally benefits from white privilege. Thus, while many people argue that the increase in interracial dating and marriages in the United States will result in the dismantling of the racial hierarchy, Bonilla-Silva does not agree. He argues that a new racial hierarchy will emerge, a triracial classification system, but whites will remain at the top. One piece of evidence he uses to make his argument that some Asian Americans and some Latinos will become honorary whites is that research finds that whites are significantly more likely to live near people that would fall into the "honorary white" category than those that fall into the "collective black/nonwhite" category (Bonilla-Silva 2010). For instance, dark-skinned Latinos face residential segregation patterns similar to that of African Americans, whereas Latinos that identify as white, such as Cubans and South Americans, are more likely to live in communities with non-Hispanic whites (Logan 2003).

The racial stratification system in Latin America is based in colorism, which implies that racial groups are internally stratified along the lines of skin color (with lighter-skinned people receiving preferential treatment and darker-skinned people experiencing more discrimination).

Race and the Millennial Generation

The "Millennial Generation," those born after 1980, is the most racially and ethnically diverse generation the United States has ever known. The youth vote strongly favored Barack Obama in the 2008 and 2012 presidential elections. In a series of focus groups conducted by the Applied Research Center, Millennials were asked their feelings about race and, specifically, the claim that the United States is a "postracial" society. While there are differences among Millennials along race and class lines as to how much race remains a factor in today's society, one of the overwhelming findings of this report is that a large majority of young people surveyed believe that racism remains a significant force today, particularly within the criminal justice system, educational institutions, economics, and in immigration debates. Research from the previous chapter describes members of this generation as more comfortable with interracial dating, which is often used as evidence of their sense that they are different from previous generations, yet they do not think our society is postracial and that they are beyond race (Apollon 2011).

Although the election of the nation's first nonwhite president is a sign of racial progress and many in the American media immediately declared the United States to be a postracial society after the election of Barack Obama, Millennials do believe that race still matters (Applied Research Center http:// www.arc.org /component / option,com _frontpage /Itemid,1). While the majority of young people in these focus groups felt that race was particularly significant in certain arenas, such as the criminal justice system and the economic sphere, there were some racial differences in how they saw racism in these institutions—interestingly, focus group participants of color were more likely to see the system as racist while white participants were more likely to view individuals within the system as responsible for the racism. Young people of color were also more likely to bring up the issue of race and racism, while white Millennials were less likely to make connections across systems when discussing racism (Apollon 2011). Millennials of color were also more likely to express concern over the increasingly hostile political climate, particularly the Tea Party movement, than were whites.

REFLECT AND CONSIDER

- How might the White racial group adapt to the change in U.S. racial demographics?
- Why is getting rid of all racial categories not the solution?

HIGHLIGHT

CHOOSE YOUR OWN IDENTITY

BY BONNIE TSUI, *THE NEW YORK TIMES MAGAZINE*

SUMMARY

In 1967 interracial marriages became legal, in 2000 the option to choose more than one race on the US Census appeared, and into the second decade of the twenty-first century multiracials are the fastest growing population. In this article, Tsui discusses the contemporary fluidity of racial identity, particularly for multiracials. There are now more options for racial identity than observed at any other time period in US history, and in evaluating the future of race, one has to take into account both the boundaries of racial classifications and individual agency.

EXCERPT FROM
"CHOOSE YOUR OWN IDENTITY"

I never realized how little I understood race until I tried to explain it to my 5-year-old son. Our family story doesn't seem too complicated: I'm Chinese-American and my husband is white, an American of English-Dutch-Irish descent; we have two children. My 5-year-old knows my parents were born in China, and that I speak Cantonese sometimes. He has been to Hong Kong and Guangzhou to visit his *gung-gung*, my father. But when I asked him the other day if he was Chinese, he said no.

 READ THE REST OF THE ESSAY:

bit.ly/identitynytimesmag

READ, LISTEN, WATCH, INTERACT!

READ

MTV/David Binder Research Study (on Millennials and Bias)
READ AT bit.ly/mtvstudy

What Happened When a Biracial Woman Was Photoshopped in 18 Different Countries

Cate Mattews, 8.8.2014, HuffPost
READ AT bit.ly/biracial18

LISTEN

Race and Medicine
Radiolab
LISTEN AT bit.ly/racemedicine

Rachel Dolezal's Story Sparks Questions About 'How People Experience Race

All Things Considered, 6.16.2015, NPR
LISTEN AT bit.ly/dolezalrace

WATCH

 Chasing Daybreak: A Film About Mixed Race in America
Justin Leroy and Matt Kelley, 2006, sponsored by MAViN Foundation
AVAILABLE AT bit.ly/chasingdaybreak

 Dear White People
Justin Simien, 2014
AVAILABLE AT bit.ly/dearwhitepeoplefilm

INTERACT

 The Hapa Project
Kip Fulbeck
INTERACT AT bit.ly/hapaproject

 The Racial Dot Map
Dustin A. Cable, Weldon Cooper Center for Public Service, Rector and Visitors of the University of Virginia, 2013

INTERACT AT bit.ly/racialdotmapdemo

FIGHTING RACIAL INEQUALITY

At this point in the course you may feel defeated and even sad about the prospects for racial equality. It's a difficult process to learn about the many ways in which race and racism are embedded into society, and the ways in which the racial hierarchy persists. At the same time, much progress has been made and a look at history shows, without a doubt, that society has moved ever closer to addressing racial inequality. The lesson is in recognizing where oppression remains, and using one's agency and collective mobilization to address it. As discussed in the first reading, "The Problem of the Twentieth Century Is the Problem of the Color Line," W. E. B. Du Bois predicted that the color line would be the problem of the twentieth century. That this has proved to be true not just for the twentieth century but for the twenty-first century as well illustrates the profundity of Du Bois's insight.

Despite Du Bois's gloomy analysis, it would be a mistake to assert that he was mired in pessimism. He showed the daunting nature of the social obstacles facing African Americans, but he also pointed to areas of life in which they had advanced. Consequently, it would be more accurate to say that Du Bois viewed the twentieth century as a time for promising struggle and uncertainty, for society in general, and for African Americans in particular. In the second reading, Howard Zinn focuses on this idea of uncertainty, and reminds us that social conditions can change over time. Taking a broad view of twentieth century history, he shows how, through struggle and resistance, various oppressed groups have improved their lot in life.

Struggle takes many forms and includes, among other things, policies that are designed to help bring oppressed groups into the mainstream of American life. Few such policies have been as contentious as affirmative action. Birthed in the liberal 1960s, it has encountered increasing backlash as American politics has moved farther and farther to the right. Considering, especially, the makeup of the US Supreme Court and recent decisions, it would not be a stretch to say that affirmative action faces significant constriction or even possible extinction. Responding to the backlash, Orlando Patterson, in the third reading, advances reasons why American society needs affirmative action. He argues that though the policy is strongly attacked because it tries to change the very assumptions undergirding inequality in America, which he refers to as "the rules of the game," affirmative action is merely an extension of struggles for inclusion that subordinated groups have been fighting for over time. In the Highlight, "The Case for Reparations," by Ta-Nehisi Coates this principle is extended by considering not simply how African Americans can be brought into the mainstream of American life, but whether they should be compensated, through reparations, for their historical oppression.

AS YOU READ

- Consider the extent to which racialized inequality in present-day America resembles or differs from such inequality in Du Bois's day.
- Evaluate the pros and cons of affirmative action.
- Reflect on how you might participate in fighting racial inequality.

THE PROBLEM OF THE TWENTIETH CENTURY IS THE PROBLEM OF THE COLOR LINE

BY W.E.B. DU BOIS

We are just finishing the first half of the Twentieth Century. I remember its birth in 1901. There was the usual discussion as to whether the century began in 1900 or 1901; but, of course, 1901 was correct. We expected great things ... peace; the season of war among nations had passed; progress was the order ... everything going forward to bigger and better things. And then, not so openly expressed, but even more firmly believed, the rule of white Europe and America over black, brown and yellow peoples.

I was 32 years of age in 1901, married, and a father, and teaching at Atlanta University with a program covering a hundred years of study and investigation into the condition of American Negroes. Our subject of study at that time was education: the college-bred Negro in 1900, the Negro common school in 1901. My own attitude toward the Twentieth Century was expressed in an article which I wrote in the Atlantic Monthly in 1901. It said:

The problem of the Twentieth Century is the problem of the color-line ... I have seen a land right merry with the sun, where children sing, and rolling hills lie like passioned women wanton with harvest. And there in the King's Highway sat, and sits, a figure veiled and bowed, by which the Traveler's footsteps hasten as they go. On the tainted air broods fair. Three centuries' thought have been the raising and unveiling of that bowed human soul; and now behold, my fellows, a century now for the duty and the deed! The problem of the Twentieth Century is the problem of the color-line.

This is what we hoped, to this we Negroes looked forward; peace, progress and the breaking of the color line. What has been the result? We know it all too well ... war, hate, the revolt of the colored peoples and the fear of more war.

In the meantime, where are we; those 15,000,000 citizens of the United States who are descended from the slaves, brought here between 1600 and 1900? We formed in 1901, a separate group because of legal enslavement and emancipation into caste conditions, with the attendant poverty, ignorance, disease and crime. We were an inner group and not an integral part of the American nation; but we were exerting ourselves to fight for integration.

The burden of our fight was in seven different lines. We wanted education; we wanted particularly the right to vote and civil rights; we wanted work with adequate wage; housing, without segregation or slums; a free press to fight our battles, and (although in those days we dare not say it) social equality.

In 1901 our education was in perilous condition, despite what we and our white friends had done for thirty years. The Atlanta University Conference said in its resolutions of 1901:

> We call the attention of the nation to the fact that less than one million of the three million Negro children of school age are at present regularly attending school, and these attend a session which lasts only a few months. We are today deliberately rearing millions of our citizens in ignorance and at the same time limiting the rights of citizenship by educational qualifications. This is unjust.

More particularly in civil rights, we were oppressed. We not only did not get justice in the courts, but we were subject to peculiar and galling sorts of injustice in daily life. In the latter half of the Nineteenth Century, where we first get something like statistics, no less than 3,000 Negroes were lynched without trial. And in addition to that we were subject continuously to mob violence and judicial lynching.

In political life we had, for twenty-five years, been disfranchised by violence, law and public opinion. The 14th and 15th amendments were deliberately violated and the literature of the day in book, pamphlet and daily press, was widely of opinion that the Negro was not ready for the ballot, could not use it intelligently, and that no action was called for to stop his political power from being exercised by Southern whites like Tillman and Vardaman.

We did not have the right or opportunity to work at an income which would sustain a decent and modern standard of life. Because of a past of chattel slavery, we were for the most part common laborers and servants, and a very considerable proportion were still unable to leave the plantations where they worked all their lives for next to nothing.

There were a few who were educated for the professions and we had many good artisans; that number was not increasing as it should have been, nor were new artisans being adequately trained. Industrial training was popular, but funds to implement it were too limited, and we were excluded from unions and the new mass industry.

We were housed in slums and segregated districts where crime and disease multiplied, and when we tried to move to better and healthier quarters we were met by segregation ordinance if not by mobs. We not only had no social equality, but we did not openly ask for it. It seemed a shameful thing to beg people to receive us as equals and as human beings; that was something we argued "that came and could not be fetched." And that meant not simply that we could not marry white women or legitimize mulatto bastards, but we could not stop in a decent hotel, nor eat in a public restaurant nor attend the theatre, nor accept an invitation to a private white home, nor travel in a decent railway coach. When the "public" was invited, this did not include us and admission to colleges often involved special consideration if not blunt refusal.

Finally we had poor press ... a few struggling papers with little news and inadequately expressed opinion, with small circulation or influence and almost no advertising.

This was our plight in 1901. It was discouraging, but not hopeless. There is no question but that we had made progress, and there also was no doubt but what that progress was not enough to satisfy us or to settle our problems.

We could look back on a quarter century of struggle which had its results. We had schools; we had teachers; a few had forced themselves into the leading colleges and were tolerated if not welcomed. We voted in Northern cities, owned many decent homes and were fighting for further progress. Leaders like Booker Washington had received wide popular approval and a Negro literature had begun to appear.

But what we needed was organized effort along the whole front, based on broad lines of complete emancipation. This came with the Niagara Movement in 1906 and the NAACP in 1909. In 1910 came the Crisis magazine and the real battle was on.

What have we gained and accomplished? The advance has not been equal on all fronts, nor complete on any. We have not progressed with closed ranks like a trained army, but rather with serried and broken ranks, with wide gaps and even temporary retreats. But we have advanced. Of that there can be no atom of doubt.

First of all in education; most Negro children today are in school and most adults can read and write. Unfortunately this literacy is not as great as the census says. The draft showed that at least a third of our youth are illiterate. But education is steadily rising. Six thousand Bachelor degrees are awarded to Negroes each year and Doctorates in philosophy and medicine are not uncommon. Nevertheless as a group, American Negroes are still in the lower ranks of learning and adaptability to modern conditions. They do not read widely, their travel is limited and their experience through contact with the modern world is curtailed by law and custom.

Secondly, in civil rights, the Negro has perhaps made his greatest advance. Mob violence and lynching have markedly decreased. Three thousand Negroes were lynched in the last half of the Nineteenth Century and five hundred in the first half of the Twentieth. Today lynching is comparatively rare. Mob violence also has decreased, but is still in evidence, and summary and unjust court proceedings have taken the place of open and illegal acts. But the Negro has established, in the courts, his legal citizenship and his right to be included in the Bill of Rights. The question still remains of "equal but separate" public accommodations, and that is being attacked. Even the institution of "jim-crow" in travel is tottering. The infraction of the marriage situation by law and custom is yet to be brought before the courts and public opinion in a forcible way.

Third, the right to vote on the part of the Negro is being gradually established under the 14th and 15th amendments. It was not really until 1915 that the Supreme Court upheld this right of Negro citizens and even today the penalties of the 14th amendment have never been enforced. There are 7,000,000 possible voters among American Negroes and of these it is a question if more than 2,000,000 actually cast their votes. This is partly from the national inertia, which keeps half of all American voters away from the polls; but even more from the question as to what practical ends the Negro shall cast his vote.

He is thinking usually in terms of what he can do by voting to better his condition and he seldom gets a chance to vote on this matter. On the wider implications of political democracy he has not yet entered; particularly he does not see the economic foundations of present civilization and the necessity of his attacking the rule of corporate wealth in order to free the labor group to which he belongs.

Fourth, there is the question of occupation. There are our submerged classes of farm labor and tenants: our city laborers, washerwomen and scrubwomen and the mass of lower-paid servants. These classes still form a majority of American Negroes and they are on the edge of poverty, with the ignorance, disease and crime that always accompany such poverty.

If we measure the median income of Americans, it is $3,000 for whites and $2,000 for Negroes. In Southern cities, 7 percent of the white families and 30 percent of the colored families receive less than $1,000 a year. On the other hand the class differentiation by income among Negroes is notable: the number of semi-skilled and skilled artisans has increased or will as membership in labor unions. Professional men have increased, especially teachers and less notably, physicians, dentists and lawyers.

The number of Negroes in business has increased; mostly in small retail businesses, but to a considerable extent in enterprises like insurance, real estate and small banking, where the color line gives Negroes certain advantages and where, too, there is a certain element of gambling. Also beyond the line of gambling, numbers of Negroes have made small fortunes in anti-social enterprises. All this means that there has arisen in the Negro group a distinct stratification from poor to rich. Recently I polled 450 Negro families belonging to a select organization forty-five years old. Of these families 127 received over $10,000 a year and a score of these over $25,000; 200 families received from $5,000 to $10,000 a year and eighty-six less than $5,000.

This is the start of a tendency which will grow; we are beginning to follow the American pattern of accumulating individual wealth and of considering that this will eventually settle the race problem. On the other hand, the whole trend of the thought of our age is toward social welfare; the prevention of poverty by more equitable distribution of wealth, and business for general welfare rather than private profit. There are few signs that these ideals are guiding Negro development today. We seem to be adopting increasingly the ideal of American culture.

Housing, has, of course, been a point of bitter pressure among Negroes, because the attempt to segregate the race in its living conditions has not only kept the more fortunate ones from progress, but it has confined vast numbers of Negro people to the very parts of cities and country districts where they have fewest opportunities and least social contacts. They must live largely in slums, in contact with criminals and with fewest of the social advantages of government and human contact. The fight against segregation has been carried on in the courts and shows much progress against city ordinances, against covenants which make segregation hereditary.

Literature and art have made progress among Negroes, but with curious handicaps. An art expression is normally evoked by the conscious and unconscious demand of people for portrayal of their own emotion and experience. But in the case of the American Negroes, the audience, which embodies the demand and which pays sometimes enormous price for satisfaction, is not the Negro group, but the white group. And the pattern of what the white group wants does not necessarily agree with the natural desire of Negroes.

The whole of Negro literature is therefore curiously divided. We have writers who have written, not really about Negroes, but about the things which white people, and not the highest class of whites, like to hear about Negroes. And those who have expressed what the Negro himself thinks and feels, are those whose books sell to few, even of their own people; and whom most folk do not know. This has not made for the authentic literature which the early part of this century seemed to promise. To be sure, it can be said that American literature to-day has a considerable amount of Negro expression and influence, although not as much as once we hoped.

Despite all this we have an increasing number of excellent Negro writers who make the promise for the future great by their real accomplishment. We have done something in sculpture and painting, but in drama and music we have markedly advanced. All the world listens to our singers, sings our music and dances to our rhythms.

In science, our handicaps are still great. Turner, a great entomologist, was worked to death for lack of laboratory; just never had the recognition he richly deserved, and Carver was prisoner of his inferiority complex. Notwithstanding this, our real accomplishment in biology and medicine; in history and law; and in the social sciences has been notable and widely acclaimed. To this in no little degree is due our physical survival, our falling death rate and our increased confidence in ourselves and in our destiny.

The expression of Negro wish and desire through a free press has greatly improved as compared with 1900. We have a half dozen large weekly papers with circulations of a hundred thousand or more. Their news coverage is immense, even if not discriminating. But here again, the influence of the American press on us has been devastating. The predominance of advertising over opinion, the desire for income rather than literary excellence and the use of deliberate propaganda, had made our press less of a power than it could be, and leaves wide chance for improvement in the future.

In comparison with other institutions, the Negro church during the Twentieth Century has lost ground. It is no longer the dominating influence that it used to be, the center of social activity and of economic experiment. Nevertheless, it is still a powerful institution in the lives of numerical majority of American Negroes if not upon the dominant intellectual classes. There has been a considerable increase in organized work for social progress through the church, but there has also been a large increase of expenditure for buildings, furnishings, and salaries; and it is not easy to find any increase in moral stamina or conscientious discrimination within church circles.

The scandal of deliberate bribery in election of Bishops and in the holding of positions in the churches without a hierarchy has been widespread. It is a critical problem now as to just what part in the future the church among Negroes is going to hold.

Finally there comes the question of social equality, which, despite efforts on the part of thinkers, white and black, is after all the main and fundamental problem of race in the United States. Unless a human being is going to have all human rights, including not only work, but friendship, and if mutually desired, marriage and children, unless these avenues are open and free, there can be no real equality and no cultural integration.

It has hitherto seemed utterly impossible that any such solution of the Negro problem in America could take place. The situation was quite similar to the problem of the lower classes of laborers, serfs and servants in European nations during the Sixteenth, Seventeenth and Eighteenth centuries. All nations had to consist of two separate parts and the only relations between them was employment and philanthropy.

That problem has been partly solved by modern democracy, but modern democracy cannot succeed unless the peoples of different races and religions are also integrated into the democratic whole. Against this large numbers of Americans have always fought and are still fighting, but the progress despite this has been notable. There are places in the United States, especially in large cities like New York and Chicago, where the social differences between the races has, to a large extent, been nullified and there is a meeting on terms of equality which would have been thought impossible a half century ago.

On the other hand, in the South, despite religion, education and reason, the color line, although perhaps shaken, still stands, stark and unbending, and to the minds of most good people, eternal. Here lies the area of the last battle for the complete rights of American Negroes.

Within the race itself today there are disquieting signs. The effort of Negroes to become Americans of equal status with other Americans is leading them to a state of mind by which they not only accept what is good in America, but what is bad and threatening so long as the Negro can share equally. This is peculiarly dangerous at this epoch in the development of world culture.

After two world wars of unprecendented loss of life, cruelty and destruction, we are faced by the fact that the industrial organization of our present civilization has in it something fundamentally wrong. It went to pieces in the first world war because of the determination of certain great powers excluded from world rule to share in that rule, by acquisition of the labor and materials of colonial peoples. The attempt to recover from the cataclysm resulted in the collapse of our industrial system, and a second world war.

In spite of the propaganda which has gone on, which represents America as the leading democratic state, we Negroes know perfectly well, and ought to know even better than most, that America is not a successful democracy and that until it is, it is going to drag down the world. This nation is ruled by corporate wealth to a degree which is frightening. One thousand persons own the United States and their power outweighs the voice of the mass of American citizens. This must be cured, not by revolution, not by war and violence, but by reason and knowledge.

Most of the world is today turning toward the welfare state; turning against the idea of production for individual profit toward the idea of production for use and for the welfare of the mass of citizen. No matter how difficult such a course is, it is the only course that is going to save the world and this we American Negroes have got to realize.

We may find it easy now to get publicity, reward, and attention by going along with the reactionary propaganda and war hysteria which is convulsing this nation, but in the long run America will not thank its black children if they help it go the wrong way, or retard its progress.

REFLECT AND CONSIDER

- What issues of racial inequality does Du Bois address that are still relevant today?
- According to Du Bois, at what point can there be real equality and cultural integration?

THE OPTIMISM OF UNCERTAINTY

BY HOWARD ZINN

In this awful world where the efforts of caring people often pale in comparison to what is done by those who have power, how do I manage to stay involved and seemingly happy?

Some quick lessons: Don't let "those who have power" intimidate you. No matter how much power they have, they cannot prevent you from living your life, thinking independently, speaking your mind.

Find people to be with who share your values and commitments, and who also have a sense of humor.

Understand that the major media will not tell you of all the acts of resistance taking place every day in the society—the strikes, protests, individual acts of courage in the face of authority. Look around (and you will certainly find it) for the evidence of these unreported acts. And for the little you find, extrapolate from that and assume there must be a thousand times as much as you've found.

Note that throughout history people have felt powerless before authority, but that at certain times these powerless people, by organizing, acting, risking, persisting, have created enough power to change the world around them, even if a little. That is the history of the labor movement, the women's movement, the anti–Vietnam War movement, the disabled persons' movement, the gay and lesbian movement, the movement of black people in the South.

Remember that those who have power and seem invulnerable are in fact quite vulnerable. Their power depends on the obedience of others, and when those others begin withholding that obedience, begin defying authority, that power at the top turns out to be very fragile. Generals become powerless when their soldiers refuse to fight, industrialists become powerless when their workers leave their jobs or occupy the factories.

When we forget the fragility of that power at the top we become astounded when it crumbles in the face of rebellion. We have had many such surprises in our time, both in the United States and in other countries.

Don't look for a moment of total triumph. See engagement as an ongoing struggle, with victories and defeats, but in the long run slow progress. So you need patience and persistence. Understand that even when you don't "win," there is fun and fulfillment in the fact that you have been involved, with other good people, in something worthwhile. You need hope.

Is an optimist necessarily a blithe, slightly sappy whistler in the dark of our time? I am totally confident not that the world will get better, but that only confidence can prevent people from giving up the game before all the cards have been played. The metaphor is deliberate; life is a gamble. Not to play is to foreclose any chance of winning. To play, to act, is to create at least a possibility of changing the world.

What leaps out from the history of the past hundred years is its utter unpredictability. This confounds us, because we are talking about exactly the period when human beings became so ingenious technologically that they could plan and predict the exact time of someone landing on the moon, or walk down the street talking to someone halfway around the Earth.

Who foresaw that, on that day in Montgomery, Alabama, in 1955, when Rosa Parks refused to move from the front of the bus, this would lead to a mass protest of black working people, and a chain of events that would shake the nation, startle the world, and transform the South?

Let's go back to the turn of the century. A revolution to overthrow the tsar of Russia, in that most sluggish of semi-feudal empires, not only startled the most advanced imperial powers, but took Lenin himself by surprise and sent him rushing by train to Petrograd. Given the Russian Revolution, who could have predicted Stalin's deformation of it, or Khrushchev's astounding exposure of Stalin, or Gorbachev's succession of surprises?

Who would have predicted the bizarre shifts of World War II—the Nazi-Soviet pact (those embarrassing photos of von Ribbentrop and Molotov shaking hands), and the German army rolling through Russia, apparently invincible, causing colossal casualties, being turned back at the gates of Leningrad, on the western edge of Moscow, in the streets of Stalingrad, followed by the defeat of the German army, with Hitler huddled in his Berlin bunker, waiting to die?

And then the post-war world, taking a shape no one could have drawn in advance: the Chinese Communist revolution, which Stalin himself had given little chance. And then the break with the Soviet Union, the tumultuous and violent Cultural Revolution, and then another turnabout, with post–Mao China renouncing its most fervently held ideas and institutions, making overtures to the West, cuddling up to capitalist enterprise, perplexing everyone.

No one foresaw the disintegration of the old Western empires happening so quickly after the war, or the odd array of societies that would be created in the newly independent nations, from the benign village socialism of Nyerere's Tanzania to the madness of Idi Amin's adjacent Uganda.

Spain became an astonishment. A million died in the civil war, which ended in victory for the Fascist Franco, backed by Hitler and Mussolini. I recall a veteran of the Abraham Lincoln Brigade telling me that he could not imagine Spanish Fascism being overthrown without another bloody war. But after Franco was gone, a parliamentary democracy came into being, open to Socialists, Communists, anarchists, everyone.

In other places too, deeply entrenched dictatorships seemed suddenly to disintegrate—in Portugal, Argentina, the Philippines, Iran.

The end of World War II left two superpowers with their respective spheres of influence and control, vying for military and political power. The United States and the Soviet Union soon each had enough thermonuclear bombs to devastate the Earth several times over. The international scene was dominated by their rivalry, and it was supposed that all affairs, in every nation, were affected by their looming presence.

Yet the most striking fact about these superpowers was that, despite their size, their wealth, their overwhelming accumulation of nuclear weapons, they were unable to control events, even in those parts of the world considered to be their respective spheres of influence.

The failure of the Soviet Union to have its way in Afghanistan, its decision to withdraw after almost a decade of ugly intervention, was the most striking evidence that even the possession of thermonuclear weapons does not guarantee domination over a determined population.

The United States has faced the same reality. It could send an army into Korea but could not win, and was forced to sign a compromise peace. It waged a full-scale war in Indochina, conducted the most brutal bombardment of a tiny peninsula in world history, and yet was forced to withdraw. And in Latin America, after a long history of U.S. military intervention having its way again and again, this superpower, with all its wealth and weapons, found itself frustrated. It was unable to prevent a revolution in Cuba, and the Latin American dictatorships that the United States supported from Chile to Argentina to El Salvador have fallen. In the headlines every day we see other instances of the failure of the presumably powerful over the presumably powerless, as in Brazil, where a grassroots movement of workers and the poor elected a new president pledged to fight destructive corporate power.

Looking at this catalog of huge surprises, it's clear that the struggle for justice should never be abandoned because of the apparent overwhelming power of those who have the guns and the money and who seem invincible in their determination to hold on to it. That apparent power has, again and again, proved vulnerable to human qualities less measurable than bombs and dollars: moral fervor, determination, unity, organization, sacrifice, wit, ingenuity, courage, patience—whether by blacks in Alabama and South Africa, peasants in El Salvador, Nicaragua, and Vietnam, or workers and intellectuals in Poland, Hungary, and the Soviet Union itself. No cold calculation of the balance of power need deter people who are persuaded that their cause is just.

I have tried hard to match my friends in their pessimism about the world (is it just my friends?), but I keep encountering people who, in spite of all the evidence of terrible things happening everywhere, give me hope. Especially young people, in whom the future rests. I think of my students. Not just the women of Spelman College, who leapt over a hundred years of national disgrace to become part of the civil rights movement. Not just the fellow in Alice Walker's poem "Once," who acted out the spirit of a new generation:

> It is true—
> I've always loved
> the daring
>   ones
> Like the black young
> man
> Who tried
> to crash
> All barriers
> at once,
>   wanted to
> swim
> At a white
> beach (in Alabama)
> Nude.

I think also of my students at Boston University and people all over the country who, anguished about the war in Vietnam, resisted in some way, facing police clubs and arrests. And brave high school students like Mary Beth Tinker and her classmates in Des Moines, Iowa, who insisted on wearing black armbands to protest the war and when suspended from school, took their case to the Supreme Court and won.

Of course, some would say, that was the Sixties. But throughout the period since, despite widespread head-shaking over the "apathy" of successive student generations, an impressive number of students continued to act.

I think of the determined little group at Boston University who, emulating groups at a hundred other schools, set up a "shantytown" on campus to represent apartheid in South Africa. The police tore it down, but the students refused to move and were arrested.

In South Africa, shortly before, I had visited Crossroads, a real shantytown outside of Cape Town, where thousands of blacks occupied places that looked like chicken coops, or were jammed together in huge tents, sleeping in shifts, six hundred of them sharing one faucet of running water. I was impressed that young Americans who had not seen that with their own eyes, had only read or seen photos, would be so moved to step out of their comfortable lives and act.

We have recently seen students all over the country campaigning for a living wage for campus employees, and against global sweatshops and pre-emptive wars. Beyond those activists, there is a much larger population of students who have no contact with any movement, yet have deep feelings about injustice.

Since I've stopped teaching, I've spent much of my time responding to invitations to speak. What I've discovered is heartening. In whatever town, large or small, in whatever state of the Union, there is always a cluster of men and women who care about the sick, the hungry, the victims of racism, the casualties of war, and who are doing something, however small, in the hope that the world will change.

Wherever I go—whether San Diego, Philadelphia, or Dallas; Ada, Oklahoma, or Shreveport, Louisiana; Presque Isle, Maine, or Manhattan, Kansas—I find such people. And beyond the handful of activists there seem to be hundreds, thousands more who are open to unorthodox ideas.

But they tend not to know of each other's existence, and so, while they persist, they do so with the desperate patience of Sisyphus endlessly pushing that boulder up the mountain. I try to tell each group that it is not alone, and that the very people who are disheartened by the absence of a national movement are themselves proof of the potential for such a movement. I suppose I'm trying to persuade myself as well as them.

Arriving at Morehead State University in rural eastern Kentucky, in the midst of the 2003 Iraq War, I found the lecture room crowded with fifteen hundred students (out of a total enrollment of six thousand). I spoke against the war and received an overwhelming reception. Earlier, when I'd been picked up at the airport by a group of faculty peace activists, one of them had brought their fourteen-year-old daughter, who'd defied her high school principal by wearing an anti-war T-shirt to school. I have found such people in all parts of the country, more and more, as evidence that the truth makes its way slowly but surely.

It is this change in consciousness that encourages me. Granted, racial hatred and sex discrimination are still with us, war and violence still poison our culture, we have a large underclass of poor, desperate people, and there is a hard core of the population content with the way things are, afraid of change.

But if we see only that, we have lost historical perspective, and then it is as if we were born yesterday and we know only the depressing stories in this morning's newspapers, this evening's television reports.

Consider the remarkable transformation, in just a few decades, in people's consciousness of racism, in the bold presence of women demanding their rightful place, in a growing public awareness that gays are not curiosities but sensate human beings, in the long-term growing skepticism about military intervention despite brief surges of military madness.

It is that long-term change that I think we must see if we are not to lose hope. Pessimism becomes a self-fulfilling prophecy; it reproduces itself by crippling our willingness to act.

There is a tendency to think that what we see in the present moment will continue. We forget how often in this century we have been astonished by the sudden crumbling of institutions, by extraordinary changes in people's thoughts, by unexpected eruptions of rebellion against tyrannies, by the quick collapse of systems of power that seemed invincible.

The bad things that happen are repetitions of bad things that have always happened—war, racism, maltreatment of women, religious and nationalist fanaticism, starvation. The good things that happen are unexpected. Unexpected, and yet explainable by certain truths that spring at us from time to time, but which we tend to forget.

Political power, however formidable, is more fragile than we think. (Note how nervous are those who hold it.)

Ordinary people can be intimidated for a time, can be fooled for a time, but they have a down-deep common sense, and sooner or later they find a way to challenge the power that oppresses them.

People are not naturally violent or cruel or greedy, although they can be made so. Human beings everywhere want the same things: They are moved by the sight of abandoned children, homeless families, the casualties of war; they long for peace, for friendship and affection across lines of race and nationality.

One semester, when I was teaching, I learned that there were several classical musicians signed up in my course. For the last class of the semester I stood aside while they sat in chairs up front and played a Mozart quartet. Not a customary finale to a class in political theory, but I wanted the class to understand that politics is pointless if it does nothing to enhance the beauty of our lives. Political discussion can sour you. We needed some music.

Revolutionary change does not come as one cataclysmic moment (beware of such moments!) but as an endless succession of surprises, moving zigzag toward a more decent society.

We don't have to engage in grand, heroic actions to participate in the process of change. Small acts, when multiplied by millions of people, can transform the world.

To be hopeful in bad times is not just foolishly romantic. It is based on the fact that human history is a history not only of cruelty, but also of compassion, sacrifice, courage, kindness. What we choose to emphasize in this complex history will determine our lives. If we see only the worst, it destroys our capacity to do something. If we remember those times and places—and there are so many—where people have behaved magnificently, this gives us the energy to act, and at least the possibility of sending this spinning top of a world in a different direction. And if we do act, in however small a way, we don't have to wait for some grand utopian future. The future is an infinite succession of presents, and to live now as we think human beings should live, in defiance of all that is bad around us, is itself a marvelous victory.

REFLECT AND CONSIDER

- What specific lessons should we follow for creating change?
- How do we maintain optimism and why is it important to do so?

WHY WE STILL NEED AFFIRMATIVE ACTION

BY ORLANDO PATTERSON

T o argue that we should begin to solve the problem of "racial" exclusion by assuming a color-blind world is to assume away the very problem we are trying to solve: only voodoo priests and rational choice theorists can get away with this kind of mumbo-jumbo. The simple truth, the simple reality, is that "racial" categorization is a fact of American life, one that we can do away with only by first acknowledging it. We must also acknowledge that Afro-Americans did not originally create or construct the social reality of their "blackness." In the West Africa of the sixteenth to eighteenth centuries from which they came there was no meaningful notion of "blackness," since everyone there looked African. Afro-Americans are the only group of persons whose ancestors were dragged here, kicking and screaming. For nearly three centuries they were held in chains here, during which time the social category of "blackness" was constructed and imposed upon them. Eventually, the logic of their situation dicrated that they accept and invert the "racial" status forced upon them in their heroic struggles to overcome the centuries of enslavement and victimization. In their struggles, they made something positive of the ethnic markers imposed upon them, even in the face of the continuing negative conception of, and response to, them on the part of still too many Euro-Americans.

The eventual goal of all but the small minority of extremist chauvinist Afro-Americans is a world in which the social fact of their ethnic difference will not have to be considered in the organizations where they work as far as evaluations of their work performance and promotion go. But to achieve such an objective, ethnic factors must be considered for some time to come, both for the reasons I have mentioned earlier and for the more obvious reasons that overt racism persists, even if it is declining.

I think it will be very difficult ever to find consensus on affirmative action. Beyond the immediate question of improving access for minorities and women looms a deeper issue. Assuming a moderate level of success in the recruitment and promotion of formerly excluded persons, the newcomers may soon begin to find that they just don't like the organizational game or the way it is played. After enormous effort to enter the executive suite, for example, many women have discovered that they do not particularly enjoy "kicking a little ass" for the hell of it, as former President Bush once so joyfully expressed it.

It is at this point that a new phase in the egalitarian struggle emerges. The struggle at this point is not about getting on the playing field or playing the game, but about the very rules of the game, about who sets the rules, and about the style and purpose of the game. And at this point we have moved well beyond the boundaries of a policy such as affirmative action, which in essence is designed to remove bias and promote access within the existing system. In defending affirmative action, or any other policy, it is important to be clear about its limits. Using it to achieve objectives for which it was not designed will result in the baby being thrown out with the bathwater. Let me therefore turn to a few of these broader egalitarian goals for which affirmative action is not appropriate.

A great deal of the heat in the debate over affirmative action, I suspect, is generated by the usually unstated assumption that changing the rules, style, and purpose of the game is really what the struggle is ultimately about. Those who control our society like to think there is something immutable and sacred about the rules of the game. Simply to bring them into question excites anxiety and outrage. If comparative and historical sociology teaches us one thing about societies, however, it is the fact that the rules by which we play in our social organizations are not like genetic codes. They can and do change.

Furthermore, we also know that the same objective can often be obtained by different means. A good case in point is provided by the differences between the American and Japanese patterns of management. For decades, many people thought that the rules of management were those encoded in the case studies of the Harvard Business School. Real culture shock reverberated when corporate America learned that there are radically different ways of maximizing profits.

My point is not to idealize the Japanese alternative, which is currently showing many signs of its own peculiar failings, but rather to illustrate the fact that the rules of the game more often reflect the interests, values, and class of those who are at the center of power than they do any hard-to-grasp essences that only the select, meritocratic few can fathom.

To put the matter another way, if we insist on running our car factories the way Detroit does, then it follows, as night follows day, that only people who look, think, feel, and behave like Lee Iacocca will ever end up at the top of the executive ladder. No Afro-American and no woman could exhibit the kind of Euro-American male executive macho with which Mr. Iacocca so obligingly regaled TV viewers in his commercial spots for Chrysler during the early eighties. The example of top executive positions in the auto industry represents the most extreme heights of power. But my argument applies to nearly all areas and levels of exclusion, from firefighting and police work to law and medicine.

We can now understand the true nature of the crisis that affirmative action creates when it is mistakenly associated with these more radical goals. It is not just the presence of the formerly excluded that presents problems for the establishment, but the fear that they might change the way we run things. These fears are indeed justified, since it is true that if women and minorities are to be included in significant numbers at the top layers of the system, the rules will have to change.

Before I am wholly misunderstood by those who wave the banner of high standards (rarely, I might add, are they those who most often achieve these standards), let me make it clear that the redefinition of rules in no way entails a lessening of standards or the abandonment of the merit principle. I am not proposing that we do away with rules and structures, but that we redefine them in a manner that makes it possible for those now excluded to play by them. I am, in short, urging a commitment to the very values that critics of affirmative action insist on, a genuine universalization of the rules of conduct. Such a universalization cannot stop short of the rules by which we change the rules.

To put the matter in somewhat more formal terms, the intensity of the debate over affirmative action may be attributed to deep-seated disagreements over three kinds of rules—what may be called the rules of allocation, of application, and of determination.

It is a struggle, first, over the age-old problem of equality and the difficulty of arriving at some acceptable conception of distributive justice. People disagree over what constitutes fair distribution of wealth and power, and even where they agree that some effort ought to be made to reduce the gap between the haves and have-nots, they disagree over the rules of allocation, the means by which we achieve less inequality. In a nutshell, those who support affirmative action believe that inegalitarian rules of allocation are fair where the objective is a more egalitarian distribution of rewards. Many of those opposed to affirmative action take the opposite view, questioning even the long-established principle of a graduated income tax—the classic example of an inegalitarian rule of allocation aimed at a more egalitarian distribution—as the unexpected surge of support for Steve Forbes's 1996 primary campaign indicated.

Second, the conflict is over the rules of application, that is, the problem of whether groups, especially noncorporate disadvantaged groups, are entitled to special claims as a result of the special damages and exclusions they have suffered historically and continue to suffer in institutional and personal terms. Supporters of affirmative action accept the legitimacy of such claims; those opposed insist that only individuals, as individuals, rather than as members of disadvantaged groups, can claim damages and are entitled to compensatory treatment, in stark contrast with the realities of the capitalist system, as I argued in the earlier essay on conservative advocacy.

Finally, the covert agenda of the struggle for affirmative action is that it seeks to change the underlying rules of determination in our society, what, to use the terminology of Daniel Bell, might be called the axial rules.[1] Affirmative action does restrain the freedom and power of some people to maintain an order that results in the chronic disadvantage of others. This is clearly a power struggle, and as with all such struggles in a democracy, it can and should be waged politically.

There are striking precedents for such political struggles. American history is a remarkable and inspiring record of the successful struggle of the disadvantaged and excluded to overcome their constraints and to be included. They accomplished their goals by personal merit, by the use of political and other means to achieve access to meaningful positions in their society and, just as importantly, by insisting on having a say in the way the rules by which they lived were defined, maintained, and changed.

The history of the Irish in America is only one, although the classic, case in point. The post-famine Irish who came to America in the nineteenth century were called every name that has been used to abuse Afro-American folks. Indeed, it was common lore among Euro-Americans that the Irish were "niggers turned inside out" and that Afro-Americans were "smoked Irish."[2] More to the point, the Irish were culturally different, "as different as could be imagined in mood and tempo from those natives of Anglo-Saxon Puritan stock," wrote William Shannon in his standard history of the group, and "they did not seem to practice thrift, self-denial and other virtues desirable in the 'worthy laboring poor.'"[3] In their struggle for inclusion, the Irish used their control of city governments to institute massive programs of "affirmative action" biased in favor of the working and middle classes of their group. There can be no gainsaying the fact that political patronage and preferential hiring in the nation's city bureaucracies were decisive factors in the rise of the Irish out of poverty into respectability.

But it is equally important to note two other elements of their success: an amazing capacity for hard work, and a deep and abiding commitment to the sanctity of their families. Even in the face of oppressively low wages and nativist hostility, including the burning of their churches and convents, the Irish worked long, backbreaking hours for their families, the men often dying young as a result. And, contrary to present sociological dogma that is poverty that creates familial dislocation, destitution and anti-Irish bigotry resulted in a tightening of familial bonds among the Irish who were seemingly trapped in the ghettos of nineteenth-century America.[4]

Another important lesson of Irish-American history confirms a point made earlier. When the Irish got on the playing fields of American politics and economics, they did not turn themselves into good little Celtic models of the Protestant ethic, meekly playing by the rules they found. Instead, once on the field they moved to the next stage of their struggle: they changed the rules of the game. "The newer Irish," wrote Shannon, "challenged the code of the community at almost every point. ... Their politicians pressed to the fore; their priests raised new issues of religious discrimination in public schools. The activities of both disturbed the smug, clublike atmosphere in which the large towns had formerly been governed. Their 'grating brogue' was heard everywhere."[5] Even in the highly traditional arena of Catholic church government, the Irish insisted on changing the rules as soon as they took over. What another historian of the Irish-Americans, George Potter, wrote of the powerful John Hughes, the first Irish-American to take over the diocese of New York in 1840, holds true of Irish rule-changing generally: "He trampled on the prudence and rejected the diplomatic suavity [of his more conformist predecessors], once saying that he did not hold with the 'generally good, cautious souls who believed in stealing through the world more submissively than suits a freeman.'"[6] Afro-American Baptists of the late twentieth century can relate to that.

The end result of this struggle, which combined politically based "affirmative action" on a grand scale for over three quarters of a century, hard work, strong family ties, and an insistence on not simply playing hard by the rules, but also changing them, is one of the great success stories of America. Contrary to common knowledge, Irish Catholics are today the second most prosperous group of people of European ancestry in America, trailing only Jews, with their household income 118 percent of the U.S. average, way above Americans of Protestant British ancestry, who ranked a distant fifth in 1989.[7]

Today, of course, the Irish no longer need affirmative action, in much the same way that, not long from now, women and Afro-Americans will no longer need it. And there is something else about the Irish-American story that informs the present debate. The men who controlled Tammany Hall and the other city governments in the earlier part of this century would have considered it laughable, if also a pretty lousy Protestant joke, had they been told that preferential treatment of the Irish poor and lower middle classes was un-American and brought into question the qualifications of worthy Irish-Americans who had succeeded solely by their merits and work ethic. These men all knew that to transcend the limitations and constraints of being Irish, they had to emphasize their Irishness. Today, there is less need for them to do so, except in a symbolic, "cutflower" kind of way or on St. Patrick's Day.

In their struggle for inclusion and prosperity, the Irish redefined themselves. By changing the rules of the game, they profoundly redefined what it is to be American. This, above all, is perhaps the greatest lesson of their prototypical American story for Afro-Americans and women. What Joseph O'Grady wrote in his book *How The Irish Became Americans* holds for all those who are still struggling for full equality and integration into the great, ever-changing cultural process that is America:

> In effect, the people of America did not bring their democracy with them, nor did they find it here. They made it from the interaction of many ideas and interests as defined by many groups. The clash of these ideas generated pressures upon both individuals and groups make decisions that, in turn, simply created new demands for new groups. In that momentum one finds the origin, meaning and purpose of America.[8]

Today, Afro-Americans and women are simply extending the struggle and renewing the momentum that is the source of America's greatness in ways that will ensure their own integration and meet their peculiar needs and interests. The affirmative action program is a start in this struggle for Afro-Americans and women, but as I indicated earlier, we are approaching its limits, and broadening its scope may simply overstrain it. The broader struggle for inclusion will have to be waged within the corporate system itself by those who gain entry through affirmative action.

The struggle is endless even at the entry level and will continue even after Afro-Americans have won their battle for full economic inclusion, because in our competitive capitalist democracy with its great tradition of immigration there will always be inequality, not to mention new outsiders to be integrated. The world will not leave America alone, because America remains its only global power, generating the world's first truly global culture, thanks in good part to the creativity of its Afro-American and Irish-American populations. Not only will some justly do better than others, but many will unjustly do so. As Rousseau saw more than two centuries ago, an inevitable tendency toward inequality in modern societies is no reason to accept inequality: "It is precisely because the force of things always tends to destroy equality that the force of legislation should always tend to maintain it."[9]

Notes

1. *See* Daniel Bell, "Ethnicity and Social Change," in Nathan Glazer and Daniel Patrick Moynihan, eds., *Ethnicity: Theory and Experience* (Cambridge: Harvard University Press, 1975), 141–174, and more generally Bell's *The Coming of Post-Industrial Society: A Venture in Social Forecasting* (New York: Basic Books, 1993).

2. Noel Ignatiev, *How the Irish Became White* (New York: Routledge, 1995), p. 41.

3. William V. Shannon, *The American Irish* (New York: Macmillan, 1963), p. 38.

4. Ibid., p. 37.

5. Ibid., p. 40.

6. George Potter, *The Golden Door: The Story of the Irish in Ireland and America* (Boston: Little, Brown, 1960), p. 407.

7. Christopher Jencks, *Rethinking Social Policy: Race, Poverty, and the Underclass* (New York: Harper Perennial, 1992), p. 28.

8. Joseph O'Grady, *How the Irish Became Americans* (New York: Twayne Publishers, 1973), prologue.

9. Jean Jacques Rousseau, *The Social Contract*, trans. Willmoore Kendall (Chicago: Henry Regnery Co., 1954), book 2, chapter 11.

REFLECT AND CONSIDER

- How does the idea of changing "the rules of the game" relate to Affirmative Action?
- Why is Affirmative Action still necessary, and at what point will it not be necessary?

HIGHLIGHT

THE CASE FOR REPARATIONS

BY TA-NEHISI COATES, *THE ATLANTIC*

SUMMARY

Many racial groups, including Native Americans, Japanese, and African Americans, have suffered at the hands of US laws. The government has attempted to account for past indiscretions by giving Native American tribes access to land and casinos. And, Japanese who were put in internment camps during World War II were given financial compensation in 1988. Thus, although there is a record of the government providing reparations to other racial groups, African Americans have yet to be given compensation. In this article by Coates, a careful analysis of racial discrimination against African Americans provides a compelling argument for creating a plan for reparations.

EXCERPT FROM
"THE CASE FOR REPARATIONS"

According to the most recent statistics, North Lawndale is now on the wrong end of virtually every socioeconomic indicator. In 1930 its population was 112,000. Today it is 36,000. The halcyon talk of "interracial living" is dead. The neighborhood is 92 percent black. Its homicide rate is 45 per 100,000—triple the rate of the city as a whole. The infant-mortality rate is 14 per 1,000—more than twice the national average. Forty-three percent of the people in North Lawndale live below the poverty line—double Chicago's overall rate. Forty-five percent of all households are on food stamps—nearly three times the rate of the city at large. Sears, Roebuck left the neighborhood in 1987, taking 1,800 jobs with it. Kids in North Lawndale need not be confused about their prospects: Cook County's Juvenile Temporary Detention Center sits directly adjacent to the neighborhood.

READ THE REST OF THE ESSAY:

bit.ly/reparationsatlantic

READ, LISTEN, WATCH, INTERACT!

READ

Apologizing for the Enslavement and Racial Segregation of African Americans

Congressional Record—Senate 2009.
READ AT bit.ly/enslavementapology

Fight Against Racism, Discrimination, and Xenophobia

UNESCO
READ AT bit.ly/unescostatement

LISTEN

Debate: Does Affirmative Action On Campus Do More Harm Than Good

NPR, 3.26.2014
LISTEN AT bit.ly/affirmativeactiondebate

How to Fight Racial Bias When It's Silent and Subtle

Shankar Vedantam, 7.19.2013, NPR
LISTEN AT bit.ly/silentracialbias

WATCH

How To Tell People They Sound Racist

Jay Smooth, 2008

AVAILABLE AT bit.ly/illdoctrine

A Guerilla Gardener in South Central LA

Ron Finley, TED

AVAILABLE AT bit.ly/guerillagardener

INTERACT

Highlander Research and Education Center

INTERACT AT bit.ly/highlandereducation

Annenberg Classroom: Resources for Excellent Civics Education

INTERACT AT bit.ly/annenbergclass

INVESTIGATE FURTHER

The readings in Investigate Further, separated by the book's sections, are an aid for further research into these topics. This list is a brief set of readings to be used as a starting point as you delve deeper into these issues. The readings are referenced in ASA (American Sociological Association) format. The first entry is a list of resources that provides contemporary statistics on a range of issues.

RESOURCES FOR CONTEMPORARY STATISTICS

American Civil Liberties Union
Brennan Center for Justice
Inequality.org
Pew Research Center
Stanford Center for Poverty and Inequality
Urban Institute
US Census Bureau

THE FOUNDATIONS OF RACE

American Sociological Association. 2003. "The Importance of Collecting Data and Doing Social Scientific Research on Race." Washington, DC: American Sociological Association. http://www.asanet.org/images/press/docs/pdf/asa_race_statement.pdf.

Black, Edwin. 2003. *War Against the Weak: Eugenics & America's Campaign to Create a Master Race.* New York: Four Walls Eight Windows.

Degler, Carl N. 1991. *In Search of Human Nature.* New York: Oxford University Press.

Gossett, Thomas. 1997. *Race: The History of an Idea in America*. New York: Oxford University Press.

Shipman, Pat. 1994. *Evolution of Racism: Human Difference and the Use and Abuse of Science*. New York: Simon and Schuster.

Smith, Andrea. 2005. *Conquest: Sexual Violence and American Indian Genocide*. Boston: South End Press.

Takaki, Ronald. 1993. *A Different Mirror: A History of Multicultural America*. Boston: Back Bay Books.

Zinn, Howard. 1980. *The People's History of the United States*. New York: HarperCollins Publishers.

THE SOCIAL CONSTRUCTION OF RACE

Cornell, Stephen, and Douglas Hartmann. 2007. *Ethnicity and Race*. Thousand Oaks, CA: Pine Forge.

Davis, James F. 2002. *Who Is Black: One Nation's Definition. Tenth Anniversary Edition.* University Park, PA: The Pennsylvania State University Press.

Hosang, Martinez Daniel, Oneka LeBennett, and Laura Pulido, eds. 2012. *Racial Formation in the Twenty-First Century*. Oakland, CA: University of California Press.

Jablonski, Nina. 2004. "The Evolution of Human Skin and Skin Color." *Annual Review of Anthropology* 33:585–623.

Lee, Sharon. 1993. "Racial Classifications in the U.S. Census: 1890–1990." *Ethnic and Racial Studies* 16(1):75–94.

Lopez, Ian Haney. 1996. *White by Law: The Legal Construction of Race*. New York: NYU Press.

Omi, Michael, and Howard Winant. 2014. *Racial Formation in the United States* (3rd ed.). New York: Routledge.

Painter, Nell Irvin. 2010. *The History of White People.* New York: W.W. Norton and Company.

STRUCTURING AMERICAN IDENTITY THROUGH IMMIGRATION

Alba, Richard, and Mary Waters, eds. 2011. *The Next Generation: Immigrant Youth in a Comparative Perspective.* New York: New York University Press.

Bashi Treitler, Vilna. 2013. *The Ethnic Project: Transforming Racial Fiction into Ethnic Factions.* Stanford, CA: Stanford University Press.

Kasinitz, Philip, John H. Mollenkopf, Mary C. Waters, and Jennifer Holdaway. 2008. *Inheriting the City: The Children of Immigrants Come of Age.* New York: Russell Sage Foundation.

King, Desmond. 2000. *Making Americans*. Cambridge, MA: Harvard University Press.

Lee, Jennifer, and Min Zhou. 2015. *The Asian American Achievement Paradox.* New York: Russell Sage Foundation.

Massey, Douglas. 2013. "America's Immigration Policy Fiasco: Learning From Past Mistakes." *Daedalus* 142 (3):5-15.

Steinberg, Stephen. 2014. "The Long View of the Melting Pot." *Ethnic and Racial Studies* 37(5):790–94.

Waters, Mary. 1990. *Ethnic Options*. Oakland, CA: University of California Press.

Wu, Frank. 2012. *Yellow*. New York: Basic Books.

RACISM: THEORIES FOR UNDERSTANDING

Anderson, Elijah. 2013. *The Cosmopolitan Canopy*. New York: W.W. Norton.

Bonilla-Silva, Eduardo. 2009. *Racism Without Racists: Color-Blind Racism and the Persistence of Racial Inequality in America.* Lanham, MD: Rowman and Littlefield.

Choo, Hae Yoon, and Myra Marx Ferree. 2010. "Practicing Intersectionality in Sociological Research: A Critical Analysis of Inclusions, Interactions, and Institutions in the Study of Inequalities." *Sociological Theory* 28(2):28–149.

Delgado, Richard, and Jean Stefancic. 2012. *Critical Race Theory: An Introduction.* New York: New York University Press.

Gallagher, Charles. 2003. "Color-Blind Privilege: The Social and Political Functions of Erasing the Color Line in Post Race America." *Race, Gender & Class* 10(4):1–17.

Glenn, Evelyn Nakano. 2009. *Shades of Difference: Why Skin Color Matters.* Stanford, CA: Stanford University Press.

Feagin, Joe. 2000. *Racist America: Roots, Current Realities, and Future Reparations.* New York: Routledge.

Hill Collins, Patricia. 2008. *Black Feminist Thought: Knowledge, Consciousness, and the Politics of Empowerment.* New York: Routledge.

Pyke, Karen, and Denise Johnson. 2003. "Asian American Women and Racialized Femininities: 'Doing' Gender across Cultural Worlds." *Gender and Society* 17(1):33–53.

Wallace, Terry. 1985. *Bloods: Black Veterans of the Vietnam War, An Oral History.* New York: Ballantine Books.

STRUCTURED RACIAL INEQUALITY

Bertrand, Marianne, and Sendhil Mullainathan. 2004. "Are Emily and Greg More Employable than Lakisha and Jamal? A Field Experiment on Labor Market Discrimination." *The American Economic Review* 94(4):991–1013.

Desmond, Matthew. 2012. "Eviction and the Reproduction of Urban Poverty." *American Journal of Sociology* 118(1):88–133.

Lewis, Amanda E., John B. Diamond, and Tyrone A. Forman. 2015. "Conundrums of Integration: Desegregation in the Context of Racialized Hierarchy." *Sociology of Race and Ethnicity* 1(1):22–36.

Massey, Douglas S., and Nancy A. Denton.1993. *American Apartheid*. Cambridge, MA: Harvard University Press.

Mills, Charles W. 1999. *The Racial Contract*. Ithaca, NY: Cornell University Press.

Oliver, Melvin, and Thomas Shapiro. 2006. *Black Wealth, White Wealth: A New Perspective on Racial Inequality*. New York: Taylor and Francis.

Pager, Devah. 2003. "The Mark of a Criminal Record." *American Journal of Sociology* 108(5):937–75.

Pattillo, Mary. 2015. "Everyday Politics of School Choice in the Black Community." *Du Bois Review* 12(1):41–71.

Peguero, Anthony A., Ann Marie Popp, and Dixie J. Koo. 2015. "Race, Ethnicity, and School-Based Adolescent Victimization." *Crime & Delinquency* 61(3):323–49.

Wilson, George, and Vincent Roscigno. 2015. "End of an Era? Managerial Losses of African Americans and Latinos in the Public Sector." *Social Science Research* 54:36–49.

RACISM IN POPULAR CULTURE

Byfield, Natalie. 2014. *Savage Portrayals: Race, Media and the Central Park Jogger Story*. Philadelphia, PA: Temple University Press.

Charnas, Dan. 2010. *The Big Payback: The History of the Business of Hip Hop*. New York: NAL.

Daniels, Jessie. 2012. "Race and Racism in Internet Studies: A Review and Critique." *New Media Society* 15(5):695–719.

Hall, Stuart. 1980. "Encoding/Decoding." In *Culture, Media, Language*, edited by S. Hall, D. Hobson, A. Lowe, and P. Willis, 117–27. New York: Routledge.

Hartigan, John. 2005. "Reading Trash: *Deliverance* and the Cultural Poetics of White Trash." In *Odd Tribes: Toward a Cultural Analysis of White People*, 135–46. Durham, NC: Duke University Press.

hooks, bell. 2009. *Reel to Real*. New York: Routledge.

Leonard, David J., and C. Richard King, eds. 2011. *Commodified and Criminalized: New Racism and African Americans in Contemporary Sports*. Lanham, MD: Rowman and Littlefield.

Mueller, Jennifer, Danielle Dirks, and Leslie Houts Picca. 2007. "Unmasking Racism: Halloween Costuming and Engagement of the Racial Other." *Qualitative Sociology* 30(3):315–35.

Thomas, James M. 2015. *Working to Laugh: Assembling Difference in American Stand-Up Comedy Venues*. Lanham, MD: Lexington Books.

CONTEMPORARY SYSTEMS OF OPPRESSION

Alexander, Michelle. 2012. *The New Jim Crow*. New York: The New Press.

Alland, Alexander, Jr. 2002. *Race in Mind: Race, IQ, and Other Racisms*. New York: Palgrave Macmillan.

Bullard, Robert, ed. 2007. *The Black Metropolis in the Twenty-First Century: Race, Power, and the Politics of Place*. New York: Rowman and Littlefield.

Cole, David. 1999. *No Equal Justice*. New York: The New Press.

Davenport, Christian, Sarah A. Soule, and David. A. Armstrong II. 2011. "Protesting While Black? The Differential Policing of American Activism, 1960–1990." *American Sociological Review* 76(1):152–78.

Holmes, Seth. 2013. *Fresh Fruit, Broken Bodies: Migrant Farmworkers in the United States*. Berkeley, CA: University of California Press.

Peffly, Mark, and Jon Hurwitz. 2010. *Justice in America: The Separate Realities of Blacks and Whites*. New York: Cambridge University Press.

Reece, Robert L., and Heather A. O'Connell. 2016. "How the Legacy of Slavery and Racial Composition Shape Public School Enrollment in the American South." *Sociology of Race and Ethnicity* 2(1):42–57.

THE FUTURE OF RACE

Alba, Richard. 2009. *Blurring the Color Line*. Cambridge, MA: Harvard University Press.

DiTomaso, Nancy. 2013. *The American Non-Dilemma: Racial Inequality Without Racism*. New York: Russell Sage Foundation.

Duster, Troy. 2003. *Backdoor to Eugenics*. New York: Routledge.

Hochschild, Jennifer L., Vesla M. Weaver, and Traci R. Burch. 2012. *Creating a New Racial Order: How Immigration, Multiracialism, Genomics, and the Young Can Remake Race in America*. Princeton, NJ: Princeton University Press.

Itzigsohn, José, and Karida Brown. 2015. "Sociology and the Theory of Double Consciousness." *Du Bois Review* 12(2):231–48.

Korgen, Kathleen. 2016. *Race Policy and Multiracial Americans*. Chicago: The University of Chicago Press Books.

Roberts, Dorothy. 2011. *Fatal Invention: How Science, Politics, and Big Business Re-Create Race in the Twenty-First Century*. New York: The New Press.

Touré. 2011. *Who's Afraid of Post-Blackness? What It Means to be Black Now*. New York: Free Press.

Vargas, Nick. 2015. "Which Latina/os Self-Classify as White and Report Being Perceived as White by Other Americans?" *Du Bois Review* 12(1):119–36.

Vickerman, Milton. 2013. *The Problem of Post-Racialism*. New York: Palgrave-Macmillan.

FIGHTING RACIAL INEQUALITY

Balint, Peter. 2016. "The Importance of Racial Tolerance for Anti-Racism." *Ethnic and Racial Studies* 39(1):16–32.

Brunsma, David L., Keri E. Iyall Smith, and Brian K. Gran. 2015. *Expanding the Human in Human Rights: Toward a Sociology of Human Rights*. New York: Routledge.

Durr, Marlese. 2016. "Removing the Mask, Lifting the Veil: Race, Class, and Gender in the Twenty-First Century." *Social Problems* 63(2):151–60.

Emerson, Michael O., and George Yancey. 2011. *Transcending Racial Barriers: Toward a Mutual Obligations Approach*. New York: Oxford University Press.

Fleming, Crystal, and Aldon Morris. 2015. "Theorizing Ethnic and Racial Movements in the Global Age: Lessons from the Civil Rights Movement." *Sociology of Race and Ethnicity* 1(1):105–26.

Gallagher, Charles A. 2007. "Ten Simple Things You Can Do to Improve Race Relations." In *Rethinking the Colorline* (3rd ed.), edited by C. A. Gallagher, 582–85. New York: McGraw-Hill.

Hill Collins, Patricia. 2010. "The New Politics of Community." *American Sociological Review* 75(1):7–30.

Wilson, William J. 1999. *The Bridge over the Racial Divide*. Berkeley and New York: University of California Press and Russell Sage.

CPSIA information can be obtained
at www.ICGtesting.com
Printed in the USA
LVHW05s1915040918
589126LV00002B/5/P